HISTORIANS' FALLACIES

Toward a Logic of Historical Thought

৯৬

HISTORIANS' FALLACIES

Toward a Logic of Historical Thought

by David Hackett Fischer

HARPER & ROW, PUBLISHERS
NEW YORK, EVANSTON, AND LONDON

The quotation on page 20 is from "Burnt Norton" in *Four Quartets* by T. S. Eliot, reprinted by permission of Harcourt, Brace & World, Inc.
The lines by Robert Frost on page 130 are from "The Lesson for Today" in *Complete Poems* by Robert Frost, reprinted by permission of Holt, Rinehart and Winston, Inc.

LIBRARY OF CONGRESS CATALOG CARD NUMBER: 69-15583

For Margaretta Frederick

CONTENTS

ૐ

PREFACE

ॐ

The poor condition of the logical analysis of history is
shown by the fact that neither historians, nor methodolo-
gists of history, but rather representatives of very unrelated
disciplines have conducted the authoritative investigations
into this important question.

—Max Weber

The problem of locating a logic of historical thought cuts across several
separate academic disciplines. For that reason, perhaps, it has been
satisfactorily studied by none of them. Many professional logicians will
refuse to recognize it as a logical problem at all. They have been at some
pains to show that their subject is an intellectual discipline in its own
right—even *the* intellectual discipline. They are customarily committed
to a search for the logic of thought about everything in general, and
nothing in particular. One philosopher, Stephen Toulmin, has proposed
a different strategy: the refinement of a plurality of field-related logics
which are designed to promote special kinds of inquiry. "Not only will
logic have to become more empirical," Toulmin writes, "it will inevitably
tend to become more historical. To think up new and better methods of
arguing in any field is to make a major advance, not just in logic, but
in the substantive field itself."[1] Toulmin's manifesto was issued more than
ten years ago. Few logicians have responded to his call. Most of them
are still moving in the opposite direction.

If there is a field-related logic of historical thought, then working
historians must help to find it. But they have contributed little of consequence in the past forty years. Their articles and books on the nature
of history tend to degenerate into mere exhortations, or manuals on the
mechanics of citation, or metahistorical mumbo-jumbo. Many academic
historians regard methodological and logical problems with suspicion
and even hostility. Incredibly, the word "logic" is often a pejorative,

1. Stephen Toulmin, *The Uses of Argument* (Cambridge, 1958), p. 257.

in their professional parlance. Sometimes it is used as a synonym for determinism by embattled antideterminists. A Scottish historian writes, "No doubt it was 'in the logic of history' that England should endeavor to absorb Scotland. None the less, the first English attempt at a wholesale conquest resulted from two dynastic accidents. . . . "[2]

A different usage carries an equally disagreeable connotation. "Logic" is sometimes understood by historians as a treacherous tangle of disjunctive snares and syllogistic delusions which are the last resort of a scholar who has run short of sources. An American historian writes contemptuously of a colleague, "He had little evidence to go upon as yet, and so he resorted frankly to logic." Another historian describes logic as "Machiavellian" in a recent monograph.[3]

This unfortunate attitude has deep roots in historians' thought. It reaches back to Carlyle's contempt for the "dead logic formula," and to Guizot's epigram that "Nothing falsifies history more than logic." In the past generation, the progress of this prejudice among historians has been promoted by the influence of relativism. That great blight upon historical scholarship is remembered as a repudiation of the empirical aspirations of "scientific history." It was also a revolt against reason. Carl Becker wrote:

> We have long since learned not to bother overmuch with reason and logic. Logic was formerly visualized as something outside us, something existing independently which, if we were willing, could take us by the hand and lead us into the paths of truth. We now suspect that it was something the mind has created to conceal its timidity and keep up its courage, a hocus-pocus designed to give formal validity to conclusions we are willing to accept if everybody else in our set will too. If all men are mortal (an assumption), and if Socrates was a man (in the sense assumed), no doubt Socrates must have been mortal; but we suspect that we somehow knew all this before it was submitted to the test of a syllogism. Logics have a way of multiplying in response to the changes in point of view. . . . The secure foundations of deductive and inductive logic have been battered to pieces by the ascertainable facts, so that we really have no choice; we must cling to the ascertainable facts though they slay us.[4]

This is indeed an irony, in a scholar who was so radically skeptical about "ascertainable facts." But his attitude retains its popularity, particularly among Anglo-American historians whose professional prejudices are powerfully reinforced by a cultural predisposition. Stanley Baldwin boasted in the year 1937, that "one of the reasons why our

2. John Duncan Mackie. *A History of Scotland* (Baltimore, 1966), p. 71.
3. Wesley Frank Craven, *The Legend of the Founding Fathers* (Ithaca, 1965), p. 120; Carl E. Prince, *New Jersey's Jeffersonian Republicans* (Chapel Hill, N.C., 1967), p. 119.
4. Carl Becker, *The Heavenly City of the Eighteenth Century Philosophers* (New Haven, 1932), pp. 25–26.

people are alive and flourishing, and have avoided many of the troubles that have fallen to less happy nations, is that we have never been guided by logic in anything we did."[5]

There is an appropriately ugly name for this prejudice: misology, or logic-hating. Its continuing existence among academic historians explains their failure to refine a logic of historical thought. When a distinguished American historian openly asserts that "a good bed book is more to be desired than another *Critique of Pure Reason*,"[6] it is not astonishing that a *Critique of Historical Reason* has failed to appear.

A good deal of relevant and important work has recently been done, not by logicians or historians, but by epistemologists. Today, a special subdiscipline of epistemology called the analytical philosophy of history is in a flourishing condition. Any historian who wishes to understand the nature of his own work has much to learn from it, and particularly from two excellent new books by Arthur Danto and Morton White.[7] But the work of Danto and White and their colleagues is not very useful in any attempt at the refinement of the thinking of working historians, for three reasons. First, analytical philosophers of history are simply not much interested in low problems of utility. "Today's philosopher of history is not a metaphysical speculator, but neither is he a methodological consultant," writes Morton White.[8] Second, historical epistemologists have not been sufficiently empirical in their procedures. They have not sufficiently attended to historical thinking as it actually happens, or to historical problems as they actually exist. Third, epistemologists have characteristically tried to analyze historical knowledge in terms of something else more familiar to them. Often in terms of some epistemological abstraction which bears small resemblance to the thinking which *anybody* actually does. Most analytical philosophers who have written on the subject attempt to force historical knowledge into a formula which the *cognoscenti* call the Hempelian model, or the Covering Law model, or the Deductive Model of Explanation. This abstraction, I believe, is seriously mistaken as an understanding of the thinking of historians, or of social scientists, or of natural scientists for that matter.[9] But all his-

5. Quoted in L. Susan Stebbing, *Thinking to Some Purpose* (Baltimore, 1961), p. 17. Winston Churchill similarly remarked that "Logic is a poor guide compared with custom. Logic . . . has proved fatal to parliamentary government." Randolph S. Churchill, *Winston Churchill, The Young Statesman* (Boston, 1967), p. 5.

6. Charles F. Mullett, in *The American Historical Review* 72 (1966): 186.

7. Arthur Danto, *Analytical Philosophy of History* (Cambridge, 1965); Morton White, *The Foundations of Historical Knowledge* (New York, 1965).

8. White, *The Foundations of Historical Knowledge*, p. 2.

9. For an extended critique by a working social scientist, see Eugene Meehan, *Explanation in the Social Sciences: A System Paradigm* (Homewood, Ill., 1968). See also chapter 4, below.

torians are made to lie down in this Procrustean bed, even if their heads must be removed to make them fit. A good many intelligent men have wasted a great deal of time and effort to reconcile this epistemological error with empirical facts which so obviously contradict it. The results are often ingenious, but rarely productive. Stirrings of a new spirit are slowly beginning to appear, but the Hempelian model, in modified forms, retains its popularity.

There are other schools of historical epistemology, which are equally unsatisfactory. One of them is organized around the central idea that to write history is to tell a story. This, I think, is partly true for some historians, but entirely false for others, and insufficient for all. I shall argue in the following chapters that history-writing is not story-telling but problem solving. Sometimes the solution takes the form of a story. But often (and increasingly today) a different kind of explanation-strategy is adopted.[10]

Still another major school of historical epistemology attempts to force all historical thought into an idealist model which derives from the work of R. G. Collingwood. I believe this "idea of history" to be fallacious, and have briefly discussed it as such in Chapter 7, below.[11]

If the analytical philosophy of history is presently in an unsatisfactory condition, professional historians have nobody to blame but themselves. "Historians," a philosopher has fairly complained, "show an almost pathological disinclination to commit themselves to general statements about their work, its aims, subject matter, and methods."[12] A few of my colleagues have even argued that a "working historian" ought not to be "talking about such matters at all."[13] Others, when asked to explain the nature of history, are apt to respond as Fats Waller (or maybe Louis Armstrong) did, when asked to explain the nature of jazz. "Man," he said, "if you don't *know* what it is, don't mess with it."

These attitudes have taken a heavy toll of modern historiography. Those historians who imagine themselves to be emancipated from philosophy are apt, in Keynes's phrase, to be the slaves of some defunct philosopher. If the logic and epistemology of historical thought are to be understood, if historical and logical and epistemological thinking are to be refined, then historians, logicians, epistemologists, and others must work together in a spirit of mutual cooperation. Each of these proud disciplines has much to teach the others—and much to learn as well.

10. The most extended statement of this understanding of history as story-telling appears in W. B. Gallie, *Philosophy and the Historical Understanding* (New York, 1964).
11. The most influential text is R. G. Collingwood, *The Idea of History* (Oxford, 1946).
12. W. B. Gallie, *Philosophy and the Historical Understanding*, p. 53.
13. Bernard Bailyn, in "The Problems of a Working Historian: A Comment," in Sidney Hook, ed., *Philosophy and History* (New York, 1963), pp. 93–94.

Many people have contributed to the writing of this book. My interest in the subject was awakened ten years ago by a philosopher, Ronald Butler, in an undergraduate course at Princeton University on the analytical philosophy of history. More recently I have learned much in conversation and correspondence with many colleagues—Jerold Auerbach, Jacob Cohen, Norman Cantor, Ray Ginger, Morton Keller, Leonard Levy, Heinz Lubasz, Eugene Meehan, and especially Marvin Meyers who always had time to talk out a knotty problem and constructive suggestions for its solution. Ramsay MacMullen kindly answered a question on Livy, and Douglas Stewart helped with problems of Greek historiography. George Billias gave me a chance to try out my ideas on some of his students, and also the benefit of his own criticism. J. H. Hexter and Arthur Danto read and criticized the manuscript, and it is better for their suggestions. A special debt is due to my students in History 97 at Brandeis University, and particularly to Hillel Schwartz and Eric Uslaner who voluntarily produced written critiques of the book.

The editorial staff of Harper & Row was, as ever, a model of encouragement and efficiency. I am especially obliged to Hugh Van Dusen and Cynthia Merman for their help, and to Antonia Rachiele for her intelligent and painstaking criticism of the manuscript. Brandeis University provided a generous grant-in-aid. Judith, my wife, made the project possible in every other way.

D.H.F.
Wayland, Massachusetts
September, 1969

INTRODUCTION

ಬಿ

When we run over libraries persuaded of these principles,
what havoc must we make?

—David Hume

This book begins with three related premises: first, that there is a tacit
logic of historical thought; second, that this logic can be raised to the
level of awareness; and third, that historical thinking itself can be refined
by its intelligent and purposeful application.

The logic of historical thought is not a formal logic of deductive
inference. It is not a symmetrical structure of Aristotelian syllogisms, or
Ramean dialectics, or Boolean equations. Nor is it precisely an inductive
logic, like that of Mill or Keynes or Carnap. It consists neither in inductive reasoning from the particular to the general, nor in deductive
reasoning from the general to the particular. Instead, it is a process of
adductive reasoning in the simple sense of adducing answers to specific
questions, so that a satisfactory explanatory "fit" is obtained. The answers
may be general or particular, as the questions may require. History is, in
short, a problem-solving discipline. A historian is someone (anyone)
who asks an open-ended question about past events and answers it with
selected facts which are arranged in the form of an explanatory paradigm.
These questions and answers are fitted to each other by a complex process of mutual adjustment. The resultant explanatory paradigm may
take many different forms: a statistical generalization, or a narrative,
or a causal model, or a motivational model, or a collectivized group-
composition model, or maybe an analogy. Most commonly it consists
not in any one of these components but in a combination of them.
Always, it is articulated in the form of a reasoned argument.[1]

1. In this book an *event* is understood as any past happening. A *fact* is a true descriptive
statement about past events. To *explain* is merely to make plain, clear, or understandable some problem about past events, so that resultant knowledge will be useful in
dealing with future problems. An explanatory *paradigm* is an interactive structure of
workable questions and the factual statements which are adduced to answer them.

To argue that there is a tacit logic of historical thinking is to assert that every historical project is a cluster of constituent purposes, and that each of these purposes imposes its own logical requirements upon a thinker who adopts them. Whether the purpose at hand is to design a proper question, or to select a responsive set of factual answers, or to verify their factuality, or to form them into a statistical generalization which itself becomes a fact, or whatever—it always involves the making of purposive and procedural assumptions that entail certain logical consequences. Every historian must learn to live within the limits which his own freely chosen assumptions impose upon him. These assumptions may differ radically from one historian to the next, but always they exist, and a historian must learn to respect them. If he does not, then he will pay a penalty in a diminution of the degree to which his purposes are attained. No man is free from the logic of his own rational assumptions—unless he wishes to be free from rationality itself.

Assuming that this logic of historical thought does tacitly exist, the next question is how to raise it to the level of consciousness. In the opinion of some intelligent men, this task is not merely difficult but impossible. Michael Polanyi has suggested that scientists do indeed proceed by a logic of tacit inference—but one which is only learned through personal experience and can never be articulated. "Any attempt to gain complete control of thought by explicit rules," he flatly declares, "is self-contradictory, systematically misleading, and culturally destructive."[2]

Polanyi's caveat would surely be correct if the object were to gain *complete* control of thought. But maybe a more humble attainment is

---

By *adduction* I do not mean what Charles Sanders Peirce appears to have intended by *abduction*. Peirce distinguished three kinds of reasoning. *Deduction* he understood in an ordinary way as "necessary reasoning" which "starts from a hypothesis, the truth or falsity of which has nothing to do with the reasoning." *Induction* he defined in a special sense as "the experimental testing of a theory," and *abduction* as "the process of forming an explanatory hypothesis." Of the latter, he wrote, "It is the only logical operation which introduces any new idea; for induction does nothing but determine a value, and deduction merely evolves the necessary consequences of a pure hypothesis. Deduction proves that something *must* be; Induction shows that something *actually is* operative; Abduction merely suggests that something *may be*." *Collected Papers* (Cambridge, 1931), V, 142, 145, 170–172. The processes which Peirce calls abductive and inductive are combined in what I call adduction—as in fact I believe them to be inseparably joined in historical thinking.

2. Michael Polanyi, "The Logic of Tacit Inference," *Philosophy* 41 (1966): 18; and *Personal Knowledge* (Chicago, 1958), passim. I am indebted to Polanyi's work for the idea of a tacit logic and for many other things, though I disagree with him on this point.

possible. Perhaps one might refine (not control) some kinds of thinking by a partial articulation of some parts of this tacit logic. It seems reasonable to expect that a man who learns much from his own experience can also learn a little from the experience of others.

Still, the problem of locating a logic of historical thinking defies a direct approach. Every attempt (there have been many) to storm the citadel by a conceptual *coup de main* has failed of its objective. But if a frontal assault is impossible, maybe the problem can be outflanked and taken from behind. A historian has written suggestively that "our present state of knowledge is one of mitigated ignorance. In such situations, the honest enquirer always has one consolation—his blunders may be as instructive as his successes."[3]

Such is the perversity of human perceptions that a blunder is apt to be more visible than a success. This psychological fact suggests a crude and eccentric method, which is adopted in this book. If there is a tacit logic of historical inquiry, then one might hope to find a tacit illogic as well, which reveals itself in the form of explicit historical errors. On this assumption, I have gone looking for errors in historical scholarship, and then for their common denominators, in the form of false organizing assumptions and false procedures. These common denominators are called fallacies in this book. A fallacy is not merely an error itself but a way of falling into error. It consists in false reasoning, often from true factual premises, so that false conclusions are generated.[4]

The object in the following chapters is not to compile a definitive catalogue of historians' fallacies, which is obviously impossible. A logician, Augustus de Morgan, wisely observed that "there *is* no such thing as a classification of the ways in which men may arrive at an error: it is much to be doubted whether there ever *can be*."[5] Surely, there can be no conclusive and comprehensive classification. Nevertheless, a list of common fallacies—however crude and incomplete—may serve a useful purpose in two respects. First, it may clearly indicate a few mistaken practices that are not sufficiently recognized as such. Second, it might

---

3. Alan Simpson, *The Wealth of the Gentry, 1540–1660* (Chicago, 1961), p. 21.
4. This definition of fallacy conforms to the third meaning of the term in Alfred Sidgwick, *Fallacies* (London, 1883). It should be clearly distinguished from several others. The literal Latin meaning of *fallax* suggests a deliberate deception. This, of course, does not apply to any of the following fallacies, all of which are self-deceptions. A fallacy has also been defined, in Jeremy Bentham's phrase, as a "vulgar error," or a common misconception. This is too broad for our purposes. Sometimes, fallacies are also understood as violations of the formal rules of deductive inference. But this is irrelevant here.
5. Augustus de Morgan, *Formal Logic, 1847* (London, 1926), p. 276.

operate as a heuristic device for the discovery of a few constructive rules of reason.

The reader might protest that this method is like telling a traveler how to get from Boston to New York by describing in detail the roads which won't take him there. If this were in fact our purpose, the project would be absurd. But it is something different. The object is not to describe the ways in which a traveler *might* get lost, but rather to identify a few common ways in which others have *actually* gone wrong. For a traveler from Boston to New York there are an infinity of wrong routes and a plurality of right ones. But real travelers who actually get lost tend to do so in a few finite ways. The Public Roads Commission does not need to put up signs everywhere but only at the doubtful intersections.

So it is with historical travelers, who set out toward a certain destination. There are many intersections along the way. Some are simple forks in the road. A few are baffling interchanges. The traveler's difficulties are compounded by the fact that well-meaning people have put up many mistaken signs for the convenience of passers-by. The signs say, "*A*, this way, seven miles," but point squarely to not-*A*.

The purpose of this book is, first, to pull down some of these wrong signs. The fact that it cannot pull down *all* wrong signs, or that pulling down is a destructive act, cannot be an argument against it. Second, the object is to put up a few crude but hopefully more correct markers at some of the simple forks in the road. Third, it is to explore some of the baffling interchanges in a preliminary way.

The object is emphatically not three other things. It is not to put up signs everywhere—there isn't enough lumber and paint in the world for that. Nor is it precisely to survey the road, which cannot be done until we have a rough sense of its location, and which will not be done until historiographical surveyors become a little more expert in the use of theodolites and trigonometry. Most important, the object is not to play traffic policeman or magistrate: it is not to flag down erring travelers and take away their licenses. In the republic of scholarship, every citizen has a constitutional right to get himself as thoroughly lost as he pleases. The only purpose here is to indicate, in an advisory spirit, a few wrong turnings which have actually been taken, and to extract from these mistakes a few rough rules of procedure.

Somebody once asked Thomas Edison about his rules of procedure and received a rude reply: "Rules!" said Edison, "Hell! There ain't no rules around here! We're tryin' to accomplish sump'n." A good many historians, particularly of the present permissive generation, which has made a cult of flexibility in its procedures, seem to have formed the same idea of their own discipline. I believe that they are wrong. There are some very strict tautological rules of historical scholarship, which are rather like the rules of chess. When a chess player sits down to a game, he must respect a rule which requires him to move his bishops on the diagonal. Nobody will arrest him if he doesn't. But if he refuses to play that way, then he isn't exactly playing chess.

There are other kinds of rules in chess, too—rough experiential rules of thumb, such as one which urges a beginning player always to seize the open file. He can violate this rule with impunity, if he is very lucky, or very good. But most players, in most situations, are properly urged to respect it.[6]

I hope that a study of the tacit logic of historical thought will yield rules of both these types. But even if not, a more precise understanding of error itself might serve a serious and constructive scholarly purpose. Karl Popper has suggested that science develops by a sequence of "conjectures and refutations." He has written that "the way in which knowledge progresses, and especially our scientific knowledge, is by unjustified (and unjustifiable) anticipations, by guesses, by tentative solutions to our problems, by *conjectures*. These conjectures are controlled by criticism; that is, by attempted *refutations*, which include critical tests."[7]

The fallacies in the following pages might be useful as some of these "critical tests" to which conjectures are submitted. As the pace of intellectual innovation continues to accelerate, we must develop devices which distinguish sound innovations from unsound ones. As we become more experimental in our thoughts and acts, we must find a way to deal with experiments that fail. In historical scholarship, the progress of interpretative revision requires a degree of critical rigor that is conspicuously absent today.

Historians must, moreover, develop critical tests not merely for their interpretations, but also for their methods of arriving at them. Today, there is a good deal of hostility against method among historians, who are apt to be contemptuous of other disciplines in which this interest is more highly developed. Among my colleagues, it is common to believe that any procedure is permissible, as long as its practitioner publishes an essay from time to time, and is not convicted of a felony. The resultant condition of modern historiography is that of the Jews under the Judges: every man does that which is right in his own eyes. The fields

---

6. I have shamelessly stolen this simile from Abraham Kaplan, *The Conduct of Inquiry* (San Francisco, 1964).
7. Karl Popper, *Conjectures and Refutations* (New York, 1962), p. vii.

are sown with salt, and plowed with the heifer, and there is a famine upon the land.

It ought to be immediately apparent that some historical methods are not as good as others, for purposes at hand. And a few methods in common use are simply no good at all, for any purpose. An investigation of fallacies in historical scholarship may provide criteria by which some of these deficiencies can be discovered and put right.

But if there are some ways in which a study of error can help historical scholarship, there are others in which it can hurt. Popper's first stage of knowledge—conjecture—in its earliest and most important phases is not presently susceptible to rational analysis. There is no logic of creative thought. Creativity makes its own rules. Genius transcends them. The aboriginal act of inspiration remains utterly mysterious to human understanding. We know when it happens, but not how or why. It would be a very grave mistake to apply a logic for the testing of conjectures to conjecturing itself.

Equally important, though logic can distinguish error from truth and truth from truism, it cannot distinguish a profound truth from a petty one. A good many historical arguments are objectionable not because they are fallacious but because they are banal, shallow, or trivial. As a remedy for these failings, logic is impotent. Indeed, as I collected material for this book, I quickly discovered that errors of the sort I was looking for were most easily found in the work of the best and brightest historians who are writing today. Many mindless monographs call to mind Davy Crockett's critique of an effusion by Andrew Jackson— "It don't even make good nonsense." There can never be a logic of grunts and grimaces, nor a logic of the great clouds of conceptual confusion which swirl around the heads of some historians. The thoughts of many historians are neither logical nor illogical, but sublogical. To their work, this book will be irrelevant.

Another qualification is also worth keeping in mind. Logical and methodological techniques are not ends but means. It would be unfortunate if historians were to become so obsessed by problems of how to do their work that no work could ever get done. Abraham Kaplan was warned against the "myth of methodology," the mistaken idea that "the most serious difficulties which confront behavioral science are 'methodological,' and that if only we hit upon the right methodology, progress will be rapid and sure." This attitude is not merely unproductive, but potentially destructive.

> By pressing methodological norms too far [Kaplan writes] we may inhibit bold and imaginative adventures of ideas. The irony is that methodology itself may make for conformism—conformity to its own favored recon-

structions. . . . And the push toward logical completeness may well make for "premature closure" of scientific conceptions. The situation in science is not unlike that in the arts: the critic with his standards discourages daubers, but he also becomes the mainstay of the Academy, and art eventually passes by him.[8]

No method exists independently of an object. None can be vindicated except in its application; none can be proclaimed to the world as The Method; and none is other than a useful tool, or more than an approximate tool. No historical method is in any sense an alternative to heavy labor in historical sources. None can serve as a substitute for creativity.

Conscious methodologies are not an indispensable prerequisite to substantive success. Max Weber has written that

> Methodology can only bring us reflective understanding of the means which have *demonstrated* their value in practice by raising them to the level of explicit consciousness; it is no more the precondition of fruitful intellectual work than the knowledge of anatomy is a precondition for "correct" walking. Indeed, just as a person who attempted to govern his mode of walking continuously by anatomical knowledge would be in danger of stumbling, so the professional scholar who attempted to determine the aims of his own research extrinsically on the basis of methodological reflections would be in danger of falling into the same difficulties.[9]

But in historical scholarship, these are distant dangers. Most historians are far removed from methodological obsessions—too far removed, for the good of their discipline. Indeed, in a strict sense, academic history today sometimes seems to be not a discipline at all, but a means of teaching and writing without one. Among my professional brethren, there is even a band of methodological *Nullbruder*, who flaunt their intellectual poverty as if it were a badge of grace, and flourish all the rusty instruments of ignorance in the face of every effort at reform.

The work of too many professional historians is diminished by an antirational obsession—by an intense prejudice against method, logic, and science. In their common speech, "scientism" has become a smear word, and "scientific history" is a phrase which is used merely to condemn the infatuation of an earlier generation. In the process of this reaction, historians have not merely severed their ties with the natural sciences, but have also turned away from science in the larger sense of a structured, ordered, controlled, empirical, rational discipline of thought.

History, it is said, is an inexact science. But in fact historians are

8. Abraham Kaplan, *The Conduct of Inquiry* (San Francisco, 1964), pp. 25–26.
9. Max Weber, "The Logic of the Cultural Sciences," in *The Methodology of the Social Sciences,* trans. Edward Shils and Henry Finch (Glencoe, Ill., 1949), p. 115.

inexact scientists, who go blundering about their business without a sufficient sense of purpose or procedure. They are failed scientists, who have projected their failures to science itself. Nothing could be more absurd, or more nearly antithetical to the progress of a potent discipline.

PART I

INQUIRY

℧

CHAPTER I

FALLACIES OF QUESTION-FRAMING

ॐ

Are we to be disgusted with science because it has not fulfilled our hopes or redeemed its promises? And are we, for this reason, to announce the "bankruptcy" of science, as is so often and so flippantly done? But this is rash and foolish; for we can hardly blame science just because we have not asked the right questions.

—Ernst Cassirer

Scissors-and-paste historians study periods; they collect all the extant testimony about a certain limited group of events, and hope in vain that something will come of it. Scientific historians study problems: they ask questions, and if they are good historians they ask questions which they see their way to answering.

—R. G. Collingwood

A moment's reflection should suffice to establish the simple proposition that every historian, willy-nilly, must begin his research with a question. Questions are the engines of intellect, the cerebral machines which convert energy to motion, and curiosity to controlled inquiry. There can be no thinking without questioning—no purposeful study of the past, nor any serious planning for the future. Moreover, there can be no questioning in a sophisticated sense without hypothesizing, and no systematic testing of hypotheses without the construction of hypothetical models which can be put to the test.

Often, this intricate process is partly hidden from a historian, as well as from his readers. Occasionally it is entirely invisible. But always it exists. Without questions of some sort, a historian is condemned to wander aimlessly through dark corridors of learning. Without questions of the right sort, his empirical projects are consigned to failure before they are fairly begun.

Specific forms of question-framing depend in a considerable degree upon the kinds of answers which are sought. There are, of course, wide variations in common practice. But there are also a few common denominators of question-framing. These elemental aspects of questioning are common to all historical inquiry, and indeed to empirical investigation in every field. They are the business of this chapter.[1]

It should be self-evident that some questions will yield empirical answers and others will not. How does one distinguish the latter from the former? This chapter will proceed first to an examination of ten fallacies of empirical question-framing which have actually—and often—occurred in historical scholarship. Ten more could easily be added. But the following fallacies account for most of the erroneous questions I have found. After a survey of these various forms of error, the chapter will end with an attempt to articulate a few affirmative axioms.

ૐ The *Baconian fallacy*[2] consists in the idea that a historian can operate without the aid of preconceived questions, hypotheses, ideas, assumptions, theories, paradigms, postulates, prejudices, presumptions, or general presuppositions of any kind. He is supposed to go a-wandering in the dark forest of the past, gathering facts like nuts and berries, until he has enough to make a general truth. Then he is to store up his general truths until he has the whole truth. This idea is doubly deficient, for it commits a historian to the pursuit of an impossible object by an impracticable method.

1. Nothing in this chapter is unique to historical inquiry. The reader will find close parallels between practices discussed here and an analysis of question-framing in survey research. Compare Stanley L. Payne, *The Art of Asking Questions* (Princeton, 1951).
2. This form of error takes its name from Francis Bacon's articulation of a method which "derives its axioms from the senses and particulares, rising by a gradual and unbroken ascent, so that it arrives at the most general axioms last of all" (*Novum Organon*, bk. 1, xix). It should be noted that this is unfair to Bacon, and inaccurate as an understanding of his thought. Bacon's larger work, of which the *Novum Organon* is but a part, did not defend an induction as simple-minded as this, but rather a more complex method of interdependent inquiry and research. Bacon was no more a Baconian than Marx was a Marxian, or Plato a Platonist. See Benjamin Farrington, *Francis Bacon: Philosopher of Industrial Science* (New York, 1949), chap. 6; and F. H. Anderson, *The Philosophy of Francis Bacon* (Chicago, 1948), p. 292, passim; and F. Smith Fussner, *The Historical Revolution* (New York, 1962), chap. 10.

Though the name is objectionable in this respect, I have adopted it because it is standard, on H. W. B. Joseph's assumption that "If it is useful to have a nomenclature of fallacies, it is useful to have a standard nomenclature." (*An Introduction to Logic* [London, 1906], p. 533.)

The impracticable method is a simple induction from the particular to the general. It cannot work, because there is an infinity of particulars in the past. Their truth value is an objective entity that exists independently of an inquirer. But their particularity is separately defined by each inquiry. If a fact is a true statement about past events, then there is no practicable limit to the number of facts which are relevant to even the smallest historical problem. "Truths are as plentiful as falsehoods," writes a distinguished logician, "since each falsehood admits of a negation which is true. Scientific activity is not the indiscriminate amassing of truths; science is selective and seeks the truths that count most."[3]

The impossible object is a quest for the whole truth—a quest which characteristically takes one of three forms. Occasionally, it consists in an attempt to know everything about everything. Sometimes it seeks to learn something about everything. Most often it is a search for everything about something. None of these purposes is remotely realizable. A historian can only hope to know something about something.

The most common everything-about-something school imagines that historical science might be constructed on the same architectural principles as the Pyramid of Khufu, with monographs stacked upon thick square monographs in one vast granite pile, the whole massy structure to be crowned some day with the gilded figure of a historiographical Newton.

But a glance at the history of historical writing suggests that this is not at all the way in which historiography develops. The monographs do not commonly come first and the general interpretations second. Instead some master architect—not master builder—draws a rough sketch of a pyramid in the sand, and many laborers begin to hew their stones to fit. Before many are made ready, the fashion suddenly changes —pyramids are out; obelisks are in. Another master architect draws a sketch in the sand, and the hewing and chipping starts all over again. A few stones can be salvaged, but most have to be cut from scratch. As Huizinga writes, "when the master builder comes, he will find most of the stones you have laid ready for him unusable."[4]

This does not mean, however, that relativists receive the last word. There are many objective truths to be told about the past—great and vital truths that are relevant and even urgent to the needs of mankind. But there is no whole truth to be discovered by a simple method of induction. Every true historical statement is an answer to a question which a historian has asked. Not to The Question. Not to questions about everything. But to questions about something.

3. Willard Van Orman Quine, *Methods of Logic* (New York, 1959), p. xi.
4. Johan Huizinga, *Men and Ideas* (New York, 1959), p. 20.

There are signs that historians are slowly beginning to learn this lesson. All the classic examples of the Baconian fallacy derive from the work of an earlier generation. The best and clearest illustration is not Bacon, or Ranke, but a distinguished French historian, Fustel de Coulanges (1830–1889). Fustel produced two great works—*The Ancient City* and a monumental *History of the Political Institutions of Ancient France*, in six erudite volumes. He was also a splendid teacher. One day, his students responded to a lecture with an ovation. "Do not applaud me," Fustel is said to have replied. "It is not I who speaks to you, but history which speaks through my mouth."

Fustel asserted that a historian should bring *no* preconceived ideas to his research—not even questions or working hypotheses:

> Since he cannot know the cause beforehand, he should not be content to study a specific category of facts; he should carefully observe all the facts, all the institutions, all regulations public or private, all the customs of domestic life, and particularly everything that relates to the possession of land. [*sic!*] He should study all of these things with equally careful attention, for he does not know beforehand from which side enlightenment will come to him. This method is slow, but it is the only one which is sure. It is not the method of the doctrinaire, but of the inquirer.[5]

Fustel conceded the possibility of error, and, indeed, affirmed that "one day of synthesis demands years of analysis. In these researches which require so much patience and so much effort, so much prudence and so much boldness, the opportunities for error are innumerable, and none can hope to escape it." But that error derived, in Fustel's thinking, not from the historian's bias, but from the gaps in his evidence. The danger in all of this is well described by G. P. Gooch, who reports that Fustel "regarded his results as independent of himself and felt criticism as something like blasphemy."[6] Moreover, he imagined that he had diminished the nationalist bias which marred the work of his many chauvinistic colleagues. But he had merely disguised it. In his major work, written immediately after the Franco-Prussian War, the main thrust was a minimization of the significance of Teutonic influences which other scholars had found in the development of French and English institutions.[7]

Historians today, several generations removed from Fustel de Coulanges, rarely commit this fallacy in so blatant a form. The relativists

---

5. Fustel de Coulanges, *Histoire des Institutions Politiques de l'Ancienne France,* 6 vols. (Paris, 1890), 5:xiii.
6. Ibid., 1:xiii, 145; G. P. Gooch, *History and Historians in the Nineteenth Century,* new ed. (Boston, 1959), p. 202.
7. See generally *Histoire des Institutions Politiques,* I, II; and also *The Origin of Property in Land,* trans. Margaret Ashley (London, 1926).

have seen to that—it was their most constructive accomplishment. But old error still survives, deep in the dark recesses of every historian's heart. Every now and then, he is apt to slip a little and allow the guilty secret to escape, like the character in an English academic novel who picked up the phone and said. "History speaking!"

Some belletristic historians occasionally yield to Dr. Johnson's irritable opinion that "questioning is not a mode of conversation among gentlemen." Samuel Eliot Morison, reviewing a book which took issue with a Morisonian interpretation, distinguished between the "realm of hypothesis" and "the realm of history," in the majestic spirit of Newton's "Hypotheses non Fingo."[8]

Other scholars hold with Kipling that "them that asks no questions, isn't told a lie." G. R. Elton skirts this position, in an essay on historical method.

> Preconceived notions are a much greater danger to historical truth than either deficiency of evidence or error in detail [he wrote]. . . . Sociologists establish "models" which they test by supposedly empirical evidence. To an historian this seems a very dangerous procedure: far too often the model seems to dictate the selection of facts used to confirm it. . . . The historian must certainly make one initial choice, of main area of study or line of approach. But after that (if he is worth considering at all) he becomes the servant of his evidence of which he will, or should, ask no specific questions until he has absorbed what it says.[9]

But one might revise Kipling's statement and assert with equal accuracy and greater relevance that "them that asks no questions isn't told a truth."

In contemporary historiography, there is a tendency not to reject this statement in an abstract way but rather to accept it in principle and to forget it in practice. There is an inherited antipathy to questions and hypotheses and models, which is apt to run below the surface of a historian's thought. The results are readily apparent in the conceptual poverty of many historical monographs—a poverty to be explained not by the stupidity of the authors, but rather by their habitual reluctance to give sufficient attention to the organization of their inquiry, to the specification of their assumptions, and to the explication of their intentions. Some younger historians, particularly an embattled group who call themselves the New Economic Historians—Douglass North, Robert Fogel, Albert Fishlow, Peter Temin, Lance Davis, and many others—have

8. *American Historical Review* 67 (1961): 89.
9. G. R. Elton, *The Practice of History* (New York, 1967), pp. 36, 38n, 62. In other parts of this work, the author adds qualifications. But his position, as I understand it, comes close to that of Fustel, and violates the succinct advice of Lord Acton: "Study problems, not periods."

begun to revolutionize their special field partly by making their own questions and hypotheses and models as carefully and consciously explicit as possible. Other historians have much to learn from their constructive example. "The wise man is not he who avoids hypotheses," a German scholar has written, "but he who asserts the most probable, and who knows best how to estimate the degree of their probability."[10]

ʃæ The *fallacy of many questions* is a common form of error, which has been variously defined as: (1) framing a question in such a way that two or more questions are asked at once, and a single answer is required; or (2) framing a question in such a way as to beg another question; or (3) framing a question which makes a false presumption; or (4) framing a complex question but demanding a simple answer.

"Have you stopped beating your wife?" This, the classic textbook example, presumes, of course, that you have already begun to do so—a presumption which is not merely ungenerous but possibly mistaken. Many wife-beating questions were deliberately concocted by that playful monarch Charles II, who enjoyed assembling the learned gentlemen of his Royal Society and asking them, with a sovereign contempt for logic as well as fact, to explain "why a live fish placed in a full bowl of water does not cause it to overflow, while a dead fish does cause it to overflow." None of his scholars dared to fault a royal question. Instead, they invented answers of magnificent absurdity as an act of homage to a man who was himself a consistent living argument for republicanism.

Historians, and others who attempt to think historically, have often committed the same error without intending it. A specimen is supplied by a distinguished sociologist, who wrote, in the context of the history of slavery in America: "There exists a major problem about American slavery, one on which a reader of even the best American historians on slavery will not be enlightened: indeed, if he limits his reading to historians he will hardly know that a problem exists. Why was American slavery the most awful the world has ever known?"[11] But *was* American slavery "the most awful the world has ever known"? Glazer frames his question in such a way as to beg another question.

Other examples fly thick and fast in the historiography of the American Reconstruction. Don E. Fehrenbacher, in an essay on the state of

10. Hans Vaihinger, *The Philosophy of "As If,"* trans. C. K. Ogden (London, 1924), p. 89.
11. Introduction by Nathan Glazer to Stanley N. Elkins, *Slavery: A Problem in American Institutional and Intellectual Life,* 2d ed. (New York, 1963), p. ix.

the literature, poses the following questions which he believes to be "especially worth asking and answering."

1. "Was Reconstruction shamefully harsh or surprisingly lenient?"
2. "Was the presidential plan of reconstruction a sound one?"
3. "Could Lincoln have succeeded where Johnson failed?"
4. "Was the latter a miserable bungler or a heroic victim?"
5. "What were the primary motives of the Radical Republicans?"
6. "How bad were the carpetbag governments?"
7. "How well did the freedman meet his new responsibilities?"
8. "What part did terrorism play in the ultimate triumph of the Southern 'redeemers'?"
9. "When did racial segregation harden into its elaborate mold?"[12]

The third question commits the fallacy of fictional questions, which is discussed below. All others are examples of the fallacy of many questions, by any of the definitions listed above. Fehrenbacher's first question assumes that Reconstruction was either "shamefully harsh" or "surprisingly lenient," but maybe it was something else again. The second question assumes that there was a single presidential plan of reconstruction, which is doubtful. The fourth commits precisely the same sort of error as the first; the fifth assumes that there were some clearly primary radical motives, and thereby encourages a simple motivational monism so common in historical writing. The sixth, literally construed, assumes that the carpetbag governments were bad in some degree; the seventh assumes that freedmen in fact had new responsibilities, which were met in some degree. The eighth assumes that the Redeemers did "ultimately" triumph. The ninth assumes that racial segregation did at some point in time harden into an elaborate mold, but maybe that institution has been continuously in process of change.

There are other complaints to be entered against Fehrenbacher's questions. They are mostly metaphysical questions and counterquestions, and they are marred by the heavy-handed moralizing which has so seriously diminished Reconstruction historiography. But the prior complaint in this chapter is that all of them commit the fallacy of many questions.

ह<> The *fallacy of false dichotomous questions* is a special form of the fallacy of many questions, which deserves to be singled out for special condemnation. It arises from the abuse of an exceedingly dangerous conceptual device. Dichotomy is a division into two parts. If it

12. Don E. Fehrenbacher, "Division and Reunion," in John Higham, ed., *The Reconstruction of American History* (New York, 1962), p. 105.

is properly drawn, the parts are mutually exclusive and collectively exhaustive, so that there is no overlap, no opening in the middle, and nothing omitted at either end. These three requirements are very difficult to satisfy in the organization of an empirical inquiry. It is rare that any two historical terms can be so related, unless one of them is specifically defined as the negation of the other. And even then, there is often trouble. The *law of the excluded middle* may demand instant obedience in formal logic, but in history it is as intricate in its applications as the internal revenue code. Dichotomy is used incorrectly when a question is constructed so that it demands a choice between two answers which are in fact not exclusive or not exhaustive. But it is used often by historians in this improper way. Indeed, a little industry has been organized around it: the manufacture of the "problems" series of pamphlets for pedagogical purposes. These works conventionally begin with a false dichotomous question, allegedly designed to "stimulate" thought. The question takes the form of "Basil of Byzantium: Rat or Fink?" Maybe Basil was the very model of a modern ratfink. Maybe that Byzantine character was neither a rat nor a fink, but something vastly more intricate, or something altogether different. But swarms of suffering undergraduates are asked to study a set of pedantical essays, half of which are exaggerated arguments for the rattiness of Basil and the other half are overdrawn portraits of Basil as a fink. The disgusted undergraduate is expected to make a choice between these unappetizing alternatives, or perhaps to combine them in some ingenious paradoxical contrivance of his own invention, which falsifies both his understanding and the problem itself.

The following examples are the actual titles of works which have been edited by reputable professional historians and issued by respectable publishers such as Holt, Rinehart; Prentice-Hall; Houghton Mifflin; Random House; and D. C. Heath:

Napoleon III: Enlightened Statesman or Proto-Fascist?

The Causes of the War of 1812: National Honor or National Interest?

The Abolitionists: Reformers or Fanatics?

Jacksonian Democracy: Myth or Reality?

Plato: Totalitarian or Democrat?

The Dred Scott Decision: Law or Politics?

The Removal of the Cherokee Nation—Manifest Destiny or National Dishonor?

John D. Rockefeller—Robber Baron or Industrial Statesman?

The Robber Barons—Pirates or Pioneers?

Huey P. Long—Southern Demagogue or American Democrat?

The New Deal—Revolution or Evolution?

Industry-Wide Collective Bargaining—Promise or Menace?

Ancient Science—Metaphysical or Observational?

Feudalism—Cause or Cure of Anarchy?

The Medieval Mind—Faith or Reason?

The Parliament of Edward I—Royal Court or Representative Legislature?

Renaissance Man—Medieval or Modern?

Martin Luther—Reformer or Revolutionary?

The Absolutism of Louis XIV—The End of Anarchy or the Beginning of Tyranny?

The Scientific Revolution—Factual or Metaphysical?

The Industrial Revolution in England—Blessing or Curse to the Working Man?

The Fall of the Russian Monarchy—Inherent Failure or Planned Revolution?

The Origins of Nazi Germany—German History or Charismatic Leadership?

What Is History—Fact or Fancy?

Many of these questions are unsatisfactory in several ways at once. Some are grossly anachronistic; others encourage simple-minded moralizing. Most are very shallow. But all are structurally deficient in that they suggest a false dichotomy between two terms that are neither mutually exclusive nor collectively exhaustive. They are also imprecise, both in the dichotomous terms and in the troublesome connective "or," which might mean "either *X* or *Y* but not both" (like the Latin *aut*), or "either *X* or *Y* or both" (like the Latin *vel*), or "either *X* or *Y* or both, or neither." This ambiguity is not often clarified in context, and the reader receives no clear indication of what he is being asked to accomplish.

The "problems" that appear in these pamphlets are not merely a result of faulty pedagogical practice. Many of these titles reflect a false dichotomy which is deeply embedded in scholarly literature on the subject at hand. They are illustrations not only of the way in which many historians teach but also of the way in which they conceptualize and carry on their own research.

What can a student do, in the face of a false dichotomy? He can try several stratagems. First, he might attempt to show that the dichotomous terms can coexist. Second, he might demonstrate that there is a third possibility. Third, he might repudiate one or the other or both alternatives. All of these devices will work, in a limited way. But all of them will have the effect of shackling the student's answer to the fallacious conceptualization he is attempting to correct. The most satisfactory response, I think, is to indicate the structural deficiencies in the question-framing and to revise the inquiry on that level, by the introduction of a more refined and more open question, which can be flexibly adjusted as the analysis proceeds.

The problem of an exclusive choice between nonexclusive alternatives is often confronted in declarative as well as interrogative sentences. The motto of the Prince of Orange was *Non rapui sed recepi,* which means, "I didn't steal; I received." But maybe he was a receiver of stolen goods, even if they were stolen in a glorious cause. In this question, as in so many others, one can only endorse the sensible observation of Reuben Abel: "The continuum in which we live is not the kind of place in which middles can be unambiguously excluded."[13]

ᔐ   The *fallacy of metaphysical questions* is an attempt to resolve a nonempirical problem by empirical means. In its most common contemporary form, this fallacy consists in the framing of a question which cannot be resolved before the researcher settles some central metaphysical problem such as "What is the nature of things?" or "What is the inner secret of reality?" And these are questions which will not be resolved before the oceans freeze over.

A prime example is the problem which is eternally popular among Civil War historians: "Was the War inevitable?" A scholar who carries this question to the archives can illustrate his answer by reference to historical events; he can add persuasive power to his metaphysical proposition by the appearance of factual solidity. But he can no more hope to resolve the issue of inevitability by empirical research than he can hope to determine by modern methods of quantification the number of angels which might be made to perch upon the head of a proverbial pin.

If Thomas J. Pressly is correct, in his study of historical interpretations of the Civil War, the problem of inevitability has been *the* central historiographical problem.[14] A few historians have repudiated it, such as Kenneth Stampp, who tried to turn away from "the fruitless and impossible task of proving or disproving that the Civil War was inevitable."[15] In the same spirit, Arthur Schlesinger, Jr., has written that "the problem of the inevitability of the Civil War, of course, is in its essence

13. "Pragmatism and the Outlook of Modern Science," *Philosophy and Phenomenological Research* 27 (1966): 50.
14. Thomas J. Pressly, *Americans Interpret Their Civil War* (Princeton, 1954).
15. Kenneth M. Stampp, *And the War Came,* 2d ed. (Chicago, 1964), p. vii.

a problem devoid of meaning."[16] And Pieter Geyl has declared that "The question of evitable or inevitable is one on which, it seems to me, the historian can never form any but an ambivalent opinion."[17]

But all of these scholars were themselves unable to keep clear of the problem they condemned. Their works are refutations of the argument that the Civil War was a "needless war," which was precipitated by a "blundering generation" of American political leaders.[18] And there are discouraging signs that the problem of inevitability is still obsessive in the consciousness of the coming generation of young American historians.[19]

"As a historian," E. H. Carr writes, "I am perfectly prepared to do without 'inevitable,' 'unavoidable.' 'inescapable,' and even 'ineluctable.' Life will be drabber. But let us leave them to poets and metaphysicians." Historians might also turn their backs upon all aspects of the metaphysical problems raised by determinism versus voluntarism, the comparative reality of individuals and groups, materialism versus idealism, and all manner of other monisms and dualisms. The progress of an empirical science of history squarely depends upon a sense of the possible. The working historian, in my opinion, is well advised to deal with these dilemmas by a method of indifference.[20]

Some historians of a humanist bent will protest that all historical problems are metaphysical problems. This is humbug. It can be argued that all historical problems can be made into metaphysical problems if

16. Arthur Schlesinger, Jr., "The Causes of the Civil War: A Note on Historical Sentimentalism," *Partisan Review* 16 (1949): 980.
17. Pieter Geyl, "The American Civil War and the Problem of Inevitability," *Debates with Historians* (New York, 1958), p. 263.
18. Stampp, p. v; Schlesinger, pp. 970–81; Geyl, pp. 244–63. For two other thoughtful critiques of the problem, see Lee Benson and Cushing Strout, "Causation and the American Civil War," *History and Theory* 1 (1960): 163–85.
19. See, e.g., Eugene D. Genovese, *The Political Economy of Slavery* (New York, 1965), pp. 4–10, passim.
20. E. H. Carr, *What Is History?* (New York, 1962), p. 126. Carr believes that the inevitability problem "attaches itself almost exclusively to contemporary history. Last term at Cambridge," he writes, "I saw a talk to some society advertised under the title: 'Was the Russian Revolution Inevitable?' I am sure it was intended as a perfectly serious talk. But if you had seen a talk advertised on 'Were the Wars of the Roses Inevitable?' you would at once have suspected some joke. The historian writes of the Norman conquest or the American war of independence as if what happened was in fact bound to happen, and as if it was his business simply to explain what happened and why" (ibid.).
But this, unfortunately, is not true, at least as far as the American Revolution is concerned. David Hawke writes, "Nothing intrigues colonial historians more than the question of why the American Revolution occurred. Was it a repressible conflict or not?" (*The Colonial Experience* [Indianapolis, 1966], p. 517.) I think it probable that historians debate the "repressibility" of every important happening which they are unable to accept unanimously as a Good Thing.

one wishes to do so. But there are many historical problems of primary importance to all inquirers, whatever their opinions may be, which are clearly *not* metaphysical. "How many people voted in the election of 1840?" "How did the price of cotton change in the 1850s?" "What did the Halfway Covenant mean to the men who made it?" "Was Franklin Roosevelt more interventionist than a majority of the American people in 1940, or less so?" Nonmetaphysical questions can be exceedingly complex and sophisticated. "How and when did habits of authority develop and decline in English and American politics?" "How did the personality patterns of Negro slaves change during the period of their enslavement?"

These are urgent questions, and they are empirical questions, which can be put to the test. The reader will note that none of them are "why" questions. In my opinion—and I may be a minority of one—that favorite adverb of historians should be consigned to the semantical rubbish heap. A "why" question tends to become a metaphysical question. It is also an imprecise question, for the adverb "why" is slippery and difficult to define. Sometimes it seeks a cause, sometimes a motive, sometimes a reason, sometimes a description, sometimes a process, sometimes a purpose, sometimes a justification. A "why" question lacks direction and clarity; it dissipates a historian's energies and interests. "Why did the Civil War happen?" "Why was Lincoln shot?" A working historian receives no clear signals from these woolly interrogatories as to which way to proceed, how to begin, what kinds of evidence will answer the problem, and indeed what kind of problem is raised. There are many more practicable adverbs—who, when, where, what, how—which are more specific and more satisfactory. Questions of this sort *can* be resolved empirically, and from them a skilled historian can construct a project with much greater sophistication, relevance, accuracy, precision, and utility, instead of wasting his time with metaphysical dilemmas raised by his profound "why" questions, which have often turned out to be about as deep as the River Platte.

It is improbable that this will happen, among historians, in the foreseeable future. "Why" questions are rooted in the literature and institutionalized in the graduate schools, and for most of my colleagues a historical discipline without them is as strange as a system of non-Euclidean geometry. But it is already beginning to happen, in a quiet way, in monographs such as Thomas Barrow's *Trade and Empire: The British Customs Service in Colonial America, 1660–1775* (Cambridge, 1967), a fine book which orthodox academic reviewers have utterly failed to understand. A young, able, but very old-fashioned scholar, Benjamin Labaree, complains in his notice of the book that "Barrow does not explain with full satisfaction *why* the Americans evaded the Acts of Trade, but he does marshal a wealth of material to show *how* they managed to disobey them."[21] One wonders what kind of "why" answer would have satisfied Labaree. The hand of God? The dialectic? Some mighty dynamic of materialism? Maybe some American merchants helped to smash up the mercantile system for the same reason that Kirillov destroyed himself in Dostoevsky's *The Possessed*—to demonstrate that they were free. These questions are not for a historian, who can only measure the motives and purposes that are part of the act itself. He can never hope to find the inner secret, maybe because it does not exist.

Be that as it may, Barrow's book is a straw in the wind. His work suggests that there is a fair and steady offshore breeze which is blowing historians clear of the rocks and shoals of metaphysics, though some seem determined (an ambiguity is intended) to know the excitement of a shipwreck, which is the only kind of metaphysical finality that is open to them.

A rigorous attempt to purge history of metaphysics will, in truth, serve to narrow historical inquiry. To those who protest that the result would be a little too narrow, one might repeat the words of Nelson Goodman: "You may decry some of these scruples and protest that there are more things in heaven and earth than are dreamt of in my philosophy. I am concerned, rather, that there should not be more things dreamt of in my philosophy than there are in heaven or earth."[22]

* The *fallacy of fictional questions* is an ancient form of error, which has recently been elevated into an explicit method and proclaimed before the world as a whole new thing in historical inquiry. It consists in an attempt to demonstrate by an empirical method what might have happened in history, as if in fact it actually had: the sort of thing that Philip Guedalla and others did in a lively work called *If, or History Rewritten* (New York, 1931), in which they ruminated upon the might-

---

21. *Journal of American History* 54 (1968): 876.
22. Nelson Goodman, *Fact, Fiction, and Forecast* (Cambridge, 1955), p. 39. Some historians have argued that the direction of historiographical change is the opposite of that which I have suggested. Miss C. V. Wedgwood writes, "The older historians concentrated more on narrative than on analysis, on the *How* rather than the *Why* of history. But now, for several generations, *Why* has been regarded as a more important question than *How*." *Truth and Opinion* (New York, 1960), p. 14. This, I think, is mistaken. Perhaps the change has been from the implicit *why* of older narrative historians to the explicit *Why* of the last generation of monographers, to the controlled *who, how, where, when,* and *what* of historians who are presently beginning to publish.

have-beens, if Booth's bullet had missed, or Drouet's cart had stuck, or Napoleon had escaped to America, or the Moors had won in Spain, or Lee had won at Gettysburg, or Byron had become King of Greece.

There is nothing necessarily fallacious in fictional constructs, as long as they are properly recognized for what they are and are clearly distinguished from empirical problems. All novels are organized around an idea of what might have happened—some very great truths have been taught to the world in this disguise. Fictional questions can also be heuristically useful to historians, somewhat in the manner of metaphors and analogies, for the ideas and inferences which they help to suggest. But they *prove* nothing and can never be proved by an empirical method. All historical "evidence" for what might have happened if Booth had missed his mark is necessarily taken from the world in which he hit it. There is no way to escape this fundamental fact.[23]

Nevertheless, fictional questions have become fashionable among a group of young economic historians who call themselves "Cliometricians" and are doing many good and revolutionary things to their discipline, in the way of an extension of empirical inquiry, a refinement of conceptualization, and a general integration of history and theory. Economic theory is theoretical in the narrow sense of the word. It deals in "if, then" propositions, unlike much social "theory," which is commonly more paradigmatic in its nature. It is understandable that economic historians, more than others, are tempted by the seductive might-have-beens of "as if" questions. A few have even attempted to combine "fictional," "counterfactual," "conditional," or "as if" questions (as they are variously called) with techniques of empirical quantification. The results are not merely false but absurd, for to quantify the conditional is to square the circle. It is simply impossible for a singular statement to be *both* counterfactual and factual at the same time.

The classic example is a controversial monograph by Robert W. Fogel, *Railroads and Economic Growth: Essays in Econometric History* (Baltimore, 1964), in which the author tries to prove that railroads were not "indispensable" to American economic growth in the nineteenth century by demonstrating how the economy might have functioned if railroads had not existed. Fogel measures "primary effects" of the transportation system in terms of the costs of haulage by railroads, as

---

23. There is an immense philosophical literature on the subject of fictional questions, or "counterfactual conditionals." The best discussion I have seen is in Nelson Goodman, *Fact, Fiction, & Forecast*, 2d ed. (Indianapolis, 1965), pp. 13–34, in which the author emphatically declares that "a counterfactual by its nature can never be subjected to any direct empirical test by realizing its antecedent" (p. 4). This is the *only* point which I mean to argue here.

against haulage exclusively by turnpikes and canals, at actual nine-teenth-century prices. He also estimates "secondary effects"—changes in spatial distribution, generation of demand for manufactures, etc. From these figures, he calculates that the "social saving" derived from the use of railroads was comparatively small, as a proportion of the gross national product. And he concludes that railroads were in fact "dispensable" to economic development in nineteenth-century Amer-ica.[24]

Fogel's book might have been called *If, or History Derailed*. His-tory is run off the rails in more senses than one. There is much to be salvaged from the wreckage—a zeal for quantification of historical problems, a determination to make questions and assumptions explicit, and an impressive conceptual sophistication. But Fogel's inquiry is flawed by three fatal inconsistencies: First, his evidence of a transportation net which might have operated in the absence of railroads is necessarily derived from a world in which railroads were present. Fogel tries to allow for this bias in his material, but only by introducing other fictional constructs which assume what he promises to prove by empirical inquiry. The cost of haulage by canal boats is merely one of many imponder-ables. Fogel bases his estimates upon a situation where canals and rail-roads coexisted. It is possible that competition between the two served in some measure to reduce rates for canal travel, but it is equally possible that if canals had been the mainstay of the transportation system, they would have been more efficient in their operations and a spur to tech-nological innovation, which might have reduced rates. Who can say which? And yet, the question is critical to Fogel's thesis. Moreover, the secondary, tertiary, etc., effects of his canals upon industry, immigration, national psychology, national politics, and such specific happenings as the Civil War cannot even be guessed, much less proved by empirical research.

Second, there is another serious flaw in Fogel's logic. He believes that "to establish the proposition that railroads substantially altered the course of economic growth, one must do more than provide information on the services of railroads. It must also be shown that substitutes for railroads could not (or would not) have performed essentially the same role" (p. 207). But this confuses two separate questions. It is one thing to ask, "Did railroads alter the process of American economic growth?"

---

24. Edward Kirkland, an economic historian of the old school, complains that there is a kind of doublethink in the work of Fogel and his friends. For the former, a social saving of 5 percent of GNP appears small. But for Douglass North, "another card-carrying Cliometrician, 'a social saving of 5 percent is a very substantial saving.'" *American His-torical Review* 72 (1967): 1494.

And quite another to ask, "Did railroads alter the process of American economic growth in a way that only railroads were able to do?" The first question is empirically verifiable. The second is not. And the first question does not require an answer to the second. It can, for example, be conclusively proved that Thomas Jefferson, as president, was the agent of certain great and grave events, such as the purchase of Louisiana. But nobody will ever know if he was "indispensable" to that result, nor is the problem of his indispensability necessarily implied by the fact of his agency. No amount of empirical research will ever suffice to prove that Timothy Pickering, had he by some horrible twist of fate been elevated to the presidential chair, would or would not have done precisely what Jefferson did. His perverse opinions on Louisiana are well known, but the opinions which he might have held in different circumstances are utterly unknowable, and irrelevant to a proper historical inquiry. And in precisely the same fashion, nobody will ever know what miracles might have been wrought by Fogel's counterfactual canal boats, which are not more mythical (if a little more plausible) than similar vessels which some enthusiasts have spied plying the alleged waterways of the planet Mars.

Third, the question of the "indispensability" of railroads is comparable to the problem of the "inevitability" of the Civil War. Fogel is leading his Cliometrical colleagues down the methodological rathole of the metaphysical question. His work is a forward step, in its explicitness, sophistication, and attempt at quantification. But it is also a step backward in its return to ancient metaphysical conundrums which have distracted many generations of historians. This aspect of the New Economic History is not new at all, but ancient, and even anachronistic.

Fogel's counterfactual canals have created an uproar among economic historians. An immense controversial literature has appeared in their journals.[25] Some of Fogel's colleagues have tried to salvage some-

25. Louis M. Hacker, "The New Revolution in Economic History: A Review Article Based on *Railroads and Economic Growth: Essays in Econometric History*, by Robert William Fogel," *Explorations in Entrepreneurial History*, 2d ser. 3 (1966): 159–75; Lance Davis, "Professor Fogel and the New Economic History," *Economic History Review*, 2d ser. 19 (1966): 657–63; R. W. Fogel, "The New Economic History: Its Findings and Methods," ibid., 624–56; R. W. Fogel, "The Specification Problem in Economic History," *Journal of Economic History* 27 (1967): 283–308; Alexander Gerschenkron, "The Discipline and I," *Journal of Economic History* 27 (1967): 443–58; Meghnad Desai, "Some Issues in Econometric History," *Economic History Review*, 2d ser. 21 (1968): 1–16; E. H. Hunt, "The New Economic History: Professor Fogel's Study of American Railroads," *History* 53 (1968): 3–18; G. R. Hawke, "Mr. Hunt's Study of the Fogel Thesis: A Comment," ibid., 18–23.

Fritz Redlich, in "New and Traditional Approaches to Economic History," *Journal of Economic History* 25 (1965): 484–85, introduces to the controversy the work of

thing from his work by arguing that counterfactuals can be used correctly "for the elucidation of relatively short-term changes, preferably in situations in which the political factor may be largely neglected. Once the period under review lengthens, the number of unconsidered and nonconsiderable factors that bear upon the outcome increases fast and the significance of the results diminishes faster."[26] One wonders what this scholar means by the "political factor." Maybe he is thinking of something like the "human factor," in which case he would rule out any historical problem involving those irritating and unpredictable things called people. But be that as it may, his attempt at compromise will not work for other reasons. The only difference between long-run and short-run counterfactuals is that the absurdity of the former is more glaringly *apparent*. It is not more extreme.

Fogel has himself replied to critics of counterfactualizing with the argument that everybody does it, that the alternative to an open counterfactual model is a concealed one.[27] But this is surely a mistake, for reasons discussed in the case of Jefferson and Louisiana, above. There is, I think, an increasing body of historical literature which is noncausal in its nature (in any meaningful or common sense of causality), and there is some which has refined the problem of causality so as to exclude problems such as inevitability and indispensability, by working closely from the assumption that things happened merely in the way that they happened and not in any other way. This is not to affirm a determinism, nor to deny that men make choices, but merely to short-circuit the problem and to get on to others that we can handle. It is always possible, of course, to convert any historical problem into a nonhistorical one, but why should a scholar go out of his way to make a difficult problem impossible? History is tough enough, as it is—as it *actually* is.

It is true that many other historians besides Fogel have resorted to explicit or implicit counterfactual models. But it is not true that they must or should do so, for the same difficulties which developed in Fogel's

---

Hans Vaihinger—mistakenly, I think. He argues that Fogel's counterfactuals are "figments" in Vaihinger's terms. But they fit more closely into Vaihinger's category called "fictions," viz., "imaginary cases." (Vaihinger, *The Philosophy of "As If,"* p. 26.) Vaihinger clearly distinguishes between "fictions" and "hypotheses." He argues that "the latter are assumptions which are probable; assumptions, the truth of which can be proved by further experience. They are therefore verifiable. Fictions are never verifiable; for they are hypotheses which are known to be false [sic], but which are employed because of their utility" (p. xlii). That is the point which is held for, here. Vaihinger observes that hypotheses are true or false, but fictions are merely expedient or inexpedient.

26. Alexander Gerschenkron, "The Discipline and I," *Journal of Economic History* 17 (1967): 457. See also Sidney Hook, *The Hero in History* (Boston, 1943), chap. 7.
27. Fogel, "The Specification Problem," p. 285.

work appear in all other cases. Consider, for example, the work of an able political historian, Eric McKitrick. In an elaborate and sophisticated study of Andrew Johnson and the American Reconstruction, which was written in the years of the Eisenhower "consensus," McKitrick wondered if "an imaginary peace-making" might have been arranged between two influential Americans—Wade Hampton, a supposititious spokesman for the South Carolina "establishment," and John Andrew, allegedly of the Massachusetts "establishment." McKitrick, who appears to believe that "establishments" are good things, and that all good things, which are mostly conservative things, must be done through them, has no difficulty demonstrating to his own satisfaction that such a peace-making was possible—thus reflecting upon the statesmanship of President Andrew Johnson, who lacked the style which McKitrick respects.[28]

It might be demonstrated that the author misinterprets the position of Wade Hampton, which was far more intransigent than McKitrick is prepared to allow.[29] But a more serious flaw consists in the attempt at empirical reification of an imaginary event, which exists only in the mind of the author. The result is merely sentimental claptrap, which calls to mind a phrase from Eliot:

> Footfalls echo in the memory
> Down the passage which we did not take
> Towards the door we never opened
> Into the rose-garden[30]

McKitrick's imaginary peacemaking brings to mind imaginary war-making, which seems almost as firmly established in the world today as war itself. German soldiers and statesmen, before they made war upon their various neighbors, formed the habit of conducting elaborate *kriegspiele* on blackboards and sandtables, which must have been as much fun as the real thing. On the eve of World War II, German leaders played a war game among themselves, in which they demonstrated to their own satisfaction that England could not and would not intervene in Poland's interest. Today this grim gamesmanship is much in fashion among semiacademic nuclear strategists at the Rand Corporation, and the Hudson Institute, and, I am told, in the Red Army Historical Section as well. Let us hope that they will not make a similar mistake, and put their trust in a method which is not merely delusive to themselves but also exceedingly dangerous to others.

28. Eric L. McKitrick, *Andrew Johnson and Reconstruction* (Chicago, 1960), pp. 214–50.
29. Joel Williamson, *After Slavery: The Negro in South Carolina During Reconstruction, 1861–1877* (Chapel Hill, 1967), pp. 276, 406–12.
30. T. S. Eliot, "Burnt Norton," *Collected Poems, 1909–1962* (New York, 1963), p. 175.

If by some miracle of rationality the Cold War were brought to an end, the *Kriegspielers* of the world would be faced with the dark prospect of occupational obsolescence. In that desperate predicament, Cold Warriors might beat their conceptual swords into historiographical plowshares and begin to dig up the past. An inkling of the possible results appears in "An Attempt to Simulate the Outbreak of World War I," by Charles F. and Margaret G. Hermann.[31] The serious student of that event may be interested to learn that according to the simulation, England considered "the initiation of war on Germany while the advantage appeared on her side" (presumably by sending the Old Contemptibles hopping over the low countries on pogo sticks). Moreover, the Austro-Hungarian decision maker in the game suddenly "revealed pacifistic tendencies and readily accepted the objections to his nation's militaristic actions" (the nature of that extraordinary conversion experience is not explained). The authors conclude with a Scotch verdict on their own efforts. "Until more validation exercises are conducted," they believe, "it is premature to accept or reject simulation as an important new tool for studying political phenomena" (p. 416).

That judgment is safe, and maybe sound (I believe otherwise). But in the meantime, Fogel and McKitrick, and the counterfactualists, and the *Kriegspielers*, might profit from the advice of those learned, if unlovable logicians, Tweedledum and Tweedledee:

> "I know what you're thinking about," said Tweedledum; "but it isn't so, nohow."
> "Contrariwise," continued Tweedledee, "if it was so it might be; and if it were so, it would be; but as it isn't, it ain't. That's logic."[32]

℘ The *fallacy of semantical questions* consists in an attempt to resolve, by empirical investigation of an object, a semantical question about the name by which that object is called, thereby confusing actual happenings with verbal descriptions of actual happenings. The problem is a difficult one, much complicated by developments in an important new discipline (linguistics), and a revolution in an old one (philosophy), both of which have spawned a vast literature of sophisticated and useful scholarship. All historical questions are semantical in some degree, in that they are attempts to establish intelligible relationships between the signs and symbols of our language on the one hand and the evidence of our past on the other.

But some questions which historians have asked are *merely* seman-

---

31. *The American Political Science Review* 61 (1967): 400–16.
32. *The Complete Works of Lewis Carroll*, Modern Library ed. (New York, n.d.), p. 181.

tical, which is to say that they are sterile disputes about word usage and not about the past happenings to which the words are supposed to refer. Semantical questions are "term questions," in the fashion of the original term question, which was not the least of many miseries inflicted by well-meaning Western missionaries upon the suffering souls of China. But in fairness to the missionaries, it should be said that the Chinese seem to be culturally predisposed to term questions. Witness the legendary Ming emperor who dealt with a dangerous river by a sort of semantical flood control project. Instead of building dikes and dams, he changed its name from "The Wild One" to "The Peaceful One."[33] So common have such "rectifications of names" been in that country, from Confucius to Chou En-lai, that this form of error might be called the Chinese fallacy.

Semantical questions are deeply embedded in our own culture as well. A classical example is the conversation between Alice and the White Knight in *Through the Looking Glass:*

> "You are sad," the Knight said in an anxious tone: "let me sing you a song to comfort you. . . . The name of the song is called '*Haddocks' Eyes*.' "
>
> "Oh, that's the name of the song, is it?" Alice said, trying to feel interested.
>
> "No, you don't understand," the Knight said, looking a little vexed. "That's what the name is *called*. The name really *is* '*The Aged Aged Man*.' "
>
> "Then I ought to have said '*That's what the song is called*'?" Alice corrected herself.
>
> "No, you oughtn't: that's quite another thing! The *song* is called '*Ways and Means*': but that's only what it's *called*, you know!"
>
> "Well, what *is* the song, then?" said Alice, who was by this time completely bewildered.
>
> "I was coming to that," the Knight said. "The song really *is* '*A-sitting On A Gate*': and the tune's my own invention."[34]

A historiographical example of the fallacy of semantical questions presently appears in a prolonged dispute among American colonial historians over the question, "Was the political structure of seventeenth-century America 'democratic' or 'aristocratic'?"

Consider two articles on the subject, one by Mrs. B. Katherine Brown, and another by Professor Roy Lokken.[35] Both quote a statement by John Cotton, addressed to a Puritan Lord in England who was con-

33. Hans Konigsburger, *Love and Hate in China* (New York, 1966), p. 9.
34. *The Complete Works of Lewis Carroll*, p. 244.
35. B. Katherine Brown, "A Note on the Puritan Concept of Aristocracy," *Mississippi Valley Historical Review* 41 (1954): 105–12; Roy N. Lokken, "The Concept of Democracy in Colonial Political Thought," *William and Mary Quarterly*, 3d ser. 16 (1959); 568–80.

cerned about the alleged absence of Orders and Distinctions in the New World. Cotton wrote:

> Nor neede your Lordship feare (which yet I speake with submission to your Lordships better judgment) that this corse will lay such a foundation, as nothing but a mere democracy can be built upon it. Bodine confesseth, that though it be a *status popularis,* where a people choose their owne governors; yet the government is not a democracy, if it be administered, not by the people, but by the governors, whether one (for then it is a monarchy, though elective) or by many, for then (as you know) it is aristocracy.[36]

Cotton and John Winthrop and others called their polity a "Mixt Aristocratie," but Mrs. Brown argues that given their definitions "Puritan 'Mixt Aristocratie' is much nearer our notion of democracy than our current meaning of aristocracy" (p. 111).

Lokken cites the same evidence to sustain a contrary proposition, that Cotton was hostile to "unmixed democracy," that there was nothing in his thought like a nineteenth- or twentieth-century sense of democracy, for "in the political ethos of the seventeenth and eighteenth century English world, representation did not involve direct responsibility to the electorate" (pp. 577–78).

This exchange has gone round and round for ten years and gives no sign of playing out. Some useful research has resulted, but in these articles of Mrs. Brown and Mr. Lokken, it has degenerated into a semantical question. What they are really concerned about, I think, is not "What was the political structure of seventeenth-century America?" but only secondarily this, and primarily "What name shall we give it?" And the dispute which has developed from that question closely resembles an argument over the question "Is a zebra a white animal with black stripes or a black animal with white stripes?"

A more intelligent and useful approach to the problem is surely possible. Suppose that all evidence of seventeenth-century New England were totally destroyed, except John Cotton's replies to Lord Say and Lord Brooke. From that source alone, much could be discovered about the polity of Massachusetts Bay, most of which Mrs. Brown and Mr. Lokken have ignored. Cotton's correspondence, both as secondary evidence of the government of the Bay and as primary evidence of the principles and prejudices of one inhabitant, shows much that has devel-

---

36. "Copy of a Letter from Mr. Cotton to Lord Say and Seal in the Year 1636," in Thomas Hutchinson, *The History of the Colony and Providence of Massachusetts-Bay,* ed. Lawrence Shaw Mayo, 3 vols. (Cambridge, Mass., 1936) 1: 416.

oped and ramified in the next three centuries of American history and much that has disappeared as well.

There is profound sense of social ranks: "Two distinct ranks we willingly acknowledge, from the Light of Nature and scripture; the one of them called Princes, or Nobles, or Elders (amongst whom gentlemen have their place) the other the people. Hereditary dignity or honours we willingly allow to the former . . . " (p. 410). But there also is, in Cotton's distinction, a repudiation of "hereditary authority and power" in formal institutional arrangements (p. 412) which exceeds, I believe, the professions and practice of any European society in the year 1636.

There is much else besides in this extraordinarily fertile document which alone is sufficient to sustain a monograph (and probably will, someday). In the meantime, the controversy might stand as a byword and an example to historians who are tempted to go rummaging through dusty records for Haddocks' eyes and Aged Aged Men and other semantical fancies.

George Boas's observation is perhaps relevant: "The song of the barnyard cock," he writes, "is *cock-a-doodle-do* in English, *cocorico* in French, and *kikiericki* in German and in Italian. Would anyone debate on which is right or whether cocks in different countries sing different songs?"[37]

⁂ The *fallacy of declarative questions* consists in confusing an interrogative with a declarative statement. It violates a fundamental rule of empirical question-framing, which requires that a question must have an open end, which will allow a free and honest choice, with minimal bias and maximal flexibility. If a historian goes to his sources with a simple affirmative proposition that "X was the case," then he is predisposed to prove it. He will probably be able to find "evidence" sufficient to illustrate his expectations, if not actually to sustain them. If, on the other hand, he asks, "Was X or Y the case?" then he has an empirical advantage, at least in some small degree. And if he asks "Was X or not-X, Y or not-Y, Z or not-Z . . . the case?" and if he designs X, and Y, and Z in such a way that his own preferences are neutralized, and if he leaves the way open to refinements in the form of X_1, Y_1, Z_1, and if he allows for still other unexpected possibilities, then the probability of empirical accuracy is still further enhanced.

A historian, like any other researcher, has a vested interest in answering his own questions. His job is at stake, and his reputation, and most

37. George Boas, *The Inquiring Mind* (La Salle, 1959), p. 45.

important, his self-respect. If he substitutes a declarative for an inter-rogative statement, then the result is literally a foregone conclusion. The best will in the world won't suffice to keep him honest.

In historical writing, declarative questions tend also to be mimetic questions, with a frequency which calls to mind an epigram (variously attributed to Max Beerbohm and Herbert Asquith), that whether or not history repeats itself, historians repeat each other. If historical research were as empirical as it can be, then we might hope to see very large heuristic hypotheses put to very small controlled tests. Now and then a study appears which suggests that this dream is more than merely a mad utopian fancy. But many historians follow a different method. In common practice, a general interpretation is fashioned by an essayist not as a heuristic hypothesis but as an affirmative proposition. In the next twenty years or so, a legion of gradgrinds manufacture monographs which reify the essay, with a few inconsequential changes. Qualifications are in-serted at the end of sentences, active verbs are changed to passive, pro-nouns of indefinite reference are converted to proper nouns, and footnotes are added at the bottom of the page. This process continues until another essayist publishes another brilliant general interpretation, and another generation of gradgrinds are wound up like mechanical rab-bits and set to running about in ever-smaller circles. The result is a dialogue between essayists and monographers which resembles the ex-change between Hamlet and Polonius:

HAMLET: "Do you see yonder cloud that's almost in the shape of a camel?"
POLONIUS: "By the mass, and 'tis like a camel indeed."
HAMLET: "Methinks it is like a weasel."
POLONIUS: "It is backed like a weasel."
HAMLET: "Or like a whale?"
POLONIUS: "Very like a whale."

There is an example in the whales and weasels of Reconstruction historiography. The first generation of academic interpretations of this problem began with the publication of a set of interpretative *Essays on the Civil War and Reconstruction* (1897) by Professor William Archi-bald Dunning of Columbia University. Mr. Dunning and a few like-minded gentlemen so dominated the American historical profession in that era that a few disenchanted contemporaries spoke of his narrow circle of acquaintances as the "history ring."[38]

Under Dunning's direct control, or indirect influence, many state

---

38. J. G. de Roulhac Hamilton, ed., *Truth in History* (New York, 1937), p. xv. Hamil-ton's introduction helps to explain the influence of Dunning, by demonstrating the extraordinary deference structure which was sustained by the power of Dunning's per-sonality, and the remarkable weight of his learning.

studies of Reconstruction began to pour out of the seminar rooms of Columbia and Johns Hopkins, most of which tended to reify the assumptions, interpretations, categories and prejudices of "the Old Chief."[39] These monographs were remarkably homogeneous in method and substance and extraordinarily consistent with Dunning's own opinions—more so than if they were merely manifestations of a common *Zeitgeist.* They tended to be elaborately detailed institutional studies, conceived as political and constitutional history, informed by racist assumptions, and colored by an antipathy to radicalism in all its forms and a particular hostility to carpetbaggers, scalawags, and all that unsavory crew. They were researched with care. But their authors willingly played Polonius to Dunning's Hamlet.

A second wave of "revisionist" academic interpretations of Reconstruction began with an article by a Negro historian, W. E. B. Du Bois, "Reconstruction and Its Benefits," published in *The American Historical Review* (15 [1910]: 781–99), and other work by Charles Beard. Though Beard never wrote at length on Reconstruction, the chapters in his *Rise of American Civilization* (2 vols., New York, 1927) were as influential as Dunning's work had previously been. The new generation of monographers was a mixed bag of semi-Marxists, white liberals, and Negro historians, whose interpretations tended to be more homogeneous than their ethnic and ideological heterogeneity suggested. These "revisionists" were more interested in economic and social history than in political and constitutional happenings and more apt to sympathize with Negroes and carpetbaggers than with their conservative white opponents. There was powerful inclination toward economic determinism in metaphysics, to relativism in epistemology, and to egalitarianism in social theory.[40]

39. They included Hamilton Eckenrode, *The Political History of Virginia During the Reconstruction* (1904); Walter L. Fleming, *Civil War and Reconstruction in Alabama* (1905); James W. Garner, *Reconstruction in Mississippi* (1901); John R. Ficklen, *History of Reconstruction in Louisiana (through 1868)* (1910); Ella Lonn, *Reconstruction in Louisiana after 1868* (1918); J. G. de Roulhac Hamilton, *Reconstruction in North Carolina* (1914); C. Mildred Thompson, *Reconstruction in Georgia* (1915); Charles W. Ramsdell, *Reconstruction in Texas* (1910); Thomas S. Staples, *Reconstruction in Arkansas* (1923); William W. Davis, *The Civil War and Reconstruction in Florida* (1913); William Starr Myers, *The Self-Reconstruction of Maryland* (1909); John S. Reynolds, *Reconstruction in South Carolina* (1905); James W. Fertig, *Secessionism and Reconstruction in Tennessee* (1898); James W. Patton, *Unionism and Reconstruction in Tennessee* (1934); and J. P. Hollis, *The Early Reconstruction Period in South Carolina* (1905).
40. Their works included Francis B. Simkins and Robert H. Woody, *South Carolina During Reconstruction* (1932); Horace M. Bond, "Social and Economic Forces in Alabama Reconstruction," *Journal of Negro History* 23 (1938): 290–348; Roger W. Shugg, *Origins of the Class Struggle in Louisiana* (1939); Vernon L. Wharton, *The Negro*

A third wave of state studies is presently beginning to appear. The most significant interpreters, the most influential teachers of graduate students, are Kenneth M. Stampp at Berkeley, David Donald at Johns Hopkins, Eric McKitrick at Columbia, and C. Vann Woodward at Yale, all of whom have published many statements of their points of view. Their approach is equally distinct from the politicoconstitutional history of Dunning and the socioeconomic history of Beard. It consists principally of a sense of the complexity of an holistic configuration called political culture, and a consciousness of the convolutions of human personality. Their histories tend to be intricate interactions of altruisms, ideologies, "styles" of behavior, rational interests, irrational feelings, and inchoate predispositions of various and sundry kinds. Their heroes tend to be people who transcend institutional, intellectual, and psychological limits and who get things done. Their antiheroes (villains are out of fashion) are blunderers and bunglers of all persuasions. A few state studies have begun to appear: Joel Williamson, *After Slavery: The Negro in South Carolina During Reconstruction* (1965); Joe M. Richardson, *The Negro in the Roconstruction of Florida* (1965); William E. Parrish, *Missouri Under Radical Rule* (1965); Alan Conway, *The Reconstruction of Georgia* (1966).

Any scholar who hopes for an empirical science of history cannot be encouraged by this sorry tale of interpretative sequacity. But there is also some rational reason for hope. Quantifiers will note that the number and variety of master interpreters is increasing geometrically in each generation, which suggests that freedom of scholarly inquiry might be sustained by something like James Madison's notion of the dynamics of republican freedom. Each generation of monographers is a little more heterogeneous than the one before.

There is another hopeful tendency as well. Each generation does not rewrite the history books; it revises them. From Dunning to Du Bois to present practitioners, there is a process of refinement which is clearly at work in Reconstruction historiography, a widening and deepening of inquiry which transcends the reversals that relativism has taught us to expect. Historians of Reconstruction *have* learned a little from their predecessors—not much, but a little. And at the same time, they have tacitly refined an ancient learning process, which the Greeks were the first to call heuristic.

This refining tendency suggests that an interpretative refinement

---

in *Mississippi* (1947); R. D. W. Conner, "The Rehabilitation of a Rural Commonwealth," *American Historical Review* 36 (1930): 44–62; and Willie M. Caskey, *Secession and Restoration of Louisiana* (1938).

might also be in order, in the terms of this essay. We began with a simple disjunction between declarative and interrogative statements. Maybe we might more accurately conceive an intricate interactive relationship between what is declarative and what is interrogative, within an operational question, which is always both declarative and interrogative in some degree. Thus refined, the object becomes not the avoidance of declarative hypotheses but careful control of the declarative part of their structure, and at the same time, a careful control of the interrogative aspect as well, so as to enlarge the empirical possibilities of historical inquiry.

* The *fallacy of counterquestions* is an attempt at a revision which becomes merely a mindless inversion of an earlier interpretation and a reiteration of its fundamental assumptions. It has been said that there are two ways of manifesting an intellectual subservience to another mind: slavish imitation and obsessive refutation. Both of these forms of servility are regrettably common in historical scholarship. As revisionism grows more respectable, and even a prerequisite to a professional career, an increasing number of historians are delivered into the latter form of bondage.

Everyone has had some experience with a mind that "moves not on wheels, but only on hinges," as Robert Hall complained of the unfortunate Dr. Chalmers.[41] A few seem seriously to believe that all minds do and should work this way. A young radical American historian, Professor Eugene Genovese, who is generally well disposed to dialectics, appears to think that historians, like lawyers, ought to operate by an adversary method. He endorses Santayana's eloquent statement that "what kills spontaneous fictions, what recalls the impassioned fancy from its improvisation, is the angry voice of some contrary fancy. Nature, silently making fools of us all our lives, never would bring us to our senses; but the maddest assertions of the mind may do so, when they challenge one another. Criticism arises out of the conflict of dogmas."[42]

This is surely false. A debate between two raving lunatics is unlikely to issue in a triumph of reason. An argument between two pathological liars is an improbable path to truth. An exchange between two fools can scarcely be expected to end in a victory for wisdom. Adversary

41. William Gerard Hamilton, *Parliamentary Logic,* ed. Courtney S. Kenny (Cambridge, 1927), p. 82.
42. Quoted in Eugene D. Genovese, *The Political Economy of Slavery* (New York, 1965), p. 11.

methods may, perhaps, be appropriate to a courtroom, where the object is the attainment of justice, but they are inappropriate to a seminar room, where the purpose is the refinement of truth. A fight between wild-eyed exponents of *X* and *Y* will help not at all if *Z* was in fact the case, as it usually is. And between *X* and not-*X* the difference is merely a cipher, a nullity, a zero.

But there is something more specifically deficient about a counterquestion. If the original question, which is under attack, is mistaken, then its basic assumptions are probably faulty. But a counterquestion, in its reflexive inversion of the original, tends to repeat the original assumptions, faults and all, and thereby to perpetuate the error. Counterquestions repudiate conclusions but reiterate premises. The resultant revision is objectionable not because it is revisionist but because its revisionism is incomplete and superficial.

Consider, for example, the case of Charles Beard's *An Economic Interpretation of the Constitution of the United States* (New York, 1913), and his most determined critic, Forrest McDonald. McDonald has published two anti-Beardian books on the constitution: *We the People: The Economic Origins of the Constitution* and *E Pluribus Unum: The Formation of the American Republic, 1776–1790* (Boston, 1965). The first volume is an elaborate refutation of Beard's interpretation; the second, a more positive statement of McDonald's views.

The labor McDonald performed was prodigious. Traveling some 70,000 miles in a battered, secondhand Plymouth,[43] he collected a wealth of information in order to construct working models of the economic and political structure of American society circa 1787 and to compile brief economic biographies of the men who participated in the Great Convention, and the state ratifying conventions as well.

But while McDonald's body was moving on wheels, his mind was moving on hinges. Unlike the mind of many another revisionist, it did so explicitly and deliberately in his first book: "The purpose of the present work is to examine Beard's thesis as history. To do so, I have followed a rather unorthodox method. For the purposes of this book I have accepted, without qualification, Beard's system of interpretation and his system of testing it."[44]

That strategy was doubly dysfunctional to McDonald's inquiry. First, it diverted his attention from the critical problem of logical and epistemological and metaphysical deficiencies in the Beardian model.

43. *We the People: The Economic Origins of the Constitution* (Chicago, 1958), p. viii.
44. Ibid., p. vii.

Second, when McDonald came to tell his own story of the Constitution, the materials at hand were dictated by Beardian assumptions. The result, in *E Pluribus Unum*, was that McDonald, in the words of one reviewer, followed "a fairly Beardian line in interpreting the movement for the Constitution. Except for a few special twists of his own, the general outline follows the economic determinist pattern: failure of the impost amendment of 1786, paper money, Rhode Island, Shays's Rebellion, conservative reaction, etc."[45]

Beard's book was built upon a conspiracy theory, and so was McDonald's. The only difference was that McDonald's conspiracies were more numerous and more complex. Beard began and finished with a confused, clouded, contradictory, quasi-determinist economic determinism, and so did McDonald. The only difference was that McDonald's interest groups were more convoluted. For both authors, the dynamics of the problem were analyzed in terms of "a handful of statesmen" who were "impelled by an irresistible and illimitable compulsion to get More."[46] The only difference is that McDonald recognized more statesmen and more ways of getting More than his predecessor had been able to imagine.

There is at least one important way in which McDonald departs from the Beardian model. He qualifies his account of the greed of the founding fathers by giving some attention to gluttony and lust. Beard delicately confined his investigation to pocketbooks; McDonald also inspected the stomachs, glands, and genitals of the Founding Fathers. But like Beard, McDonald tended to forget that men have minds and hearts, and feet to stand on and spines to stand straight. In this respect, McDonald became more Beardian than Beard.

Other parts of McDonald's second book, which are not merely anti-Beardian but anti-Jensen and anti-Farrand in the same obsessive way, suggest that his counterquestions were not merely methodological but temperamental in their nature. His reviewer complained of a reflexive tendency toward the "categorical reversal of orthodox interpretations." And though McDonald is an honest and an able scholar, he tended also, in the process of turning things upside down, to give the evidence a twist as well. A counterquestion tends to operate, in this respect, as a declarative question. It does not open the inquiry, but ends it.

There are many other historiographical examples of the fallacy of

45. E. James Ferguson in *The William and Mary Quarterly*, 3d ser. 23 (1966): 149.
46. *E Pluribus Unum*, p. 116.

counterquestions, and indeed, some very great and useful ones: Burckhardt and Huizinga, Tawney and Trevor-Roper, Weber and his many critics, Hegel and Marx, English Whig historians and Namierites, enemies and friends of the French Revolution, creators of the "Black Legend" in Latin American historiography, and others who have responded with a whitewash. In American history, one thinks of Parrington and Perry Miller on seventeenth-century New England, Thomas Jefferson Wertenbaker and Wilcomb Washburn on seventeenth-century Virginia, the Whig interpretation of the American Revolution and the Imperial School, Henry Cabot Lodge and Edward Channing on the politics of the early republic, Turner and Abernethy on the frontier, Fiske and Jensen on the "critical period," Ulrich Phillips and Kenneth Stampp on slavery, and others too numerous to mention.

In each of these historiographical pairs, the second man, or group, is guilty of the fallacy of the counterquestion. In many cases, his work was an improvement upon what went before, but it might have been better still if counterquestions had been avoided and problems studied without allowing assumptions to be established and problems to be limited by earlier investigators.

ᢙᢦ The *fallacy of tautological questions* is the framing of questions in such a way that they are true by definition and cannot be empirically contradicted without self-contradiction. A tautological question is not really a question at all, but a declaration. Moreover, it is doubly declarative, for it asks nothing and asserts the same thing twice.

There are three common varieties of tautological questions in historical writing. The first and most common form of this error is a simple proposition that all things which are *P* are in fact *P*. Calvin Coolidge's famous first law of political economy is a familiar example. "When people are out of work," he is alleged to have said, "unemployment results." But Coolidge's second law is not tautological, though it may appear to be so. "The business of America is business," said he, which is an equivocation. "Business" is used in two different senses to sustain an argument that America's primary concern should be capitalism.

A historiographical example of this simple species of "*P* is *P*" tautology is an article on radicalism and reform in *The New York Times Magazine*, June 18, 1961, by Eric Goldman. Goldman asked, "Why do some spectacular agitators forward their cause, and others do not?" Before an audience of thousands, the author groaned and twisted upon his bed of conceptual agony, and at last, with a great rush of crimson adjectives, he delivered himself of the following hypothesis: "All-out agitators, to be successful, must be moving with history" (pp. 10–11). But if the phrase "moving with history" means anything at all, it must be something like a synonym for success. And if this is so, Mr. Goldman's profundity consists in a hypothetical proposition that "all-out agitators, to be successful, must be successful."

Another example of the same sort of error occurs in *The Rise of Puritanism*, a distinguished work of creative synthesis by William Haller. But one of its major theses is a "*P* is *P*" proposition. "The cause of the steady development of the centrifugal tendencies of Puritanism," writes Mr. Haller, "was the Puritan fostering of individualism in religion in the course of the accelerating democratization of English society." A close critic of this work has complained that, given Haller's definitions, he comes "near to saying that individualism was the cause of individualism growing in conditions favorable to individualism."[47]

A second kind of tautology consists in a proposition that all things which are both *P* and *Q* are *P*. For example: "all red wagons are red." Dr. Benjamin Spock somewhere sternly reminds American mothers that "all babies are young." Dr. Barrington Moore solemnly reminds American conservatives that all radical revolutionary change is violent— which looks fine on first impression. But Barrington Moore's idea of a radical revolution begins with violence as a central and limiting characteristic. He singles out the most bloody chapter of American history, the Civil War, as its most revolutionary chapter and ignores other periods and processes which were more revolutionary and also more radical in their effects, but less violent, and even nonviolent, in their development. Moore's argument thus becomes an hypothesis that "all violent radical revolutionary change is violent."[48] To forestall an accusation of ideological special pleading, I hasten to add a conservative example. President William McKinley once declared that "our past has gone into history"—this in a speech at Memphis, Tennessee, April 30, 1901, shortly before Mr. McKinley himself went into history.

The tautology "All things which are both *P* and *Q* are *P*" should, however, be clearly distinguished from "All things which are *P* are *P* and *Q*," which is tautological in "*P* is *P*" but more than merely a tautology. Consider the statement attributed to Marshal Turenne, "He who has

---

47. William Haller, *The Rise of Puritanism*, 2d ed. (New York, 1957), p. 179; Richard B. Schlatter, "The Problem of Causation in Some Recent Studies of the English Revolution," *Journal of the History of Ideas* 4 (1943): 364 n.
48. Barrington Moore, *Social Origins of Dictatorship and Democracy* (Boston, 1966), pp. 4, 20, 426–30, 505–8.

never made mistakes in war has never made war," which is not the same as the statement "He who makes mistakes in war makes war" or "He who makes mistakes in war makes mistakes."

A third general form of tautology is the assertion that something is either *P* or it is not *P*. This sort of statement is very common in the works of sixteenth-century historians, who were trained in dichotomous reasoning. The writings of Machiavelli are chock-full of *"P-or-not-P"* tautological hypotheses. "All states," he wrote in *The Prince*, ". . . are either republics or monarchies." But he defined a republic in the usual way as any state not monarchical. Similarly, Machiavelli hypothesized often in the form, "The nobles are to be considered in two different manners; that is, they are either to be ruled so as to make them entirely dependent on your fortunes, or else not."[49]

Consider also the following irreverent proposition:

> First come I. My name is Jowett.
> There's no knowledge but I know it.
> I am Master of this College,
> What I don't know isn't knowledge.

All three forms of tautology appear in hypotheses which are proposed by Professor Bruce Mazlish in *The Railroad and the Space Program* (Cambridge, 1965), pp. 34–35: He begins by defining "social invention" as "an invention which is technological (e.g., missile launching pads), economic (e.g., involving large scale employment, widespread use of materials), political (e.g., involving new forms of legislation and new dispositions of political forces), sociological (e.g., affecting kinship groups, communities, classes), intellectual (e.g., changing man's views of space and time), and so forth" (p. 11). Then he proceeds to the following hypotheses:

> A. All social inventions are part and parcel of a complex—and have complex results. Thus, they must be studied in multivariate fashion.
> B. No social invention can have an overwhelming and uniquely determining economic impact . . . because no completely new innovation is possible in reference to any set of economic objectives.
> C. All social inventions will aid some areas and developments, but will blight others.
> D. All social inventions develop in stages, and have different effects during different parts of their development.
> E. All social inventions take place in terms of a national "style," which strongly affects both their emergence and their impact.

According to Mazlish's definition of "social inventions," all of his hypoth-

49. Niccolò Machiavelli, *The Prince and the Discourses*, Modern Library ed. (New York, n.d.), pp. 4, 37.

eses are truistic and tautological—and all three forms of tautology are included.

It has sometimes been argued that all hypotheses, or at least all explanatory hypotheses, are tautological.[50] But this is surely a mistake. Crane Brinton's explanatory generalization hypothesis that sociopolitical revolutions tend to happen in societies which are relatively prosperous, progressive, and "on the upgrade economically" is not a tautology. Pieter Geyl's explanatory causal hypothesis that the difference between the Flemings and Hollanders was caused not by differences of a racial character but by the "geographical situation of Holland" is not a tautology. Bernard Bailyn's explanatory descriptive motivational hypothesis that Americans went to war against England partly because they feared that a deliberate conspiracy was directed at the destruction of their freedom is not a tautology. Max Weber's explanatory paradigmatic hypothesis that there was a functional interaction between the Protestant ethic and the spirit of capitalism is not a tautology. An explanatory theoretical hypothesis such as the quantity theory of money, in the form of an assertion that, all things being equal, the value of money is directly proportional to the amount of money in circulation and the velocity of its circulation—this is not a tautology. All of these explanatory hypotheses may be right or wrong, but they are not tautological. But to insist, as some analytic philosophers of history would, that they are not explanations *is,* itself, a tautology.

Tautologies can be exceedingly useful in the clarification of conceptualization. If they are used intelligently, they can also be effective rhetorical devices. But they ought not to be confused with heuristic, open-ended questions of the sort which can be resolved by empirical research.

ठ‍ॐ The *fallacy of contradictory questions* is the framing of a question which is false by definition and contradicts itself. If a truistic question is a tautology, then a contradictory question is a naughtology.

One might pose a simple hypothetical example. An essayist asks brightly, "What *really* happened in the summer of 1422, when, as every schoolboy knows, an irresistible force met an immovable object?" The question is contradictory, for if there are irresistible forces then there can be no immovable objects. But our essayist is not dismayed. With a flourish of hyphens and exclamation points he continues, "I'll tell you what really happened in the horrible hot summer of 1422,

50. Eugene J. Meehan, *Explanation in Social Sciences: A System Paradigm* (Homewood, Ill., 1968), p. 67.

when an irresistible force met an immovable object—there was one Hell of a crash!"

This form of error is sometimes found in the bravura essays which were much in fashion among historians of an older generation, who worked themselves into impossible predicaments by framing contradictory questions and then worked their way out by dodging them. The object, I think, was to make historical writing appear difficult (and thereby to magnify the apparent skill of the historian) by means of a method which is impossible.

I am thinking particularly of the virtuoso pieces of A. J. P. Taylor, the Paganini of historical prose, who likes to open an essay with a paradox and to close it with a *petitio,* or else to begin with an insoluble puzzle and end with an insidious quibble. One of his essays starts with the question, "How has the continent of Europe escaped political unification? [Immovable object.] Everything in Europe seems to call for it. [Irresistible force.]" Mr. Taylor proceeds to deal with this difficult problem by rejecting both his major premises. With dark logic, but with a brilliant display of rhetorical fireworks, he argues that the irresistible force was not a force at all and that the immovable object was actually in motion. And he caps off his exercise with a conclusion which is altogether as perverse as his premises. Unification, Mr. Taylor believes, did not come to "this most uniform of continents" because "rejection of uniformity was the one thing uniform to the inhabitants of Europe."[51]

Mr. Taylor does it again in a famous essay on Napoleon III. He begins with a conventional complaint that the more we learn about Napoleon III, the less we really know. "The more we strip off [the] disguises, the more new disguises appear. Such was Louis Napoleon, the man of mystery. Conspirator and statesman; dreamer and realist; despot and democrat; maker of wars and man of peace; creator and muddler; you can go on indefinitely. . . ."

But Taylor is not discouraged. He piles one puzzle upon another in a great towering pyramid of cleverness and confusion. The reader scarcely has time to study any one of them before it disappears beneath others. In the end, there is a conundrum: "It was easy to be against Napoleon when he turned out to be the man of Sedan. It was his doom that he was branded from the start, and branded in history, as the man of December," which is ambiguous, obscure, and irrelevant to the question which Taylor originally raised.[52]

51. A. J. P. Taylor, "Napoleon and Gentz," in *From Napoleon to Lenin: Historical Essays* (New York, 1966), pp. 12–20.
52. "The Man of December," ibid., pp. 76–81.

It is important, however, to distinguish clearly between a contradictory question and a paradoxical question—which is to say, between a contradiction and a seeming contradiction. The latter is much exploited by historians, not merely for rhetorical purposes but for sound research purposes as well. The works of an American historian, David W. Noble, are a case in point: *The Paradox of Progressive Thought* (Minneapolis, 1958) and *Historians Against History* (Minneapolis, 1965). The first title could read, "Progressives against Progress"; the second, "The Paradox of Historical Thought." Noble's answers may be mistaken, but his questions are workable.

&⤜ The *fallacy of "potentially verifiable" questions* consists in the mistaken and mischievous idea that a division of labor is both possible and desirable between historians who identify hypotheses which might be put to the test and other historians who test them. The mistake of this method lies in an attempt to separate two interdependent parts of a single process. Any such attempt to divide history, like physics, into "theoretical" and "experimental" branches would probably impoverish both aspects of a historian's task.

Question-framing cannot be undertaken independently of question-answering, for no hypothesis can be demonstrated to be potentially verifiable except in the degree to which it has been partially verified. When a historian says, "I have reason to believe that the question 'Was X or Y the case?' can be answered," he means that he has some evidence to suggest that either X or Y *was* the case, but that the evidence is incomplete or inconclusive. Moreover, so vastly complex is the process of verification, and so utterly unpredictable are the obstacles which lie hidden along the way, and so intimate is the functional relationship between the design of questions and the attempt to resolve (and refine) them, that the two processes cannot be separated, except at a heavy cost to the quality of conceptualization and research which is accomplished.

This truth does not need to be taught to working historians, who have learned it by bitter experience. But it is, perhaps, a lesson which *they* can teach to a distinguished sister discipline. In 1949, a prominent sociologist wrote of his own colleagues that "sociologists (including this writer) may discuss the logical criteria of sociological laws without citing a single instance which fully satisfied these criteria."[53]

Professor Merton's statement applies with greater accuracy to

53. R. K. Merton, *Social Theory and Social Structure* (Glencoe, Ill., 1949), p. 92.

sociology today than it did twenty years ago. His discipline has become, if anything, even less empirical than it used to be. "The weakness of much social thought, it seems to me," writes an English historian, "is that it is so largely concerned with packing its bag (or even with working out a general theory about the way in which a bag should be packed) for a journey which is never taken."[54]

To complain that sociologists have habitually tended to commit the fallacy of potentially verifiable questions, is not, however, to issue an invitation to another interdisciplinary slugging match, from which nothing good can come. E. H. Carr's fine epigram can bear repeating many times: "The more sociological history becomes, and the more historical sociology becomes, the better for both. Let the frontier between them be kept wide open for two-way traffic."[55] But let us hope that the two-way traffic will keep to the right side of the road. If sociological history and historical sociology are conceived as a combination of the conceptual sophistication of the best sociologists and the dogged if often undirected empiricism of the best historians, then the prospects are very bright indeed. But one might also imagine an interdisciplinary effort which combined the worst of both worlds— the stupidity of historians and the ignorance of sociologists.

This unfortunate tendency is apparent in the early work of Professor Lee Benson, a historian who has tended to borrow the vices of other disciplines and to surrender the virtues of his own. Prominent among his takings from sociology was the idea of the "potentially verifiable" question, which he elevated into an explicit method and urged upon his colleagues as a new tool of historical inquiry.[56] Happily, this well-intended but ill-founded advice has not been heeded, even by historians who have adopted some of Professor Benson's more constructive suggestions. We shall have occasion, in a later chapter, to consider the toll which this erroneous method has taken of his own work.

The potentially verifiable question is perhaps a manifestation of Abraham Kaplan's myth of methodology.[57] Let us hope that historians will hear the advice of a sociologist, Professor T. H. Marshall, who has written. "There was a compelling persuasiveness about the famous cry —'Give us the tools and we will finish the job.' One may be forgiven

54. Alfred Cobban, *The Social Interpretation of the French Revolution* (Cambridge, 1964), p. 23.
55. E. H. Carr, *What Is History?*, p. 84
56. Lee Benson, "Research Problems in American Political Historiography," in Mirra Komarovsky, ed., *Common Frontiers of the Social Sciences* (Glencoe, Ill., 1957), pp. 113–81.
57. See above, p. xx.

for responding less eagerly to the scholar, be he sociologist or anything else, who says—'Give me a job, and I will spend the rest of my life polishing the tools.' "[58]

    ᠔᠊ These eleven common fallacies of factual question-framing suggest a few affirmative axioms, which, however simple they may be, are often honored in the breach.

First, a proper historical question must be *operational*—which is merely to say that it must be resolvable in empirical terms. This simple requirement has been elevated into an ism by philosophers who speak of "operationism," or "operationalism," and define it as "the demand that the concepts or terms used in the description of experience be framed in terms of operations which can be unequivocally performed."[59] But this is merely a common-sense notion.

Second, a question should be *open-ended,* but not wide-open. It should dictate the kinds of facts which will serve to solve a problem, without dictating the solution itself. It must be a genuinely interrogative statement, but at the same time it must guide the inquiry through masses of information. If it does not perform the latter function, the historian will share Alice's confusion, as she went a-wandering in Wonderland:

> "Cheshire-Puss," she began, rather timidly. . . . "Would you tell me, please, which way I ought to go from here?"
> "That depends a good deal on where you want to get to," said the Cat.
> "I don't much care where—" said Alice.
> "Then it doesn't matter which way you go," said the Cat.[60]

One way to balance the difficult dual requirement of freedom *and* control is to begin with a cluster of questions, and for each of them, a cluster of answers which are generated by hunches and preliminary explorations and refined into alternative hypotheses, which can be enlarged or altered as research may require. These clusters of questions and hypotheses can and indeed must be designed in such a way as to neutralize a predisposition to actualize any one of them. There is no other way to keep honest and at the same time to keep one's momentum through masses of source material:

Third, a question should be *flexible.* A historian must learn to resist that form of debilitation which has been called "hardening of the

58. T. H. Marshall, *Sociology at the Crossroads* (London, 1947), p .19.
59. Carl G. Hempel, *Fundamentals of Concept Function in Empirical Science* (Chicago, 1952), pp. 39–50; Percy Bridgman, *The Logic of Modern Physics* (New York, 1948), p. 5, passim.
60. *The Complete Works of Lewis Carroll*, p. 72.

categories."[61] He must learn to conceive his questions and hypotheses as approximations, which are open to infinite refinement. A question cannot be framed wholly from historical sources—a historian must start with something. But it can be adjusted and amended, revised and ramified.

Fourth, a question must be *analytical,* which is to say that it must help a historian to break down his problem into its constituent parts, so that he can deal with them one at a time. It has been wisely and wittily observed that "the only practical problem is what to do next."[62] A proper question must serve to assist in this process, by separating sequential steps of inquiry.

Fifth, a question must be both *explicit* and *precise.* Its assumptions and implications must be spelled out in full detail, not merely for the sake of the reader, but for the sake of the researcher himself. Nothing is more deleterious and more absurd than the common tendency of some historians to confuse open-mindedness with imprecision, and flexibility with befuddlement, and wisdom with obscurity.

Finally, a question must be *tested.* No hypothesis can be conceived as "empirically verifiable" except in the degree to which it is verified. "Questions are not put by one man to another man, in the hope that the second man will enlighten the first man's ignorance by answering them," wrote R. G. Collingwood. "They are put, like all scientific questions, by the scientist himself."[63]

61. F. H. Underhill, quoted in Toynbee, *Reconsiderations* (New York, 1961), p. 1.
62. I. J. Good, *The Scientist Speculates: An Anthology of Partly Baked Ideas* (New York, 1962), p. 213.
63. Collingwood, *The Idea of History,* p. 274; and *Autobiography,* A30–31, 37.

CHAPTER II

FALLACIES OF FACTUAL VERIFICATION

ह्य

> One of the first duties of man is not
> to be duped.
> —Carl Becker

The best historical questions are no better than the answers which they generate—true answers, which are the object of all empirical inquiry. It is no easy matter to tell the truth, pure and simple, about past events; for historical truths are never pure, and rarely simple. And the process of historical truth-telling itself is even more intricate than the truths which historians tell. Every true statement must be thrice true. It must be true to its evidence, true to itself, and true to other historical truths with which it is colligated. Moreover, a historian must not merely tell truths, but demonstrate their truthfulness as well. He is judged not simply by his veracity, but by his skill at verification.

Anyone who has followed the progress of historical scholarship in the past generation will probably agree that this fundamental skill of factual verification has not been sufficiently attended to. The incidence of simple factual error in academic history today is nothing short of appalling. Two conventional attitudes are, I think, commonly responsible. First, the requirement is so fundamental that it is too often taken for granted. Few graduate programs in history deliberately teach students how to discover particular truths, and how to demonstrate truthfulness. It is merely assumed that historians will do so. An English scholar writes condescendingly,

> It is no doubt important to know that the great battle was fought in 1066 and not in 1065 or 1067, and that it was fought at Hastings and not Eastbourne or Brighton. The historian must not get these things wrong. But when points of this kind are raised, I am reminded of Housman's remark that "accuracy is a duty, not a virtue." To praise a historian for his accuracy

is like praising an architect for using well-seasoned timber or properly mixed concrete in his building. It is a necessary condition of his work, but not his essential function. It is precisely for matters of this kind that the historian is entitled to rely on what have been called the "auxiliary sciences" of history—archaeology, epigraphy, numismatics, chronology, and so forth.[1]

This haughty attitude is a very unfortunate habit, which many eminent historians have fallen into. The apparent fact that historians often assume that particular statements will be accurate, or that somebody else is responsible for their accuracy, may serve to explain why so many historical statements are in fact inaccurate. There are *no* auxiliary sciences to which a historian can conveniently dispatch his verification problems, and none to relieve him of his responsibility in this respect.

Carr's argument is also objectionable because it simplifies a vastly complicated process, which is inseparable from historical inquiry and functionally related to its most intricate conceptual parts. An inspection of the following fallacies will, I hope, suffice to demonstrate the fact that erroneous understandings of the verification process have caused able historians to adopt dysfunctional methods and procedures, which are utterly destructive of empirical scholarship.

Second, historical accuracy has also been diminished, during the past generation, by the progress of historical relativism. This absurd and pernicious doctrine became a popular delusion in the 1930s, when many historians suddenly discovered the disturbing fact that history was something which happened to *them*. The effect of that uncomfortable revelation was reinforced by the failure of history to develop as satisfactorily as the natural sciences, and by the fact that a good deal of humbug had been proclaimed to the world as the objective truth of history, and by a great falling away from first principles in the Western world, and especially in the Western democracies.

Relativism became particularly powerful in the United States, where the polemics of Charles Beard and Carl Becker reached many historians born in the generation 1890–1930, and indirectly, much of the general public as well. The way was prepared by a profound Pyrrhonism in the popular culture which was perfectly exemplified by Poor Richard's saying that "historians relate, not so much what is done, as what they would have believed," or in General George Meade's Philistine assertion that "I don't believe the truth will ever be known, and I have a great contempt for history."

But historical relativism was also an international phenomenon,

1. E. H. Carr, *What Is History?* (New York, 1962), p. 8.

which has appeared in formal treatises by a great Chilean historian, a distinguished French scholar, and an Hungarian-born historical sociologist, to name but a few.[2] A full-fledged cultural history of this intellectual movement would embrace a major school of German historical and philosophical thought, the epistemology of Fascism,[3] Stalin's hostility to "archive rats" and "bourgeois objectivism," the great Japanese movie *Rashomon* and several popular anthologies of Hindu folk legends, the novels of Aldous Huxley, Thomas Mann and André Gide, the essays of Renan and Croce, the poetry of Edward Arlington Robinson and E. E. Cummings, the theology of Reinhold Niebuhr, and the aesthetics of abstract art.

In poetry and painting, relativism was a harmless error, but whenever it appeared in historical scholarship, the results were disastrous. The fallacies committed by relativists have been sufficiently exposed by philosophers.[4] They require no laborious discussion here. There is, of

2. Francisco A. Encina, *La Literatura Histórica Chilena y el Concepto Actual de la Historia* (Santiago, 1936); Raymond Aron, *Introduction à la Philosophie de l'Histoire* (Paris, 1938); Karl Mannheim, *Ideology and Utopia: An Introduction to the Sociology of Knowledge* (New York, 1936).

3. Svend Ranulf, *Hitlers Kampf gegen die Objektivität* (Copenhagen, 1946).

4. A good brief discussion of Beard's relativism is in Arthur C. Danto, *Analytical Philosophy of History* (Cambridge, 1965), chap. 6. Karl Mannheim's "relationism," which was actually a form of relativism even less defensible than Beard's, is refuted in Charles Frankel, *The Case for Modern Man*, 2d ed. (Boston, 1959), chap. 7. Every historian can profit by a reading of these two critiques. In brief, the errors of relativism consist in the following:

First, there is a confusion between the way knowledge is acquired and the validity of that knowledge. An American historian may chauvinistically assert that the United States declared its independence from England in 1776. That statement is true, *no matter what the motives of its maker may have been*. On the other hand, an English historian may patriotically insist that England declared its independence from the United States in 1776. That assertion is false, and always will be.

Second, relativism mistakenly argues that because all historical accounts must be partial in the sense of incomplete, that they must also be partial in the sense of false. An incomplete account *can* be an objectively true account; it cannot be the whole truth. In this respect, the relativists continued to bootleg the idea of telling the whole truth in their work.

Third, relativism makes false distinctions between history and the natural sciences. Beard in particular did this, and his error consisted in rendering a special judgment upon historical science for its use of hypotheses, etc., which are also characteristic of natural science. Arthur Danto comments, "It is as though a man were to lament that it is a sad thing to be a Frenchman, for all Frenchmen die. . . . History is no more and no less subject to relativistic factors than science is" (Danto, p. 110). Mannheim made the same error in *Ideology and Utopia* (p. 79).

Fourth, relativists all argued that they and their friends were exempt from relativism in some degree. Thus, Beard's special pleading for an economic interpretation; and Mannheim's, for the intelligentsia. Both scholars were inconsistent, and understandably so. Cushing Strout has observed that "a consistent relativism is a form of intellectual

course, something that is profoundly right in relativism. It is true that history is something which happens to historians. And it is correct to argue that no historian can hope to know the totality of history as it actually happened. But it is wrong to conclude that objective historical knowledge is therefore impossible. The conventional wisdom of contemporary historiography still consists in the common idea that "a historian cannot know what *really* happened, but he has a duty to try." It is not surprising that historians have not tried very hard. Among the results are the following fallacies.

&❧ The *fallacy of the pseudo proof* is committed in a verification statement which seems at first sight to be a precise and specific representation of reality but which proves, on close inspection, to be literally meaningless.

Consider the work of a single scholar—Carl Bridenbaugh of Brown University, an able and distinguished author of many monographs about American colonial history, a president of the American Historical Association, a pioneer in the development of American social history, and one of the best and most useful men in his historiographical generation. But the methodological faults of that generation frequently appear in his work, which is grossly impressionistic in style and substance. Many of his conclusions are sustained by one fact at most, and some by a pseudo fact.

In a book entitled *Cities in Revolt* (New York, 1955), Bridenbaugh argued that Bostonians were heavily taxed in the period 1743–1760. His evidence consisted in an exclamatory assertion that "at the close of this period the levy on the 'Estates Real and Personal' of Bostonians amounted to 13s. 6d. in the pound, or 67 percent!"[5] But this statement, in itself, tells the reader nothing. Were those thirteen shillings and sixpence extracted from a pound of property at market value or from an assessed valuation of estates? Bridenbaugh doesn't tell us. Let us assume the latter, which was probably the case. If so, what were the assessment rates in proportion to real value—100 percent? 50 percent?

suicide" (*The Pragmatic Revolt in American History: Carl Becker and Charles Beard* [New Haven, 1958], p. 84).

Finally, the idea of subjectivity which the relativists used was literal nonsense. "Subjective" is a correlative term which cannot be meaningful unless its opposite is also meaningful. To say that all knowledge is subjective is like saying that all things are short. Nothing can be short, unless something is tall. So, also, no knowledge can be subjective unless some knowledge is objective. (See Christopher Blake, "Can History be Objective?" *Mind* 72 [1955]: 61–78.)

5. P. 7.

5 percent? If rates were high, then Bostonians were very heavily taxed, in whatever year Bridenbaugh found his figure. But if they were low, then the Boston tax rate might have been absurdly small. Bridenbaugh's "fact" helps not at all to clarify the confusion. As it is presented to the reader, it has no more evidential value than the exclamation point which ends his sentence.

This may serve as a specimen of one sort of pseudo fact, in which a relative quantity is stated in absolute terms, without a clarification of its reference. Another example of precisely the same species appears in Bridenbaugh's *The Colonial Craftsman* (2d ed. [Chicago, 1961]), which is studded with impressionistic statements of prices, wages, profits, and investments, all expressed in pounds and shillings. But pounds and shillings in what currency? Bridenbaugh helpfully identifies one figure as pounds sterling, and another as pounds, Massachusetts currency, which had a different and changing value. The rest of his figures are for the most part unspecified, and therefore unclear. What were these pounds worth, in purchasing power? Bridenbaugh cheerfully provides two conflicting estimates, one of which equates a "pound" to $30; the other, to $25, at "present day values." But which "pound" and what "present day"—the date of the first edition (1950) or the second (1961)? Every point pounded is confusion compounded. Bridenbaugh's method adds something to the weight of the book but nothing to its value.[6]

A second species of pseudo fact is the reversible reference—a chameleonlike statement which changes its color with its context and which might variously be used to prove the proposition that X is the case or that not-X is the case, as the author wishes. Here again, Bridenbaugh's books provide a plenitude of examples. In *Cities in the Wilderness* ([New York, 1955], p. 18), he asserts that the streets of colonial towns were strewn with trash: "Casting rubbish and refuse of all kinds into the streets without let or hindrance was a confirmed habit of both English and American town-dwellers," he wrote confidently. It may have been so, but his supporting evidence for Manhattan consists of three reversible references—that a law was passed against littering in New Amsterdam in 1657, that the law was enforced upon an early American litterbug named John Sharp in 1671, and that provision was made in 1670 for weekly trash removal by the car men of the city. Each of these impressionistic snippets of pseudo-factual information is consistent with a thesis that (1) the streets of New Amsterdam were knee-deep in trash; or (2) the streets of New Amsterdam were kept spotlessly clean by the

6. Pp. 42, 44, 128, passim.

tidy Dutch inhabitants, by means of laws which were enforced and by regular trash removal; or (3) any statement between these two extremes. The problem of the reversible reference rises whenever a historian tries to draw an inference directly from law to life. A law against *X* can be interpreted as evidence for the existence of *X* or for its nonexistence.

Another error of this same sort appears in Bridenbaugh's *Myths and Realities* (Baton Rouge, La., 1952), where he attempts to demonstrate that eighteenth-century Virginians were not much interested in music. To sustain this statement, he quotes Thomas Jefferson, who complained that he lived in a country where music "is in a state of deplorable barbarism."[7] But Jefferson was part of this society, and his statement is primary evidence that at least one eighteenth-century Virginian *was* interested in music, and secondary evidence of the barbarism of his neighbors. It might be a more accurate indicator of the quality of Jeffersonian expectations than of the musicological decadence of the Old Dominion. In the absence of clarifying evidence it is meaningless. Whenever a historian quotes an allegation by a member of group *A*, to the effect that *A* is not sufficiently interested in *B*, he is in danger of perpetrating a pseudo fact.

A third kind of pseudo fact is close to another fallacy in the following chapter. It consists in the precise quantification of imprecise entities. Bridenbaugh solemnly tells us that "at this time [no date] at least eight drawing schools drew their support from the wish of Charles Town's young ladies to learn the rudiments of a fashionable art."[8] This "fact" is at first sight an impressive testimony to the painterly propensities of Charleston belles—until one begins to wonder what precisely a drawing school could be. Bridenbaugh's statement *could* refer to eight splendid institutes with white marble steps and a faculty of French masters. Or it could mean eight old women with a community paint brush. Surely the truth is somewhere in the middle. But Bridenbaugh leaves us merely in a muddle.

ह&➤ The *fallacy of the irrelevant proof* consists in asking one question and answering another. Suppose, for example, that a historian asks, "Was Senator X a thief?" And suppose, moreover, that Senator X was a very great thief. But our hypothetical historian, who is an admirer of Senator X, proceeds to prove that Senator X had often declared that honesty was the best policy. He demonstrates that Senator X was acquit-

7. P. 48.
8. *Myths and Realities*, p. 111.

ted of theft by a jury (without mentioning that all the jurymen became postmasters immediately after the trial). He publishes an affidavit in which Senator X's mother solemnly swore that *her* son could never be a thief. He establishes that Senator Y was a bigger thief than Senator X, and that the Senate itself was a den of thieves. He shows that Senator X only stole from the government, and was kind to his children, and faithful to his wife, and loyal to his party. He proves that Senator X used some of his money to pay for an operation which was desperately needed by a crippled orphan in Cincinnati, Ohio. He argues, in a learned Keynesian disquisition, that Senator X was a big spender in a state where money was scarce, and that his spending, compounded by many multipliers and linkage effects, brought prosperity to thousands, and factories, jobs, schools, and churches. All of these statements may in fact be true, and yet Senator X remains a thief.

Something very similar to this hypothetical example actually appeared in the *American Historical Review* over the signature of a great and gifted historian—Allan Nevins. The point at issue was the validity of Henry Demarest Lloyd's allegations against John D. Rockefeller and the Standard Oil Company, in a polemic called *Wealth Against Commonwealth*. Allan Nevins had, at one time, shared Lloyd's point of view. In his biography of Grover Cleveland, Nevins characterized *Wealth Against Commonwealth* as "a searching exposure, amply buttressed by detail," and an accurate rendering of a "sordid record of business piracy," in "more than five hundred calm, unemotional pages." But a few years later, Nevins published a biography of Rockefeller in which he condemned Lloyd's work as "almost utterly worthless" and even dishonest.

One of Nevins's colleagues, Chester McA. Destler, replied with a critical essay in the *American Historical Review,* in which he defended Lloyd's book against Nevins's strictures. Specifically, Destler checked some 420 footnotes in *Wealth Against Commonwealth,* and found all but ten of them to be fair and accurate (the ten exceptions were inaccurate in insignificant ways). He checked 241 unsupported statements by Lloyd, and found 229 of them to be true and just. Destler concluded, persuasively, that Lloyd was correct in charging Standard Oil and Rockefeller with the bribery of public officials, the corruption of judges and juries, the negotiation of illegal pooling agreements, shoddy treatment of inventors, and sundry acts of espionage, coercion, fraud, and physical violence against competitors. He conceded that Lloyd had wrongly condemned Rockefeller for having allegedly bilked a Cleveland widow out of her life savings. But otherwise, he insisted, Lloyd's indictment of the methods of Standard Oil and Rockefeller was substantially accurate and just.

To this, Nevins made the rebuttal that John D. Rockefeller was a "hard-working, home-loving, religious" man, that he founded the University of Chicago, and that "his house was filled with missionaries and social workers." Nevins argued at some length that Rockefeller did not defraud the Cleveland widow out of her property (a point which Destler had granted). To a charge that Standard Oil bought a seat in the U.S. Senate for Henry B. Payne by bribing the Ohio legislature, Nevins seriously replied that the Ohio legislature made an investigation of this charge and found it to be unsustained. To the accusation that the Standard Oil Company had engaged in physical violence against its rivals and bribed a jury to acquit the perpetrators or to let them off with a trivial fine, Nevins replied that the alleged perpetrators had been acquitted, or let off with a trivial fine. "Men guilty of trying to blow up a factory are not treated so lightly," Nevins piously declared.[9]

చ్ The *fallacy of the negative proof* is an attempt to sustain a factual proposition merely by negative evidence. It occurs whenever a historian declares that "there is no evidence that X is the case," and then proceeds to affirm or assume that not-X is the case. He may have spent all the years of his youth in the Antiquarian Society, feverishly seeking the holy X and never finding it. He may have examined every relevant scrap of evidence in every remote repository, without reward. He and every other reasoning being on this planet may know in their bones that not-X is the case. But a simple statement that "there is no evidence of X" means precisely what it says—no evidence. The only correct empirical procedure is to find affirmative evidence of not-X—which is often difficult, but never in my experience impossible.

An example of the fallacy of negative proof occurs in a recent essay by Mary and Oscar Handlin, *The Popular Sources of Political Authority: Documents on the Massachusetts Constitution of 1780* (Cambridge, Mass., 1966). Constitution-making in Massachusetts was a complex process, of central relevance to any interpretation of political development in the early American republic. Great clouds of controversy swirl around this chapter of our history, and they have grown dense and dark with time. Among many urgent and unresolved problems is the question of social and cultural correlates with political commitments.

The Handlins, however, airily dismissed this issue with a simple statement that "the editors have been unable to establish a meaningful correlation between the social conditions of specific towns and the at-

9. Chester McA. Destler, "Wealth Against Commonwealth, 1894 and 1944," *American Historical Review* 50 (1944–45): 49–72, and reply, pp. 679 ff.

titudes expressed in the responses [to constitutional questions]." They insisted that "no conclusion was possible from an examination of the returns." Evidence collected by other historians has suggested that there was at least a clear pattern of denominational response to those parts of the Constitution which concerned religion—towns with large Baptist populations being averse, unsurprisingly, to a state-supported Congregationalist establishment. But Mr. and Mrs. Handlin simply state that "even in this matter the correlation was not exact," and drop the question.[10]

The authors, in short, declared categorically that there is no evidence that X is the case, instead of presenting affirmative evidence of not-X. But affirmative evidence of not-X could have been obtained (if in fact not-X was the case) by the calculation of correlation coefficients between, for example, the number of Baptist churches in the towns and the town votes on religious provisions of the Constitution. A low correlation would stand as positive evidence of not-X. Something similar might have been done with respect to the wealth of the towns, their demographic characteristics, and their political identities.

Had the Handlins collected such positive evidence, in my opinion, their thesis would have collapsed. It is exceedingly likely that in fact X, rather than not-X, was the case, and that many correlations between social, religious, and economic variables on the one hand, and political variables on the other, can be found. But the Handlins, able and honest historians, seem not much interested in finding correlations of this sort, perhaps partly because such findings would contradict some of their most cherished beliefs about American history in particular, and humanity in general.

A good many scholars would prefer not to know that some things exist. But not knowing that a thing exists is different from knowing that it does not exist. The former is never sound proof of the latter. Not knowing that something exists is simply not knowing. One thinks of Alice and the White Knight:

> "I see nobody on the road," said Alice.
> "I only wish *I* had such eyes," the King remarked in a fretful tone. "To able to see Nobody! And at that distance too!"[11]

⁄ The *fallacy of the presumptive proof* consists in advancing a proposition and shifting the burden of proof or disproof to others.

---

10. Pp. 933, 475.
11. *The Complete Works of Lewis Carroll*, Modern Library ed. (New York, n.d.), p. 223.

An example comes from Erik H. Erikson's fine monograph *Young Man Luther*. That controversial psychoanalytic interpretation of the reformer is grounded in an assumption that many specific Freudian and post-Freudian insights into human behavior are equally valid in Erikson's era and in Luther's. The author writes, with specific reference to the Oedipus complex, "I will not discuss here the cultural relativity of Freud's observations nor the dated origin of his term; but I assume that those who do wish to quibble about all this will feel the obligation to advance specific propositions about family, childhood and society which come closer to the core, rather than go back to the periphery of the riddle which Freud was the first to penetrate."[12]

Aside from Erikson's unfortunate condemnation of his critics in advance, as mere "quibblers," this passage, which is centrally important to the validity of his interpretation, is seriously objectionable. There is a burden of responsibility which rests squarely upon Erikson, and not upon his quibbling critics, to advance specific propositions which come closer to the core.

The raw application of timeless ideas about identity crises and Oedipus complexes—which are surely dependent in some degree upon family structure, child-rearing practices, and sundry other changing cultural conditions—to a man whose cultural environment was far different from Freud's, or Erikson's, without a satisfactory attempt to allow for those differences, is a disconcerting quality of Erikson's book.

❧ The *fallacy of the circular proof* is a species of a question-begging, which consists in assuming what is to be proved. A hypothetical example might help to clarify the point. A researcher asks, "Do gentlemen prefer blondes?" He discovers that Smith, Jones, and James prefer blondes, and tacitly assumes that Smith, Jones, and James are therefore gentlemen. He concludes that three gentlemen out of three prefer blondes, and that the question is empirically established, with a perfect correlation. His argument runs through the following stages:

> Inquiry: Do gentlemen prefer blondes?
> Research: Smith, Jones, and James prefer blondes.
> (Tacit Assumption): Smith, Jones, and James are gentlemen.
> Conclusion: Therefore, gentlemen prefer blondes.

Absurd as this fallacy may appear in a hypothetical way, it is exceedingly common in empirical scholarship. Consider the following case

12. Erik H. Erikson, *Young Man Luther: A Study in Psychoanalysis and History*, 2d ed. (New York, 1962), p. 257.

by a historian of old Ireland. "The question has been posed," writes Jeremiah O'Sullivan, "whether St. Patrick and Palladius were one and the same person. Tírechán in his *Memoir of St. Patrick* states that Palladius also had the name of Patrick and changed his name as Patrick did. The best proof that they were not one and the same seems to be that St. Patrick died in Ireland in 461, whereas the time and circumstances of Palladius's death are uncertain."[13]

This may indeed be the best *available* proof, but it is not good enough to carry the question. If Palladius were known to have died in 470, somewhere in Germany, then we would have very good evidence that he and Patrick were not the same. But the uncertain circumstances of Palladius's death are clarified in a way which is consistent with O'Sullivan's hypothesis only if we assume that his hypothesis is correct.

Other examples appear in a provocative new book on English Puritanism by Michael Walzer, who seeks to demonstrate by an appeal to historical evidence that a certain complex of ideas and feelings specifically attached to Puritanism. But when he finds an expression of these ideas and feelings, he assumes that the thought of the man who expressed them was "Puritanical" simply because he expressed them. This happens even in the case of men who are known to have been hostile to the movement conventionally called Puritanism.[14]

In other words, Walzer argues that Puritans were men who thought *X*, but he attempts to prove his thesis by assuming that men who thought *X* were Puritan. This is a convenient way to collect vast quantities of evidence. But it might make the Pope himself into a Puritan. In the same fashion, Walzer seeks to prove that certain other patterns of thought were abandoned by the Puritans. But when Puritans expressed those thoughts, Walzer explains those expressions away by arguing that Puritans really didn't mean them.[15]

The fallacy of the circular proof, or question-begging, also has its converse, which is described by Augustus de Morgan.

> There is an opponent fallacy to the *petitio principii*, which, I suspect, is of the more frequent occurrence [he writes]. It is the habit of many to treat an advanced proposition as a begging of the question the moment they see that, if established, it would establish the question. Before the advancer has more than stated his thesis, and before he has time to add that he proposes to prove it, he is treated as a sophist on his opponent's perception of the relevancy (if proved) of his first step. Are there not persons who

13. Jeremiah O'Sullivan, "Old Ireland and her Monasticism," in Robert McNally, ed., *Old Ireland* (New York, 1965), p. 91.
14. See, e.g., the discussion of Henry Crosse in Michael Walzer, *The Revolution of the Saints* (Cambridge, 1965), pp. 207–11.
15. Ibid., pp. 176, 186, 189, 193, passim., on organic imagery and ideas of the family.

think that to prove any previous proposition, which necessarily leads to the conclusion adverse to them, is taking an unfair advantage?[16]

Something like this, without any presumption of rhetorical dirty dealing, appears in an English textbook on logic which uses a statement by Arnold Toynbee as a specimen of a *petitio*. Toynbee wrote, with his usual obscurity,

> We may perhaps take it as having been already demonstrated that an historian's professed inability to discern any plot, rhythm, or predetermined pattern is no evidence that blind Samson has actually won his boasted freedom from the bondage of "Laws of Nature." The presumption is indeed the opposite; for, when bonds are imperceptible to the wearer of them, they are likely to prove more difficult to shake off than when they betray their presence and reveal something of their shape and texture by clanking and galling.[17]

The English logician, E. R. Emmet, interprets this to mean "In other words:

> Invisible bonds are hard to shake off
> X cannot see any bonds
> Therefore they are hard to shake off
> Therefore, the presumption is that they are still there.[18]

But Mr. Toynbee is saying something more than this. Leaving out blind Samson and chains and bonds and clanking and galling, Toynbee is arguing at very great length in volume 9 that all historians should generalize intelligently and accurately, and that it is impossible to generalize intelligently and accurately without generalizing consciously and deliberately. Therefore, all historians should generalize consciously and deliberately. This argument may or may not be substantively correct (I think it is), but it is structurally sound, and can be articulated in syllogistic form. But no sooner did Mr. Toynbee get part of the statement out, in a great jumble of confused imagery, than the logician pounced.

The *fallacy of the prevalent proof* makes mass opinion into a method of verification. This practice has been discovered by cultural anthropologists among such tribes as the Kuba, for whom history was whatever the majority declared to be true.[19] If some fearless fieldworker

16. Augustus de Morgan, *Formal Logic, 1847* (London, 1926), pp. 296–97.
17. Arnold J. Toynbee, *A Study of History*, 12 vols. (New York, 1935–61) 9:196.
18. E. R. Emmet, *The Use of Reason* (London, 1960), p. 226.
19. Jan Vansina, *Oral Tradition* (Chicago, 1965), pp. 104–5.

were to come among the methodological primitives who inhabit the history departments of the United States, he would find that similar customs sometimes prevail. There are at least a few historians who would make a seminar into a senate and resolve a professional problem by resorting to a vote. I witnessed one such occasion (circa 1962) as a student at the Johns Hopkins University. A scholar who was baffled by a knotty problem of fact literally called for a show of hands to settle the question. An alienated minority of callow youths in the back of the room raised both hands and carried the day, in defiance of logic, empiricism, and parliamentary procedure.

If the fallacy of the prevalent proof appeared only in this vulgar form, there would be little to fear from it. But in more subtle shapes, the same sort of error is widespread. Few scholars have failed to bend, in some degree, before the collective conceits of their colleagues. Many have attempted to establish a doubtful question by a phrase such as "most historians agree . . ." or "it is the consensus of scholarly opinion that . . ." or "in the judgment of all serious students of this problem. . . ."

A historian has written, for example, "While the role of dope in damping social unrest in early industrial England has not been extensively investigated, every historian of the period knows that it was common practice at the time for working mothers to start the habit in the cradle by dosing their hungry babies on laudanum ('mother's blessing,' it was called)."[20] This statement is often made, and widely believed. But it has never, to my knowledge, been established by empirical evidence. The reader should note the hyperbole in the first sentence. When an historian asserts that "*X* has not been extensively investigated," he sometimes means, "I have not investigated *X* at all."

A fact which every historian knows is not inherently more accurate than a fact which every schoolboy knows. Nevertheless, the fallacy of the prevalent proof commonly takes this form—deference to the historiographical majority. It rarely appears in the form of an explicit deference to popular opinion. But implicitly, popular opinion exerts its power too. A book much bigger than this one could be crowded with examples. One will suffice here, for the sake of illustration. Every schoolboy knows, and most schoolmasters, too, that Mussolini made the trains run on time. But did he? Ashley Montagu observes that "there was little or no truth in it: people who lived in Italy between the March on Rome (October 22, 1922) and the execution at Como (1945) will bear testimony to the fact that Italian railroads remained as insouciant as ever with regard to time-

20. Theodore Roszak, "Capsules of Salvation," *The Nation*, April 8, 1968, p. 470.

tables and actual schedules."[21] And yet, the myth still runs its rounds, with a regularity that *Il Duce* was unable to bring to his railroads.

  The *fallacy of the possible proof* consists in an attempt to demonstrate that a factual statement is true or false by establishing the possibility of its truth or falsity. "One of the great fallacies of evidence," a logician has observed, "is the disposition to dwell on the actual possibility of its being false; a possibility which must exist when it is not demonstrative. Counsel can bewilder juries in this way till they almost doubt their own senses."[22] This tactic may indeed prove to be forensically effective in an Anglo-American court of law, but it never proves a point at issue. Valid empirical proof requires not merely the establishment of possibility, but an estimate of probability. Moreover, it demands a balanced estimate of probabilities pro and con. If historians, like lawyers, must respect the doctrine of reasonable doubt, they must equally be able to recognize an unreasonable doubt when they see one.

Consider the following example, from the work of an American historian, Professor J. S. Auerbach. In a recent essay, Auerbach attempted to impeach the authenticity of a statement widely attributed to Woodrow Wilson. Many texts and treatises assert that, on the night before Wilson delivered his war message to Congress, he confessed to a journalist friend that "he'd never been so uncertain of anything in his life," and that he foresaw among the consequences of his act a "dictated peace, a victorious peace" imposed upon Germany, and "illiberalism" imposed upon America.

"Once lead this people into war," the President allegedly said, "and they'll forget there ever was such a thing as tolerance. To fight you must be brutal and ruthless, and the spirit of ruthless brutality will enter into the very fibre of our national life, infecting the Congress, the courts, the policeman on the beat, the man in the street. . . . the Constitution would not survive it . . . free speech would have to go."[23]

Did Wilson actually speak these words? Auerbach says no: "The sources for the conversation, its content, the circumstances of its publication, and all that we know about Woodrow Wilson strongly suggest that the President never spoke the words so frequently attributed to him."[24]

21. Ashley Montagu and Edward Darling, *The Prevalence of Nonsense* (New York, 1967), p. 19.
22. Augustus de Morgan, *Formal Logic, 1847*, p. 321.
23. John L. Heaton, *Cobb of "The World"* (New York, 1924), pp. 268–70.
24. J. S. Auerbach, "Woodrow Wilson's 'Prediction' to Frank Cobb: Words Historians Should Doubt Ever Got Spoken," *Journal of American History* 54 (1967): 609–17.

But that conclusion rests upon a fallacious method of proof. Auerbach attempts to demonstrate that Wilson probably did not make his "prediction" by dwelling primarily upon the possibility of error in the evidence. First, he shows that the earliest published account of the alleged conversation was "hearsay evidence, twice removed," which first appeared in John L. Heaton's biography of the journalist-confidant Frank Cobb. Heaton heard the story from Maxwell Anderson and Laurence Stallings, who allegedly heard it from Cobb, who allegedly heard it from Wilson. Heaton's book came out in 1924, seven years after the event, three years after the death of Wilson, and one year after the death of Cobb. A third of Auerbach's essay is an attempt to impeach the credibility of Anderson and Stallings in this respect.

Second, Auerbach writes that there is "no evidence whatsoever" that Frank Cobb visited the White House on the night of April 1, 1917 —the night before Wilson's war message and the night when the conversation allegedly took place.[25] He asserts that "it is conceivable that such a meeting could have passed unrecorded. But it is also conceivable that the absence of documentation, in conjunction with other evidence, indicates that the words that presumably were spoken at a nonexistent meeting on April 2 never were spoken at all."[26]

Third, Auerbach argues that the words attributed to Wilson are suspiciously similar to phrases which did not become common until after 1917, particularly the reference to a "dictated peace."

All of this may seem to establish a plausible case against the authenticity of the alleged conversation. But it does not establish a probable case. Auerbach's method merely establishes that the conversation might *possibly* have been imaginary. There is no presumptive evidence of probability. Hearsay evidence is not categorically invalid in historical research, nor is it always inadmissible in a court of law, popular belief notwithstanding. The "no evidence" of Cobb's visit is precisely what it says—no evidence—a fallacy of negative proof. The "dictated peace" argument, on the other hand, commits the fallacy of the partial proof. The invalidation of a literal phrase in the purported conversation, even if it were accomplished by Auerbach (it is not), would not suffice to invalidate the substantive version of the conversation.

There is, however, another approach to the problem. Did Wilson say similar things to other people at the same time that he allegedly had his conversation with Frank Cobb? Auerbach says no—the content of the

---

25. Auerbach quotes from Arthur S. Link's *Wilson: Campaigns for Progressivism and Peace, 1916–1917* (Princeton, 1965), pp. 398–99.
26. Auerbach, p. 612.

Cobb conversation runs "completely counter to the President's words and deeds." But this is factually false. In the memoirs of Josephus Daniels, there is an account of a conversation sometime early in 1917, in which Wilson reportedly said:

> There are two reasons why I am resolved to keep our country out of this war if possible:
>
> 1. If we go to war thousands of young men will lose their lives. I could not sleep with myself if I do not go to the extreme limit to prevent such mourning in American homes.
>
> 2. Every reform we have won since 1912 will be lost. We have got new tariff, currency, shipping and trust legislation. These new policies are not thoroughly set. They will be imperilled or lost if we go to war. We will be dependent in war upon steel, oil, aluminum, ships and war materials. They are controlled by Big Business. Undoubtedly many captains of industry will be patriotic and serve their country, but when the war is over those whose privileges we have uprooted or started to uproot will gain control of government and neither you nor I will live to see government returned to the people. Big Business will be in the saddle. More than that—Free speech and other rights will be endangered. War is autocratic.[27]

This evidence is something less than impeccable. It was published long after the event, by a man whose memory was less than infallible. But it serves in some degree to confirm the substantive authenticity of the Cobb conversation. There is more evidence in interviews which Wilson held with Ida Tarbell, in transcripts of speeches delivered by Wilson during the campaign of 1916, in Wilson's scholarly writings on American history, and sundry other sources, all of which suggest that Wilson did agonize most deeply over the coming of war in 1917, did fear the effect of war upon his program, did believe that war was autocratic and hostile to freedom, and did desire to preserve civil liberties as he understood them—though not, perhaps, as Auerbach understood them.

Auerbach did not conduct his inquiry in such a way as to elicit this factual information. He did not do research in the appropriate sources, in order to establish the balance of probability by a comparative analysis of the content of the Cobb conversation in relation to other relevant evidence for Wilson's thoughts. Instead he confined himself largely to a discussion of the possibility of error in the evidence at hand.

>> The *fallacy of the hypostatized proof,* as identified and defined by Perrell F. Payne, "consists in identifying the received theory about

27. Josephus Daniels, *The Wilson Era, Years of Peace, 1910–1917* (Chapel Hill, N.C., 1944), pp. 581–82.

X . . . with *X* itself, and hence rejecting some variant theory of *X* on the grounds that it does not do justice to the nature of *X*."[28] In historical scholarship, this form of error commonly occurs when a historian reifies a historiographical interpretation and substitutes it for the actual historical event it allegedly represents, and then rejects contradictory interpretations or affirms compatible ones.

An example appears in Michael Paul Rogin, *The Intellectuals and McCarthy: The Radical Specter* (Cambridge, 1967), in which the author discusses the Federalists. He hypostatizes Louis Hartz's interpretation of the Federalists—an interpretation which is far off the mark—and then proceeds to reject all variant interpretations. A few scraps of allegedly empirical evidence are introduced as reinforcement—scraps and snippets from Madison and John Adams, who were not representative Federalists, and indeed scarcely Federalists at all.

&» The *fallacy of the appositive proof* is a common but complex form of empirical error, which consists in an attempt to establish the existence of a quality in *A* by contrast with a quality in *B*—and *B* is misrepresented or misunderstood. This is an invidious mistake, which silently insinuates itself upon the understanding of both the author and his readers, for *A* is frequently the focus of both the readers' attention and the author's research, and the erroneous *B* is bootlegged into the book without warning or conscious control. The result is a little like the old army shell game, in which many a raw recruit is swindled out of his savings by being invited to guess which shell covers the pea, and his attention is diverted from the sergeant's sleight of hand at a crucial moment. But this fallacy is unlike the shell game in one important way: no swindle is involved. The perpetrator is the principal victim.

There are many examples. One of them appears in Samuel Eliot Morison's biography of his ancestor, Harrison Gray Otis. Despite its many merits, the book tends to be a vindication of Otis and an apology for the principal acts of his career. Morison is at some pains to show that his great-grandfather was a statesman and a successful practitioner of moderate conservative politics. But unfortunately for this interpretation, Otis was himself the author and abetter of several unstatesmanlike and spectacularly unsuccessful proposals—most notoriously, the radical innovations recommended by the Hartford Convention in 1814. Morison makes his case not by denying these plain and familiar facts but by con-

28. Perrell F. Payne, Jr., "A Note on a Fallacy," *Journal of Philosophy 55* (1958): 124–28.

trasting Otis with a semimythical society of stubborn malcontents called the Essex Junto, who purportedly possessed great power in New England politics, and a great desire to smash up the Union after they lost control of it. Morison suggests that the measure of Otis's moderate statesmanship was his skill in keeping New England off the rocks and shoals of Essex Junto extremism. To demonstrate more clearly his ancestor's proficiency in political navigation, he tries to show that the rocks were dangerous, and the shoals were treacherous, and the current strong. The more powerful and reactionary the Essex Junto appears, the more statesmanlike seems Otis. By this means, the great political disaster which was the Hartford Convention is suddenly converted into a shining triumph of unselfish and successful moderate statesmanship. There is one mistake in all of this: the fabled Essex Junto is a myth.[29] Morison's error is like Macaulay's who is said to have made pygmies of all Europe in order to flatter William III.

A second example is Daniel Boorstin's *The Americans: The Colonial Experience* (New York, 1958). Boorstin contrasts the uniqueness of America with Europe—the "active enterprises of the American" against the "contemplative tradition of European man"; the intellectual freedom of Americans against the abstract and sterile system-building of "garret-spawned illuminati." Boorstin believes that in the eighteenth century "the best European minds of that age labored to build new-model walls in which they were to be confined." He lumps together Kant and Hume, d'Alembert and Diderot, Voltaire and Condorcet, Holbach and Adam Ferguson in one great musty neo-Thomistic system.

Boorstin's interpretation of the European enlightenment, an interpretation which owes much to Carl Becker's *Heavenly City of the Eighteenth-Century Philosophers,* is simple-minded, uninformed, and seriously inaccurate. It is fundamental to his interpretation of American uniqueness, and it is insinuated into the book in such a way that the attention of the reader (and the author) is deflected from its deficiencies and is focused instead upon Boorstin's stunning epigrams and appeals to self-evidence in his discussion of America.

A third example appears in recent works on American Negro slavery and Negro personality. It is argued by Frank Tannenbaum, Stanley Elkins, and others that slavery in the United States was uniquely dehumanizing in its effects on the enslaved, that no other form of slavery so thoroughly deprived a slave of all the rights and responsibilities of

---

29. S. E. Morison, *The Life and Letters of Harrison Gray Otis,* 2 vols. (Boston, 1913). See also my article, "The Myth of the Essex Junto," *William and Mary Quarterly,* 3d ser. 21 (1964): 191–235.

humanity. There is, I think, a sound and significant element of truth in this interpretation, but it is distorted by an overdrawn contrast between Anglo-America and Latin America. Slavery in the latter colonies is stereotyped, and maybe even a little romanticized, by Elkins, Tannenbaum, and Klein in their juxtaposition of the two.[30]

To condemn this fallacy is not, of course, to condemn the flourishing discipline of comparative history. The most dangerous examples of the fallacy of appositive proof often appear in works that are not avowedly comparative but implicitly and erroneously so. The remedy for comparative error is not less comparative history but more of it, more that is explicit and more that is empirical.

ɤ The *fallacy of misplaced literalism* is a form of context error, which consists in the misconstruction of a statement-in-evidence so that it carries a literal meaning when a symbolic or hyperbolic or figurative meaning was intended; or the attribution of a general meaning where a special or specific one was meant. Messrs. Barzun and Graff comment, "Misplaced literalism . . . has many forms, and it is particularly insidious because the reporter must *begin* by being literal. He must ascertain with all possible precision what his original text tells him. . . . [But] if he remains baldly literal and contents himself with quoting extracts, he invariably ends by showing his human subject to have been a mass of contradictions. . . . Misplaced literalism makes a shambles of intellectual history."[31]

John Marshall declared in the Virginia ratifying convention, "We, Sir, idolize democracy." That statement is surely not to be taken literally. A glance at the contours of John Marshall's career suggests that he did not idolize Jeffersonian democracy, or Jacksonian democracy, or indeed democracy in any accepted meaning. The word "democracy" in his statement is as hyperbolical as the word "idolize." In context, Marshall merely meant that he and his Federal friends were prepared to acquiesce in a particular kind of popular election.

Misplaced literalism can also make a shambles of institutional history. An example comes from the history of industrialization in England.

30. Frank Tannenbaum, *Slave and Citizen*, 2d ed. (New York, 1963); Stanley Elkins, *Slavery: A Problem in American Institutional and Intellectual Life*, 2d ed. (New York, 1963); Herbert S. Klein, *Slavery in the Americas: A Comparative Study of Cuba and Virginia* (Chicago, 1967).
31. Jacques Barzun and Henry Graff, *The Modern Researcher*, 2d ed. (New York, 1962), pp. 127–28.

In a work published in 1619, there appears the following description of a factory which was allegedly visited by Henry VIII:

> Within one room being large and long
> There stood two hundred looms full strong
> Two hundred men, the truth is so,
> Wrought in these looms all in a row.
> By every one a pretty boy
> Sat making quils with mickle joy.
> And in another place hard by
> An hundred women merrily,
> Were carding hard with joyful cheer
> Who singing sat with voices clear.
> And in a chamber close beside
> Two hundred maidens did abide
> In petticoats of Stamell red
> And milk white kerchers on their head
> These pretty maids did never lin
> But in that place all day did spin.

This source has been literally interpreted by historians as evidence of the existence of factories in the sixteenth century. The alleged owner, Jack of Newbury, has been identified as a great textile magnate. But Peter Laslett observes that "this Jack of Newbury was as much of a myth as Jack and the Beanstalk."[32] The poem appeared in a novel which is as suitable to a literal interpretation by a student of sixteenth-century England as *Gargantua* and *Pantagruel* might be for a student of sixteenth-century France. Imagine what might happen if all evidence for the latter were destroyed except the works of Rabelais.

Still another specimen of misplaced literalism occurs in Darrett B. Rutman's monograph *Winthrop's Boston: Portrait of a Puritan Town, 1630–1649* (Chapel Hill, 1965). The author argues that the founders of Boston wished to establish a "medieval monastery," in which society would be "perfectly united in thought, speech, judgment, and, above all, God's holy love." Much of Rutman's thesis rests upon a lay sermon which John Winthrop delivered on board the ship *Arbella* in passage to New England. Rutman quotes excerpts from this source as literal evidence of Winthrop's expectations. The most famous line—"Wee shall be as a Citty upon a Hill"—brings forth the following comment: "Winthrop's expression was much more than a literary conceit borrowed from the Gospel of Matthew. It reflected the core of his thinking about the society he and his fellows intended to establish."[33]

32. Laslett, *The World We Have Lost* (New York, 1965), pp. 152–53.
33. P. 4

But did it, exactly? Rutman makes a sermon into a social blueprint, a hortatory message into a measure of both a man's specific purpose and his general sense of prospects and possibilities. Imagine a football team which is losing, 42–3, at the end of the first half. In the locker room, the coach says, "Let's go, you guys: We need six quick touchdowns: And I *know* that you will do it!" Rutman's method would convert this expression of hope into an indication of what the coach really plans and expects. More likely, the coach had already called his wife and said, "I'll be home early. No bonfire tonight!"

A reviewer of Rutman's book complains, "My only regret is that the author has pursued what is essentially [sic] a literary device to a point where it seems to affect his assessment of the Puritans. In taking an exhortation as a statement and in using it as a reference point throughout the book, he makes Winthrop and the other founders appear more naive than they were."[34]

Misplaced literalism does not appear only in the interpretation of literary evidence. The same mistake is easily made in the use of other kinds of sources, too. Consider, for example, the party in the White House following Andrew Jackson's inauguration. The goings-on were described by an eyewitness, Mrs. Margaret Bayard Smith:

> What a scene did we witness! The *Majesty of the People* had disappeared, and a rabble, a mob, of boys, negros, women, children, scrambling fighting, romping. What a pity what a pity! No arrangements had been made no police officers placed on duty and the whole house had been inundated by the rabble mob. We came too late. The President, after having been *literally* nearly pressed to death and almost suffocated and torn to pieces by the people in their eagerness to shake hands with Old Hickory, had retreated through the back way or south front and had escaped to his lodgings at Gadsby's. Cut glass and china to the amount of several thousand dollars had been broken in the struggle to get the refreshments, punch and other articles had been carried out in tubs and buckets, but had it been in hogsheads it would have been insufficient, ice-creams, and cake and lemonade, for 20,000 people, for it is said that number were there, tho' I think the estimate exaggerated. Ladies fainted, men were seen with bloody noses and such a scene of confusion took place as is impossible to describe—those who got in could not get out by the door again, but had to scramble out of the windows. At one time, the President who had retreated and retreated until he was pressed against the wall, could only be secured by a number of gentlemen forming round him and making a kind of barrier with their bodies, and the pressure was so great that Col Bomford who was one said at one time he was afraid they should have been pushed down, or on the President. It was then the windows were thrown open, and the torrent found an outlet, which otherwise might have proved fatal. . . . The

34. Edmund S. Morgan in *American Historical Review* 71 (1966): 664.

noisy and disorderly rabble in the President's House brought to mind descriptions I had read, of the mobs in the Tuileries and at Versailles, I expect to hear the carpets and furniture are ruined, the streets were muddy, and the guests all went thither on foot.[35]

This little "scene of confusion" has often been used as a key to that larger scene of confusion called the Jacksonian era—as apparent evidence of the rise of the Common Man, whoever he may have been. Now, let us assume that things happened precisely as Mrs. Smith reported them—a doubtful assumption, for Mrs. Smith's descriptions of things Jacksonian were a little like her friend Mrs. Bomford's inauguration gown, deep scarlet, richly trimmed with embroidery. But let us assume it to be correct. Even so, it is not a literal proof of political equality in the Jacksonian era. There were similar goings on at the coronations of medieval kings. At the coronation banquet of Charles VI of France in 1380, "the throng of spectators, guests and servants was such that the constable and the marshal of Sancerre had to serve up the dishes on horseback." At the coronation of Henry VI of England, in 1431, "the people force their way at daybreak into the great hall where the feast was to take place, 'some to look on, others to regale themselves, others to pilfer or to steal victuals or other things.' " During the "inauguration" of Louis XI, it is said that the disorder was such that "the princes of the blood were nearly squeezed to death in their seats of honour."[36]

To assume that Jackson's inaugural reception was a literal reflection of the Jacksonian movement itself is surely a fallacy.

&ঌ The *fallacy of misplaced precision* is an empirical statement which is made precise beyond the practical limits of accuracy. One fanatical quantifier in the sixteenth century was curious to know the weight of a stone cannon ball, 10¾ inches in diameter. There was, of course, considerable variation in the size and weight of stone cannon balls, even those prepared for a single specific gun. And there was undoubtedly some small change in the weight of any single shot, as it was rubbed and chipped by careless gunners, etc. But our inquirer figured the weight of a 10¾ inch ball as "61 lb., 1 oz., 2 drams, 1 scruple and $15 \frac{685644}{1414944}$ grains," thus attempting to ascertain the weight of a various and variable object within a millionth part of the weight of a grain of barley. The modern scholar who reported this episode commented that

35. Margaret Bayard Smith to Jane Kirkpatrick, March 11, 1829, as published in *The First Forty Years of Washington Society* (New York, 1906), pp. 295–96.
36. Johan Huizinga, *The Waning of the Middle Ages* (Garden City, N.Y., 1954), p. 50.

it showed "a kind of theoretical meticulousness which is quite medieval in flavor."[37] But it is one which we shall see more of in modern historiography as quantification becomes increasingly fashionable.

> "Prove everything," saith St. Paul, "and hold fast to that which is good." Historians are likely to agree in principle, but not in practice. Specific canons of historical proof are neither widely observed nor generally agreed upon. There is no historiographical Wigmore, Stephen, or Thayer and no body of precedents which is recognized as a reliable guide.

But there are, I think a few simple rules of thumb, which are the inversion of the fallacies discussed in this chapter. First, as Wigmore has exhaustively argued, sound evidence consists in the establishment of a satisfactory relationship between the *factum probandum,* or the proposition to be proved, and the *factum probans,* or the material which is offered as proof. That is sufficiently obvious. But it is not so obvious to many scholars that the criteria for a satisfactory *factum probans* depend in large degree upon the nature of the *factum probandum.*[38] This is a pedantical way of saying that every fact in history is an answer to a question, and that evidence which is useful and true and sufficient in answer to question B may be false and useless in answer to question A. A historian must not merely get the facts right. He must get the right facts right. From this a simple rule of relevance may be deduced: historical evidence must be a direct answer to the question asked and not to some other question.

Secondly, an historian must not merely provide good relevant evidence but the best relevant evidence. And the best relevant evidence, all things being equal, is evidence which is most nearly immediate to the event itself. The very best evidence, of course, is the event itself, and then the authentic remains of the event, and then direct observations, etc. We shall call this the rule of immediacy.

Third, evidence must always be affirmative. Negative evidence is a contradiction in terms—it is no evidence at all. The nonexistence of an object is established not by nonexistent evidence but by affirmative evidence of the fact that it did not, or could not exist, as, for example, in a low coefficient of correlation, in the case of a comparative analysis. In the case of a journalist who did not in fact call upon a President, proof

37. Michael Lewis, "Armada Guns: A Comparative Study of English and Spanish Armaments. Section V. The Guns of the Spanish Fleet, 1588," *The Mariner's Mirror* 29 (1943): 3–39, 8 n.
38. John Henry Wigmore, *A Treatise on the Anglo-American System of Evidence in Trials at Common Law. . . ,* 3d ed., 10 vols. (Boston, 1940), 1, sect. 2.

requires affirmative evidence from the journalist or the President, or evidence that the journalist was somewhere else at the time, or evidence that the president's time was entirely taken up with other things. If proof of this sort cannot be found, then the point cannot be proved, and a historian must candidly accept uncertainty. This is the rule of affirmation.

Fourth, the burden of proof, for any historical assertion, always rests upon its author. Not his critics, not his readers, not his graduate students, not the next generation. Let us call this the rule of responsibility.

Fifth, all inferences from empirical evidence are probabilistic. It is not, therefore, sufficient to demonstrate merely that A was possibly the case. A historian must determine, as best he can, the probability of A in relation to the probability of alternatives. In the same fashion he cannot disprove A by demonstrating that not-A was possible, but only by demonstrating that not-A was more probable than A. This is the rule of probability.

Sixth, the meaning of any empirical statement depends upon the context from which it is taken. No historical statement-in-evidence floats freely outside of time and space. None applies abstractly and universally. The statement that a Norman army defeated a Saxon army at Hastings in 1066 is meaningless without reference to a map of England, and also to our calendar. For a Moslem, the same event has the different date of 459. The relativity of a date to a calendrical frame of reference is self-evident. But the contextual relativity of many other "facts" is not.

Seventh, an empirical statement must not be more precise than its evidence warrants. And degrees of precision, of course, vary greatly from one piece of evidence to another. Someday, historians may take a leaf from statisticians and specify the quantitative "significance" of their statements. In the meantime, the same effect can be accomplished by nuances of language. We shall call this the rule of precision.

These seven rules of thumb are ones that good historians feel in their bones and apply without thinking. If such rules are raised to the level of consciousness, practices might hopefully improve in at least some small degree. The factual errors which academic historians make today are rarely deliberate. The real danger is not that a scholar will delude his readers, but that he will delude himself.

CHAPTER III

FALLACIES OF FACTUAL SIGNIFICANCE

ಶಿ

No one reads or writes history in a fit of total absent-mindedness, though a fair amount of history has been written by people whose minds seem in part to have been on other things.

—G. R. Elton

To write history, or even to read it, is to be endlessly engaged in a process of selection. No part of the job is more difficult or more important, and yet no part has been studied with less system, or practiced with less method. Many facts are called, but few are consciously chosen, on explicit and rational criteria of factual significance.

Historians have, I think, deliberately resisted the refinement and rationalization of this aspect of their task. For some of them, the idea of a chosen fact is hateful in itself. Others think that the process of selection is not merely an unknown but a mystery. Both of these beliefs are utterly mistaken. The process of selection can and must be clarified if history is to develop beyond its present condition. Criteria of factual significance can and must be specified, or else historians will be running through records like rats in a maze, without even a rudimentery notion of the nature of their predicament.[1]

In every historical inquiry, the process of factual selection operates in several separate ways. One species of selection, commonly called "sampling," consists in the selection of representative facts of a certain predetermined kind, within a closed universe of investigation. This undertaking, difficult as it often is in practice, presents comparatively few

1. An important beginning has been made by two able philosophers of history: Arthur C. Danto, *Analytical Philosophy of History* (Cambridge, 1965), pp. 1–16, 132–39; and Morton White, *The Foundations of Historical Knowledge* (New York, 1965), pp. 237–270.

conceptual problems. We shall consider it in a later chapter. A much tougher problem is presented by the complex selection process that precedes sampling—namely, the selection of the kinds of facts to be sampled. This involves the determination of fundamental criteria of factual significance.

Significance is the sort of word which sends shudders down the spine of every working historian. But if he turns his back upon the problem, he will operate upon covert criteria of factual significance, which may be incompatible with his own objectives. "He who is deficient in the art of selection," Macaulay wrote, "may, by showing nothing but the truth, produce the effect of the grossest falsehood."[2] And he who is deficient in his ideas of significance is sure to be equally so in the art of selection.

There are a few common fallacies in this respect, a few criteria of factual significance which are inconsistent with empiricism in history. In each of the following instances, the fallacy consists not in the criteria themselves but rather in an attempt to combine them with the methods and objects of empirical inquiry. Every historian, of course, has the inalienable right to do any kind of history that pleases him—a constitutional right to go wrong in his own way. But no historian is liberated from the logical consequences of his own assumptions. The object of this chapter is not to condemn certain deviations from narrow academic norms. It is rather to demonstrate that all historians operate upon certain criteria of factual significance in their work, and that those criteria must be aligned with *their* own purposes, and methods.

ે≱ The *holist fallacy* is the mistaken idea that a historian should select significant details from a sense of the whole thing. This method seems plausible at first sight. But it would prevent a historian from knowing anything until he knows everything, which is absurd and impossible. His evidence is always incomplete, his perspective is always limited, and the thing itself is a vast expanding universe of particular events, about which an infinite number of facts or true statements can be discovered.

An extreme example of holism is Hegel's *The Philosophy of History,* which is clearly and cogently discussed by Bertrand Russell:

> The view of Hegel and of many other philosophers, is that the character of any portion of the universe is so profoundly affected by its relations to the other parts and to the whole, that no true statement can be made

2. Thomas Babington Macaulay, "History," *Complete Writings,* 20 vols. (Boston, 1900), 11:245.

about any part except to assign its place in the whole. Thus there can be only one true statement; there is no truth except the whole truth. . . . Now this is all very well, but it is open to an initial objection. If the above argument were sound, how could knowledge ever begin? I know numbers of propositions of the form "A is the father of B," but I do not know the whole universe. If all knowledge were knowledge of the universe as a whole there would be no knowledge. This is enough to make us suspect a mistake somewhere.[3]

A historian who swears to tell nothing but the whole truth, would thereby take a vow of eternal silence. A researcher who promises to find the whole secret for himself condemns himself to perpetual failure. The whole truth, at any stage of an inquiry, is an ideal that ought to be abolished from historiography, for it cannot ever be attained. Historians are bound to tell the best and biggest truths they can discover, but these truths are very different from the whole truth, which does not and cannot exist. A scholar who seeks the whole truth is on a road which can only end in the intellectual suicide of relativism, or else in that condition of methodological anomie which characterizes so many of my colleagues.

Georg Wilhelm Friedrich Hegel, poor twisted Teutonic soul that he was, is an easy mark for a methodologist. Most of the fallacies in this book could be illustrated by his arguments. But there are many other examples of the holist fallacy, which is an exceedingly common form of error. All metahistorians, by definition, are guilty of this mistake—Toynbee, Spengler, Sorokin, Marx, Comte, Kant, Condorcet, Vico—and others who have tried to discover *the* "meaning" of *the* whole past.[4]

The extravagant holism of metahistory is held in deserved contempt by most working historians. But the same form of error also comes in smaller sizes. Many a monographer has set his sights upon the whole of a little subject, like William James's Adirondack hunter who shot a bear by aiming, not at his eye or heart, but "at him generally."[5]

3. Bertrand Russell, *A History of Western Philosophy* (New York, 1945), pp. 743, 745.
4. Arthur Danto reaches the same conclusion by a different argument. He argues that the significance of events is always, in part, dependent upon later events; and therefore, that the significance of past events is partly dependent upon future events; and thus, that substantive philosophers of history are condemned to failure in their quest for the whole truth, for their method would require a "history of events before the events themselves have happened" (*Analytical Philosophy of History*, p. 14). This is *not* to say that the past can change, for events happened in the way that they happened, and not in any other way. But facts, or true statements about past events, can and will change, as other events occur.
5. William James, *The Principles of Psychology*, 2 vols. (New York, 1890), 2:333–34.

A classical example is Macaulay, whose essay on history is a disquisition on selection and significance. But his criteria of significance are holistic. "No history," he knew, "can present us with the whole truth; but those are the best . . . histories which exhibit such parts of the truth as most nearly produce the effect of the whole. . . . The perfect historian is he in whose work the character and spirit of an age is exhibited in miniature."[6]

But if the whole of history is unattainable, so also is the whole of any historical age. Macaulay himself noted, inconsistently, that "if history were written thus, the Bodleian library would not contain the occurrences of a week."[7] And if the whole of an "age," or any such part of history can never be known, it can never be exhibited in miniature.

The idea is absurd, and yet it persists. Many modern historians continue to dig themselves into wholes, large and little, and it isn't easy to root them out again. Professor G. R. Elton, in a historiographical how-to-do-it manual, stubbornly insists that "all good historical writing is universal history in the sense that it remembers the universal while dealing with a part of it."[8] Professor Jacques Barzun, in his romantic way, writes blissfully of "the intelligibility of the whole."[9] The holistic fallacy has been much invigorated by the fashionable idea of cultural history; many scholars flatter themselves, as Barzun does, that they have discovered in "culture" the whole secret for themselves.

The great UNESCO history project, which is presently in progress, is a serious attempt to synthesize the sum of all human memories and to recapture the "past in its entirety." The second volume of this Quixotic venture promises to tell the whole truth about the ancient world, from 1200 B.C. to A.D. 500.[10] It was prepared by thirty-seven contributors and consultants. The result is a catastrophe on an appropriately monumental scale. A critic comments, "Rarely, if ever, can so many learned men have labored so long on a history to so little purpose."[11] The book is as bland and trivial as if the members of the Security Council had collaborated on a treatise of political theory. A project designed to explain everything ends, predictably, by explaining nearly nothing.

6. Macaulay, "History," pp. 244–45, 280.
7. Ibid., p. 244.
8. G. R. Elton, *The Practice of History* (New York, 1967), p. 16.
9. Jacques Barzun, "Cultural History as a Synthesis," in Fritz Stern, ed., *The Varieties of History* (New York, 1956), p. 393.
10. Luigi Pareti, et al., *The Ancient World, 1200 BC to AD 500: History of Mankind, Cultural and Scientific Development* (New York, 1965).
11. Laurence Lee Howe, *The American Historical Review* 71 (1966): 520.

The holist fallacy may be developing in a fresh new form today, thanks to the electronic revolution. An economist, Kenneth E. Boulding, seriously proposes that the whole of recorded history should be programed on one gigantic IBM machine. "One visualizes a computer on which the totality of recorded history has been coded and from which then samples can be taken, relations perceived, discrepancies identified, and continuously new questions asked and gaps in the data discovered. The problem of coding would indeed be a difficult one, but it is surely not beyond the capacity of the historian's intelligence."[12]

Some recorded history is presently being encoded into a computer-readable form, in various data banks throughout the Western world. We shall all gain much from these immense projects. But nobody will ever program the whole of recorded history into a computer—merely a few selected kinds of material. Enormous though they may be, their selection will require the same careful and explicit criteria of significance which smaller projects now demand.

The *fallacy of essences* begins with the old idea that everything has something deep inside it called an essence, some profound inner core of reality. According to this view, facts about a man, a nation, an age, a generation, a culture, an ideology, or an institution are significant in the degree to which they display the essence of the entity in question.

This most durable of secular superstitions is not susceptible to reasoned refutation. The existence of essences, like the existence of ghosts, cannot be disproved by any rational method. But it *is* possible to demonstrate that a belief in essences, like a belief in ghosts, involves an empiricist in certain difficulties. This has been done at some length by Karl Popper, who persuasively suggests that the progress of empirical knowledge requires, not a search for essences, which cannot be found by any empirical method, but rather a search for patterns of external behavior.[13] The essentialist's significant facts are not windows through which an observer may peek at the inner reality of things but mirrors in which he sees his own a priori assumptions reflected.

The fallacy of essences is, nevertheless, very common in historical writing. It is psychologically gratifying, for it supplies a sense of completeness and it encourages a sense of certainty. But these are illusions which an empiricist must learn to live without. Popper believes

12. *History and Theory* 7 (1968): 90.

13. Karl Popper, *The Open Society and Its Enemies*, 2 vols. (New York, 1963), 1, chap. 3, pt. 6; *The Poverty of Historicism* (Boston, 1957), chap. 1, pt. 10.

that natural scientists have learned to live without them. He correctly complains that "the problems of the social sciences, on the other hand, are still for the most part treated by essentialist methods. This is, in my opinion, one of the main reasons for their backwardness."[14]

Essentialism is, I think, closely related to holism, for knowledge of the "essence" of a thing implies knowledge of the whole thing, which is impossible. Consider, for example, the case of Sir Lewis Namier, a great historian and a gross Tory (the organic bias of classical conservatism perhaps explains the particular susceptibility of conservatives to holism and essentialism). Sir Lewis was no enemy of chosenness in either facts or people. He was, indeed, a confirmed Zionist in both respects. The role of selection in historical writing and the importance of "significant detail" were explicitly acknowledged in his works.

But Namier so conceptualized the selection process as to undercut its very existence and at the same time to diminish the empirical aspect of historical knowledge.

> The function of the historian [he wrote] is akin to that of the painter and not of the photographic camera: to discover and set forth, to single out and stress that which is of the nature of the thing, and not to reproduce indiscriminately all that meets the eye. To distinguish a tree you look at its shape, its bark and leaf; counting and measuring its branches would get you nowhere. Similarly what matters in history is the great outline and the significant detail; what must be avoided is the deadly morass of irrelevant narrative. History is therefore necessarily subjective and individual.[15]

The essentialist fallacy appears in Namier's notion of "the nature of the thing," which, if it means anything at all, must mean some intuitive sense of the inner essence of the thing. The holist fallacy appears in the "great outline," which is a holistic greatness, because it is general and all-inclusive. One must surely agree with Namier as to "significant detail," but not as to his standard of significance, which is not a method of selection at all but a pious and stubborn hope, against all reason and experience, that a historian will be able to operate intuitively without one.

A second example comes from the opposite end of the political spectrum and suggests a relationship between the fallacy of essences and another form of error, which we shall come to in this chapter—the antiquantitative fallacy. Barrington Moore, in *Social Origins of Dictatorship and Democracy* (Boston, 1966), attacks all statistics that contradict his radical presuppositions. "Statistics," he writes, "are

14. Popper, *The Open Society and Its Enemies*, 1:33.
15. Sir Lewis Namier, "History," *Avenues of History* (London, 1952), p. 8.

misleading traps for the unwary reader when they abstract from the *essence* of the situation the whole structural context in which social osmosis takes place. As statistics are fashionable now, it is worthwhile stressing this point."[16] I shall have something more to say about this statement later in this chapter. Here, one might note that Moore has things backwards. It is not external facts which are abstracted from essences by observers, but essences from external facts. Moore's understanding of the essence of historical events is a radical vision of the progress of humanity toward some egalitarian Utopia. All external facts and statistics which sustain this vision are significant for Moore; all those which contradict it are not. Can anything be more absurd?

Namier and Moore are not alone in their essentialism. In between, many historians have made the same error. Morton White suggests that any historian who argues that "Europe was essentially characterized by a Renaissance at one time, and at another by an Enlightenment, may think along similar lines."[17] And similarly, "even the most cautious and unmetaphysical of historians are prepared to speak in some such vein of the 'line' that the main stream of American 'actuality' has followed."[18] White is referring to the "Jefferson-Jackson-Franklin Roosevelt" line and the "Federalist-Whig-Republican line" which many historians have identified as the "essence" of American history.

The fallacy of essences is tempting to historians, because many of them begin with an article of faith (which I happen to share) that history happened in the way that it happened and not in any other way. But it does not follow from this premise that there is one "essential" inner reality, which can be hunted and found. There are many factual patterns—an infinite number of them—which can be superimposed upon past events. A historian's task is to find patterns which are more relevant to his problems, and more accurate and more comprehensive than others, but he cannot hope to find that "essential" pattern, any more than he can hope to know all of history, and to know it objectively. Here again, the progress of historical science depends squarely upon a sense of the possible.

ᘒᕳ The *prodigious fallacy* mistakes sensation for significance. It is the erroneous idea that a historian's task is to describe portents and prodigies, and events marvelous, stupendous, fantastic, extraordinary, wonderful, superlative, astonishing, and monstrous—and further,

16. P. 37; italics added.
17. White, *The Foundations of Historical Knowledge*, p. 244.
18. Ibid., p. 244.

that the more marvelous, stupendous, etc., an event is, the more historic and eventful it becomes. This absurd standard of significance is older than history itself. Herodotus, the putative "father of history" (grandfather might be more correct), composed his great work on the explicit assumption that a historian should entertain his readers with tales of true "wonders." The result was a perpetual tension in his work between that which was true and that which was wonderful, a tension which was profoundly dysfunctional to the historicity of his interpretation.[19]

Today, this form of error is widely disseminated by the mass media. Journalists use the word "historic" to describe earthquakes, hurricanes, five-alarm fires, floods, state funerals, typhoons, train wrecks, quintuplets, transatlantic canoe trips, and other curiosities or catastrophes which are chiefly remarkable for the fortunate fact that they rarely occur, or for the unfortunate fact that they occur at all.

War reportage from Vietnam is studded with these fallacies, which are known to their perpetrators as "the left-handed battalion commander syndrome." A journalist explains: "It was a function of journalistic desperation to differentiate one military operation from another. An enormous effort was made to establish a 'first' or 'most' or 'least' in the lead of a newspaper article. It was surmised that the classic lead for the nonevent of a fruitless operation [*sic*] would be that a left-handed battalion commander, 'for the first time,' led it into battle."[20]

One expects to see this sort of thing on the sports page, where history is made by an infield triple, or a one-armed shortstop, or the most Texas Leaguers in a ten-inning game. But somehow it always comes as a surprise to find it on the editorial page of *The New York Times,* where the defection of Stalin's daughter was played up for many months in 1967 as one of the "historic" events of the century. And it is even more disconcerting to hear a good journalist-turned-historian, William Manchester, saying that "the abdication of Edward VII [*sic*] . . . was the greatest story since the Resurrection."[21]

In the genre called popular history, many prodigious fallacies are perpetrated by historians who appear to have mistaken their muse for Miss Dorothy Kilgallen, and their mission for the titillation of illiterate thrill-seekers. Almost any given volume in Doubleday and Company's disastrous *Mainstream of America* series can serve as an

19. *The History of Herodotus,* trans. George Rawlinson, ed. Manuel Komroff (New York, 1956), pp. 36, 134, 149, 187, 213, 267.
20. Ward S. Just, *To What End?* (Boston, 1968), p. 15.
21. Quoted in John Corry, *The Manchester Affair* (New York, 1967), p. 86.

example. A particularly serious specimen is Paul I. Wellman's *The House Divides* (Garden City, N.Y., 1966), which purports to be a serious popular history of the United States from the end of the War of 1812 to the start of the Civil War. Wellman appears to have believed that the best way to bring history to life is to crowd it with as many violent deaths as possible. In his fourth chapter, ostensibly about the early career of Andrew Jackson, I counted 1,452 violent killings. Many are described in graphic detail. A few are described twice. This butcher's bill for Chapter 4, it should be noted, does not include the battle of New Orleans, which has Chapter 1 all to itself— an entire celebratory chapter dedicated to the sublimity of that epic slaughter.[22]

Political history, in Wellman's book, is retailed in a sequence of anecdotes and apocrypha—the false fable about Stephen Van Rensselaer and the election of 1824 (p. 68); the alleged vote of an invalid in Switzerland County, Indiana, which "made Texas a state and brought on the Mexican War" (p. 213); the Peggy Eaton affair, which is interpreted as a "trigger" of the Civil War; and other assorted marvels, mostly false, about Abraham Lincoln's first sight of slavery (p. 286); the defense of the Alamo (p. 157); Daniel Webster's seventh-of-March speech (p. 330); and the underground railroad (p. 236).

Economic history is largely left out of sight. The only extended discussion of a manufacturing process is a recipe for "Injun Whiskey." As for social, intellectual, cultural, and educational history, Jim Bowie receives more space than all major figures in these areas combined. Chief Justice John Marshall gets seven lines; James Marshall, the mechanic who found gold in the American River, gets sixty-three.

Wellman's book is not much worse than many others in the same series, which has been widely distributed by Doubleday, and often, I fear, urged upon innocent children by well-meaning librarians and school teachers.[23]

22. For violence, see in addition to chap. 4, pp. 1–12, 15–21, 26, 30–36, 37–55, 74, 78, 80, 99, 100, 118–19, 130, 135, 144–45, 148–63, 184–86, 188, 190–92, 194, 196, 199, 201, 202, 207, 216–80, 288–89, 295, 299, 300–1, 313–14, 345–49, 350–53, 354–62, 367, 378–79, 380–81, 388, 389, 400, 415–17. For sex, see pp. 25, 33, 60, 65, 73, 75, 76, 78–79, 86, 87, 91–92, 106–7, 120–23, 161, 206, 248–49, 253, 291, 294, 296–98, 352, 377–78.

23. A few *Mainstream of America* volumes are exceptional. They tend to be books avowedly on military subjects, such as Bruce Catton's *This Hallowed Ground*, C. S. Forester's *Age of Fighting Sail*, and Edward Hamilton's *French and Indian Wars*. Volumes of colonial history by Harold Lamb and Marion Starkey are at least accurate. And David Lavender's *Land of Giants* is a good history of the Pacific Northwest. For deficiencies in the others, the reader might consult critical reviews by competent authorities. I recommend for Hodding Carter's *The Angry Scar* the review in the *Journal*

But popular historians have no monopoly on prodigious fallacies. Academic historians tend to commit them more delicately but not less frequently. There are examples even in the *Oxford History of England* series, magisterially edited by Sir George Clark. The most recent volume is *English History, 1914–1945*, by A. J. P. Taylor (Oxford, 1965). The reader is invited to locate Taylor's standards of significance, in the following biographical notes:

[2]George V (1865–1936), second son of Edward VII: married Princess Mary of Teck, 1893; king, 1910–1936; changed name of royal family from Saxe-Coburg to Windsor, 1917; his trousers were creased at the sides, not front and back [p. 2n].

[2]David Lloyd George (1863–1945): educ. Church school; Liberal M.P., 1890–1945; chancellor of the exchequer, 1908–15; minister of munitions, 1915–16; secretary for war, 1916; prime minister, 1916–22; leader of the Liberal party, 1926–31; cr. Earl Lloyd-George, 1945. A master of improvised speech and of improvised policies. Though he was dangerous to most women, he gave his heart to few. After leaving office, he farmed ambitiously, though unprofitably, and propagated the 'Lloyd-George' raspberry. He disliked his correct surname, 'George,' and imposed 'Lloyd George' on contemporaries and posterity [p. 5n].

[1]Asquith was the first prime minister since the younger Pitt who is said to have been manifestly the worse for drink when on the Treasury Bench. George Robey was uncomfortably near the mark when he sang:
Mr. Asquith says in a manner sweet and calm:
Another drink won't do us any harm [p. 15n].

[2]Walter Long (1854–1924): educ. Harrow and Oxford; M.P., 1882–1921; president of local government board, 1915–16; colonial secretary, 1916–18; first lord of the admiralty, 1918–21; cr. Viscount, 1921. Chesterton wrote (incorrectly):

---

of Southern History 25 (1959): 400–402; for Clifford Dowdey's *The Land They Fought For*, ibid., 21 (1955): 541–42; for John Dos Passos' *Men Who Made the Nation*, *William and Mary Quarterly*, 3d ser. 15 (1958): 120–21; for Bruce Lancaster's *From Lexington to Liberty*, ibid., 12 (1955): 665–67; for Irving Stone's *Men to Match My Mountains*, see *Pacific Historical Review* 26 (1957): 79–80; and for Paul Wellman's earlier volume, *Glory, God, and Gold*, ibid., 24 (1955): 80–81. Stewart Holbrook's *The Age of the Moguls* is reviewed in *The Saturday Review of Literature*, Oct. 10, 1953, and his *Dreamers of the American Dream*, in ibid., Oct. 26, 1957. I did not find good reviews of Kenneth Davis's *The Experience of War*, which promiscuously mixes fiction and fact; or Saunders Redding's *Lonesome Road*, which is a moving human document, but not a sound or reliable history of the Negro in America.

Such works as these are not commonly reviewed in learned journals, which is unfortunate. If *The American Historical Review*, crowded though it is, were to make an effort to stimulate careful critiques of popular histories, and then to distribute those critiques to librarians and public school teachers, the quality of pop history would soon improve. If the reader will forgive a hackneyed phrase, pop history is much too serious a business to be left to pop historians and businessmen.

> Walter, beware! scorn not the gathering throng . . .
> It suffers, but it cannot suffer Long [p. 40n].

There are many other "true wonders" in Taylor's notes, and more in his text, and a few even in his index. Some are more wondrous than true.[24] Together, they suggest that the youthful spirit of Herodotus has revived in the ripe old age of English academic history. Professor Taylor has, I think, hunted down his smoking-room stories in the same Herodotean spirit which caused that ancient author to journey all the way from Halicarnasus to Arabia to investigate reports of winged serpents, and to regale his readers with strange tales of giants and dwarfs, men with horns and oxen without them, savage tribes who worshiped their parents and others who ate them.[25]

ၜ➤ The *furtive fallacy* is the erroneous idea that facts of special significance are dark and dirty things and that history itself is a story of causes mostly insidious and results mostly invidious. It begins with the premise that reality is a sordid, secret thing; and that history happens on the back stairs a little after midnight, or else in a smoke-filled room, or a perfumed boudoir, or an executive penthouse or somewhere in the inner sanctum of the Vatican, or the Kremlin, or the Reich Chancellery, or the Pentagon. It is something more, and something other than merely a conspiracy theory, though that form of causal reduction is a common component. The furtive fallacy is a more profound error, which combines a naïve epistemological assumption that things are

---

24. Henry Pelling, "Taylor's England," *Past and Present* 33 (1966): 149–58.
25. Taylor is not the only academician who has slipped into his "Herodotage," as Malinowski called it. Occasional lapses are apparent in the work of all scholars—even duly licensed American Ph.D.s! Eugene L. Cox, in a fine book called *The Green Count of Savoy* (Princeton, 1967), was unable to resist the following marvel:

"The conflicting claims of the Pope and Bernabo Visconti finally led to Bernabo's excommunication. Milanese chroniclers recount that the Lord of Milan was sitting with some of his men on a bridge over the Lambro when the papal envoys approached with the bull of excommunication. The terrible Bernabo is supposed to have seized the bull, perused it with darkening brow, then gazed for a moment down at the swift waters of the river. Glaring at the envoys, he asked them if they would rather eat or drink. The frightened ambassadors, knowing Bernabo's grotesque sense of humor and certain that if they expressed a preference for drinking they would soon find themselves in the river, chose to eat. They were accordingly seized by Visconti men-at-arms and forced to eat the papal bull itself, parchment, seals and all, while their tormenter looked on with sadistic amusement."

To this extraordinary story, which Cox included in the text of his book, the following footnote was appended: "To paraphrase Winston Churchill, tiresome investigators have undermined this excellent tale, but it should still find its place in any history worthy of the name." Eugene L. Cox, *The Green Count of Savoy* (Princeton, 1967), p. 155.

never what they seem to be, with a firm attachment to the doctrine of original sin.

There is a little of the furtive fallacy in us all—enough to sustain the common truth of Ralph Barton Perry's observation that "facts, like sinners, gain something from an unsavory reputation."[26] But there is more of it in some people than in others. And when there is much of it, we are apt to summon a psychiatrist. In an extreme form, the furtive fallacy is not merely an intellectual error but a mental illness which is commonly called paranoia.[27]

Sometimes paranoia is an epidemic disease. There are periods in the past when men ran mad in packs, and when their madness took precisely this form. Sometimes, such outbreaks have been followed by great cataclysms. The relationship of cause to consequence is cloudy, but a symptomatic significance, at least, seems clear. If it is correct, then nothing is more ominous in our own time than the prevalence of furtive fallacies in every ideological camp. Witness the appalling success of *Macbird,* and the tone of the campaign against Axel Springer, and miscellaneous fears of furtive acts by soldiers and students, Negroes and Jews, Communists and capitalists, the Mafia, Maoists, the Kennedy clan, President Johnson, General de Gaulle, and many others. Reasonable men of all persuasions have an interest, and a duty, to oppose this ugly tendency. The furtive fallacy has a self-fulfilling quality. Men who believe it begin to act furtively. Nothing is more dangerous to the peace of the world or more deleterious to the progress of humanity.

The furtive fallacy is, however, nothing new in the world. A rounded history of this delusion would carry us back to the great Homeric treacheries and far beyond. We might merely return sixty years, or so, to muckraking journalists of America's "Progressive era." If Richard Hofstadter is correct, they operated upon an assumption that reality was a "rough and sordid" thing. "It was hidden, neglected, and off-stage. . . . Reality was the bribe, the rebate, the bought franchise, the sale of adulterated food. . . . Reality was a series of unspeakable plots, personal iniquities, moral failures."[28]

Historians in the Progressive era showed the same habit of thought. A socialist scholar, Algie Simons, led the pack in their reinterpretation of that sacred ark of republicanism, the United States Constitution. In

---

26. Ralph Barton Perry, *Puritanism and Democracy* (New York, 1944), p. 53.
27. Of course, I do not mean to suggest that the historians whose works are used as examples of this error are paranoid. The argument, rather, is that a fallacy which appears in their thought has sometimes become paranoia in the thought of others.
28. Richard Hofstadter, *The Age of Reform,* Vintage ed. (New York, 1960), pp. 201–2.

rhetoric which "sweats with rural superstition,"[29] he informed his readers that "the organic law of this nation was formulated in secret session by a body called into existence through a conspiratory [sic] trick, and was forced upon a disfranchised people by means of dishonest apportionment in order that the interests of a small body of wealthy rulers might be served."[30]

Close behind Simons was the mightiest muckraker of them all, Charles Beard, author of the most famous monograph in American history, *An Economic Interpretation of the Constitution* (New York, 1913), in which the furtive fallacy was deeply embedded. Beard claimed otherwise, and several times insisted that his thesis was misunderstood. But in fact it was misconceived. For Beard, as for Simons, the Constitution was "essentially an economic document," which was "written by a small and active group of men" who were "with a few exceptions, immediately, directly and personally interested in, and derived economic advantages from, the establishment of the new system."[31]

Beard's book, for all the controversy which it caused, was a very moderate specimen of the furtive fallacy. No imputation of paranoia can attach to his work. Nobody, not even his worst critics, wished to call a psychiatrist (though President Nicholas Murray Butler of Columbia may have wished to call the police). But his interpretative model, in the events which it made significant, was false and misleading.

Beard's last major book, on the origins of American intervention in World War II, was even more deeply flawed by the furtive fallacy in its thesis that Franklin Roosevelt and his cronies secretly manipulated American policy by a series of subtle and sordid tricks to bring their nation into the war. There is no evidence that Beard deliberately falsified his account.[32] The errors and distortions in his interpretation are rather the result of his erroneous assumptions—not merely in the conceptualization of the specific historical problem which he was studying, nor simply in his political prejudices, but in the way he believed history happened. That fundamental error was a constant in Beard's

29. Stanley Elkins and Eric McKitrick, *The Founding Fathers: Young Men of the Revolution* (Washington, D.C., 1962), p. 8. I am heavily endebted to this essay, in the following interpretation.

30. Algie M. Simons, *Social Forces in American History* (New York, 1911), p. 99; quoted in Elkins and McKitrick, p. 8.

31. *An Economic Interpretation of the Constitution*, new ed. (New York, 1935), pp. 324–25; cf. pp. xvi, 73.

32. Cushing Strout notes that Basil Rauch in *Roosevelt from Munich to Pearl Harbor* (New York, 1950) "attacks Beard's devil-theory of Roosevelt at the price of creating a devil-theory of Beard by accusing him of deliberate falsification of the record." *The Pragmatic Revolt in American History: Carl Becker and Charles Beard* (New Haven, 1958), p. 150 n.

career, from the *Economic Interpretation* in 1913 to *President Roosevelt and the Coming of the War, 1941: A Study in Appearances and Realities* (New Haven, 1948).

If the furtive fallacy is a link between the early Beard and the late Beard, it is also a bond between Beard and the anti-Beardians. We have already considered the fallacy of counterquestions in this connection. The mistake perpetrated by Beard was perpetuated by his most able critic. In Forrest McDonald's history of the Constitution, there is a furtive fallacy which is so gross that I have sometimes wondered if it was intended as a practical joke.

McDonald tells us, with a straight face, that the critical compromise which made the Constitution possible was a secret deal between Connecticut land speculators, represented by Roger Sherman, and South Carolina planters, represented by John Rutledge. The arrangement was made in a smoke-filled room, on the evening of June 30, 1787, but almost came unstuck in another smoke-filled room, where Charles Pinckney (who was in on the secret), and Luther Martin (who was not), went off on a great roaring drunk together. This alcoholic bout might be called the first anti-Federal party. Sometime after the seventh drink, bibulous "blackguard-Charlie" whispered the secret to the cunning "Brandy Bottle" Martin, who proceeded to rally the opposition. But Oliver Ellsworth and John Rutledge, who are compared to Samuel Rayburn and Lyndon Johnson, managed to put the deal back together again, by some sly parliamentary skulduggery.[33]

This remarkable interpretation is developed with imaginative detail, in a work which might be enjoyed as a masterpiece of black humor, worthy of comparison with the best of Terry Southern (with James Madison in the role of Candy), or Pynchon (with the Constitution as V), or Donleavy (with Robert Morris as Sebastian Dangerfield), or John Barth himself. I suppose that it *might* have happened—even Barth's scatalogical secret history of Captain John Smith *might* have happened. But there is no evidence to sustain McDonald's interpretation, and much to the contrary. There is no good evidence even that the alleged meetings took place, much less that such bargains were made.

This furtive fallacy is central to McDonald's interpretation. But there are also many smaller ones, in a work which is rum-and-strumpet history, with a vengeance. What, for example, *really* went on, in that green paradise called New Hampshire? McDonald believes that reality was something like this: "Winters in eighteenth-century New Hampshire were uncommonly long and cold: so cold that all men save the most

33. Forrest McDonald, *E Pluribus Unum: The Formation of the American Republic, 1776–1790* (Boston, 1965), chap. 6, pp. 176–84.

industrious stayed indoors, making their wives pregnant and praying to a Fundamentalist, Calvinist God to make it warmer; and so long that when Spring finally broke, all men save the most industrious got fiercely drunk and made other men's wives pregnant" (p. 114). Who *really* was an obscure Maryland politician, Daniel of St. Thomas Jenifer? "Jenifer was a petty local official who customarily had his hand in the public till or was helping someone else's to reach it" (p. 166). What was the *real* story behind the Jay-Gardoqui treaty? "Gardoqui flattered Jay and showered Jay's wife (whom Jay adored) with attention and gifts, whereupon Jay agreed to ask Congress for permission to surrender American claims to rights of navigation on the Mississippi" (p. 82).

In the misbehavioral science of Beard and McDonald, reality is always the *underlying* fact, always something more than meets the eye. But there is also another curious inversion of the furtive fallacy, which is grounded in an increasingly fashionable assumption that reality is something *less* than meets the eye. An example is a work by Joseph Hamburger on the philosophic radicals and the English reform bill. His thesis, as summarized by a critic, is that "their threat of violence and revolution was a calculated bluff, a threat they neither intended nor desired to carry out, and that their strategy succeeded not because everyone was taken in by the bluff, but because some politicians, recognizing it as such, chose to submit to it for tactical reasons of their own." Reality is reduced to a set of shadows, flickering behind a curtain of flimsy rhetoric.[34]

  The *moralistic fallacy* selects edifying facts. In Michael Oakeshott's phrase, it makes the past into "a field in which we exercise our moral and political opinions, like whippets in a meadow on Sunday afternoon."[35]

In the fields and meadows which surround most American universities, there are hordes of hairy graduate students who are crying up this error, as a Whole New Thing in historical scholarship. But it is a very old thing—as ancient as Dionysius of Halicarnasus, who characterized history as "philosophy by examples." And it is inconsistent with a serious and disciplined empirical inquiry into what actually happened. It would make history a handmaid of moral philosophy, as it actually was in most American colleges, during much of the nineteenth century.[36]

34. Gertrude Himmelfarb, *American Historical Review* 61 (1966): 1344. The book is Joseph Hamburger's *James Mill and the Art of Revolution* (New Haven, 1963). See pp. 115, 125.
35. Michael Oakeshott, *Rationalism in Politics and Other Essays* (London, 1962), p. 165.
36. See, e.g., Wilson Smith, *Professors and Public Ethics* (Ithaca, N.Y., 1956).

This fallacy is exceedingly difficult to define precisely. Most reasonable men would agree that all historians, without exception, must and should make value judgments in their work. But they would also agree that some historians moralize upon past events in ways which are inconsistent with empiricism. There is a thin line, somewhere in between, which is not easy to locate.

Historians with whom I have discussed this problem have variously suggested five separate criteria for distinguishing acceptable moral judgments from unacceptable moralizing:

1. Moral judgments are good, true, or sensitive judgments; moralizing is bad, crude, shallow, false, or stupid.

2. Moral judgments are moderate; moralizing is immoderate.

3. Moral judgments are empirically accurate; moralizing is empirically false.

4. Moral judgments consist in judging people by their own standards; moralizing is judging them by other people's standards.

5. Acceptable moral judgments are functional, or neutral, to empirical inquiry; unacceptable moralizing is dysfunctional.

All but one of these notions seem clearly untenable. The first, I think, is circular. Though it conforms to common usage among historians, it tends to become, in practice, mere special pleading, like the statement "I make moral judgments; you moralize; he is a self-righteous prig." The second distinction is also invalid, because it makes moderation the measure of truth. It is a classic example of argument *ad modum,* discussed in chapter XI below.

The third distinction seems equally unacceptable in its premise that ethical problems are susceptible to empirical resolution. Without plunging into the philosophical thickets of ethical objectivism, which I am not qualified to discuss, it appears to me that moral judgments are, in context, a priori in their nature. The fourth distinction implies an ethical relativism which is as hateful and suicidal as historical relativism.

By process of elimination, we are left with the fifth distinction, which makes more sense to me than any other. What does one mean by moral judgments which are functional or neutral or dysfunctional to empirical inquiry? Merely this: every historian possesses a complex structure of value assumptions, which he cannot adjust to his empirical projects, and cannot keep out of his work. But he can adjust his project to his values in such a fashion as to neutralize or to control his moral preferences. The first step in that process would be to make his values as fully explicit, to himself and others, as possible. The second step would be to design a research problem in which his values allow an open end.

Imagine two historians, one a southern white supremacist and the other a black militant. Each possesses many values which are separate from white supremacy or black militancy, but we will confine our attention to these elements alone. (The nature of the problem does not change as it becomes more complex.) Neither of these scholars, however honest and well-intentioned they may be, can ever hope to write a rounded general history of Negroes in Reconstruction without moralizing upon their subject in a dysfunctional way.

Our hypothetical black militant wishes, of course, to write a history of Blacks. Within the general area, he can find problems in which his moralizing propensity is controlled. He might try his hand, for example, at a comparative study of black slavery and anti-black prejudice in Spanish, French, Dutch, Portuguese, Danish, and English colonies—a study which we very much need at the present moment. His values would be engaged in the problem, but functionally engaged, for he has an open end in his inquiry. Our imaginary southern white supremacist, on the other hand, wants to study the history of the American South. Maybe he could do a comparative analysis of regional white culture patterns within the South and bring a functional intensity of moral purpose to his work without moralizing upon it in a dysfunctional way.

We might, in light of these observations, refine our first, approximate, definition of the moralistic fallacy, which becomes not merely, in Michael Oakeshott's metaphor, exercising our moral opinions in history like a whippet in a meadow on Sunday afternoon. It is exercising the whippet without a leash.

A classical example of an unleashed moralizer is a great Roman historian, Tacitus, who possessed a glorious gift for vivid and, I think, exact analysis of historical problems. His remarkable characterizations, like the Roman sculpture of the same period, gain a universal meaning from their profound particularity. But that splendid talent coexisted with an incompatible purpose. "This I regard as history's highest function," he wrote, "to let no worthy action be uncommemorated, and to hold out the reprobation of posterity as a terror to evil words and deeds."[37] Tacitus gave this moralizing method a famous twist in the *Germania,* where the chastity, simplicity, freedom, and fidelity of a primitive people are set up as an antithesis to the debauchery and corruption which he despised in his own culture. The book is punctuated with sarcastic side comments about the ignoblest Romans of them all. Classical historians have argued endlessly about the priority of his purposes. Did he mean to describe Germans as they were, or Romans as he wished them to be? The only

37. Tacitus, *Annals,* 3. 65.

sensible answer, I think, is that he tried to do both at the same time, and therein lies the fallacy, for his moral judgments were dysfunctional to his historical interpretation of the Germans.[38]

From the age of Tacitus to our own time, the moralistic fallacy has flourished in a thousand forms. My favorite is *The Mirror for Magistrates,* a versified raid upon English history, probably first conceived in the twelfth century, and much enlarged by "dyuers learned men" through the next four hundred years. The work was addressed to the "nobilitye and all other in office," in the hope that "For here as in a loking glas, you shall see (if any vice be in you) howe the like hath bene punished in other[s] heretofore, whereby admonished, I trust it will be a good occasion to move you to the soner amendment. This is the chiefest ende, whye it is set furth, which God graunt it may attayne."[39]

In the moral universe of the *Mirror,* everyone received his just reward:

> Humber the king of the Hunnes shewes how he minding to conquere this land was drowned, &c. . . . Morindus a bastarde, declares how hee was exalted to the kingdome, waxed cruell, and at laste was deuoured by a monster, the year before Christe 303. . . . King Emerianus for his tirany was depose, about the year before Christ, 225. . . . King Chirinnus giuen to dronkennesse raygned but one year. Hee died about the yeare before Christ, 137.[40]

A noble gentleman who glanced into the *Mirror* could see "How Guiderious . . . became desirous to winne all the worlde, spoyled France, Germany and a great part of Italy: and lastly, how hee was miserably slayne in a tempest of thunder. . . . This history is a synguler ensample of God's vengeance, against pride and arrogancy." He could learn "Howe Vter Pendragon was inamoured of Duke Garelus wife, and howe by laweless loue he lost his kingdome. This example is most necessary for the present time. . . ." and "How Sigebert was thrust from his throne, and miserably slayne by a Heardman. This tragedie dooth teach both Prince and suiect his duetie at large."[41]

The "ensampling" method of the *Mirror for Magistrates,* of course, is as faithful a representation of the reality of history as a fun-house mirror. For every sinner who has been struck by lightning, or providentially slain by a shepherd, a hundred have lived happily ever after.

---

38. A juxtaposition of primitive virtue and civilized corruption is a common variant of the moralistic fallacy, which mars many modern works in history and anthropology. It is deeply embedded in the curious cult of "structuralism" which has formed in France around the work of a great ethnologist, Claude Lévi-Strauss.

39. Lily B. Campbell, ed., *The Mirror for Magistrates* (Cambridge, 1938), pp. 65–66.

40. Lily B. Campbell, ed., *Parts Added to The Mirror for Magistrates* (Cambridge, 1946), pp. 74, 185, 282, 283.

41. Ibid., pp. 386, 452.

But, alas, even that fact has been made into a moralistic fallacy by the Swiss historian, Jacob Burkhardt. "Every violent deed that prospers is, to say the least, an offense; that is to say, a bad example. The only thing to be learned from successful misdeeds of the mighty is not to value life in this world more highly than it deserves."[42]

ได้ The *pragmatic fallacy* selects useful facts—immediately and directly useful facts—in the service of a social cause. Most historians hope that their work is, or will be, useful to somebody, somewhere, someday. In the conclusion we shall consider how utility *can* function in history. But the pragmatic fallacy short-circuits the problem. It consists in the attempt to combine scholarly monographs and social manifestoes in a single operation. The result is double trouble: distorted monographs and dull manifestoes.

Consider a recent work by Eric Williams, a trained scholar and a prominent West Indian statesman, who explicitly pursued two entirely different and incompatible purposes. The first was to do an "accurate," "adequate," and "informed" history, in which the author attempted, in a Rankean spirit, "to let the documents speak for themselves."[43] But the second was something else: "The aim in writing the book, however, was not literary perfection or conformity with scholarly canons," Mr. Williams wrote. "The aim was to provide the people of Trinidad and Tobago on their Independence Day with a National History, as they have already been provided with a National Anthem, a National Coat of Arms, National Birds, a National Flower and a National Flag."[44]

These emblems, for Williams, were meant to be both useful and ornamental. He industriously collected facts which promoted two particular purposes: the "integration of the races" in Trinidad and Tobago and "integration of the separated Caribbean territories." The "national history" of Trinidad and Tobago which resulted, closely resembled its national flag in more respects than one—a great heavy black diagonal, snug between two thin bands of white (Spaniards and British, I presume), all superimposed upon a red field (Williams's interpretation is predominantly Marxist). Facts are selected to show that "in Trinidad the Negro, the Indian, French and Spaniard, English and Portuguese, Syrian and Lebanese, Chinese and Jew, have all messed out of the same pot, all are victims of the same subordination, all have been tarred with the

---

42. Quoted by Ernst Cassirer in *The Problem of Knowledge*, p. 275.
43. Eric Williams, *History of the People of Trinidad and Tobago* (Port-of-Spain, 1962), p. vii.
44. Ibid.

same brush of political inferiority. Divergent customs and antipathetic attitudes have all been submerged in the common subordinate status of colonialism."[45] And that thesis is as false and misleading as it is possible for a thesis to be.

But it is not more false or misleading than other patriot histories which have been written in all nations for the same purpose of national integration. There is no appreciable difference in this respect between Williams' interpretation and that of national historians of Britain, who equally condemned Oliver Cromwell as a great bad man and James II as a tyrant-fool, all in the cause of nation-building; or American historians—maybe the worst of the lot—who have filled the heads of little children with functional fairy tales about the good Pilgrim fathers and wicked witch-burning Puritans; about bad King George and the demigods who wrote the Constitution, the Monroe Doctrine, the Great Emancipator, the Glorious Melting Pot, and all the dirty Indians, Frenchmen, English, Scots, Hessians, Algerians, Mexicans, Spaniards, Filipinos, Nicaraguans, Prussians, Italians, Japs, Koreans, Chinese, and Vietnamese who had to bite the dust so that the world would be made safe for Peace, Brotherhood, and the Universal Yankee Nation. The fairy tales I was taught, in a schoolroom below the Mason and Dixon line, were a little different. But the fallacy was much the same.

Today, there isn't much of this nation-building variant of the pragmatic fallacy in the serious scholarly literature of the United States and Britain. But the same form of error is still very common in the service of other causes. A case in point is the work of a young radical American historian, Staughton Lynd. He is a scholar who is possessed of extraordinary gifts—intelligence, industry, imagination, integrity, candor, a sense of perspective, a sense of proportion, and even a sense of humor. By temperament and conviction he is not an observer but a participant. He enthusiastically endorses an aphorism paraphrased from Marx's *Theses on Feuerbach:* "The Historians have interpreted the world; the thing, however, is to change it."[46] To this declaration, Lynd adds a rhetorical question of his own: "Should we be content with measuring the dimensions of our prison instead of chipping away, however inadequately, against the bars?"[47]

For many years Lynd has been working like a beaver at the prison bars—not with a file but with a file card.[48] It would appear to be arduous

---

45. Ibid., p. 280.
46. Staughton Lynd, "Historical Past and Existential Present," in Theodore Roszak, ed., *The Dissenting Academy* (New York, 1967), p. 107.
47. Ibid.
48. The task is tough enough, given Lynd's choice of tools. But the trouble is compounded by the fact that Lynd and his radical friends believe that the great penitentiary in which they live—i.e., American society—is cunningly constructed with *invisible* bars.

and unrewarding toil. But Lynd is determined to demonstrate that a "professor of history" (in a literal sense) should be a historical protagonist in one and the same act. He believes specifically that a historian should promote the transcendent purpose of class revolution in the American republic. Now, to have a class revolution, one must have class conflict. One major group of his writings is organized around this object. For Lynd, a significant fact is a useful fact, and a useful fact is a fact which demonstrates the reality of class conflict in America and even promotes it. To this end he has published a monograph and several articles, mostly about affairs in Dutchess County, New York, mainly in the period 1760–1790. It is work of high professional quality which genuinely deals in facts—true statements about the past. But there is a fallacy in the true statements which Lynd chooses to make and in the criteria of factual significance upon which he bases his choice. The author himself is his own best critic. Writing five years after the monograph was published, he candidly observes,

> I am now more conscious that I selected a range of data which I could be pretty certain would substantiate the thesis I hoped was true. I studied opposition to the United States Constitution in Dutchess County, New York, because Dutchess County had a history of landlord-tenant conflict very likely to be connected with how groups aligned themselves for or against ratification of the Constitution. The bias involved in my selection of Dutchess County did not necessarily invalidate my findings, but it raised serious question as to their generalizability. I believe this is how bias characteristically operates in the work of other historians, too: not in the deliberate mishandling of evidence, but in the selection of research design.[49]

Other batches of Lynd's essays are devoted to the discovery of other kinds of useful facts. One group of them represents an attempt to locate an authentic radical tradition in American history. "As one considerably alienated from America's present," he writes, "I wanted to know if there were men in the American past in whom I could believe."[50] A third group of articles, which are functionally related to Lynd's

---

He has worked for years at what he thinks is an invisible bar, only to discover that it is really a space between them, and that the work must begin again. This cycle has been repeated several times in Lynd's scholarly career.

49. Ibid., p. 10. The monograph is *Anti-Federalism in Dutchess County, New York: A Study of Democracy and Class Conflict in the Revolutionary Era* (Chicago, 1962). The articles are reprinted in *Class Conflict, Slavery, and the United States Constitution* (Indianapolis, 1967).

50. "A Profession of History," p. 10. These works include *Nonviolence in America: A Documentary History* (Indianapolis, 1966); and "Beard, Jefferson and the Tree of Liberty," in *Class Conflict, Slavery, and the United States Constitution*, pp. 247–69; and *Intellectual Origins of American Radicalism* (New York, 1968).

participation in the civil rights movement, centers upon Negro slavery in American history. Lynd argues that the Peculiar Institution was a key, maybe *the* key to American history, the significance of which has been underestimated by American historians. He suggests that the issue of slavery was *the* issue in the politics of the early republic, and particularly in the framing of the Constitution. In these articles, I think, unlike the Dutchess County essays, Lynd does not make true statements. He means to make them, but his pragmatic criteria of factual significance lead him to exaggerate grossly a few scraps of evidence, mostly circumstantial, into an interpretation, mostly false. Most American historians would surely agree that slavery was the predominant issue in American politics from 1820 to 1860. But to argue that it was equally so in the preceding forty-year period is simply wrong.[51]

An introduction to one of Lynd's collections of essays has been written by a radical English historian, whose works provide many other examples of the same sort of error. E. P. Thompson is a little more heavy-handed than his American colleague. His introduction is a ritual incantation against "mutton-fisted narks of academe," but he is also a serious and gifted scholar who has written a work of great importance on the English working class.[52] His work, however, is seriously flawed by his standards of factual significance, which lead him to select facts which are useful to the preservation of the culture and identity of the working class against a variety of enemies, imagined and real.[53]

Radical historians have no monopoly on the pragmatic fallacy. The same error is committed by historians who are located at many different points in the spectrum of social ideology. A familiar and flagrant example is the recent work of Arthur Schlesinger, Jr., in his writings on the New Deal.[54] Turning to a conservative historian, we find a different form of the pragmatic fallacy, as well as a different substance—a form which is not merely deleterious in its methodological consequences but exceedingly dangerous as well. Scholars who take a pragmatic view of their task and collect facts that are weapons for a cause are faced with the problem that some facts exist which are useful to their enemies. More than a few able historians, caught up in this predicament, have proposed a kind of fact control, which is profoundly hostile to free inquiry.

In the early stages of the Cold War, the American Historical As-

51. Lynd, "On Turner, Beard and Slavery," and "The Compromise of 1787," in *Class Conflict, Slavery, and the United States Constitution*, pp. 135–52, 185–213.
52. *The Making of the English Working Class* (New York, 1964).
53. Another excellent work, similarly flawed, in much the same way, is Richard Hoggart, *The Uses of Literacy* (London, 1957), p. 280.
54. See, e.g., *The Coming of the New Deal*, pp. 1–2, 16, 20–23, 102, 169–70, 175–76, passim.

sociation elected as its president Conyers Read, a distinguished historian of Tudor England, a deep believer in "the relativity of all history," and a dedicated anti-Communist. Seriously concerned about the fate of free institutions in the postwar world, he advocated a little fact control in historical scholarship.

> We must assert our own objectives, define our own ideals, establish our own standards and organize all the forces of our society in support of them. Discipline is the essential prerequisite of every effective army whether it march under the Stars and Stripes or under the Hammer and Sickle. . . . Total war, whether it be hot or cold, enlists everyone and calls upon everyone to assume his part. The historian is no freer from this obligation than the physicist. . . . If historians, in their examination of the past, represent the evolution of civilization as haphazard, without direction and without progress, offering no assurance that mankind's present position is on the highway and not on some dead end, then mankind will seek for assurance in a more positive alternative, whether it be offered from Rome or from Moscow. . . . This sounds like the advocacy of one form of social control as against another. In short, it is. But I see no alternative in a divided world. Probably in any planned world we can never be altogether free agents, even with our tongue and our pen. The important thing is that we shall accept and endorse such controls as are essential for the preservation of our way of life. . . . This need not imply any deliberate distortion of the past in the interests of any ideology. Always it will be our obligation as historians to consider the present developing civilization in all its aspects. We shall still, like the doctor, have to examine social pathology if only to diagnose the nature of disease. But we must realize that not everything which takes place in the laboratory is appropriate for broadcasting at the street corners. . . . I am inclined to think that the first prerequisite of a historian is a sound social philosophy. Actually he finds in the past what he looks for.[55]

Professor Read, now in his grave, was a scholar and a gentleman. But his doctrine is utterly despicable and very dangerous to historical science. It is, I fear, one of the many poisoned fruits of relativism and of the Cold War altogether. And it is still very much alive.

There is something equally ugly in American radicalism, of which the principal manifestation is a book by Herbert Marcuse and others, called *A Critique of Pure Tolerance* (Boston, 1965), in which Mr. Marcuse demands "new and rigid restrictions on teachings and practices in educational institutions," and specifically the withdrawal of tolerance from anyone who promotes "armament," "chauvinism," or "discrimination on the grounds of race and religion," or who opposes the "extension of public services, social security, medical care, etc."

The spectacle of an impotent radical minority threatening to with-

---

55. Conyers Read, "The Social Responsibilities of the Historian," *American Historical Review* 55 (1950): 283–85.

draw tolerance from the moderate mass would be amusing if it were not so profoundly hostile to a principle which has been very slow to take root in the world, and which is still very fragile. Experience suggests that the repressive form of the pragmatic fallacy is highly contagious—it can spread swiftly if it is not actively contained.

• The *aesthetic fallacy* selects beautiful facts, or facts that can be built into a beautiful story, rather than facts that are functional to the empirical problem at hand. It consists in an attempt to organize an empirical inquiry upon aesthetic criteria of significance, or conversely in an attempt to create an *objet d'art* by an empirical method. To do so is to confuse two different kinds of knowledge and truth.

To the truth of art, external reality is irrelevant. Art creates its own reality, within which truth and the perfection of beauty is the infinite refinement of itself. History is very different. It is an empirical search for external truths, and for the best, most complete, and most profound external truths, in a maximal corresponding relationship with the absolute reality of the past events. Any attempt to conduct that search according to aesthetic standards of significance (most commonly in an attempt to tell a beautiful story) is either to abandon empiricism or to contradict it.

The aesthetic fallacy is an ancient form of error, which appeared full blown in Aristotle's notorious opinion that history was an inferior form of particularized poetry, roughly on an intellectual plane with lyre plucking.[56] That Aristotle should have come to this conclusion is understandable, for the aesthetic fallacy appears in the writing of every ancient historian whose works have survived into the modern age, particularly in historians of the fourth century B.C.[57]

But the logical extension of the aesthetic fallacy appears later, in the Roman historian who is reputed to have said that he would have made Pompey win the battle of Pharsalia if the turn of the sentence had required it. This extraordinary statement is attributed to Livy by Lytton Strachey, who thought it a perfectly sensible idea.[58]

56. *Poetics*, ed. Richard McKeon, *The Basic Works of Aristotle* (New York, 1941), chaps. 1, 4, 9.
57. J. B. Bury, *The Ancient Greek Historians* (New York, 1958), pp. 160–78. An exception is a great fifth-century historian, Thucydides, who specifically condemned the errors of poets "who exaggerate the importance of their themes," and wrote his speeches, especially, in a style which is a schoolboy's despair, a Greek style so crabbed and ugly that one wonders if he contrived it deliberately, to demonstrate that he wished to tell the unvarnished truth.
58. Lytton Strachey, *Spectatorial Essays* (London, 1964), p. 13.

The attribution is probably incorrect. Indeed, one wonders if Livy was made to say it for the turn of Lytton Strachey's sentence. But, there was, in truth, more than a little of this madness in Livy's method. A learned student of his works has compared him to Sir Walter Scott. "Like a novelist," writes R. M. Ogilvie, "he subordinated historical precision to the demands of character and plot. He indulged freely in invention and imagination in order to present a living picture. He would have disclaimed the title of a 'Historian' in a modern sense."[59]

Strachey's alleged quotation would be even more accurately descriptive of the Roman poet-historian Lucan than Livy. Lucan actually wrote a long epic poem, commonly called the *Pharsalia*. Though he did not reverse the outcome of the battle for poetic effect, he revised nearly everything else, in the interest of aesthetic perfection. For the sake of his meter he rearranged the geography of the Mediterranean, substituting *Emathios* for *Thessalios* in the first line, because *Thessalios* would not scan after the opening *Bella per*.[60] He removed the capital of Parthia from crude, clumsy-sounding Ctesiphon, to beautiful, euphonious Babylon.[61] Like many another Roman poet after Virgil, he made the battles of Pharsalia and Philippi take place on the same spot, though more than 150 miles lay in between. He changed the sequence of consuls when it suited his poetic purpose, promiscuously mixed real and fictitious persons, improved the inconvenient topography of Greece, reversed the Persian Gulf and the Red Sea, revised the career of Pompey, and brought Cicero to the battlefield for dramatic effect.[62]

Lucan is long gone and little mourned. But the aesthetic fallacy appears to be immortal. There are many examples in the modern world of both historians and novelists who have ignored Virginia Woolf's sound maxim that "truth of fact and truth of fiction are incompatible."[63] Two able and deservedly distinguished modern historians may serve as examples: first, A. L. Rowse, an English historian who rarely publishes a volume without a prefatory barrage of angry epithets, aimed at academic colleagues who fail in his judgment to fulfill the aesthetic potential of their discipline. Nobody can read, or rather study, a representative doctoral thesis without sympathizing in some degree. But Rowse seems to have a curious conception of his discipline. "History," he writes, "is a great deal closer to poetry than is generally realised; in truth, I think, it is in essence [that word!] the same."[64] Rowse's meaning, in context, is

59. *The Listener*, Nov. 3, 1960.
60. Robert Graves, ed., *Lucan, Pharsalia* (Baltimore, 1957), p. 17.
61. J. D. Duff, ed., *Lucan* (London, 1951), p. 3.
62. Duff, ed., *Lucan*, pp. 52–53, 268, 320, 328, 359, 369, 372, 412.
63. Virginia Woolf, *Collected Essays*, 4, 234.
64. A. L. Rowse, *The Use of History* (London, 1946), p. 55.

unclear. But I understand him to argue the ancient Aristotelian proposition that history is particularized poetry and to urge upon his colleagues the double standard of beauty and empirical truth—a double mode of selection, in which events are significant both for their functional relation to the historical problem, and for their aesthetic quality. But the two standards are incompatible, and some of Rowse's work falls between them. A reviewer of one of his books complains that "details are often murky and sometimes inaccurate; biased judgments and dubious points of history are frequently put forward as established fact."[65]

A second example is Bernard De Voto, an American novelist who became an American historian. But the conversion was incomplete. He called history a "spectacle"—something to be staged for the aesthetic gratification of the reader. And he undertook to write a book about American events in the year 1846, "because 1846 best dramatizes personal experience as national experience."[66] The book characteristically begins with a splendid story, which De Voto describes as "doubtless more beautiful than true." It concerns a group of American trappers in the spring of 1846, who, after a violent thunderstorm, saw the image of an eagle in the red western sky, superimposed upon the sun. This tale is followed by another baroque paragraph describing an omen which is equally spectacular in its literary effect: Biela's comet, in that *annus mirabilis,* split in two on its way toward perihelion, thus prefiguring the fate of the Republic.

Throughout the rest of the book, there is much more in the same spirit. The great Western eagle screams and flaps his wings, and lots of brave but wretched little Mexicans scurry to and fro across the countryside. History becomes alternately a tragic "drama" of heroes who are undone by their virtues, and a low "vaudeville show of swollen egotism, vanity, treachery, incompetence, rhetoric, stupidity and electioneering." De Voto clearly makes every effort to be accurate. But one cannot read his books without concluding that he is torn between two inconsistent objects—to tell what actually happened, and to tell a beautiful story. In pursuit of his two purposes, he operates at cross-purposes and diminishes the degree to which either is fulfilled.[67]

A third example is also an American historian, Samuel Eliot Morison, who believes deeply in "history as a literary art." In an essay pub-

65. Darrett B. Rutman, in *William and Mary Quarterly,* 3d ser. 18 (1961): 134–36; reviewing *The Elizabethans and America* (New York, 1959).
66. Catharine Drinker Bowen, et al., *Four Portraits and One Subject* (Boston, 1963), pp. 1–27.
67. Bernard De Voto, *The Year of Decision* (Boston, 1943), pp. 4–5, 234, 496–97 passim.

lished under that title,[68] he urges young historians not to "bore and confuse the reader with numerous 'buts,' 'excepts,' 'perhapses,' 'howevers,' and 'possiblies.' " Instead they are advised to tell beautiful stories for the aesthetic intoxication of their readers. But this, I would think, would be storytelling in more senses than one. A historian who omits all the ugly "buts," "excepts," "perhapses," etc., is falsifying the record. I do not mean to suggest that Morison is a deliberate falsifier—far from it. But his method has a falsifying effect. It is profoundly dysfunctional to serious historical study.

ટે≫ The *quantitative fallacy* is the latest form of insignificance, which consists in the idea that the facts which count best count most. It should not be confused with quantification proper—an important tool, long used by historians and presently in process of a revolutionary refinement.[69] To "quantify" is merely to count; "quantifiers" thus include schoolboys who are taught to tally the Five Points of Calvinism on their fingertips, as well as scholars who employ sophisticated techniques of regression analysis, and an IBM computer. Surely no reasonable man will deny that counting has always been useful to historical inquiry and that it will ever continue to be so; and that every historian should count everything he can, by the best available statistical method.

But the quantitative fallacy is something else: a criterion of significance which assumes that facts are important in proportion to their susceptibility to quantification. There is an epigram, perhaps apocryphal, attributed to Lord Kelvin, that everything which exists, exists in quantity. Enthusiastic quantifiers have amended Lord Kelvin's statement to read, "Unless a thing can be measured quantitatively, it does not exist significantly." Therein lies a fallacy.

There are many significant things in the world today that nobody knows how to measure. Someday, maybe, somebody will. But in the meantime one must acknowledge their existence. Many ideational and emotional problems, which lie at the heart of historical problems, cannot be understood in quantitative terms. To move to the periphery, because

68. Samuel Eliot Morison, "History as a Literary Art," *By Land and By Sea* (New York, 1953) pp. 289–298, 294.
69. For an early specimen of quantification, see A. Lawrence Lowell, "The Influence of Party Upon Legislation in America," American Historical Association, *Annual Report for 1901*, 319–542, a roll-call analysis of party regularity in the British Parliament, 1836–1899, and the U.S. Congress, 1844–1899. In professional discussions of quantification, as in public discussions of automation, there has been a good deal of nonsense about the newness of it all, and an appalling lack of historical perspective.

things can be measured there, is to behave like the man in Abraham Kaplan's parable.

"There is a story," Kaplan writes, "of a drunkard searching under a street lamp for his house key, which he had dropped some distance away. Asked why he didn't look where he had dropped it, he replied, 'It's lighter here!' "[70]

To make this argument is not to endorse the usual humanistic blather about quantification as the enemy of the human spirit. There are many critics of quantification in history who hold with Carlyle that "He who reads the inscrutable book of Nature as if it were a Merchants Ledger, is justly suspected of having never seen that Book, but only some school Synopsis thereof; from which, if taken for the real book, more error than insight is to be derived."[71] The argument here is a different one—that the Book of Nature, like a merchant's ledger, might be kept in double-entry style, one column listing phenomena which can be quantified and another listing things which can be qualitatively known. The latter is always longer than the former and can never be dismissed.

Criteria of significance should not be methodological, but substantive in nature. They should always be grounded in the nature of the problem itself and not in the tools of problem solving. The purpose of historical inquiry is not to vindicate a method but to discover what actually happened. Every efficient means to this end is legitimate, but none alone can be erected into a standard of legitimacy.

Behaviorists have reacted violently to this argument without meeting it.

> For some time [writes Warren E. Miller] it has been fashionable to argue against the behavioral mode of research by insisting that one must beware of becoming a prisoner of one's methods. The argument comes most often from the traditional scholar who notes correctly that behavioral science tends to ignore questions that accumulated wisdom has properly defined as important. The argument is seldom sensitive to the possibility that traditional workways often have taken a nettle for a rose and have ignored many other questions—or have answered them badly—because the methods were not equal to the task of mastering available information.[72]

But this is an *ignoratio,* compounded by an *ad hominem.* The complaint is not against the behavioral method of research, but rather against mak-

70. Abraham Kaplan, *The Conduct of Inquiry* (San Francisco, 1964), p. 11.
71. Thomas Carlyle, "On History," *Critical and Miscellaneous Essays*, 5 vols. (New York, 1899), 2:91.
72. Warren E. Miller, "Promises and Problems in the Use of Computers: The Case of Research in Political History," in E. Bowles, ed., *Computers in Humanistic Research* (Englewood Cliffs, N.J., 1967), p. 84.

ing that method into a standard of substantive significance. And Miller
cannot meet it by entering a complaint against somebody else's method.

In the past few years, historians who have issued manifestoes for
quantification have, by and large, been remarkably moderate in their
claims for that method. The restraint of W. O. Aydelotte, Samuel Hays,
and even Lee Benson, and the generally sympathetic, if not entirely
enthusiastic, response of their colleagues, is a hopeful sign that history may
avoid that unfortunate polarization into behavioralism and antibehavior-
alism, which largely explains the appalling poverty of political science as
a serious discipline during the past decade.

But scholars who have used quantification in historical research have
sometimes tended to be a little less cautious. One example is Jackson
Main's *The Social Structure of Revolutionary America* (Princeton,
1965), an important and useful inquiry into social class in America,
circa 1760–1790. Main's work has none of the most refined and esoteric
symbols which are the hallmark of a card-carrying quantifier. Nevertheless, his book is quantitative in its method and a specimen of the
quantitative fallacy. Main largely confined his attention to things he
could count—income and property, consumption patterns, occupations,
economic mobility. Even in a chapter on "contemporary views of class,"
he tended to count the number of classes which Americans recognized. In
consequence of his tacit assumption that things which count best count
most, his conclusions were both inaccurate and a little superficial. Main
believes, with many other scholars, that "the indigenous class structure"
of Revolutionary America "was based upon property rather than inherited
status."[73] That statement is surely true in *some* degree—but in what
degree? Property is something which can be counted with comparative
ease. Inherited status, however, involves such problems as deference,
which are much more difficult to manage in quantitative terms. Main's
quantitative bias, in his criteria of significance, tends to skew his conclusions toward a property-based class system and away from the component
of hereditary status. And in so far as he dealt with hereditary status, he
tended to do so in terms of material emblems which inaccurately represent the problem. Main would have had to shift to a qualitative strategy
to attain a more fair and accurate approximation of his subject.

The superficiality of Main's book is equally serious and also closely
related to his quantitative bias. A reviewer writes:

> That the book lacks a greater importance is in part the result of an exagger-
> ated insistence on quantification which weakens rather than strengthens
> one's confidence in the conclusions reached and limits the subtlety of
> both the questions asked and the answers given. On certain occasions,

73. P. 283.

when comprehensive figures are missing, individual cases that happen to permit quantification are selected and are used without apparent justification as models of the whole.[74]

The same reviewer also criticizes Main's questions for their simplicity, for their failure to incorporate recent and sophisticated work in social stratification, and for their operational inflexibility. These deficiencies, I think, generally attach to merely quantitative questions and can only be corrected by other techniques, which impose methodological deficiencies of their own which quantification in turn helps to diminish. The only sensible strategy is a methodological pluralism, which is necessary to any complex and important project.

A second example of the quantitative fallacy is Richard L. Merritt's *Symbols of American Community* (New Haven, 1966). The author's object is to measure the growth of community awareness in the American colonies by "content analysis" of seven colonial newspapers in the period 1735–1775. Specifically he counted the number of times words like "America" and other American symbols appeared, as against the number of times that "His Majesty's Colonists," "British colonists," or other British symbols appeared, in articles with British and American datelines. He reached many conclusions: that the growth of community awareness was a slow process; that British writers tended to speak of America before Americans did; that the development of a sense of community preceded a demand for communitarian integration of institutions; that individual colony patterns were different in several specific ways but tended to become more congruent as time passed; that colonial wars tended to retard the growth of American community awareness, which was cyclical in nature, like "a typical learning curve" (p. 184).

But all of this is deduced merely from the quantity of British and American symbols found in the newspapers. He does not sufficiently deal with important qualitative aspects of his problem, such as the contexts in which the symbols appeared, or even with the question of whether the references to Britain or America were favorable or unfavorable in their connotation. The problem is exceedingly complex—much too complex, in the present condition of our knowledge, to be resolved in terms of quantity. A simple "favorable-unfavorable" index would not have sufficed. Someday, historians may work out ways of using a many-valued symbolic logic in the quantification of such problems. But at the moment, answers must be sought in qualitative terms.

By Merritt's strictly quantitative standard of significance, an entirely false conclusion can obtain. As the author himself suggests, Adolf Hitler

74. Bernard Bailyn, *American Historical Review* 71 (1966): 1432.

would appear to have had a sense of community with the Jews, according to a content analysis of Jewish symbols in his speeches and writings. And the John Birch Society would appear to have a fraternal bond with the Communist party.

ૐ The *antinomian fallacy,* on the other hand, is the erroneous idea that facts which count best, count least. Two old-fashioned American historians have publicly committed themselves to this absurdity, which is more generally assumed than asserted. One of them was Carl Bridenbaugh, who delivered before the American Historical Association a presidential address that was in the nature of a jeremiad. The professor, like the prophet, pronounced a fearful judgment upon all the cities of Judah. Among the sins which he singled out for special condemnation was quantification.

Bridenbaugh allowed some latitude to counting, but not enough. "The finest historians," he wrote, "will not be those who succumb to the dehumanizing methods of social science, whatever their uses and values, which I hasten to acknowledge. Nor will the historian worship at the shrine of the Bitch-Goddess QUANTIFICATION. History offers radically different values and methods."[75] Something of the same spirit appears in a statement by Arthur Schlesinger, Jr.: "As a humanist, I am bound to reply that almost all important questions are important precisely because they are not susceptible to quantitative answers."[76]

An intense hostility to quantification also appears among radical historians, who have painfully discovered that counting does not easily coexist with their ideological preconceptions. An English historian, E. P. Thompson, bitterly attacks "the orthodoxy of the empirical economic historians, in which working people are seen as a labor force, as migrants, or as the data for statistical series." His quarrel with quantification consists in his belief that it tends "to obscure the agency of the working people, the degree to which they contributed, by conscious efforts, to the making of history."[77]

A more moderate manifestation of the same phenomenon is Barrington Moore's *Social Origins of Dictatorship and Democracy* (Boston, 1966), which invokes essentialism against statistics. "Statistics," he

75. Carl Bridenbaugh, "The Great Mutation," *The American Historical Review* 68 (1963): 326.
76. Arthur Schlesinger, Jr., "The Humanist Looks at Empirical Social Research," *American Sociological Review* 27 (1962): 770.
77. E. P. Thompson, *The Making of the English Working Class* (New York, 1966), pp. 12, 196–223.

writes, "are misleading traps for the unwary reader when they abstract from the essence of the situation the whole structural context in which social osmosis takes place. As statistics are fashionable now, it is worthwhile stressing this point."[78] Moore is careful to qualify his objections. "I still have no patience with the machine breaking mentality that rejects figures out of hand," he writes. "To name this deformation of humanist mentality after the Luddites is actually unfair to them; they were rather more intelligent."[79] But this statement is made in an appendix called "A Note on Statistics and Conservative Historiography," which is an obscurantist critique of three important quantitative studies that reach conclusions contradicting Moore's ideological assumptions. Mr. Moore comes close to arguing that statistics which sustain his interpretation of modernization are valid; but statistics which contradict it are false.[80]

But it is among conservative scholars that the antinomian fallacy is most often apparent, and that an attendant metaphysical bias is most clearly visible. Historical antinomianism commonly begins with the assumption that regularities do not exist in history, or that they do not exist significantly. It holds that every historical event is unique. This idea, of course, is self-contradictory. If all historical events were unique, then they would be alike in their uniqueness, and therefore in that respect they would not be unique. Moreover, they would be alike in their eventfulness and in their historicity, and therefore not unique in three important ways. If every historical happening were *sui generis,* no language could be found to communicate its nature. The past would become a "wilderness of single instances," in Tennyson's phrase. To argue that every event is unique in its sum and essence is to commit the fallacy of holism, and the fallacy of essences, which have already been discussed.

"Historical understanding," writes Raymond Aron, "consists of perceiving differences among similar phenomena *and* similarities among different ones."[81] The two ideas of similarity and difference must coexist, if they are to exist at all. Each is meaningless without the other. An historical interpretation which is cast merely in terms of one, without the other, is not false but absurd.

78. P. 37.
79. P. 510.
80. Pp. 508–23. The three works which he attacks are D. Brunton and D. H. Pennington, *Members of the Long Parliament* (London, 1954); G. E. Mingay, "The Size of Farms in the Eighteenth Century," *Economic History Review,* 2d ser. 17 (1964): 381–88; and Donald Greer, *The Incidence of Terror during the French Revolution* (Cambridge, Mass., 1935).
81. Raymond Aron, "Evidence and Inference in History," in Daniel Lerner, ed., *Evidence and Inference* (Glencoe, Ill., 1959), p. 27.

Nevertheless, many able historians obsessively persist in the pursuit of uniqueness. A prime example is an American historian, Daniel Boorstin, who bitterly complains that "the rising social sciences have deprived the historian of his traditional vocation as the high priest of uniqueness." He continues:

> If the historian has any function in the present welter of the social scientific world, it is to note the rich particularity of experience, to search for the piquant aroma of life. As contrasted with the abstract, antiseptic dullness of numbers, "cases," and prototypes [sic]. The historian as humanist is a votary of the unrepeatability of all experience, as well as of the universal significance of each human life. Of course the unique cannot be seen as unique except by reference to a universal (and the word "unique" itself is such a one), yet there are important practical differences of emphasis. Today the historian is qualified for a kind of emphasis on individuality which is too rare in our world. Social scientists are preoccupied with what are called the "modal" approach; they are dominated by the statistical notion of "the category, value, or interval of the variable having the greatest frequency." They focus upon such concepts as "status," "personality types," and "occupational mobility" which transcend time and place. And historians who boast of having become interdisciplinary are often only confessing that they no longer burn any tapers before the altar of human uniqueness.[82]

This extraordinary statement is no casual outburst but an extended commitment, upon which Boorstin is building a major interpretation of American history in three volumes—a brilliantly suggestive work in many of its remarkable insights, but at the same time a fallacious attempt to characterize American culture in terms of qualities which are unique to it. The result is a history of American religion in which Jonathan Edwards is an unperson; a history of American politics in which political parties scarcely exist, and in which Hamilton and Jefferson do not have a serious difference of opinion; a history of American culture in which Herman Melville appears mainly as an unsuccessful lecturer; a history of American regionalism in which the plantation states are exiled to a distant island of metaphysical alienation, somewhere far below the southern horizon.[83]

Boorstin suggests that a demarcation line might be drawn between two academic disciplines, with historians responsible for uniqueness and sociologists, I suppose, responsible for universality. But this surely will not do. The deficiencies of Boorstin's historical works demonstrate

---

82. Daniel Boorstin, *America and the Image of Europe* (New York, 1960), p. 66.
83. Two volumes of Boorstin's trilogy have appeared: *The Americans: The Colonial Experience* (New York, 1958); and *The Americans: The National Experience* (New York, 1965). The best review which I have seen is Kenneth Lynn's, in *Kenyon Review* 28 (1966): 116–22.

that the unique and the universal must be combined in each inquiry. An English historian takes a more tenable position.

No historian really treats all facts as unique; he treats them as particular. He cannot—no one can—deal in unique fact, because facts and events require reference to common experience, to conventional frameworks, to (in short) the general before they acquire meaning. The unique event is a freak and a frustration; if it is really unique—can never recur in meaning or implication—it lacks every measurable dimension and cannot be assessed. But to the historian, facts and events (and people) must be individual and particular: *like* other entities of a similar kind, but never entirely identical with them. That is to say, they are to be treated as peculiar to themselves and not as indistinguishable statistical units or elements in an equation; but they are linked and rendered comprehensible by kinship, by common possessions, by universal qualities present in differing proportions and arrangements.[84]

8∾ The *fortuitous fallacy* is committed by any scholar who abdicates his arduous responsibility of rational selection and allows the task to be performed for him by time and accident. There is madness in this method, for it would reduce scholarship to mere sciolism—a smattering of superficial nuggets of knowledge without point or plan or purpose.

Nevertheless, at least one great popular historian has erected this method sans method into an avowed standard of selection. He was Giles Lytton Strachey (1880–1932), English author of *Eminent Victorians* (1918), *Queen Victoria* (1921), *Elizabeth and Essex* (1928), and many other volumes which may have reached a larger public than the work of any other historian in his generation, except Winston Churchill.

Lytton Strachey began his best-remembered work, *Eminent Victorians,* with the following assertion: "The history of the Victorian Age will never be written: we know too much about it. For ignorance is the first requisite of the historian—ignorance, which simplifies and clarifies, which selects and omits, with a placid perfection unattainable by the highest art."[85]

But the inconvenient presence of excess knowledge did not dismay Strachey. On the apparent assumption that if ignorance does not exist it can always be invented, he explored Victorian England as a small boy plays blindman's buff, covering his eyes and groping over strange dark objects, and suddenly seizing upon familiar ones.

The careless impressionism of Strachey's method is best communi-

---

84. G. R. Elton, *The Practice of History* (New York, 1967), p. 11.
85. Giles Lytton Strachey, *Eminent Victorians* (New York, 1918), Preface.

cated by his own imagery. "It is not by the direct method of a scrupulous narration that the explorer of the past can hope to depict that singular epoch," he wrote. "If he is wise, he will adopt a subtler strategy. He will fall upon the flank, or the rear, he will shoot a sudden revealing searchlight into obscure recesses, hitherto undivined." The metaphor seems more than a little indelicate when we remember that it was Florence Nightingale's flank which Strachey fell upon, with such unseemly, and uncharacteristic, enthusiasm.[86]

But in all seriousness, such a method is exceedingly ineffectual for all but the most paltry of popularizing purposes. The reader is diverted by it, but so is the historian, from his difficult obligation to select factual statements according to explicit criteria of significance and to tell truths which are as clear and comprehensive as mortal intelligence will allow. Any fool can write a readable history, if Strachey's method is all that is required. Any literary hack can popularize a complicated problem by this technique, but the nature of that problem cannot be communicated accurately by it. Such a method guarantees falsehood and gross distortion; moreover, it prevents the author from knowing how false and distorted his interpretation actually is.

Lytton Strachey was neither a fool nor a hack. He possessed a rare and truly remarkable creative gift, and a splendid talent for exposition. His characters seem so real that the reader thinks they *must* be true. But they are merely fantastic inventions.

Strachey's intuitions and expository gifts were perfectly compatible with a better method of research, which would not have required more labor than he actually performed. By all accounts, he worked long and hard in both research and writing. But an improved method would have taken a toll of Strachey's intentions in one important way. It would have confined him within limits with which he was apt to be more than a little impatient—the limits of truth. It would have told him when he was falsifying, and that was something which Strachey did not wish to hear.[87]

Strachey's work had a very great impact, not merely upon the reading public, but upon the writing of biography as well.

> As for Strachey [writes Louis Kronenberger] he was not just a brilliant biographer, he was a revolutionizing one. An *Eminent Victorians* had, indeed, a greater immediate effect than a *Ulysses* or a *Wasteland*, for at one stroke it antiquated a method and enthroned a manner. When *Eminent Victorians* appeared, biography while displaying an anarchy of form, was all too lacking in freedom of speech. Strachey gave it the polish of style,

---

86. Ibid.
87. For a different interpretation, cf. Michael Holroyd, *Lytton Strachey, A Critical Biography*, 2 vols. (New York, 1968), 2:261–305.

the sting of plain speaking, the tensions of fiction, and brought along with his new kind of technique, a new kind of target.[88]

If this statement is more than a little exaggerated, it nevertheless contains a good deal of truth. After *Eminent Victorians* there would be many another biography conceived by the same method, with similar results. No academic historian has, to the best of my knowledge, openly and explicitly committed the fortuitous fallacy in print, with the literary bravado of Lytton Strachey. But there is much of it in the careless, casual impressionism which still infests much, if not most, historical writing. Many scholars persist in conducting their research according to the Strachian spirit, idly falling upon one fascinating fact after another, without method or control.

&➤ This chapter could be extended indefinitely, for there is no fixed limit to the number of inconsistent standards of significance which historians might adopt. But the nature of history, historiography, and historians is practically such that a few finite forms of error are predominant. The aesthetic fallacy, the pragmatic fallacy, and the moralistic fallacy have been deeply rooted in historical writing for 3,000 years. Even the quantitative fallacy might be traced back to Plato's assertion that God always geometrizes, or to the Pythagorean idea that all things are numbers. Other fallacies are probably transitory, for there are fashions in error as well as truth. The antinomian fallacy is, I hope, ephemeral. But other forms of error, equally egregious, will probably take its place.

Nevertheless, there are a few constant and comprehensive rules of thumb for the determination of sound criteria of factual significance. First, these criteria must be substantive rather than methodological in nature. They must be formed from the nature of the subject itself and from the purpose for which it is studied, rather than from procedures and techniques. Second, they must be empirical, unlike the pragmatic and moralistic and aesthetic fallacies. Third, they must be capable of fulfillment, unlike the holist and essential fallacies. Fourth, they must be made explicitly, for the only alternative to overt criteria of significance are covert commitments, which are not merely inappropriate but actually falsifying in their function.

Finally, criteria of significance must not violate what philosophers call the principle of nonvacuous contrast. There are some words in the world which are merely meaningless if they are made to stand alone. It makes no sense to say that all things in the world are short. "Short" is

88. *The Atlantic*, May, 1968, pp. 85–88.

meaningless unless some things are tall. This reasoning, I think, can be applied as an operational test to many criteria of significance which historians actually make. It rules out such criteria as uniqueness, and many others which historians have been industriously applying. Any attempt to identify all the vacuous contrasts which historians have made would yield a list which is very long and yet very incomplete. In place of this strategy, it may be sufficient merely to point out the principle itself.

If false criteria of significance are such as appear in this chapter, and such as violate these rules, what then might true ones be? The answer, I think, is that a true standard of factual significance is one which is generated by a sound model of historical explanation.

Historians who seek to frame factual questions and to verify factual answers almost always do so in order to elicit a historical explanation of some sort. They rarely do so for the sake of the facts themselves. A historical explanation is an attempt to relate some historical phenomenon in a functional way to other historical phenomena. Nothing is literally self-explanatory. An explanation, properly executed, relates the unknown to the known in a series of orderly inferences. It always explains sentences —complete sentences. Nobody can hope to have an explanation merely of "Jeffersonian Democracy," but only of something about Jeffersonian democracy, something which can be cast in a rounded sentence with a subject and a predicate.

A fact becomes significant in proportion to its relevance to an explanation model. Historians actually seek to explain things by means of many different, but sometimes overlapping, explanation models. They use generalization models, narration models, causation models, motivation models, composition models, analogy models, and undoubtedly many others. The nature of these models is very complex. A separate chapter is therefore assigned to each of them in the following pages.

There is another set of sound standards of factual criteria of significance which is not precisely explanatory, but expository and evocative. A significant fact for most historians is one which helps them to make a case for their explanation and to communicate its nature to the reader. The latter partakes of the irrational process which the Germans call *Verstand*—a word for which no English equivalent exists. There cannot be a logic of *verständliche* criteria of significance. But there is a tacit logic of rational explanation. The next six chapters attempt to specify it.

PART II
EXPLANATION

CHAPTER IV

FALLACIES OF GENERALIZATION

ટ~

What distinguishes the historian from the collector of historical facts is generalization.

—E. H. Carr

Pour faire de l'histoire, il faut savoir compter. [To do history, one must know how to count.]

—Georges Lefebvre

Scholars still solemnly engage in controversies over questions such as "Should a historian generalize?" One might as well ask "Should a historian use words?" Generalizations are embedded in his language, in his thought, and in his explanation models. There are, of course, other modes of explanation. But none is more common, or more commonly abused, than generalization.

The term "generalization," in ordinary usage, means everything and nothing. In a recent discussion of the problem, an attentive critic found nine distinguishable conceptions of generalization:

1. "Labeling," or "classificatory," concepts; e.g., "feudalism."

2. Universal "laws" or regularity statements; e.g., "Ideas follow trade routes."

3. "Limited," or summative, general statements, specifying the conditions that obtained in a particular geographical area or during a determinate period of time; e.g., "Successful revolution occurred [in the eighteenth century] only where the agricultural population generally collaborated with middle-class leaders."

4. Statements asserting the existence of a trend or tendency; e.g., "The Speaker was a power in the House, but as the Elizabethan period went on, his power was on the wane."

5. Statistical regularities.

6. General characterizations of some particular historical figure with regard to his motivation, activities, etc.

7. Particular explanations or interpretations of events.

8. Evaluative assessments.

9. Procedural rules for the selection of historical material and data, the authentication of evidence, etc.[1]

In this chapter, generalization will refer to statements of statistical regularity, a category which cuts across all others on the list. A statistical generalization is a descriptive statement which is inferred from particular facts by a special process of reasoning. It is often built into a complex explanation model with other components and is sometimes employed as an explanation in its own right. To explain is, in common usage, merely to make plain, clear, and understandable. This is precisely what a statistical generalization does. It explains what, how, when, where, and who. It does not explain why, but often we don't need or wish to know why.

Historical science presently hovers naked and trembling on the edge of quantification, with Clio in the huddled, hesitant posture of September Morn. But it is already irretrievably committed to the logic of statistical reasoning, in many quasi-quantitative ways. Statistical generalizations are implicit not merely in impressionistic adjectives like "some" and "most" and "many," but also in nouns like "majority" and "democracy" and verbs like "expand" and "grow." A single term can serve to summarize an implicit statistical statement; a single impressionistic sentence can contain an appalling number of implicit statistical series.

It is still uncommon for a historian to make explicit and formal use of statistical reasoning. Consequently, the statistical fallacies which historians commonly commit are, at present, of an elementary and transitional nature. They often consist in a confusion of quantitative and impressionistic procedures. As practices change, historians will probably learn to make more sophisticated blunders. But in the meantime, our business is with crude low-order mistakes of the sort which commonly occur in everyday thought. All of them are procedural errors, by which false inferences are derived from true particulars.

ह**ම** *Fallacies of statistical sampling* occur in generalizations which rest upon an insufficient body of data—upon a "sample" which

1. Patrick Gardiner, reviewing Louis Gottschalk, ed., *Generalization in the Writing of History and Theory* 3 (1965): 351.

misrepresents the composition of the object in question. Sound methods of sampling have been satisfactorily discussed at length by statisticians with a degree of clarity and accuracy which no historian can hope to attain.[2] But when it comes to unsound sampling, historians qualify as experts, by reason of their long experience in the ways of error. Rarely have so many generalized so much from so little as have impressionistic historians in the past generation.

One example is an assertion, sometimes made by historians of the framing of the United States Constitution, that there was a significant age difference between Federalists and Antifederalists. A recent statement of this thesis is by Stanley Elkins and Eric McKitrick, in *The Founding Fathers: Young Men of the Revolution* (Washington, 1962). Elkins and McKitrick attempted to develop a generational interpretation of the fight over the Constitution as an alternative to Charles Beard's battered economic thesis. These two historiographical knights errant boldly attacked the problem, as Beard himself said of another scholar, sans fear and sans research. Their argument rests upon a so-called sample of nine Federalists and nine Antifederalists:

Federalists	*Antifederalists*
Robert Morris, b. 1734	Samuel Adams, b. 1722
John Jay, b. 1745	Patrick Henry, b. 1736
James Wilson, b. 1742	R. H. Lee, b. 1732
Alexander Hamilton, b. 1755?	George Clinton, b. 1739
Henry Knox, b. 1750	James Warren, b. 1726
James Duane, b. 1733	Samuel Bryan, b. 1750?
George Washington, b. 1732	George Bryan, b. 1731
James Madison, b. 1751	George Mason, b. 1725
Gouverneur Morris, b. 1752	Elbridge Gerry, b. 1744

The authors conclude that "the age difference between these two groups is especially striking. The Federalists were on the average ten to twelve years younger than the Anti-Federalists." The arithmetic is slovenly—the average (mean) difference is in fact 9.8 years. But more serious is the validity of the sample, which is absurdly small and extremely biased.

It is easy to invent a different list of equal length which would support an opposite conclusion.

2. For a good introduction see W. Allen Wallis and Harry V. Roberts, *Statistics, A New Approach* (New York, 1956), chap. 11, passim.

Federalists	*Antifederalists*
Robert Morris, b. 1734	Patrick Henry, b. 1736
James Duane, b. 1733	George Clinton, b. 1739
George Washington, b. 1732	Elbridge Gerry, b. 1744
Benjamin Franklin, b. 1706	John Francis Mercer, b. 1759
James Madison, b. 1751	John Lansing, Jr., b. 1754
Nathaniel Gorham, b. 1738	Benjamin Austin, b. 1752
John Rutledge, b. 1739	Luther Martin, b. 1748?
Roger Sherman, b. 1721	Samuel Bryan, b. 1750?
W. S. Johnson, b. 1727	Melancton Smith, b. 1744

These Antifederalists are, on the average, 13.9 years *younger* than the Federalists. Adding the Elkins-McKitrick arithmetical inflation quotient, we conclude, "The age difference between these groups is especially striking. The Federalists were, on the average, 14 to 16 years older than the Antifederalists."

A more comprehensive study, by Jackson T. Main, suggests that both lists are invalid. Working from a much larger sample, he found no significant age difference between friends and foes of the Constitution. "In Pennsylvania the Antifederalists were older by two years," he writes, "but in New York there was no difference at all; in South Carolina the median age of eleven Antifederalists was 33; of thirty-two Federalists, only 29; in Massachusetts, the average Antifederalist was 52, the Federalist 51. All told, the Federalists were about two years younger than their antagonists. It is hard to see how this could have made any difference."[3] Other generational interpretations of the same problem might be entertained. It is conceivable that extremists in both camps were younger than moderates; and Westerners were younger than Easterners. But the generational lines appear to have crossed party lines at right angles, *if* Main's work is correct. (Maybe it isn't.)

The probability of a sampling error tends to diminish as the size of the sample increases. But size alone is no protection. The classic example was a massive effort by the *Literary Digest* to forecast the presidential election of 1936. More than 10,000,000 ballots were sent out. Something like 2,367,523 came back, mostly marked for Alf Landon. The poll predicted 370 electoral votes for the Republican candidate, and 161 for Roosevelt. In the real election, Roosevelt won 523 votes, Landon 8. What went wrong? The *Digest,* it seems, sent

3. Jackson T. Main, *The Antifederalists: Critics of the Constitution* (Chapel Hill, 1961), p. 259. Main's conclusions may in turn be corrected by other inquiries, now in progress.

ballots to addresses collected from the subscription lists of magazines and also from telephone directories and automobile registration lists. But magazines, telephones, and automobiles were not randomly distributed among the American population in 1936, as many will ruefully recall.

This famous statistical disaster was not the only sampling error which was made during the presidential campaign of 1936. In October of that year, a Republican leader in Chicago discovered that demands for Alf Landon buttons greatly exceeded those for the Democratic emblems. On this basis, he wrote to Landon's headquarters, confidently predicting that the Kansas governor would carry the city. But a demand for Landon buttons was not equivalent to a demand for Landon. The Republicans had distributed a gorgeous badge for their candidate—a brown tin disk set against a yellow felt background, in the image of a Kansas sunflower. For the possession of this splendid trinket, many a red-blooded American boy in 1936 might cheerfully have sold his mother into slavery. According to one learned scholar, the exchange rate among small boys in Chicago was two or three plain, ordinary Roosevelt buttons to one of Landon's.[4] Most Americans sensibly chose the best from both parties—the Republican campaign badge and the Democratic candidate.

There are many other examples of sampling errors in historical scholarship, some of which are explicitly statistical and others implicitly so. One scholar, Edward Pessen, examined election returns in Boston during the Jacksonian era. He concluded that workingmen more generally voted Whig than Democratic and that they either rejected or ignored so-called workingmen's candidates. But another scholar sharply criticized Pessen for failing to "use some tool of analysis that will neutralize the effect of the general level of voting in the area and allow us to see to what degree voting Whig or Democratic is related to the socio-economic nature of the wards." Working from the same sources by a different and more defensible method, the critic concluded that "Jackson and his political allies did get their support from working class groups," and that there was a good inverse correlation between votes for Democratic and workingmen's candidates and an economic index.[5]

.   Another case of an explicitly statistical sampling error appears in Robert E. Brown's attempt to show that something which he calls a

---

4. Donald R. McCoy, *Landon of Kansas* (Lincoln, 1966), p. ix.
5. Edward Pessen, "Did Labor Support Jackson?: The Boston Story," *Political Science Quarterly* 64 (1949): 262–74; Robert T. Bower, "A Note on 'Did Labor Support Jackson?: The Boston Story,'" ibid., 65 (1950): 441–42.

"middle class democracy" existed in pre-Revolutionary Massachusetts and that property was widely and equitably distributed, and the franchise as well. But Brown's thesis is much exaggerated in both respects, and the exaggeration is partly sustained by serious errors in the sampling of probate records, tax lists, and voter lists.[6]

Other sampling errors are implicitly, rather than explicitly, statistical. They occur in simple impressionistic statements, such as the following observation by the late V. O. Key on the alleged suicidal tendencies of Southern literati: "A depressingly high rate of self-destruction prevails among those who ponder about the South and put down their reflections in books," he wrote. "A fatal frustration seems to come from the struggle to find a way through the unfathomable maze formed by tradition, caste, race and poverty."[7]

A friend of Key's asked how many suicidal Southern writers he could name. There were only three—W. J. Cash, Clarence Cason, and another whose name Key couldn't recall.[8] Some Southern historians may consider W. J. Cash to be a host within himself, but not for the purposes of quantification.

Impressionistic sampling errors are sometimes so gross than nobody is taken in by them—probably not even the author. A Russian historian, B. I. Bukharov, has used opinions expressed in the *Daily Worker* as representative of American opinion generally.[9] But other errors can be very subtle and insidious. The difficulties entailed in statistical sampling have sometimes tended to make statistics generally suspect in the eyes of some historians, more than a few of whom are prepared to accept Disraeli's famous statement that there are lies, damned lies, and statistics. But statistics themselves do not lie—only statisticians, and if they lie, they are apt to lie to themselves, in Dostoevski's phrase. And their confusions are clarity itself compared to the impressionistic muddles which so many historians get themselves into by an even more dangerous method.

With skill, practice, and a little luck (impressionists need a lot of luck), statistical sampling can be very reliable indeed. Anglo-American intelligence officers in World War II used a sampling method to estimate German production figures from serial numbers on cap-

6. Robert E. Brown, *Middle-Class Democracy and the Revolution in Massachusetts, 1691–1780* (Ithaca, 1955); John Cary, "Statistical Method and the Brown Thesis on Colonial Democracy," *William and Mary Quarterly*, 3d ser. 20 (1963): 251–64, with a rebuttal by Brown, 265–76.
7. V. O. Key, *Southern Politics in State and Nation* (New York, 1947), p. 664.
8. Joseph L. Morrison, *W. J. Cash: Southern Prophet* (New York, 1967), p. 140.
9. See Ernest May's review in *American Historical Review* 67 (1961): 87.

tured equipment. Their estimates are alleged to have been more accurate than those of the German government itself, and more quickly available than inventory estimates. Many historians, still wedded to the whole truth, will find themselves at a disadvantage comparable to that of the Germans. To repudiate samples and to count everything is an arduous undertaking which is not only unnecessary in many cases but undesirable as well. The incompleteness of historical evidence is itself an argument for scientific sampling, rather than an argument against it.

→ The *fallacy of the lonely fact* is the logical extension of a small sample, which deserves to receive special condemnation. It may be defined as a statistical generalization from a single case. There is a story, perhaps apocryphal, of a scientist who published an astonishing and improbable generalization about the behavior of rats. An incredulous colleague came to his laboratory and politely asked to see the records of the experiments on which the generalization was based. "Here they are," said the scientist, dragging a notebook from a pile of papers on his desk. And pointing to a cage in the corner, he added, "there's the rat."

There are many astonishing and improbable generalizations in historical scholarship in which the critical reader will smell a singular rat. As long as the majority of historians continue to conduct their "research" impressionistically and to cast their findings in a simple narrative, the fallacy of the lonely fact is likely to flourish. A special stylistic device has developed around it. Whenever the reader sees a mighty generalization, followed by a minute example, and the telltale phrase "for instance," or "for example," he should be on his guard against this error.

But often the fallacy of the lonely fact occurs without warning. The only defense is research in depth, of the sort which readers are rarely equipped to carry out. In the past half century, many (perhaps most) interpretations of the thought and conduct of the members of the Federalist party have derived primarily from the case of a single eccentric West Indian—Alexander Hamilton. In the past twenty years, a bold revisionary trend has set in. Textbook writers and political scientists now generalize upon the Federalists from *two* cases, an eccentric West Indian and an eccentric New Englander—Hamilton and John Adams. Similarly, many broad generalizations about the Jeffersonian party are precariously based upon the behavior of Thomas

Jefferson himself. But as we learn more about the politics of the early republic, Jefferson is beginning to appear as a very special sort of Jeffersonian. These three statesmen—Hamilton, Adams, and Jefferson—were exceptional men in more senses than one. Each of them, in his own way, was *sui generis*. This is not to argue that they had nothing in common with their political colleagues. But common qualities can never be located by investigation of themselves alone.

The most successful recent survey of American political history, Richard Hofstadter's *The American Political Tradition and the Men Who Made It* (New York, 1948), contains many examples of this fallacy. The book is a sequence of single facts, punctuated by sweeping generalizations. Jefferson, Jackson, Calhoun, Lincoln, Wendell Phillips, Bryan, Wilson, Hoover, and the two Roosevelts are each individually sketched as representative of "main currents of American political sentiment."[10] In only two chapters out of twelve is a different strategy developed. Hofstadter's book surely deserves its splendid reputation— what it lacks in the breadth of its empirical base, it more than matches in the depth of its remarkable intuitions. But had the author's intuitive excellence been wedded to the discipline of a better method, a very great book indeed would undoubtedly have been the result.

Other specimens of this fallacy have occurred in the field of pre-history, where archaeologists and historians have generalized broadly from a single find. Some of them concluded from a skeleton found at La Chapelle-aux-Saints that Neanderthal man had the posture of a pretzel and the locomotion of a crab—that "the head was so balanced on the spine that it hung forward; the structure of legs and feet permitted only a shuffling gait." But re-examination of the same evidence has suggested that the individual in question had a bad case of arthritis, and that normal Neanderthal men stood straight and strode confidently in pursuit of their prey.[11] It is as if an archaeologist, a millennium hence, were to generalize upon the stature of twentieth-century *Homo americanus* from the Brobdingnagian bones of Wilt-the-Stilt Chamberlain.

     ⇝ The *fallacy of statistical special pleading* occurs whenever an investigator applies a double standard of inference or interpretation to his evidence—one standard to evidence which sustains his generalization and another to evidence which contradicts it.

Imagine a scholar who hypothesizes that Republican ladies tend to have blond hair, while Democratic females are brunette. He carefully

10. P. x.
11. Gordon Childe, *What Happened in History*, new ed. (Baltimore, 1964), p. 40.

conducts his research at two national conventions, and when he tabulates his results, he discovers to his horror that they are:

	Blondes	Brunettes	Other
Republican ladies	20	40	10
Democratic ladies	20	40	10

But our scholar is not so easily discouraged. He proceeds to the second stage of his inquiry, which is called "interpretation" of the evidence. First, he re-examines his twenty blond Democrats, discovers that ten of them dyed their hair, and shifts them to the brunette column. Second, he studies the forty brunette Republicans, discovers that twenty-five of them had been blond in childhood, and shifts them to the blond column. Third, he takes a look at the miscellaneous column, which in each party includes five ladies with red, white, gray, etc., hair, and five ladies with dark-blond or light-brown hair. The latter, if Republican, he classifies as dark blond; but if Democrat, light brunette. He adds the dark blondes to the blond column, and the light brunettes to the brunette column. The results read:

	Blondes	Brunettes	Other
Republicans	50	15	5
Democrats	10	55	5

He works out his coefficients of correlation and triumphantly publishes the results in *The American Behavioral Scientist*. None of these manipulations necessarily involves an outright fraud. It is possible that our scholar did not deliberately fudge any of his figures. He may have been utterly unaware of his own errors.

There are many examples of this fallacy in actual historical practice. One of them is David Donald's *The Politics of Reconstruction* (Baton Rouge, 1965). Donald tried to explain why Republican congressmen in the Thirty-ninth Congress (1866–1867) voted as "radicals" or "moderates" on legislation before them. He hypothesized that the difference between them lay not in "personality, ideology, geographical origins, or social and economic status" but rather in their political situation—specifically, that Republicans who held safe seats—with wide electoral margins—tended to be radical, while Republicans who were elected by narrow and precarious pluralities tended to be moderate. Unfortunately for Donald's hypothesis, the result of his research showed that margins of electoral victory for both radicals and moderates were almost identical—59.3 percent to 59.2. But Donald proceeded to "interpret" his evidence until it conformed to his hypothesis. He argued that in some states, where there was an allegedly powerful Republican organization, a majority of 52 percent was security itself for a radical, but that in another state, a majority of 58 percent was too small to serve the same purpose. One qualification was heaped upon another with an industry and an ingenuity which were worthy of a better cause.

> To maintain his propositions [one reviewer wrote] Donald is forced to resort to a "cake and eat" approach. A Radical's election by a large vote is prima facie evidence of a safe seat. But when Moderates take office with large margins Donald introduces the realm of psychology, that is, his guess as to how secure the congressman felt. . . . There is no shortage of ingenious explanations here, but there seems to be little sense in accumulating data only to shuffle and disregard it.[12]

A second and more impressionistic example is a recent work by Alan Heimert. In *Religion and the American Mind from the Great Awakening to the Revolution* (Cambridge, 1966), he argued the thesis that there was a correlation between the religious divisions between Old Light opponents of the Awakening and New Light friends of it, on the one hand, and the political cleavage between friends and enemies of the Revolution. This interpretation is supported not with quantitative evidence but with qualitative interpretations of thought and expression. But Heimert applies a double standard of inference and interpretation to his evidence. He is often forced to argue that his historical subjects really meant the opposite of what they said.

One critic has complained,

> For Professor Heimert things are seldom what they seem, but if we know which side of the cleavage a man stands on, we need have no difficulty in penetrating the disguises of reality. . . . The world he offers us has been constructed by reading beyond the lines of what men said; and what he finds beyond the lines is so far beyond, so wrenched from the context, and so at odds with empirical evidence, that his world, to this reviewer at least, partakes more of fantasy than of history.[13]

Maybe this judgment is a little on the harsh side, but I think it is roughly correct. Heimert has so seriously overstrained his interpretation by an unfortunate—and certainly unintentional—double distortion of his evidence that it is quite impossible to know how much credence to put into his thesis until another scholar undertakes a more careful analysis of the same problem by means of a better method. Nothing

12. David Rothman in *Political Science Quarterly* 81 (1968): 334–36.
13. Edmund S. Morgan, in *William and Mary Quarterly*, 3d ser. 24 (1967): 454–59.

is more pathetic than so many years of labor utterly wasted and undone by a procedural fallacy of this sort.

It would, of course, be a great mistake to assume that statistical special pleading is a sign of fraud whenever it appears. It is extraordinarily easy for a historian to distort his evidence in this way without ever intending consciously to do so. A great English economic historian of an older generation, Sir John Clapham, once observed, "It is very easy to do this unawares. Thirty years ago I read and marked Arthur Young's *Travels in France,* and taught from the marked passages. Five years ago I went through it again, to find that whenever Young spoke of a wretched Frenchman I had marked him, but that many of his references to happy or prosperous Frenchmen remained unmarked."[14] The same thing has happened in almost everybody's work.

ٮ The *fallacy of statistical impressionism* occurs whenever a historian casts an imprecise, impressionistic interpretation into exact numbers. The result tends to be speciously specific or specifically specious.

An example of a historian who casts impressions into numbers is Lee Benson, in *The Concept of Jacksonian Democracy: New York as a Test Case,* 2d ed. (New York, 1964). Benson's book is both a polemical plea for quantification in history, and an intensive analysis of the New York elections of 1844 as a case study in political ecology. It is, I think, more successful as a manifesto than as a monograph, for its major points are either inaccurate or unsubstantiated. The reader finds much of the rhetoric of quantification in Benson's book but little of its reality. *The Concept of Jacksonian Democracy* combines the worst of both methodological worlds—history is researched as an art and written as a science.

Chief among the theses of this controversial book is an argument that there can be no clear and simple correlation between party affiliation and economic wealth, in the New York elections of 1844 in particular, and American political history in general. Instead, Benson suggests a six-part multivariate analysis of voting patterns in terms of previous voting behavior, economic groups, ethnocultural groups, religious groups, residential groups, and regional groups.

Benson's thesis is asserted rather than proved. One looks in vain, through 340 pages crowded with numbers, footnotes, and tables, for any comprehensive and unequivocal attempt to calculate the correlation

14. Quoted in Edward P. Thompson, *The Making of the English Working Class* (New York, 1964), p. 210.

of political affiliation with economic wealth. Instead, there are declarative sentences punctuated with impressionistic scraps of statistics such as the following:

> Perhaps the most dramatic way to illustrate the inaccuracy of traditional claims about voting behavior is to present the data for the two towns in the state that received the highest and lowest Democratic vote. Clarkstown in Rockland County was a "very prosperous" ($629) Hudson River town, but its 89.9% Democratic vote established it, by a considerable margin, as that party's banner unit. The second highest Democratic unit (83.9 per cent) was an extremely "poor" ($494), isolated interior town (Croghan in Lewis County). The lowest Democratic unit was Putnam, a "marginal" town ($339) in Washington County, where the Democratic vote was 18.5 per cent of the total.[15]

These impressionistic figures lend a sense of statistical authority to Benson's book, but little substance. Another inveterate historical quantifier has wisely observed that "to support an argument by a few examples, though it may be a persuasive rhetorical device, is not logically adequate. There are exceptions to most historical generalizations, and, if the citation of occasional instances were accepted as proof, it would be possible to prove almost anything."[16]

Though Benson asserts, or implies, that he systematically compared economic and political data throughout the state, he strangely omits anything in the way of a comprehensive statistical generalization which bears upon that critical question.

He comes close twice. There is only one table, out of many in the book, which displays the two variables side by side for any area of the state—a tabulation of towns in Delaware County. This table shows the average valuation of dwellings in eighteen towns, the percentage of the Democratic vote in sixteen of them, and their rank order in both. But there is nothing at the bottom of the table, in the way of a summary

15. P. 150. The dollar values refer to the average (assessed) value of dwellings per family.
16. William O. Aydelotte, "Quantification in History," *The American Historical Review* 71 (1966): 805. Another quantifier has commented directly on Benson's book, "Despite his concern for theoretical explication, Professor Benson's work sometimes falls short of the standards that many behavioural scientists consider essential. One searches the first edition of *The Concept of Jacksonian Democracy* in vain for any detailed discussion of the methods by which he selected his indicator precincts, or of the numbers of voters in his sample, or of correlations or significance tests underlying the party preference percentages which he ascribed to the various ethno-cultural groups living in New York during the 1830s and 1840s." Allan G. Bogue, "United States: The 'New' Political History," *Journal of Contemporary History* 3 (1968): 11. In the second edition, Benson added a descriptive methodological statement which appears to have satisfied Bogue. But an explicit description of a bad method does not thereby convert it into a good one. The fatal flaws remain.

or a statistical generalization, and nothing in the text but statistical snippets.

I took the sixteen towns for which both economic and political data appear in the table and tried three experiments: First, a simple two-by-two table, in which the towns were equally divided on two axes: the eight most Democratic, the eight least Democratic, the eight most wealthy, and the eight least wealthy. The results were:

	8 most wealthy	8 least wealthy
8 most Democratic	2	6
8 least Democratic	6	2

This appears to contradict Benson's thesis and also to undercut the impressionistic examples which he extracted and discussed in his text.

Next I averaged the wealth of the towns which the Democrats carried by more than 50 percent ($331) as against those in which they received less than that percentage ($414). The results once again contradicted Benson's assertion that "no significant relationship existed between wealth and voting in 1844." Finally, I calculated a Spearman rank correlation coefficient for the sixteen towns and got a positive correlation of .3, which leaves the issue in doubt. That marginal figure neither confirms nor refutes Benson's sweeping generalization but requires further evidence of the sort which he does not provide.[17]

A second piece of evidence which appears to bear directly on the issue of wealth and politics is Benson's analysis of a directory called *Wealth and Biography of the Wealthy Citizens of New York City, Comprising an Alphabetical Arrangement of Persons Estimated to Be Worth $100,000, and Upwards—With the Sums Appended to Each*

17. The disparity of results obtained by these three different statistical tests may serve to suggest the need for historians to study the mathematical assumptions embodied in the statistical tools at their command. Lancelot Hogben has remarked upon the "feverish concern of biologists, sociologists and civil servants to exploit the newest and most sophisticated statistical devices with little concern for their mathematical credentials or for the formal assumptions inherent therein." Historians are beginning to use the oldest and least sophisticated statistical techniques in precisely the same uncritical spirit. Lancelot Hogben, *Statistical Theory: The Relationship of Probability, Credibility and Error* (New York, n.d.) p. 13.

Name, published by Moses Beach in 1845.[18] Benson examined a sample of a few names and concluded that Democrats and Whigs appeared in almost equal numbers. But another scholar has recently studied the whole list in a comprehensive fashion and discovered a very close and symmetrical correlation between wealth and Whiggery.[19]

Benson's methodological misdemeanors are not a mark of depravity. They are not a proof of the inherent inadequacy of quantification in history. The remedy is not less quantification but more. And Benson himself has, I think, done more than any other single individual to make possible more thorough and exact quantification in American political history. His work in the organization of the American Historical Association's program for the computer programing of political and social data, a program which is already sufficiently advanced to be useful and even indispensable to American political historians, is a giant step forward. But *The Concept of Jacksonian Democracy* was in some respects a step back.

និ✍ The *fallacy of statistical nonsense* serves as a catchall category for a miscellany of statistical mumbo jumbo, all of which has one quality in common: it is, *in context,* literally meaningless. Sometimes it consists in a statistical generalization which may be accurate and important in some other context, but which is irrelevant to the problem at hand. A historian has argued, for example, that a measure of the effectiveness of Communism in the U.S.S.R. appears in the fact that "the number of doctors in Russia had increased from 1,380 in 1897 to 12,000 in 1935."[20] But the meaningful comparison for this problem is the increase in the number of doctors from 1917 to 1935. The Soviet regime has often received statistical credit for economic and social development at the end of the czarist period.

Another example of the same sort of error is from American political history, where one scholar attempted to measure the degree of party cohesion in the first session of the Second Congress by recording

18. Reprinted in Henry Wysham Lanier, *A Century of Banking in New York: 1822–1922* (New York, 1922), pp. 151–84.
19. Frank O. Gatell, "Money and Party in Jacksonian America: A Quantitative Look at New York's Men of Quality," *Political Science Quarterly* 82 (1967): 235–50. There are several signs of trouble in Gatell's essay, too. I compared the Beach list with other overlapping directories for Brooklyn and found that old established wealth tended to be more completely represented than new wealth, and wealthy citizens of English and Dutch descent more than Irish wealth, such as it was. This suggests that the Beach list is skewed toward Whiggish wealth, and that Gatell's conclusions require qualification. But they demonstrate a gross and serious inaccuracy in Benson's use of the Beach list.
20. Bernard Pares, *Russia* (New York, 1949), p. 137.

the number of times the votes of each congressman agreed or disagreed with the vote of James Madison. The figures are accurate, but they are not an appropriate test of party regularity, for Madison himself was something of a swing-voter at this time. Moreover, to categorize party patterns in these terms is to permit only two patterns to emerge—a pattern of consistent divergence from Madison's record and one of agreement with it. It would exclude the discovery of multiparty patterns.[21]

The second general category of nonsensical statistical generalizations includes statements which float in an interpretive vacuum, without an adequate control group as a reference point. Thus, David Donald attempted a statistical analysis of abolitionist leadership and found that the median age was twenty-nine, that 85 percent came from the Northeast, 60 percent from New England, and 30 percent from Massachusetts; that there was a preponderance of Congregationalists and Presbyterians and Quakers; that most were from respectable families, neither rich nor poor; that few were immigrants; that few were born in the city; and that few had any connection with industrial activity. These statistical generalizations are not, however, weighed against national norms, or the leadership of other movements, or any other control. Without such a control, they are largely empty of meaning.[22]

The third general category of statistical nonsense consists in shifting statistical bases as a correlation is run. James Sterling Young, in *The Washington Community,* tried to prove that there was a pattern of residential segregation in the District of Columbia during the Jeffersonian era, with congressional legislators living in one community and executive officers in another. But he compared legislative residences in one period (1807, apparently) with executive residences in another (1800-1828, apparently mostly toward the end of this period), and both in turn with a control from a third period (1800). All of this was at a time when Washington was being built, and residential patterns were changing, and the changes cut against the author's thesis.[23]

Other examples of comparable errors appear in statistics textbooks, which also supply illustrations of a fourth category of statistical nonsense, not much in evidence in historical writing—yet. But it is one which is likely to become more common as quantification becomes more routine. This fallacy of the fourth type consists in a shifted statis-

21. Noble Cunningham, *The Jeffersonian Republicans: The Formation of Party Organization, 1789–1801* (Chapel Hill, N.C., 1957), pp. 22, 267–72.

22. David Donald, "Toward a Reconsideration of the Abolitionists," *Lincoln Reconsidered* (New York, 1956), pp. 19–36.

23. James Sterling Young, *The Washington Community 1800–1828* (New York, 1966), pp. 67, 69.

tical method, which has the same results as a shifted statistical base. It includes a variety of technical errors of various degrees of sophistication, in which medians, modes, and means are mixed up, or averages of any sort are confused with ranges of dispersion, and stupid, careless mistakes in which "natural" and "common" logarithms are mistaken for one another, or one unit of measurement is substituted for another.[24]

Historiographical examples have, however, already begun to appear. In Terry G. Jordan's *German Seed in Texas Soil: Immigrant Farmers in Nineteenth Century Texas* (Austin, 1966) there is an attempt to compare statistically the condition of German and Anglo-American farmers. But the author relies principally on averages, without applying information as to ranges and dispersions and medians, all of which are functional to his thesis.

ᐤ   *Fallacies of statistical probability* are numerous, and sometimes very technical, and as yet rarely committed in historical scholarship. We might, however, briefly note two of them. The first is the error of assuming that the most probable distribution will occur, exactly, in any given instance. Abraham Kaplan writes,

> This point played an historic part in the Dreyfus trial, where the prosecution argued that Dreyfus' correspondence must be in code because the frequency distribution of the letters of the alphabet contained in the correspondence deviated from what is "normal" for the French language. The testimony of Poincaré for the defense that the most probable distribution is highly improbable was not very convincing, in spite of its being correct. (Possibly a contributing factor was that Poincaré had identified himself on the stand as the greatest living expert on probability, a tactical error which he later justified to his friends by pointing out that he was under oath at the time.)[25]

A second and related simple form of probability error is the familiar gambler's fallacy, which is the error of assuming that if a coin has come down heads one time, it is more likely to come down tails the next, because the probability (assuming the coin to be symmetrical) is .5 for heads and .5 for tails. But the "law of averages" does not work this way. The odds are always even in every single toss.

24. Darrell Huff, *How to Lie with Statistics* (New York, 1954); Ernst Wagemann, *Narrenspiegel der Statistik* (Bern, 1950); J. B. Cohen, "The Misuse of Statistics," *Journal of the American Statistical Association* 33 (1938): 657–74; W. Allen Wallis and Harry V. Roberts, *Statistics: A New Approach* (New York, 1956), chap. 3; Hans Zeisel, *Say It with Figures,* rev. 4th ed. (New York, 1957), passim; M. J. Moroney, *Facts From Figures,* rev. 3d ed. (Baltimore, 1956), passim.
25. Abraham Kaplan, *The Conduct of Inquiry* (San Francisco, 1964), p. 224.

&⤳ The *ecological fallacy* is a false form of statistical inference which is common in quantitative research. Its popularity is sustained by the fact that it *appears* to be a shortcut to a significant statistical conclusion. It is a form of error which is more easily committed than characterized, and most clearly explained by an example.

W. S. Robinson, who discovered and named this fallacy, provides a good illustration. He attempted to estimate the statistical relationship between illiteracy and race (white-Negro), by three statistical methods. First, he correlated marginal percentages between Negroes and illiteracy in nine standard census regions of the United States. The result was a positive Pearson correlation coefficient of .946. Next, he correlated percentages of Negroes and illiterates in the forty-eight states. This time he obtained a different estimate—a positive Pearson coefficient of .773. Finally, he attempted to run a correlation, not between ecological areas, but between individuals—white and Negro, literate and illiterate. The result was still a third figure: a low positive Pearson coefficient of .203. The ecological fallacy consists in a confusion of the first two ecological correlations with the third individual correlation.[26]

An individual correlation is one between discrete and indivisible objects—namely, people, in this case. An ecological correlation is between percentage figures which refer to classes of individuals—areal, or geographical or ecological classes. The ecological fallacy occurs when classes are used which do not coincide with the variable being measured. The degree of error is regressive, as the classes increase in number and diminish in size, and also in proportion with the degree of coincidence with the variable under investigation. Suppose, for instance, that General Sherman had his way, and Negroes were *entirely* segregated by region from whites in the United States. Suppose all Negroes lived in census region one, and all whites in regions two through ten. Then, an ecological correlation should yield the same results as an individual correlation.[26a] But not otherwise. It is possible, by the use of regression techniques, to derive individual correlations from ecological data.[27] But it is incorrect to use an ecological correlation itself as an interchangeable substitute for an individual correlation. This point, important as it is for sociologists, is still more important for historians who seek to use quantitative materials. If Robinson, in his example,

26. W. S. Robinson, "Ecological Correlations and the Behavior of Individuals," *American Sociological Review* 15 (1950): 351–7; Leo Goodman, "Ecological Regression and the Behavior of Individuals," and "Some Alternatives to Ecological Correlation," in ibid. 18 (1953): 663–4; and *American Journal of Sociology* 64 (1959): 610–25. A bibliography of other discussions of this problem appears in Otis Dudley Duncan et al., *Statistical Geography* (Glencoe, 1961).
26a. If variances of the ten groups are similar.
27. Goodman, op. cit.

were concerned with race and literacy in 1840, he would not have been able to run an individual correlation directly. The only data available to him would have been aggregate census data. He would, therefore, have to use regression techniques on his data to obtain an answer.

The ecological fallacy is not well named, for precisely the same sort of error can be committed in the use of any kind of aggregate data. The ecological fallacy could appear, for example, in the analysis of generational as well as areal classes—in classes which are temporal rather than spatial in nature. Historians, therefore, have still another reason to be wary of this problem.

ॐ The *fallacy of false extrapolation* is a statistical series which is stretched beyond the breaking point. It occurs in a variety of forms. The most clear and simple is a generalization from a true series *A, B* to a false *A, B, C*. The average size of the American family was reported by the Census Bureau as 3.71 persons in 1940 and 3.54 persons in 1950. To extrapolate from these known quantities, on the assumption that the American family is shrinking at an arithmetical rate of 0.22 persons per decade, to the conclusion that the American family, in 2070, will consist of 0.90 persons, is absurd. The Census Bureau estimated that family size actually increased from 3.54 to 3.65 in the decade 1950–1960. To extrapolate from these figures on the assumption that families are growing in geometrical ratio (the increment, let us say, is doubling every decade) to the conclusion that the average American family in 2070 will include 228.82 persons is not merely absurd but inconceivable, in every sense of the word.

Many terrifying predictions of a great demographic Götterdämmerung lying just around the corner—not in 2070, but in 1970, or 1975, or 1980—are not absurd, but they may be equally fallacious. There is clear evidence that birth rates have been rising at a formidable rate. But there has been a good deal of loose talk about population explosions that fails to take into consideration the increase in contraception, the cumulative effect of education and affluence upon birth rates, and other countervailing phenomena. There *is* an ongoing crisis, but maybe not the incipient catastrophe which some of our Cassandras so confidently expect.

There was an eighteenth-century American clergyman, Rev. Ezra Stiles, who loved to weigh and measure things. He often talked of his findings with his many visitors, and sometimes he even weighed and measured them as well. But he outdid himself in 1760 with the following projection of the denominational demography of New England:

A.D.	Episcopalians	Friends	Baptists	Congregationalists
1760	12,600	16,000	22,000	440,000
1785	23,200	32,000	44,000	880,000
1810	46,400	64,000	88,000	1,760,000
1835	92,800	128,000	176,000	3,520,000
1860	185,600	256,000	352,000	7 MILLIONS*

* Quoted in Carl Bridenbaugh, *Mitre and Sceptre* (New York, 1962), p. 12.

Small wonder that this incorrigibly optimistic Congregational divine could plan a monument for himself with a sketch of the universe on one side and the Stiles family tree on the other! It is said that the only biblical injunction which New England Congregationalists consistently obeyed was the one which required them to increase and multiply—but not precisely according to Stiles's projections.[28]

The field of demography is littered with discarded extrapolations that seemed the soul of reason at the time they were made. The Negro population of the United States appeared to fall sharply from 1860 to 1880, which led many intelligent Americans to predict the imminent extinction of Negroes in this nation. A little later, others predicted from an inverse correlation between IQs and fertility rates that the Republic would soon be inhabited by a race of morons. Still others, from a differential in the reproductive rates of members of various religious groups, predicted that the United States would become a fief of the Pope. A satirical specimen of the fallacy of false extrapolation is supplied by Mark Twain, who wrote:

> The Mississippi between Cairo and New Orleans was twelve hundred and fifteen miles long one hundred and seventy-six years ago. It was eleven hundred and eighty after the cut-off of 1722. It was one thousand and forty after the American Bend cut-off. It has lost sixty-seven miles since. Consequently, its length is only nine hundred and seventy-three miles at present.
>
> Now, if I wanted to be one of those ponderous scientific people, and "let on" to prove what had occurred in the remote past by what had occurred in late years, what an opportunity is here! Geology never had such a chance, nor such exact data to argue from! Nor "development of species," either! Glacial epochs are great things, but they are vague—vague. Please observe: In the space of one hundred and seventy-six years the lower Mississippi has shortened itself two-hundred and forty-two miles. That is an average of a trifle over one mile and a third per year. Therefore, any calm person, who is not blind or idiotic, can see that in the Old Oölitic Silurian Period, just one million

28. The number of Congregational *churches* is thought to have increased from 465 in 1750 to 1,706 in 1850. But the number of Congregationalists seems to have increased in a smaller ratio even than this. See Edwin S. Gaustad, *Historical Atlas of Religion in America* (New York, 1962), pp. 62, 167, 168.

years ago next November, the lower Mississippi River was upward of one million three hundred thousand miles long, and stuck out over the Gulf of Mexico like a fishing-rod. And by the same token any person can see that seven hundred and forty-two years from now the Lower Mississippi will be only a mile and three-quarters long, and Cairo and New Orleans will have joined their streets together, and be plodding comfortably along under a single mayor and mutual board of aldermen. There is something fascinating about science. One gets such wholesale returns of conjecture out of such a trifling investment of fact.[29]

Another kind of false extrapolation occurs in the form of $a:b::A:B$, where a, b, and A are known, and an unknown B is falsely extrapolated. An example may appear in a group of ingenious essays by two naval historians, Michael Lewis and Lieutenant Commander D. W. Waters, R.N., on the argument of the Spanish Armada. The authors were especially interested in the number of long-range guns (culverins) carried by the great galleons of that mighty fleet. No direct evidence exists to answer this question. Lewis and Waters were compelled to operate by means of an extrapolation from three knowns to an unknown—from a known number of Spanish galleons (a) carrying a known number of culverins (b) to the unknown total number of culverins (B) carried by all the galleons in the fleet (A). But galleons came in many assorted sizes, and culverins, too. In the opinion of some learned students of this question, it is probable that Lewis and Waters, for all their care and ingenuity, overestimated the number of long guns in the Spanish fleet by this method.[30]

੩❧ The *fallacy of false interpolation* is a form of overgeneralization, in which a line is inaccurately run between two known points in order to estimate the location of an unknown point in between. It is, in other words, a false estimate of an unknown B from a known A and C. There is no sure defense against this fallacy except full factual information. But there are two logical rules of thumb which, obvious though they may be, are often overlooked.

First, the accuracy of interpolations of unstable indices must necessarily vary inversely with the degree of their instability and with the number of known index points. A grossly unstable index ought to be interpolated with great caution and reluctance. Few indices are as unstable as the level of voter participation in a free and open polity. In early American presidential years, participation fluctuated wildly from one

29. Mark Twain, *Life on the Mississippi* (New York, 1917), pp. 155–56.
30. Michael Lewis, "Armada Guns: A Comparative Study of English and Spanish Armaments. Section V. The Guns of the Spanish Fleet, 1588," *The Mariner's Mirror* 29 (1943): 3–39; D. W. Waters, "The Elizabethan Navy and the Armada Campaign," ibid., 35 (1949): 90–138; cf. Garrett Mattingly, *The Armada* (Boston, 1959), p. 416 n.

election to another and from one state to the next. Moreover, the number of known index points is small. In New Hampshire, the percentage of adult males voting in three elections was:

1808	62.1%
1812	75.4%
1828	76.4%

If anybody tried to interpolate the turnout in 1824, solely from these figures, he would be far off the mark. According to Richard McCormick, who made the estimates above, only 16.8 percent of New Hampshire's adult males came to the polls in 1824![31]

A second obvious rule of thumb is that an interpolation can be no stronger than its weaker pole. A cautionary example is an article by Professor George Rogers Taylor called "American Economic Growth before 1840: An Exploratory Essay" in *The Journal of Economic History* 24 (1964): 427–44.

Taylor's purpose was to develop a preliminary hypothesis, from scattered statistical snippets and impressionistic material, as to per capita growth rates in early America. He began with the work of another economist who studied the same problem by working backward from the period 1840–1959 where statistical evidence was comparatively good, and the per capita growth rate seems to have been something like 1⅝ percent per year. Could this rate apply to the period 1676–1840? The other economist, Raymond Goldsmith, did not think so, for it would require absurdly small levels of per capita income at the beginning of the period. Instead, Goldsmith suggested an extended average growth rate before 1840 of 0.6 percent per year, which never rose, in his opinion, in any fifty-year part of this early period to as much as one percent per year.

Taylor accepted much of this, but not the presumption of a steady low growth rate. Instead he hypothesized from a variety of demographic and economic materials that the per capita rate of growth in the period 1710–1775 was "relatively high for a preindustrial economy," perhaps as high as one percent, maybe even higher. From this conclusion he interpolated the additional conclusion that the *average* per capita growth rate in the period 1775–1840 approached zero. "Per capita income in 1840 was about the same or at least not substantially higher than in the early 1770's," he guessed.

This interpolation is logically tenable. If Taylor's estimates of

31. Richard P. McCormick, "New Perspectives on Jacksonian Politics," *American Historical Review* 65 (1960): 288–301.

growth rates before 1775 and after 1840 are correct, then his interpolation of a zero-sum in the intervening period must be right, too. But if one of the guesses is wrong, then the interpolation collapses. Taylor's figures for the post-1840 period seem acceptable. But his estimates for the period 1710–1775 are derived from partial and contradictory evidence. A more open hypothesis would, in my judgment, be more serviceable to sustained research.[32]

ૄ੭ The *fallacy of the insidious generalization* is committed by a historian who swears up and down that he cannot and will not generalize upon his subject, and then proceeds to bootleg generalizations into his work, without recognizing their existence or controlling their content. An example is H. A. L. Fisher, an English academic historian who prefaced one of his books with the following assertion: "One intellectual excitement has, however, been denied me. Men wiser and more learned than I have discerned in history a plot, a rhythm, a predetermined pattern. These harmonies are concealed from me. I can see only . . . one great fact with respect to which, since it is unique, there can be no generalizations."[33]

This statement is followed by a considerable number of generalizations, some of which are quite as absurd as the disclaimer which preceded them. "The Athenian empire, the brilliant growth of two generations, shared the fate of every polity which rises by the repression of local liberties," Fisher wrote. Again: "It is the property of polytheism to be tolerant." And again: "Men once embarked on the ocean of political strife are apt to be carried further than they intended."[34]

One might note, in Fisher's prefatorial statement, a common confusion in the author's mind between generalizations concerning the whole of history and generalizations of a limited sort within history. A good many historians, I think, have condemned both of these things together.

The fallacy of the insidious generalization commonly occurs in a form even more insidious than Fisher's errors. Impressionistic historians, who bitterly inveigh against quantification and its dehumanizing tendencies, are quick to use the words "few," "some," "most," "many," "singular," "typical," "exceptional," "common," "customary," "normal," "regular," "recurrent," "periodic," "widespread," "often," and many others. These terms imply numbers, and numbers need counting. And

32. For a historiographical model of interpolation by a series of orderly inferences, see Willi Apel, *Gregorian Chant* (Bloomington, Ind., 1966), pp. 33, 507–15.
33. H. A. L. Fisher, *A History of Europe*, 3 vols. (London, 1935), 1:vii.
34. Ibid., 1:32, 45, 67.

yet they are used without quantification, by scholars who believe that quantifying is no part of their job. The inaccuracy of much impressionistic history is an inevitable result. Other historians make statements in which even these words are implicit. The results are even worse. So common is this form of error that the reader can pick up almost any work of history from his shelves, turn to almost any page, and find an example.

&~ The *fallacy of the double-reversing generalization* is the opposite of many errors in this chapter—a halting generalization rather than a hasty one, an understatement rather than an overstatement. It is a species of interpretative bet-hedging, which in an extreme form becomes no interpretation at all but a maze of mutual qualifications or a cunning balance of casuistical contradictions, or a trackless wilderness of pettifogging detail, or a slippery ooze of substantive (as well as semantical) shilly-shally.

A familiar example is Theodore Roosevelt's first presidential state paper, in which the author, with uncharacteristic restraint, tried to play things both ways on a number of controversial issues of the day. The most famous part of this document concerned public regulation of corporate enterprise—a passage which the inimitable Mr. Dooley took great pleasure in satirizing: "Th' trusts," says he, "are heejoous monsthers built up be th' enlightened intherprise iv th' men that have done so much to advance progress in our beloved country," he says. "On wan hand I wud stamp thim undher fut; on th' other hand not so fast."

There are many comparable examples in historical scholarship. More than a few monographers have timidly advanced a tentative thesis in Chapter 1, only to withdraw it in Chapter 2 with an "on th' other hand not so fast." An example is Alfred F. Young's *The Democratic Republicans of New York: The Origins, 1763–1797* (Chapel Hill, N.C., 1967). This distinguished work possesses many great merits in the breadth and depth of its accurate and painstaking research. But it is more satisfactory in its parts than in the whole. The author's idea of truth, like Burke's idea of liberty, seems to be "a sort of middle" between interpretative extremes. There is, of course, no necessary fallacy in moderation. But Young's assertions are so thoroughly amended by strings of qualifications that the main point is neutralized, or obscured. And sometimes he declares unequivocally that X was the case, only to declare unequivocally a little later that not-X was the case.

What, for instance, was George Clinton's conception of the economic role of the state government? On page 56 Young characterizes it as "essentially negative." On page 570 he calls it essentially "positive" on the same questions.

What was the nature of the relationship between Federalist leaders and their constituents? We are informed on one page that "most Federalist support was uncoerced," but also that "to a considerable extent Federalist electoral strength continued to be a vote of economic dependents" (p. 569). A reconciliation is conceivable between these two statements, but none is supplied by the author.

What, precisely, was the degree of continuity and discontinuity between the political groups of 1788 and the parties of the 1790s? The author seems to stress elements of continuity, but there is no clear and conclusive estimate of this difficult problem. Instead the reader learns that "In the leadership of the Federalists, the continuities in New York politics from the Revolution through the 1790's were striking. . . . There were also discontinuities. . . . The leadership of the Republicans showed similar continuities and discontinuities . . ." (pp. 566–67).

The ambivalence of Young's interpretation of the impact of the French Revolution upon New York politics is captured in the tension between the beginning and the end of his essay on that question. The chapter is called "The Spirit of 1776 Rekindling." But the author concludes "it was not quite true of New York, as Jefferson said of the country as a whole, that 'all the old spirit of 1776 is rekindling.' " Nevertheless, he insists "a fire had indeed been lit," and this reader, at least, lost his way in billowing clouds of conceptual smoke (pp. 345–65).

A good deal of the confusion in Young's book is a consequence of impressionistic research and of his attempt to compress an analytical thesis into a narrative form; but much, I think, is substantive as well. The complaint is not that he took a middling position, but rather that his position tends to shift within an unstable range of middling possibilities.

Another example is Norman K. Risjord's *The Old Republicans: Southern Conservatism in the Age of Jefferson* (New York, 1965). A fair judgment upon this work is passed by Noble Cunningham:

> The author begins by picturing the old Republicans in traditional shades as a group who appeared in reaction to the surge of nationalism following the War of 1812, men who took to heart the compact theory of government and adhered to the "principles of 1798." Although this theme is later restated, it is so modified in other places as to raise the question of how well the author has thought through his interpretations. While stating as fact that the old Republicans appeared as a reaction to postwar nationalism, the author later writes that this "is generally assumed" but "only partially true." . . . Throughout the work, shifting emphasis and conflicting interpre-

tations leave no clear picture of the old Republicans or of Southern conservatism.[35]

ह The *fallacy of the overwhelming exception* is a generalization which is a good deal less general than it appears to be. The authors of *1066 and All That* assert, for instance, that "Magna Charta was therefore the chief cause of Democracy in England, and thus a *Good Thing* for everyone (except the Common People)."[36]

A serious example appears in an essay by an American business historian, Gordon C. Bjork, who argued the thesis that "the relatively slow rate of population growth in the [American] seaport cities under consideration for the period 1790 to 1825 must be blamed, in large part, on the failure of foreign trade to expand." He contended that something called "trade gain per capita" fell from a base of 100 in 1790 to 30 in 1825—in Boston, New York, Philadelphia, and Baltimore.

Bjork's critical index of "trade gain per capita" is a complicated thing, calculated from three other indices, all of which are incorrect. But our business is merely with his estimates of the expansion of commerce in the cities. We discover that he omitted cotton from his calculations, though it was the most expansive domestic commodity of the period and important even in the trade of ports as far north as Boston. Moreover, he excluded re-exports, which other scholars have found to account for much of the expansion of American commerce during the period 1790–1807. Bjork justified his exclusions on the ground that cotton and re-exports were not produced in the western hinterlands of the seaport cities—which is irrelevant to any estimate of trade volume. All four of these cities had southern hinterlands as well as western ones; all of them were engaged both in the re-export business and in the transshipment of cotton.

These exclusions are not readily apparent to a casual reader of Bjork's paper. But they are vital to his interpretation. To make such sweeping exclusions is to make nonsense of the subject.[37]

---

35. *American Historical Review* 71 (1966): 1062.
36. Walter C. Sellor and Robert J. Yeatman, *1066 and All That,* new ed. (London, 1965), p. 34.
37. Gordon C. Bjork, "Foreign Trade," in David Gilchrist, ed., *The Growth of the Seaport Cities* (Charlottesville, 1967), pp. 54–61. The accuracy of Bjork's interpretation is diminished by other errors. A *weighted* average of the four seaport cities would show a different result from the one which he calculated. Moreover, Bjork appears to have inflated his population index, and his calculation of terms of trade contradicts, without explanation, the source which he cites: Douglass North's *The Economic Growth of the United States, 1790–1860* (Englewood Cliffs, N.J., 1961).

ह≫ Positive rules for the construction of sound statistical generalization need not be discussed here. They are thoroughly explored in statistics texts. But there is something of another sort which needs to be said. The structure and function of generalization in history has been considerably confused by the errors of a reigning school of epistemologists, who hold that every explanation in history (and indeed everywhere else) must consist in referring the thing to be explained to a "general law" or "universal hypothesis" or "hypothesis of universal form." These three phrases, suitably shrouded in shudder-quotes, come from the classic argument for this interpretation by Carl G. Hempel. His thesis is:

> The explanation of the occurrence of an event of some specific kind E at a certain place and time consists, as it is usually expressed, in indicating the causes or determining factors of E. Now the assertion that a set of events—say, of the kinds C_1, C_2 . . . , C_n—have caused the event to be explained, amounts to the statement that, according to certain general laws, a set of events of the kinds mentioned is regularly accompanied by an event of kind E. Thus, the scientific explanation of the event in question consists of
> (1) a set of statements asserting the occurrence of certain events $C_1, \ldots C_n$ at certain times and places.
> (2) a set of universal hypotheses, such that
> (a) the statements of both groups are reasonably well-confirmed by empirical evidence,
> (b) from the two groups of statements the sentence asserting the occurrence of event E can be logically deduced.

Hempel's criteria for a "general law" or "universal hypothesis" are rigorous. A law must be universally true in *all* cases where a certain complex of conditions is satisfied. And an explanation model must be "logically conclusive," in the literal sense that the conclusion must follow *necessarily* from the premises. The only complete explanation is an explanation which is "deduced by logical reasoning" in this way. An explanation is not complete unless "it might as well have functioned as a prediction."[38]

---

38. Hempel, "The Function of General Laws in History," as reprinted in Patrick Gardiner, ed., *Theories of History* (Glencoe, Ill., 1959), pp. 344–56. Hempel's classic article, published in 1942, was not, of course, the first statement of the "Hempelian model." The idea that explanation consists in showing that something obeys a law has been traced back to Berkeley, and probably appeared much earlier. (E. Meyerson, *De l'Explication dans les Sciences*, 2d ed. [Paris, 1927]). More recently it appeared in forms very close to Hempel's in Karl Popper's *Logik der Forschung* (Vienna [1934]), and in Morris Raphael Cohen, *Reason and Nature* (New York, 1931). It is called by many different names—the "regularity interpretation" (Patrick Gardiner, *The Nature of Historical Explanation*, p. 65); the "covering law model" (Willian Dray, *Laws and Explanation in History*, p. 1); and the "deductive model" (Michael Scriven, "Truisms as Grounds for Historical Explanations," *Theories of History*, p. 444.

But these conditions cannot be met in historical writing. Consider a whimsical example of a universal law which is presented by another philosopher, Morton White. "Let us assume that the statement 'Whenever Chinese eat, they eat with chopsticks' is true," he writes. But this statement, as it stands, is of course untrue, in a way which invalidates other alleged universal laws in history. First, Chinese have not always eaten with chopsticks. The earliest humanoid inhabitants of the Yellow River valley probably lapped up their dinners like dogs. Moreover, today's Chinese do not eat with chopsticks everywhere. It is unlikely that a well-mannered Mandarin, however loyal he may be to the ways of his ancestors, would eat with chopsticks at Maxim's. Most important, even when the use of chopsticks was at its peak in China, most Chinese did not use them some of the time (i.e., mourning periods), and some Chinese did not use them most of the time (i.e., fingerless Chinese). One must, therefore recast White's statement to read, "Within certain limits of time and space, Chinese tended to eat with chopsticks."

This statement differs from a universal law in two respects. First, it applies differentially through time within a closed temporal frame of reference. Second, it is a statistical statement. An explanation model which includes a temporalized statistical generalization statement of this sort cannot support the sort of deduction which the Hempelian model requires. A probability statement asserts that C is sometimes followed by E, and sometimes not. Maybe E happens 999 times out of 1,000, but if it doesn't happen once there can be no necessary and certain deduction

---

In revisions of his thesis, Hempel has stressed a second kind of covering law model, in which the *explanans* does not include a universal law, but rather a statement of statistical probability. This second model is more relevant to the explanations which historians (and natural scientists) actually make. And it is radically different, in its logical behavior, from the deductive model of explanation. But even with this salutary modification, serious problems remain. Hempel still seems to insist that all explanations must conform to one or the other of his models. (He would allow "explanation sketches" which are understood as incomplete statistical statements to be filled in by some future empiricist.) Now, if it is true that no historian (or natural scientist) can hope to find a universal law of the sort required by Hempel's first model, then it follows that *all* explanations in history (and in the natural sciences) must be statistical or proto-statistical in nature. And this, I think, is the quantitative fallacy, which returns to the Pythagorean error of thinking that all significant things are numbers.

Moreover, Hempel seems to argue that only statements of very high ("close to 1") probability can be used in explanations. This is surely unsatisfactory. How close to 1? What criteria can there be? And what, precisely, is the logical relationship between an *explanandum* and an *explanans* which contains a statistical statement? Is it different from an explanation model which contains a narrative statement, or a motivational statement, or a group composition statement? I don't see how. In each of these types, the bond between an *explanans* and an *explanandum* must be presently understood in psychological and/or pragmatical terms, perhaps because it conforms to a logic we don't yet understand.

from the premises to the conclusion. This is true, I think, equally in the natural sciences, where universal laws are equally elusive. Albert Einstein wisely asserted that "As far as the laws of mathematics refer to reality they are not certain, and as far as they are certain they do not refer to reality."[39] The same thing might be said of Hempel's general laws.

Philosophers of history have recently squandered a good deal of time and effort in a vain attempt to adjust the Hempelian model to the plain fact that historians do not use universal laws in their work. A few have attempted to adjust the plain fact to the Hempelian model. Some extraordinarily ingenious arguments have been invented, but the enterprise is, at bottom, absurd. Analytical philosophers have failed, I think, to be sufficiently empirical in their own work. They have failed to give sufficient attention to historical thought as it actually happens. And they have erected a deductive standard which is so exalted that no mortal empiricist can ever begin to meet its requirements. One wishes that analytical philosophers might harken to the words of Robert Frost:

> As ever when philosophers are met,
> No matter where they stoutly mean to get,
> Nor what particulars they reason from,
> They are philosophers, and from old habit
> They end up in the universal whole
> As unoriginal as any rabbit.[40]

39. James R. Newman, ed., *The World of Mathematics,* 4 vols. (New York, 1956), 3:1646.
40. Robert Frost, "The Lesson for Today," *Complete Poems* (New York, 1965), p. 474. To this unkindness, analytical philosophers could conceivably reply with a poem which is not by Robert Frost. It is called "The Lesson for Yesterday."

> Historians, rather like primitive moles,
> Live purposeless lives in particular holes,
> Which they dig with their noses, or else with their toeses
> (A few have invented small shovels and hoeses).
> They're burrowing blindly in Byzantine tunnels
> Constructed like sinuous serpentine funnels;
> They're burrowing busily, back to the past:
> A steady regression to nowhere—fast.

CHAPTER V

FALLACIES OF NARRATION

૪৯

Historians begin by looking backward. They often end
by thinking backward.
                    —Nietzsche

Most historians tell stories in their work. Good historians tell true
stories. Great historians, from time to time, tell the best true stories which
their topics and problems permit. Narration is not the only form of
explanation they use, but it is one of the more common and most
characteristically historical forms.[1]

A story explains how and what—not why. For many epistemologists
this is no explanation at all. But if explaining is understood to mean
what every dictionary says it means, and what common usage makes it
mean—namely, making clear, plain, and understandable—then story-
telling is a form of explanation which is common not merely in historical scholarship but in a dozen other disciplines and in daily life as
well. When a policeman arrives at the scene of an accident and asks,
"What happened?" he wishes to hear a true story. When a child asks,
"What was World War II?" or "Who was Winston Churchill?" he wants

1. This point, important as it is, has recently been exaggerated by epistemologists. Note
three errors in the following statement: "The difference between history and science is
not that history does and science does not employ organizing schemes which go beyond what is given. Both do. The difference has to do with the *kind* of organizing
schemes employed by each. *History* tells true stories." (Arthur C. Danto, *Analytical
Philosophy of History* [Cambridge, 1965], p. 111).

First, *history* tells no tales—*historians* tell them. Second, scientists are storytellers
too. All scientists use story schemas some of the time; some use them nearly all the
time. Examples are geologists, paleontologists, and astronomers. Third, historians use
many other organizing schemes in their work, occasionally in place of narratives, and
often in addition to them. It is, I think, an error to distinguish history from the sciences
on epistemological grounds alone.

and usually gets an explanation in the form of a short narrative history of the war or a simple narrative biography of the statesman.

Sometimes narrative explanations are very short and simple and yet sufficient to the task at hand. The question "What happened at the battle of Gettysburg?" might be answered by the shortest story imaginable—Lee lost. No generalizations are required, and no cause, no motive, no elaborate composite-models, no analogies, and no pedantical detail.

But in anything more than this atomic form, storytelling becomes exceedingly complex. This chapter will be confined to merely one elementary aspect of an immensely intricate subject—the problem of time and temporal integrity in a narrative. A sense of time is not a simple thing. Time is something which people must painfully learn to think clearly about—something, indeed, which they must be taught. And there are many obstacles in the path of understanding it. It is difficult enough in this day and age for a person to imagine that there really was a past and that there will be a future. But even when that lesson is learned, one must master the idea that there are many different pasts and futures, and many different degrees of pastness and futurity. A child's history of the United States is likely to locate all past events on a single plane. Winthrop, Washington, Lincoln, and Kennedy are dimly perceived as chronological contemporaries, without depth, breadth, or temporal discrimination.

Psychologists have demonstrated that these discriminations are difficult for a young mind to master. It is hard for children to understand that Philadelphia is simultaneously north of Baltimore and south of New York—particularly if they happen to live in Boston. In precisely the same way, they cannot quickly grasp the idea that Washington was simultaneously in Winthrop's future and Lincoln's past. Adults often have this trouble, too. The dimness of their temporal perceptions may be the deeper reason for many so-called factual mistakes. It was said of Mrs. Disraeli, for example, that "she could never remember who came first, the Greeks or the Romans."[2] Mrs. Disraeli's difficulty may have derived from the fact that Greeks and Romans really existed for her as chronological contemporaries.

The memories of many professional historians seem to work a little better than Mrs. Disraeli's. But not much better. Some symptoms of time trouble are the following fallacies.

ॐ The *fallacy of anachronism* is the common denominator of most forms of error in this chapter. It generally consists in the description,

2. Robert Blake, *Disraeli* (New York, 1968), p. 146.

analysis, or judgment of an event as if it occurred at some point in time other than when it actually happened. If the event is located too early in time, then the error is sometimes pedantically called a "prochronism." If it is made to happen too late, then the result is a "metachronism."

Anachronisms flourish in a profusion of particular forms. A simple mistaken date is technically an anachronism, as when a recent student of Benjamin Franklin somehow made his hero die in the wrong year.[3] So also is a single misplaced object, event, or word. The title of William Allen White's biography of Calvin Coolidge provides two examples in four words—*A Puritan in Babylon.*[4]

These howlers are unimportant in themselves, except as signs of more serious analytical anachronisms, by means of which many historical problems have been grossly misconceived. Consider the case of an iconoclastic book called *Jefferson and Civil Liberties: The Darker Side* (Cambridge, 1963), in which the author, Leonard Levy, committed an analytical anachronism of serious proportions.

Levy argued that there was "a strong pattern of unlibertarian or even antilibertarian thought and behavior extending throughout Jefferson's long career," and specifically that Jefferson countenanced loyalty oaths, internment camps, bills of attainder, Blackstonian prosecutions for seditious libel, censorship of books and words and even thoughts, infringements of academic freedom, and violations of various provisions of the Bill of Rights. This indictment is accompanied by epithets such as "obnoxious," "abhorrent," "sophistical," "narrow and ritualistic," and many disparaging comments upon Jefferson's mind and character.[5]

Critical reviewers have brought some of Levy's factual statements into dispute.[6] But there is a deeper deficiency in the book. Levy asserts that "during Jefferson's lifetime, there was never an issue for which incontestably familiar libertarian standards were lacking to guide his judgment. Experience with the application of certain of those standards may have been slim, yet the standards themselves had been established."[7]

This, I believe, is a very great mistake on Levy's part. It is factually

---

3. John H. Best, *Benjamin Franklin on Education* (New York, 1962), p. 7.
4. (New York, 1938); see also H. P. Gambrell, *Mirabeau Buonaparte Lamar: Troubadour and Crusader* (Dallas, 1934); Carleton Mabie, *American Leonardo: A Life of Samuel F. B. Morse* (New York, 1943); and S. H. Brockunier, *The Irrepressible Democrat: Roger Williams* (New York, 1940).
5. See, e.g., pp. xii, 27, 40, 42, 50, 55. An exception is the first chapter, in which Jefferson is praised for his religious libertarianism.
6. A good and fair review by Joseph H. Harrison, Jr., appears in *The William and Mary Quarterly,* 3d ser. 21 (1964): 451–54.
7. P. 20.

false to argue that there were incontestably familiar libertarian standards in Jefferson's own day. Levy himself, and others, have demonstrated that there were many different ideas of liberty which were eminently contestable—and constantly contested in that era. There were new ideas of free expression, which some of Jefferson's younger supporters avowed but which Jefferson did not. And there were other conflicting ideas in various stages of development, with a good deal of confusion in between.

Moreover, there were many difficult problems in the early Republic for which no "incontestably familiar libertarian standards" exist, even today: the problem of civil liberties in wartime, the problem of the extension of liberty to people who are determined to destroy the liberty of others—these are questions for which there are no easy answers. Jeffersonian answers were sometimes of the sort which Levy and the American Civil Liberties Union condemn as "unlibertarian." But always Jefferson's responses were of such a nature that Jefferson himself could honestly and consistently reasonably claim them as libertarian—according to his lights.

Levy formed in his own mind an idea of what civil liberties *should* entail—an idea which has *some* relevance in *some* of its particulars to *some* of Jefferson's associates (men younger than Jefferson himself). Then he proceeded to condemn Jefferson, sometimes explicitly, sometimes by innuendo, for not living up to this exalted atemporal standard. In short, Levy analyzed and evaluated Jefferson by measuring his acts and attitudes against the standards of the ACLU and tallying all the discrepancies. The result is objectionable not merely because it is unfair to Jefferson but also because it distorts and falsifies the texture of Jeffersonian thought.

Anachronisms of this sort are sometimes so subtle and intricate that they consistently elude analysis and understanding. A disturbing case in point is the work of Douglas Southall Freeman, who possessed an extraordinary talent for seven-volume studies of Victorian gentlemen—which Robert E. Lee was, but George Washington emphatically wasn't. Nevertheless, Freeman clapped a cocked hat on the head of General Lee, and called him General Washington. The underlying errors are exceedingly difficult to locate with precision. But somehow the psychic processes are wrong—the attitudes and responses of Freeman's Washington belong to a man born in 1807 rather than in 1732.[8]

Complex anachronisms are not merely matters of sterile academic

8. Cf. the criticism of Perry Miller in *The William and Mary Quarterly*, 3d ser. 9 (1952): 226–29.

interest. They are snares that have caught up many people in the world. Consider the case of the Cox Commission report, an attempt by a group composed mostly of lawyers to produce something like a history of the student rebellion at Columbia University in 1968. The authors were able and intelligent men, but their honest attempt to understand the thought patterns of another generation was marred by analytical anachronism. They sought to explain the discontent of student rebels by quoting a character in J. D. Salinger's *Franny and Zooey*! My students laughed uproariously at this gaffe. They suggested that the Commission might as well have studied the works of Scott Fitzgerald.[9]

&ᴥ The *fallacy of presentism* is a complex anachronism, in which the antecedent in a narrative series is falsified by being defined or interpreted in terms of the consequent. Sometimes called the fallacy of *nunc pro tunc*, it is the mistaken idea that the proper way to do history is to prune away the dead branches of the past, and to preserve the green buds and twigs which have grown into the dark forest of our contemporary world. Imagine two historians, both studying the same problem, which happened thus:

	Time	Events				
(Past)	1	A	B	C	D	E
	2	B	C	D	E	F
	3	C	D	E	F	G
	4	D	E	F	G	H
(Present)	5	E	F	G	H	I

A total of twenty-five events actually happened, in this hypothetical matrix of pastness.[10] Suppose that each historian can select fifteen of them. The presentist chooses the following:

9. Archibald Cox et al., *Crisis at Columbia: Report of the Fact-Finding Commission Appointed to Investigate the Disturbances at Columbia University in April and May, 1968* (New York, 1968), p. 23.
10. This matrix, like those which follow, is meant merely as an heuristic device. There is, of course, no such symmetry in any past problem. A more realistic representation might be provided by the following method. Take a Jackson Pollock painting and cut it into a jigsaw puzzle with a hundred thousand parts. Throw away all the corner pieces, two-thirds of the edge pieces, and one-half of the rest. What remains is a little closer to the problems historians actually study.

Time		Events			
(Past)	1					E
	2				E	F
	3			E	F	G
	4		E	F	G	H
(Present)	5	E	F	G	H	I

The other historian, who is not a presentist, selects the same number of events by a different method of sampling. The result is:

Time		Events				
(Past)	1	A	B	C	D	E
	2					
	3	C	D	E	F	G
	4					
(Present)	5	E	F	G	H	I

The latter pattern not merely provides a more satisfactory sense of the configuration of past events, but also a more enlightening perspective upon the present. The presentist method is self-contradictory. In the name of modernity and relevance and utility, it sacrifices precisely that kind of knowledge which historians can most usefully provide: knowledge useful in the establishment of present trends and future tendencies.

There are many examples in historical scholarship. One of them is a standard textbook in intellectual history, John Herman Randall's *The Making of the Modern Mind,* first published in 1926. The author's avowed purpose was "to explore the mind of the present generation, to unravel the many threads that enter into its tangled fabric and trace them back to their first appearance in the loom of history."[11] The result is the usual humbug about Hebrews and Greeks, the "modernity" of the Renaissance and the "democracy" of the Reformation.[12] Each of Randall's backward projections of present phenomena so grossly distorts the past that the reader receives an utterly erroneous idea of events in earlier periods, and of tendencies in his own as well. A reader who wishes to discover the damage which is done by Randall's unfortunate method might examine his version of Copernicus, whom he makes into a John-the-Baptist for Isaac Newton, and compare it with a contrasting interpretation by an excellent historian of science, Thomas

11. John Herman Randall, *The Making of the Modern Mind,* rev. ed. (Boston, 1940), p. 4.
12. Ibid., pp. 144, 165.

S. Kuhn.[13] In terms of our matrices, Randall interpreted Copernicus in period one as E; Kuhn represented him as ABCDE. The two results are radically different, and Kuhn's is surely superior.

The fallacy of presentism is a common failing in historical writing by men who have never been trained in the discipline of history. A very great man, in his own field, may serve as a second example. Bernard Berenson was an art critic of splendid gifts. But he wasn't a historian —which was unlucky for him, and unhappy in its consequences, for he wrote several fat volumes of what are commonly called "art history." In a lively little volume called *Aesthetics and History* he included a chapter on "significant events in history," in which he made explicit his criteria of selection. Berenson's view was precisely the same as Randall's.

> Significant events [he wrote] are those events that have contributed to making us what we are today . . . art history must avoid what has not contributed to the main stream, no matter how interesting, how magnificent in itself. It should exclude, for instance, most German and even Spanish and Dutch art. It should dwell less and less on Italian art after Caravaggio, and end altogether by the middle of the eighteenth century with Solimena and Tiepolo. Except for Ribera, Murillo, Velasquez and Goya in Spain, and Schongauer and Dürer and Holbein in German lands, the painters of these countries are neither in the main line of development nor of universal appeal to cultivated Europeans.[14]

Berenson was a historical relativist when he wrote this book. He allowed that every culture must have its own art history. But for himself and his culture, he casually dismissed as nonevents all artistic accomplishments "from western Kamchatka to Singapore, from Greenland's icy mountains to Patagonia's stormy capes, in Africa and on the islands of the sea." And he was equally cavalier with all "the arts of China and of India, remarkable and deeply human as they are."[15] They might do for a Chinaman or an Indian, he conceded, but they "are not history for us Europeans," he wrote.

Berenson's outlook, I think, differs from that of many other art historians only in the degree to which its assumptions are spelled out, and in the zeal with which they are extended to their logical conclusion. Other art historians are more moderate in their statements, if not in their thoughts. But a glance at the syllabus of an art history survey course or the contents of a text in this field suggests that more than a

---

13. Thomas S. Kuhn, *The Copernican Revolution* (Cambridge, Mass., 1957); *The Structure of Scientific Revolutions* (Chicago, 1962).
14. Bernard Berenson, *Aesthetics and History* (New York, 1948; 2d ed., 1954), pp. 257–58.
15. Ibid., p. 257.

few art historians are still chugging along Berenson's main line, pulling passenger cars full of culture-hungry coeds. The main line isn't quite as narrow-gauged as it used to be, there are more side excursions, and the locomotives are a little more powerful. But the trip itself is much the same.

Academic historians are not exempt from the same error. Consider the case of Geoffrey Barraclough, a distinguished medievalist, now converted to "contemporary history." Barraclough has published two enthusiastically present-minded volumes, premised upon the notion that since 1943, or thereabouts, traditional European historiography has been reduced to irrelevance. "The traditional Europe—the Europe of our history books, the Europe of Louis XIV and Napoleon and Bismarck—is dead and beyond resurrection, and we may disabuse our minds of the illusion that there is any special relevance, from the point of view of contemporary affairs, in studying those neolithic figures," he believes.[16]

I can't imagine that Barraclough means to be taken literally, but he clearly intends to be taken seriously.

> It [is] only a pardonable exaggeration [he writes], to say that, for me, it was the Russian victory at Stalingrad in 1943 that made a total revision of European history imperative. I realized with consternation that three years in an English and two years in a German university had left me for all practical purposes ignorant of eastern European history, save at a few points where it caught the limelight. . . . I knew a great deal of the machinery of the papal chancery in the thirteenth and fourteenth centuries, and of writings of the canonists; but I knew nothing of the Piasts, Przemyslids and the Ruriks. . . . I had some notion of the place of the emperor Charles IV in history, but knew little more than the names of his contemporaries, Louis the Great of Hungary and Casmir the Great of Poland. I had read all the surviving letters of St. Boniface, the apostle of the Germans, but nothing of St. Cyril and St. Methodius, the apostles of the Slavs.[17]

It is impossible not to sympathize with Barraclough in his protest against the narrow parochialism of so many (though not all) European historians during the past two centuries. But his method would mark the end not merely of Eurocentric history but of history itself. What, one wonders, would be the task of ancient and medieval historians if the Germans had won the battle of Stalingrad? By Barracloughian logic, Peter the Great, Alexander I, and even the great Lenin himself would then become unpersons, instead of Bismarck & Co.; and our survey courses would serve up a spicy schnitzel of Aravisci, Vangiones, and Triboci, in place of a goulash of Piasts, Przemyslids, etc.

16. Geoffrey Barraclough, *History in a Changing World* (Oxford, 1955), p. 217.
17. Ibid., p. 10.

Surely any standard of significance which requires a 180-degree turn in interpretations of the history of Europe before the fourteenth century, because of the outcome of a battle in 1943, is not merely mistaken but absurd.[18]

No discussion of presentism in history can be complete without the classic example of the "Whig interpretation of history," which has been defined by Herbert Butterfield as the "tendency in many historians to write on the side of Protestants and Whigs, to praise revolutions provided they have been successful, to emphasise certain principles of progress in the past and to produce a story which is the ratification if not the glorification of the present."[19]

I have heard historians use the pejorative phrase "Whig history" as a synonym for any kind of presentism, which is unfair to Whiggery. The same sort of error appears in works by scholars of all political persuasions. There is, for instance, an anti-Whig history which commits the same fallacy in an inverted form. Examples include the later works of Henry Cabot Lodge and Henry and Brooks Adams. The latter, it is said, used to greet each day by singing a song of his own invention, which consisted entirely of three repeated words: "God damn it! God damn it! God damn it!" For these gentlemen, history was indeed one goddamned thing after another—a steady spiral running downward toward the left, and culminating in some dark catastrophe—lava flowing through the streets of Quincy, or a tidal wave crashing upon Nahant, or a wild-eyed mob of Jews and Irishmen smashing in the doors of the Boston Athenaeum and scribbling madly in the margins of books.

Presentism equally appears in the new-liberal narratives of Arthur Schlesinger, Jr., where American history is the steady progress of pragmatic liberalism from Jefferson to Jackson to Franklin Roosevelt. Finally, the Kennedys become Top Family, and History comes to a .

The so-called New Political History does not display this deficiency in so gross a form. As historians begin to fill their monographs with more sophisticated analyses, the temptations for this species of simplicity tend to diminish. But presentism still appears, in some surprising forms. A case in point is William Nisbet Chambers' *Political Parties in a New Nation,* an analytical history of the development of party structure in the United States. For Chambers, parties are a Good Thing. "If party

18. Pieter Geyl, "Geoffrey Barraclough, or the Scrapping of History," *Encounters in History* (Cleveland, 1961), pp. 336–40.
19. Herbert Butterfield, *The Whig Interpretation of History* (London, 1931), Preface. Butterfield took a different position in a subsequent work, *The Englishman and His History* (Cambridge, 1944), thus permitting E. H. Carr to have a little fun with "the proto-Butterfield" and "the deutero-Butterfield," in *What Is History?* (New York, 1962), p. 51.

politics are contrasted with the near-chaos of faction politics that preceded the formation of parties," he wrote, "it becomes apparent that even a loose party system brings substantial advantages in both democratic responsibility and coherence."[20]

Chambers understands faction politics as pre-party politics. He defines the antecedent in terms of the consequent, and the result is a falsification of the former. Faction politics, of course, were not at all a condition of near-chaos, before Jefferson and John Beckley brought order and light. Factions functioned very well indeed in a different kind of political environment. As that environment changed, new party forms were created to serve new functions. Chambers' retrospective symmetry, in short, distorts both the factions which preceded parties and the parties themselves.

The problem of retrospective symmetry in historical narration is a tough one, for without retrospection there can be no history, and without symmetry there can be no narrative. But whenever retrospective symmetry takes such a form that parts of the story are falsified, then the fallacy of presentism results.

ჽა The converse of presentism is the *antiquarian fallacy,* for which a brief note should suffice. An antiquarian is a collector of dead facts, which he stuffs full of sawdust and separately encloses in small glass cases. Often, he is a gentleman (or lady) of respectable origins who is utterly alienated from the present. The past serves him as a sanctuary from a sordid world which he neither accepts nor understands. His matrix of pastness looks a little like this:

	Time	Past events
(Past)	1	A B C D
	2	B C D
	3	C D
	4	D
(Present)	5	$@#%?!*¢#**!!

At the Boston Athenaeum, one may discover flocks of tiny birdlike old gentlemen, who nest in eery piles of dirty yellow paper and brood their myths and memories into monumental Lives-and-Letters. In every

20. William Nisbet Chambers, *Political Parties in a New Nation* (New York, 1963), Foreword.

New England town library, there is likely to be an ancient Puritan virgin, shriveled and dried in the snows of sixty Massachuetts winters and suitably shrouded in black bombazine, who has been at work for the past twenty years on the story of her home town from 1633 to 1933, when Franklin Roosevelt was inaugurated and history came to an end. In the Maryland Historical Society one might find a retired colonel, impeccably dressed, with the Bronze Star in one buttonhole and the rosette of the Company of Military Collectors in the other, who is writing a monograph on the smallclothes of the Continental Army. At the American Jewish Historical Society there may be an elderly gentleman at work on an article called "A Jewish Tourist at the Battle of Bladensburg." In the New York Public Library there may be a desiccated country clergyman, in black oxfords and white athletic socks, who is at work on a county history of his denomination, from King William's War to the Peace of Ghent, in two octavo volumes, illustrated. Three years ago, the University of Oklahoma Press published a book by a petroleum geologist who is said to possess the world's largest private collection of barbed wire, which he apparently treasures in the proper antiquarian spirit.[21]

But the antiquarian fallacy is not confined to antiquarians. Whenever a professional historian deliberately tries to cut himself off from his own time in order to study somebody else's, he commits the same mistake. Winthrop Jordan, author of a splendid scholarly work on white American attitudes toward Negroes before 1812, is an example. "I have attempted, indeed, to avoid reading widely in the literature of the present crisis because it is frequently so tempting to read the past backwards— and very dangerous," he writes.[22] One may sympathize with Jordan's desire to avoid the presentist fallacy, but deliberate ignorance is no defense.

Many other historians (the number is diminishing) have argued that a history of ongoing events ought not to be attempted, because objectivity is impossible, evidence is incomplete, and perspective is difficult to attain.[23] But all these complaints also apply to ancient history, if not precisely in the same degree. Most reasonable men would agree, I think, that the history of contemporary events presents some special

21. Francis T. and Henry D. McCallum, *The Wire That Fenced the West* (Norman, Okla., 1965).

22. Winthrop D. Jordan, *White over Black* (Chapel Hill, N.C., 1968), p. ix.

23. Geoffrey Barraclough discusses this controversy, which has been going on for forty years and more in the English journal *History,* in *An Introduction to Contemporary History* (New York, 1965), pp. 11–20.

difficulties but many other opportunities. To rule out events because they are living is as mistaken as the opposite error.

&ν The *fallacy of tunnel history* is identified by J. H. Hexter, and so-named after the tendency of many historians to

> split the past into a series of tunnels, each continuous from the remote past to the present, but practically self-contained at every point and sealed off from contact with or contamination by anything that was going on in any of the other tunnels. At their entrances these tunnels bore signs saying diplomatic history, political history, institutional history, ecclesiastical history, intellectual history, military history, economic history, legal history, administrative history, art history, colonial history, social history, agricultural history, and so on, and so on. At first glance one might think that these kinds of history came into being as a consequence of a rational attempt at an exhaustive classification of what is knowable about the past, and that history continues to be written under these headings *because* the classification represents the best way to deal with the past. Nothing could be further from the truth. Whether or not the current classification provides the best means for exploring the past, it did not come into being as a result of any conscious aiming at the best on the part of historians.
>
> What mainly determined the way historians split up history during the past century was a ridiculously adventitious set of circumstances: the way in which public authorities and private persons tended to order the documents which suited their purposes to preserve. The basis of constitutional history was the preservation and segregation of the commands of the superior public authorities, of administrative history the care with which accountable public servants preserved the documents for which they were responsible, of intellectual history the irrepressible urge of intellectuals and literary folk to hand on their maunderings to posterity and to display their erudition by references to the writings of other intellectual and literary folk, and so on.[24]

In terms of a hypothetical historical matrix, tunnel history takes a problem which happened thus:

	Time	Past events				
(Past)	1	A	B	C	D	E
	2	B	C	D	E	F
	3	C	D	E	F	G
	4	D	E	F	G	H
(Present)	5	E	F	G	H	I

and converts it into

24. J. H. Hexter, *Reappraisals in History* (Evanston, Ill., 1961), pp. 194–95.

	Time	Past events
(Past)	1	A
	2	B
	3	C
	4	D
(Present)	5	E

or maybe

	Time	Past events			
(Past)	1				E
	2			E	
	3		E		
	4	E			
(Present)	5	E			

Each of these versions of the past is not merely incomplete but seriously inaccurate, which is what happens when a complex problem of development is taken apart and its components are extruded into long thin ribbons of change.

Unpleasant things are apt to happen when one grimy historical tunneler bumps into another, somewhere in the dark, and disputes the right of way with pick and shovel. In these altercations, the fallacy of essences is apt to be the ultimate weapon. Charles Beard, for example, insisted that the United States Constitution was "essentially an economic document." To this, Henry Steele Commager made the absurd reply that it "was, and is, *essentially* a political document."[25] Surely the Constitution was in some respects an economic document and in other respects a political document, and essentially neither, and indeed *essentially* nothing.

The same delusion is much more dangerous when it appears in arguments over American strategy in Vietnam. Some insist that a successful policy must be "essentially political" or "essentially social" or "essentially military" or "essentially educational" or "essentially economic" or "essentially cultural." Again, the tunnelers (few of whom, in this instance, are academic historians) meet in the dark and fight it out, and everybody loses.[26]

25. Charles A. Beard, *An Economic Interpretation of the Constitution* (New York, 1935), p. 324; Henry Steele Commager, *The Search for a Usable Past* (New York, 1967), p. 60.
26. Cf. Hexter, *Reappraisals in History*, p. 199.

There are many different kinds of tunnels in historiography. Among the narrowest and darkest are the ethnic tunnels. And of all the ethnic tunnels, none is quite so dark and narrow as that which is called "Jewish history." There are many important and even urgent things to be written about the history of the Jewish people, but the present mode of writing and research is a scandal and an abomination in its profound provinciality. Jewish historiography converts a matrix such as:

	Time	*Past events*				
(Past)	1	F	G	H	I	J
	2	G	H	I	J	K
	3	H	I	J	K	L
	4	I	J	K	L	M
(Present)	5	J	K	L	M	N

into:

	Time	*Past events*				
(Past)	1				J	
	2			J		
	3		J			
	4	J				
(Present)	5	J				

The American Jewish Historical Society, for instance, dutifully subscribed for many years to a large number of historical journals, some of which are rare today. But the librarians of that institution believed it their duty to snip out everything in the journals which explicitly referred to Jews and to throw away the rest. One might doubt that any chosen people are quite as chosen as all that.

It ought to be apparent that people who are commonly called Jews by reason of their membership in an ethnic-religious group are also at the same time members of many other groups. No problem in their history can be resolved within the single aspect of their Jewishness. This fact, which many Jews and non-Jews alike are reluctant to acknowledge, is the great antidote to the poison of anti-Semitism which has caused so much suffering and hatred and death in the world.

 క్కు   The *fallacy of false periodization* consists in assigning inappropriate temporal limits to a historical problem. It is sometimes asserted that all periodization is necessarily false and artificial. This, I think, is incorrect. Maitland's famous epigram that history is a "seamless web" betrays the holist bias of that great historian. History is a web of many seams. The problem is not that a scholar must make one out of whole cloth, so to speak, but that he must choose one out of many, and that he may make a mistaken choice.

One common kind of false periodization might be called hecto-history. It happens when history is neatly chopped into Procrustean periods, each precisely a hundred years long. The fascination of a rounded number is irresistible. "We tend to count by centuries," Marc Bloch complained.

> We no longer name ages after their heroes. We very prudently number them in sequence every hundred years, starting from a point fixed, once and for all, at the year 1 of the Christian era. The art of the thirteenth century, the philosophy of the eighteenth, the "stupid nineteenth": these faces in arithmetical masks haunt the pages of our books. Which of us will boast of having never fallen prey to the lures of their apparent convenience?[27]

This species of distortion may be particularly serious in France, owing to an accident of language, by which the single word *siècle* has an unfortunate double meaning—both "century" and "period." English-speaking historians are a little luckier in this respect. Nevertheless, the fallacy of hectohistory often appears in the United Kingdom and the United States. What Thomas Hardy called the "centuried years" are commonly yoked together: "Each century seen in perspective, has its own unique pattern. The thirteenth century was one of deep contrasts: of consummate skill and real elegance side by side with barbaric and primitive ignorance; of cruelty and corruption on the one hand and saintly courage on the other."[28]

Hectohistory is undoubtedly useful to undergraduates, as it was to T. E. Lawrence, sometime of Arabia. It is reported that "In his History Finals at Oxford he spoke merely in centuries—'in the beginning of the twelfth' or 'towards the end of the fifteenth century,' etc. Only once he named a date—in brackets: 'about the middle of the eleventh century (1066).' . . ."[29]

The same generic form of error has imposed itself on history in

27. Marc Bloch, *The Historian's Craft* (New York, 1953), pp. 181–82.
28. T. Beamish, *Battle Royal: A New Account of Simon de Montfort's Struggle Against King Henry III* (New York, 1966), p. 31; for another example see Henry Horowitz, *Revolution Politicks: The Career of Daniel Finch, Second Earl of Nottingham* (Cambridge, 1968), p. vii.
29. Sir Lewis Namier, "Lawrence: As I Knew Him," *In the Margin of History* (London, 1939), p. 279.

many other forms. More than a few Christian scholars have made most things divisible by three. Others have been obsessed with a periodization based upon the four monarchies in the prophecy of Daniel (2:40). Still others have divided the past into six ages, according to the six days of creation. A few medieval scholars sundered things seven ways, in proportion to the seven planets. In Vietnam, nine is a lucky number. Among astrologers, twelves seem more natural than tens.[30]

A different form of false periodization appears when a historian takes a time scheme which may be valid and functional in problem *A* and transfers it to problem *B,* where it is invalid and dysfunctional. American history is still periodized in the textbooks by presidential administrations, which are perfectly proper for a history of the presidency but not for the development of American society, which possesses its own set of inaugurations and retirements.[31] This unfortunate method of periodization is quite as primitive as that which traditionally prevailed in the oral history of the Congo, where history was reckoned in rainy seasons and dry.[32]

Another kind of periodization error is one in which the historiographical medium provides the method. A classic example is that species of quasi-historical writing which appears in newspapers and newsmagazines. Academic historians are often contemptuous of the historical interpretations of journalists—and properly so. Those failings are attributable not to the cultural barbarism of the fourth estate, but rather to the scheme of periodization which is forced upon it. Time, for a newspaperman, is measured in the intervals between editions. His often desperate effort to find some significant happening in each of these periods explains his shallowness, rather than ignorance or illiteracy or the company he keeps.

A fourth kind of periodization error is a kind of temporal reduction, in which a very large temporal period scheme is hung upon a very small peg. A famous example is Michelet's division of the reign of Louis XIV into two periods, "avant la fistule" and "après la fistule"—a great epoch in the history of a great nation, periodized by a painful anal fistula on the bottom of the man at the top.[33]

---

30. Wallace K. Ferguson, *The Renaissance in Historical Thought* (Cambridge, 1948), p. 6, passim; Philippe Ariès, *Centuries of Childhood* (New York, 1962), pp. 18–25.
31. Thomas C. Cochran, "The 'Presidential Synthesis' in American History," *American Historical Review*, 53 (1948): 748–59.
32. Jan Vansina, *Oral Tradition* (Chicago, 1965), p. 100.
33. G. J. Renier, *History, Its Purpose and Method* (New York, 1965), p. 118, notes that this interpretation "can be disproved through the study of the diary kept by the physicians of the *Grand Monarque*. This manuscript, which was published in the nineteenth century, reveals that the health of Louis had been extremely bad for many years before a *fistula*

ஃ The *telescopic fallacy* makes a long story short. It appears in interpretations which reduce an extended trend to a momentary transformation. This form of error is common today, and likely to become still more so, as historians become increasingly interested in putting big questions to little tests. When they do so, they must be careful not to attempt to find a solution to the entire problem within the narrow range of the period tested.

Three generalized examples should suffice. First, there has been a good deal of loose talk about *the* historical revolution, i.e., *the* moment of a great expansion in historical consciousness. The historical revolution has been located by various monographers in ancient Sumer, ancient China, ancient Israel, ancient Greece, and ancient Rome; in the thought of a miscellany of medieval Christians, Jews, and Arabs; in the twelfth-century Renaissance; in fifteenth-century Italy, seventeenth-century England, eighteenth-century France, nineteenth-century Germany, and various twentieth-century movements. There was probably a development of historical consciousness in all these periods and places. But *the* development of historical consciousness occurred in none of them. Any attempt to locate a protracted trend in a brief period, as, for instance, F. Smith Fussner does in *The Historical Revolution: English Historical Writing and Thought, 1580–1640* (New York, 1962), is fallacious.

Another example is the problem of the decline of deference in English society. Lawrence Stone located this extended development in the early seventeenth century. Virginia Woolf, on the other hand, placed it in the twentieth century with remarkable precision.

> In or about December, 1910 [she wrote], human character changed, I am not saying that one went out, as one might into a garden, and there saw that a rose had flowered, or that a hen had laid an egg. The change was not sudden and definite like that. But a change there was nevertheless; and since one must be arbitrary, let us date it about the year 1910. The first signs of it are recorded in the books of Samuel Butler, in *The Way of All Flesh* in particular; the plays of Bernard Shaw continue to record it. In life one can see the change, if I may use a homely illustration, in the character of one's cook.[34]

Other scholars have dated the decline of deference in still other ways—in eighteenth- or nineteenth-century England, for example. It seems reasonable to guess that so extraordinary a transformation occurred gradually (not steadily) over many generations. Maybe human

---

analis was diagnosed, and that this new illness was not an exceptional phenomenon in the career of this coarse contemner of hygiene and sensible living."

34. Virginia Woolf, "Mr. Bennett and Mrs. Brown," *Collected Essays*, 4 vols. (London, 1966), 1:321.

character *did* change a little, in December, 1910, but also in 1810, and 1710. One wonders if trend can be stretched back as far as 1610 without breaking. The apparent intensity of deference politics in late seventeenth-, eighteenth-, and nineteenth-century England would appear to contradict Stone's thesis. But let us give him the benefit of the doubt and assume that there was, indeed, something like a decline of deference in his period. The next question concerns the relationship of that decline to developments in other periods. Stone does not help us find the answer. He telescopes the problem into his period, and, except for a few brief and inconclusive passages, he ignores other eras.[35]

A third academic example of the telescopic fallacy occurs in a book called *The Strange Career of Jim Crow,* by C. Vann Woodward.[36] The author argues for the "relative recency" of the establishment of racial segregation in the South—specifically that "bonds of intimacy" existed between the races during slavery, that there was a period of "forgotten alternatives" after the Civil War, and that the "capitulation to racism" occurred in the South during the 1890s and afterward. Woodward's purpose, apparently, was to demonstrate to Southerners that their allegedly "immutable folkways" were in fact modern mutations, which, having changed once recently, could change again.

This thesis was greeted with enthusiasm by many of Woodward's colleagues—some of whom proclaimed to the world that "racial segregation in the Old South had been unknown," and that Jim Crow "did not spring directly from slavery or from the timeworn customs of many generations," and that before the Civil War, "the circumstances which later gave rise to the segregation codes could not exist."[37]

These unguarded statements, and the more moderate thesis from which they stem, are classic examples of the telescopic fallacy. Much recent work has demonstrated in great detail that Woodward's argument is wrong in all its major parts—wrong because he made a long story short. There is abundant evidence of a "capitulation to racism" by Americans, both above and below the Mason-Dixon line, long before 1890. No period of "forgotten alternatives" existed after the Civil War— racial segregation was immediately imposed by law and custom. Even before the war, segregation formally existed wherever free Negroes could

---

35. Lawrence Stone, *The Crisis of the Aristocracy: 1558–1641* (New York, 1965), pp. 7–17, 746–53 passim.
36. (Oxford, 1955).
37. Barton J. Bernstein, "*Plessy* v. *Ferguson*: Conservative Sociological Jurisprudence," *Journal of Negro History* 48 (1963): 200; John S. Ezell, *The South Since 1865* (New York, 1963), p. 184; Charles Crowe, ed., *The Age of Civil War and Reconstruction* (Homewood, Ill., 1966), p. 439; quoted in Roger A. Fischer, "Racial Segregation in Ante Bellum New Orleans," *The American Historical Review* 74 (1969): 926–27.

be found. And most important, slavery functioned in the Southern states not merely as a labor system but also as an instrument of social control which was itself a form of racial segregation (physical as well as social) more extreme in many ways than the most elaborate Jim Crow codes. In short, the history of racism *and* racial segregation in Anglo-America is a very long story indeed. Woodward telescoped it into the narrow span of his own special period, and thereby falsified it.[38] There were undoubtedly important changes in the quality of racist thought, and in the shape of racist institutions, during Woodward's narrow period—changes which affected a far larger area than merely the South. But the fact remains that the thesis of the *Strange Career of Jim Crow* truncates one of the enduring themes of American history.[39]

This form of the telescopic fallacy—in which distant origins are forgotten—is its most common form. It is a serious problem in historians' sources as well as in their own writings. Survey research has yielded solid evidence that respondents often tend to telescope their retrospections. Historians face similar problems in retrospective accounts of events.[40]

Precisely the same error often occurs today in discussions of contemporary problems. How many commentators on the consequences of "automation" have assumed that the introduction of labor-saving machinery is something which our generation is the first to face? It is an incredible error, and yet one which is very common and very deleterious in its influence upon strategies designed to deal with the problem. Sometimes it makes a mighty difference to know how long ago something began to happen.

⊱ Conversely, the *interminable fallacy* makes a short story long, or a long story longer than it ought to be. It is a temporal form of a

38. Among many recent revisionary works, see Joel Williamson, *After Slavery* (Chapel Hill, 1965); Richard C. Wade, *Slavery in the Cities: The South, 1820–1860* (New York, 1964); Leon Litwack, *North of Slavery* (Chicago, 1961); V. Jacque Voegeli, *Free but Not Equal: The Midwest and the Negro During the Civil War* (Chicago, 1967); and Winthrop Jordan, *White over Black* (Chapel Hill, 1968).

39. Through two revisions, the author has held his ground with a tenacity worthy of a better cause. The result is another fallacy—the overwhelming exception (see above, chapter 4). We are now told that the interpretation applies to all Southern institutions *except* churches, schools, militia, hotels, restaurants, public buildings, jails, hospitals, asylums, gardens, railroads in several states, and the New Orleans Opera House. It applies to all Negroes but freedmen, hired slaves, urban Negroes, South Carolina Negroes, and in some respects Negro field hands (1957 ed., p. 15; 1966 ed., pp. 12, 13–17, 25–26).

40. John Neter and Joseph Waksberg, "A Study of Response Errors in Expenditures Data from Household Interviews," *Journal of the American Statistical Association* 59 (1964): 18–55.

false extrapolation—a developmental trend stretched beyond the breaking point.

A familiar example is that omnipresent cliché of modern European historiography, the "rise of the middle class." This group has been found rising most remarkably in every period from the twelfth century to the twentieth. It has been used to explain the Renaissance and the Reformation, absolutism and liberalism, monarchy and republicanism, conservatism and radicalism, nationalism and internationalism, romanticism and rationalism, fascism and communism, the commercial revolution, the managerial revolution, the agricultural revolution, the industrial revolution, the Puritan revolution, the American Revolution, the French Revolution, the Russian Revolution, etc., etc.

If the middle class had in fact been rising as powerfully as this, it should presently be somewhere in the disciplinary jurisdiction of astronomers, who alone could measure its continuous ascension with their powerful instruments.

This risible phenomenon surely requires no extended refutation. But the interested reader might examine an unfortunate book by Louis B. Wright called *Middle-Class Culture in Elizabethan England* (Chapel Hill, 1935), and an excellent critique by J. H. Hexter, called "The Myth of the Middle Class in Tudor England." Wright found a close interactive causal connection between the rise of the middle classes and the rise of the Tudors, an allegedly "bourgeois" dynasty. Hexter correctly complains of the tautological nature of this thesis, in which everybody who appears to be rising is admitted to the middle class. Hexter wonders not merely whether or not the middle class was rising in Tudor England, but whether it was there at all, in any meaningful sense. He finds that "there is little evidence, then, that the Tudor period saw any extraordinary development in the middle class of group conciousness, group pride, or will to power," and no proof of the proposition that Tudor monarchs favored commerce in any special way, or that they manifested "middle-class" characteristics in any intelligible sense.[41]

ɞ* The *fallacy of archetypes* consists in conceptualizing change in terms of the re-enactment of primordial archetypes which exist outside of time. It is a method in which an event acquires meaning as a re-enactment of some aboriginal and atemporal model. Mircea Eliade supplies many examples, all of which manifest the same primitive ontological conception—that "an object or an act becomes real only insofar

---

41. Hexter, *Reappraisals in History*, p. 99.

as it imitates or repeats an archetype. Thus, reality is acquired solely through repetition or participation; everything which lacks an exemplary model is 'meaningless,' i.e., it lacks reality. Men would thus have a tendency to become archetypical and paradigmatic. This tendency may well appear paradoxical, in the sense that the man of a traditional culture sees himself as real only to the extent that he ceases to be himself."[42]

In archaic societies, the myth of the eternal return to aboriginal archetypes may be merely "paradoxical," as Eliade calls it. But when the myth becomes a modern interpretation of historical change, the paradox becomes a fatal contradiction. The myth of the return is an antithesis to time, change, and history itself. When it is used by a historian to conceptualize his subject, then it becomes a fallacy, for the myth implies that what is real does not change. His time series is bent back upon itself in a sterile series of cyclical enfoldments.

The classical examples of this fallacy are those monumental works of melancholy genius, Arnold Toynbee's *A Study of History* and Oswald Spengler's *The Decline of the West*. Both authors conceived all "civilizations" according to fixed archetypal patterns which transcend time. There are many complaints to be entered against these interpretations. But much of their absurdity flows from a sense of time which is a perfect example of Mircea Eliade's idea of primitive prehistorical thought.

Toynbee's "civilizations" are all converted into conceptual contemporaries. When this is done to Sumerian "civilization" on the one hand and Western "civilization" on the other, the result may be the most gigantic anachronism in recorded historiography. The vast developmental changes from one to the other are either ignored or discounted. Similarly, between "Sumerian" and "Sinic" civilization, between "Minoan" and "Christian" civilization, there are contrasts of complexity and scale which are so great that any simple-minded archetypical interpretation is at bottom absurd.[43]

---

42. Mircea Eliade, *Cosmos and History: The Myth of the Eternal Return* (New York, 1959) pp. 34–43, passim.

43. There are also many small single examples of archetypical thinking in historiography—examples which are significant only in a symptomatic sense. A petty specimen appears in a fine history of Scotland by John Duncan Mackie, in which that excellent author asserts that "history had repeated itself exactly . . . the year 1286 was come again [in 1542]." Similarly, G. A. Williamson writes in another context, "No one can read Eusebius's account of how the cathedral of Tyre, with all its elaborate symbolism, rose from the ashes, without thinking of Coventry. Truly that generation and this are one." Whenever these phrases appear before a reader's eye, a klaxon horn should sound a warning in his ear. See J. D. Mackie, *A History of Scotland*, 2d ed. (Baltimore, 1966), p. 141; and Eusebius, *The History of the Church from Christ to Constantine*, ed. G. A. Williamson (New York, 1966), p. 10. Another example suggests that the warning sound might well be a few bars from *Le Retour à la Vie*. See Jacques Barzun, *Berlioz and His Century* (New York, 1956), p. 10.

The fallacy of archetypes is an erroneous form of historical consciousness, but it is not restricted to the conciousness of erroneous historians. There are many people in modern industrial societies who still live in the grip of Mircea Eliade's "archaic ideology of ritual repetition" and dream of the return to the eternal archetype. In Cornwall, today, there is a band of fanatics who seriously predict the second coming of King Arthur.[44] Others dream of—who knows what? The second coming of Charlemagne, or Christ, or Thomas Jefferson; the recovery of the primitive church, or the garden of Eden, or some other Shangri-la for which real people are ready to butcher other real people who seem to stand in the way. Here is another fatal fallacy that cannot be allowed to endure in a complex world.

&~ The *chronic fallacy* is a kind of misplaced temporal literalism in which a historian forces his story into an overrigid chronological sequence and tells everything in the precise order of its occurrence, with results that are dysfunctional to his explanatory purpose. It is not easy to define this form of error exactly, for a historian must begin by respecting the chronology of events. But sometimes he can be overly obsequious to the tyranny of time.

One might imagine a better method. A scholar should seek the pattern of change in his problem and organize his narrative around it, rather than according to a strict observance of the calender. This pattern always exists, but never coincides exactly with the ticking of a clock. Imagine, for example, the history of generational responses to a given theme. An older generation may clearly express its attitudes at time 1, 3, 5, 7, and 9. A younger generation might do so at time 2, 4, 6, 8, and 10. It surely makes better sense to tell this story in the sequence 1, 3, 5, 7, 9, 2, 4, 6, 8, 10, and not in a straight numerical order, which would make literal nonsense of the story.

If the chronic fallacy is not easy to define, it is unmistakable in its commission. There are many examples in the work of great nineteenth-century historians, who were trained to think narrowly in terms of linear narration and never to take a liberty with a date.

But the error survives in our own era. Witness John A. Garraty's biography of Henry Cabot Lodge, which tells everything with an engaging simplicity but explains nothing in a satisfactory way. The complex rhythms of Lodge's career are reduced to the mindless cadence of a metronome. The resultant narrative structure is not a vehicle for ex-

44. George Thayer, *The British Political Fringe* (London, 1965), Chap. 9.

planation but a means of compiling 400 pages without one.[45] No satisfactory sense of the quality of Lodge's conservatism is communicated to the reader, nor any extended awareness of the psychic, social, and cultural contexts within which Lodge lived. There is, I think, an important developmental sequence in Lodge's public career—a measured development through time, though not precisely Eastern standard time. There is a kind of counterpoint of environment, attitude, and act, which imposes its own chronology upon the problem. But in Garraty's book, *Anno Domini, dominus est.*

&» The *static fallacy* broadly consists in any attempt to conceptualize a dynamic problem in static terms. This form of error represents an intermediate stage of historical consciousness, in which change is perceived merely as the emergence of a nonchanging entity. Such was the shape and texture of much Christian historiography, which often represented past events in terms of a slow unfolding of a preordained divine plan. The same conception, semisecularized, appears in George Bancroft's great history of the unfolding of the American plan. Bancroft's chapter on the earliest Anglo-American settlements is titled, "England Takes Possession of the United States."[46]

Even in our own time, a good many liberal textbook historians of the American republic tend to conceptualize their dynamic subject in terms of the unfolding of a static idea of democratic society, which slowly reveals itself through three centuries, without ever really changing in the process. The result is a historiographical equivalent of the Dance of the Seven Veils, featuring the damsel Democracy herself, and half a dozen willing helpers. First, Roger Williams helps her out of a somber shroud of Puritan black. Then Benjamin Franklin rends a red coat with his lightning rod, and Thomas Jefferson tugs off a covering of Hamiltonian buff and blue, to expose an earthy homespun of Old Hickory brown. This rude garment falls to pieces, revealing a cloak of Confederate gray, which Lincoln removes with magnanimous gestures. Next there is a gilded robe, embroidered with Black Fridays and costly touches of Tweed, which miraculously yields to a checkered cloth of Populist red and Progressive lily white, with a free-silver lining. The last veil finally falls away, and beauteous Columbia stands revealed, with a blue eagle tattooed on her belly.

In all seriousness, any scholar who tries to organize a book called

45. John A. Garraty, *Henry Cabot Lodge: A Biography* (New York, 1953).
46. George Bancroft, *History of the Colonization of the United States*, 15th ed. (Boston, 1852), 1:74.

The Growth of the American Democracy around the emergence of a single static democratic idea will soon find himself tied up in conceptual knots. If, on the other hand, the theme is shifted from the emergence of democracy to democratization, and if the latter is understood not as the maximization of an immutable idea, but rather as a series of fluid ideas each of which are qualitatively in motion on several separate axes, then at least a few of the obstacles in the path of historical understanding are removed.

The number of "-izations" in the lexicon of history is rapidly increasing, as our understanding of change is steadily refined. But the static fallacy still appears in sophisticated disguises. American political historians, for example, stand ready to argue at the drop of a cocked hat, over the question "When did the first modern party system appear in the United States?" Many find the answer in the Jacksonian era. A few date the development during the 1840s. Some go back to the 1790s. Others locate the first really modern party system in the Jeffersonian era.

This academic dispute, to which I regret that I have contributed, is wildly unhistorical when it is cast in these terms. It derives from a faulty question, which rests in turn on the false idea of a modern party as something that exists statically outside the flow of time but slowly unfolds within it. Any attempt to locate a single model of the modern party system for purposes of historical analysis is not merely arbitrary, but absurd.

ह्र्ल्ट्र्व्ह् The *fallacy of presumptive continuity* and the *fallacy of presumptive change* are two fundamental forms of error which came to mind in a reading of Barrington Moore's *Social Origins of Dictatorship and Democracy*. Moore criticizes his colleagues for an assumption of social inertia in their work.

> There is a widespread assumption in modern social science [he writes] that social continuity requires no explanation. Supposedly it is not problematical. Change is what requires explanation. . . . The assumption of inertia, that cultural and social continuity do not require explanation, obliterates the fact that both have to be recreated anew in each generation, often with great pain and suffering. To maintain and transmit a value system, human beings are punched, bullied, sent to jail, thrown into concentration camps, cajoled, bribed, made into heroes, encouraged to read newspapers, stood up against a wall and shot, and sometimes even taught sociology. To speak of cultural inertia is to overlook the concrete interests and privileges that are served by indoctrination, education, and the entire complicated process of transmitting culture from one generation to the next.[47]

47. Pp. 485–86.

As an example of an "assumption of inertia," Moore cites the work of Talcott Parsons,[48] who does indeed explicitly commit this error. But I wonder if Moore has committed the counterfallacy of presumptive change. They are both equally indefensible. Probably no form of bias is more difficult to eradicate from one's work than this one, and yet its consequences can be exceedingly serious. One thinks of those two countervailing schools of American historiography—the consensus-continuity school of B. F. Wright, Louis Hartz, and Daniel Boorstin, and the conflict-change school of an earlier generation of progressive historians. What is clearly needed is a set of mediating terms and concepts which might help to neutralize these opposite biases.

ñ The *genetic fallacy* mistakes the becoming of a thing for the thing which it has become. In other words, it is the erroneous idea that "an actual history of any science, art, or social institution can take the place of a [nontemporal] logical analysis of its structure."[49]

Much was made of the genetic fallacy by the so-called New Critics of the interbellum era—T. S. Eliot and others who invigorated their discipline by insisting that a history of a literary work is something different from an analysis of its aesthetic structure. A few went further and argued that literary history is no part of a literary critic's business, and no use to him in his work. This counterfallacy, which confuses a thing-which-has-become for a thing's becoming, has been amply condemned by the so-called New-New Critics, such as Leslie Fiedler and others.[50] Both kinds of organizing schemas—temporal and nontemporal alike—are surely useful and constructive tools of analysis and explanation. But they are not interchangeable. The New Critics were correct in drawing a clear distinction between them.

The most hateful forms of the genetic fallacy are those which convert a temporal sequence into an ethical system—history into morality. This pernicious error was embedded in a movement called historicism,

48. *The Social System* (Glencoe, 1951), p. 205.
49. Morris R. Cohen and Ernest Nagel, *An Introduction to Logic and the Scientific Method* (New York, 1934), pp. 388–90. I think it incorrect to distinguish, as Cohen and Nagel do, between a temporal and logical order. A narrative is itself a special kind of logical order. If so, the proper distinction is therefore a temporal logic on the one hand and a nontemporal logic on the other.
To argue that narrative possesses a logical structure of its own is *not*, however, to suggest that past happenings themselves possess an inherent logic of their own, but rather that a study of past happenings must be conducted in a logical manner, and that the resultant interpretation must be organized in a logical form if it is to be intelligible.
50. For an extended critique of the "new criticism" in this respect, see E. D. Hirsch, Jr., *Validity in Interpretation* (New Haven, 1967).

which flourished in Germany during the period 1790–1930—a school which stretched from the early work of Herder, Hegel, Schiller, and Schelling to the later work of Troeltsch and Meinecke. Historicism was many things to many people, but in a general way its epistemology was idealist, its politics were antidemocratic, its aesthetics were romantic, and its ethics were organized around the nasty idea that whatever is becoming, is right.[51]

The classical expression of ethical historicism is Schiller's epigram *"die Weltgeschichte ist das Weltgericht."* This doctrine reduced ethics (and much else) to a province of historiography. And it was radically destructive, not merely of other ethical systems but of itself as well. Ethical historicism commonly took one of two untenable forms. Some historicists—Ranke is an eminent example—unwittingly smuggled an ethical system into history, and then discovered it as the objective teaching of history itself. Others later converted ethical historicism into an ethical relativism. Meinecke, for instance, asserted that "nothing can be immoral which comes from the innermost individual character of a being."[52] This doctrine must necessarily become an ethical nihilism. It would prevent any moral judgment against the filth which flowed from "the innermost individual character" of many Nazi beings. Historicism, relativism, nihilism. There is *no* stopping place in this downward descent to nothingness.[53]

German historicism is dead, or dying, but the same ethical version of the genetic fallacy still appears in other forms. It seems to find a certain popularity in what the authors of *1066 and All That* called "Top Nations." American historians such as Daniel Boorstin came close to arguing in the 1950s that *Die americanische Geschichte ist das Weltgericht,* and they were not alone in that assumption. Something of the fallacy of ethical historicism appears in the absurd and dangerous idea that America's rise to power and prosperity is a measure of its moral excellence—that the history of the Republic can be seen, in short, as a system of morality. How many of us have not, at some time, silently slipped into this error?

---

51. The many conflicting (and sometimes contradictory) definitions of historicism are a measure of the movement's range and complexity. The best and fullest account in English is Georg G. Iggers, *The German Conception of History* (Middletown, Conn., 1968), with a good bibliography.

52. *Weltbürgertum und Nationalstaat,* in *Werke* (Munich, 1959), 5:83; as quoted in Iggers, *The German Conception of History,* p, 271.

53. The doctrines of historicism are sometimes condemned as the cause of Nazism, as if Herder puffed up a great cloud of Teutonic humbug and out marched Adolf Hitler. This is unfair, inaccurate, and illogical: a misreading of German history, in my opinion; and a classic example of an argument to consequences. Historicism remains profoundly hateful, but for itself, and not for its putative effects.

On the other side of the ideological divide, another contemporary variant of the fallacy of ethical historicism might be diagnosed as Carr's disease, after an English socialist scholar who seems to think that morality marches triumphant through history, always on the side of the big battalions. Carr marches through history with them, too. He is not a citizen of a Top Nation, but a strenuous advocate of a Top Notion.

One wonders how Carr measures the bigness of his big battalions— a tough perception problem which cannot be resolved merely by the quantification of muster rolls. Psychologists have demonstrated that a symbol of something which is valued looks physically bigger than a symbol of something which is not.[54] Their discovery applies to Carr's big battalions, and to much else besides. In that degree his argument becomes circular, as all ethical historicisms are. An ethical system is bootlegged into history, and then proclaimed to the world as the lesson of history itself. Or else, all ethical systems are undercut, so that nothing remains. The only remedy is a radical recognition that a temporal series cannot be converted into an ethical system, under any circumstances, without self-contradiction.

&ver; The *didactic fallacy* is the attempt to extract specific "lessons" from history, and to apply them literally as policies to present problems, without regard for intervening changes. There are several special types and subdivisions of this fallacy—e.g., the attempt to revive past precepts, or creeds, or codes for the purification of the present; or the attempt to repeat past political successes by returning to the programs of successful politicians; or the attempt to study problem A and to apply conclusions obtained from it to problem B, though B may be very different from A, and far removed in time and place from A.

Many pundits today are in the habit of misquoting Santayana's epigram, "Those who cannot remember the past are condemned to repeat it."[55] Maybe some people have come to grief this way, but they are probably fewer than those who have fallen into the opposite error. "One is apt to perish in politics from too much memory," Tocqueville wrote somewhere, with equal truth and greater insight.

This is not to argue that historical study itself is useless or dangerous. It is not to endorse Hegel's maxim that "the only thing one learns

54. J. Bruner and L. Postman, "Symbolic Values as an Organizing Factor in Perception," *Journal of Social Psychology* 27 (1948): 203 ff. Carr's position appears in *What Is History?*, chaps. 2, 5, and 6; and *The New Society* (New York, 1957), passim.
55. George Santayana, *The Life of Reason: Reason in Common Sense* (New York, 1905), p. 284.

from history is that nobody ever learns anything from history." It is
rather to suggest that the utility of historical knowledge consists, among
other things, in the enlargement of substantive contexts within which
decisions are made, and in the refinement of a thought structure which is
indispensible to purposeful decision making about men, societies, time,
and change—a kind of logic which this book is an effort to define.
Historical study, in short, equips men to think historically. That intellectual discipline is the only remedy against such errors as the following.

Consider the case of Field Marshal Douglas Haig, a Scottish soldier
who was centrally responsible for the bloody shambles at Passchendaele
in 1917. Some critics have attributed his costly blunders to sheer ignorance and stupidity. But that is not correct. Haig's mistakes were errors
of intelligence and learning. An able military historian has observed
that Haig

> was not an uneducated soldier. Unlike so many cavalrymen of his day, he
> had studied war, and, strange to say, this was to be his undoing, because
> he was so unimaginative that he could not see that the tactics of the past
> were as dead as mutton. We are told he held that the "role of cavalry
> on the battlefield will always go on increasing," and that he believed
> bullets had "little stopping power against the horse."[56]

Other examples appeared in the next war, when, as always, many
soldiers and statesmen were superbly prepared to refight the last one.
There is a continuing controversy about Hitler's decision to halt his
panzers when they were but a few miles from Dunkirk. Chester Wilmot
provides a sensible explanation in his excellent history of World War II.

> The Dunkirk decision [he wrote] was Hitler's first great military mistake,
> but it was not so irrational and short-sighted as some German generals have
> asserted. Although Hitler was influenced by the lure of Paris, the goal of
> all German conquerors, a more important factor was his determination to
> avoid the costly mistakes of 1914. *He* would not falter and be stopped
> at the Somme, as von Moltke had been stopped on the Marne through
> excessive concern about the British on the flank.[57]

On the other side, General George S. Patton prepared himself in a
curious way, on the eve of OVERLORD, for his extraordinary campaign
against the Wehrmacht in 1944.

> I also read *The Norman Conquest* by Freeman [he wrote in his Diary]
> paying particular attention to the roads William the Conqueror used in
> his operations in Brittany and Normandy. The roads used in those days
> had to be on ground which was always practicable. Therefore using these

---

56. J. F. C. Fuller, Introduction to Leon Wolff, *In Flanders Fields* (New York, 1960),
p. 9.
57. Chester Wilmot, *The Struggle for Europe* (New York, 1952), p. 21.

roads, even in modern times, permits easy by-passing when the enemy resorts, as he always does, to demolition.[58]

Fortunately for Allied arms, General Patton seems not to have had an opportunity to apply these "lessons of history" very closely. Had he done so, it is conceivable that the Third Army might still be hacking away at the *bocage*.

More specimens of the same sort of error appear in political history. Franklin Roosevelt during World War II appears to have been dangerously obsessed with the failures of Woodrow Wilson in World War I.[59] De Gaulle, who was at one time a professor of history at St. Cyr, may have learned some "lessons" of French history all too well. Stalin seems to have done the same with respect to the "lessons" of the history of Russian foreign relations. And Winston Churchill, at Cairo in 1943, had a haunting conversation with Harold Macmillan. Late one night, Churchill observed, "Cromwell was a great man wasn't he?"

"Yes, sir," said Macmillan, "a very great man."

"Ah," Churchill said, "but he made one terrible mistake. Obsessed in his youth by fear of the power of Spain, he failed to observe the rise of France. Will that be said of me?"

Churchill was, of course, referring to Germany and Russia. But the opposite is said of him, increasingly, these days—that he was obsessed too much with Russia, with serious consequences for the postwar world.[60]

The didactic fallacy is particularly dangerous to conservative thought. One case in point is an unusually intelligent, and much maligned, American president, Herbert Hoover. A historian, Herbert Feis, fairly remarks,

> President Hoover was not an insensitive or inhumane man; quite the contrary. But he could not grasp or would not face the grim realities which called for deviations from principles and practices that he deemed essential to American greatness and freedom. The policies and proposals which he expounded so earnestly might have served to end the depression, let us say, in the 1870's or 1880's, but not the ones by which the United States was then [after 1929] beset.[61]

The same sort of mistake is contained in the atomistic conservatism of Barry Goldwater's *Conscience of a Conservative*. Goldwater is an intelligent and rational man, though the nature of his intellect and

58. George S. Patton, Jr., *War as I Knew It* (Boston, 1947), p. 92.
59. Eric Goldman, *Rendezvous with Destiny* (New York, 1952), pp. 398–400, 447–50.
60. Randolph S. Churchill, *Winston S. Churchill, The Young Statesman* (Boston, 1967), p. 274.
61. Herbert Feis, *1933: Characters in Crisis* (Boston, 1966), p. 7.

rationality is so far removed from that of many American academicians that they are only able to understand him by presuming some degree of insanity. He has made a very great *rational* error in his thought, in an attempt to revive precepts and principles that were functional in nineteenth-century America but which are today dysfunctional and even dangerous to the peace and prosperity of the world, for they ignore great demographic, technological, social, and cultural changes. Walter Bagehot has truly written that "the whole history of civilization is strewn with creeds and institutions which were invaluable at first and deadly afterwards."

    What positive principles of narrative explanation can be extracted from these fallacies? A few random thoughts come to mind.

First, a historian must distinguish between an analysis of the becoming of an object and an analysis of the object as it has become. The narrative history of the writing of a poem is something distinct from an analysis of its poetic structure. A narrative history of ethics is something different from an ethical system. By the same token, a narrative history of events in Southeast Asia is something other than a structural analysis of the situation which presently exists. This lesson is not an easy one for a historian to learn, for it requires him to recognize the limits of his own expertise. And its converse is equally unwelcome to nontemporal structural analysts of various persuasions. Some questions which we ask about the world require explanatory answers of a narrative-descriptive sort. Other questions require a different strategy. There is nothing to be gained by a condemnation of either method out of hand—and much to be lost by their confusion.

Second, the analysis of the becoming of a thing must be cast in appropriately dynamic conceptualizations. Historians for many years attempted to analyze dynamic problems in static terms, with seriously dysfunctional results. Many scholars are slowly learning to employ more fluid and flexible conceptual units. Conceptual flexibility is not conceptual imprecision, but rather precision of a new kind, in which the dynamics of change and continuity are carefully specified but not frozen into a static structure. The stuff of history is things that happen—not things that are. The historian's object, in Ranke's classic phrase, is not to tell what actually *was,* but what actually *happened.*

Third, the logic of any narrative scheme must conform to the logic of the problem at hand and not to some extraneous structure. Many distractions must be resisted. Calendars and clocks are the worst of temporal tyrants, which reduce narrative histories to slavish chronicles. The institutional structures within which historians live—academic departments in America, for example—supply other snares which Hexter has described in his attack on tunnel history. Antitemporal archetypes still take their toll of serious research, and so also do many irrelevant schemes of periodization.

Fourth, within an appropriate time scheme, events must be located with accuracy and precision. A historian must preserve an uncompromising respect for the temporal integrity of his story and of its various components. He must beware of the temptations of retrospective symmetry, in which antecedents are defined in terms of consequents. And he must be on guard against anachronisms in every form.

Fifth, a historian must develop interpretative devices which neutralize bias toward continuity or change. A device has been created by an imaginative historian of science, Thomas S. Kuhn, from whom historians in every field have much to learn. The history of science, in the past, resembled an Old Testament genealogy. Copernicus begat Tycho, and Tycho begat Kepler, and Kepler begat Newton, and the world was filled with light. Kuhn has worked out a more satisfactory method, which he has described in *The Structure of Scientific Revolutions* (Chicago, 1962).

Kuhn's conceptualization of change and continuity in the history of science is organized around a series of "shared paradigms"—sets of scientific methods and understandings which were consistent with what was known when they were established, and which persisted until anomalies generated a crisis. The old paradigm was blurred, and then disrupted; then a new paradigm was generated, and the process began again. Kuhn writes:

> Historians of science have begun to ask new sorts of questions and to trace different and often less than cumulative, developmental lines for the sciences. Rather than seeking the permanent contributions of an older science to our present vantage, they attempt to display the historical integrity of that science in its own time. They ask, for example, not about the relation of Galileo's views to those of modern science, but rather about the relationship between his views and those of his group, i.e., his teachers, contemporaries and immediate successors in the sciences. Furthermore, they insist upon studying the opinions of that group and other similar ones from that viewpoint, usually very different from that of modern science— that gives those opinions the maximum internal coherence and the closest possible fit to nature.[62]

62. Kuhn, *The Structure of Scientific Revolutions*, p. 3. One might compare Kuhn's paradigms with a distinguished piece of retrospective symmetry, C. C. Gillespie's *The Edge of Objectivity* (Princeton, 1960), to see what a difference a method can make.

Narrative history is still consistent with Kuhn's paradigms, but it becomes a more profound and more intricate narrative, in which the story consists not in a progressive unfolding of the present, but rather a series of structural reformations (in a literal sense). Kuhn's method may be marred by an excessive reaction to the linearity of earlier efforts, but it is a closer approximation to the requirements of the subject than anything we have had before. And it is relevant to all fields of historical inquiry. Political history can be constructively conceived in precisely the same paradigmatic terms—a certain congruence is established in a polity, and then eroded by a sequence of new problems and purposes. The old polity is at last overturned, there is a period of confusion, a new polity is created, which possesses a congruence of its own, and the process begins again. The cyclical implications of this approach need not be taken very seriously, for the nature of the paradigmatic relationship is itself in motion, and it must vary greatly from one phenomenon to another. To accept Kuhn's model is not to argue that history itself is a right- or left-handed spiral, a sine curve, a merry-go-round, a roller coaster, or a loop-the-loop. The method can coexist with any of these absurd abstractions; it entails none of them. Instead, it is a flexible, empirical device which means not the end of narrative history but the beginning of a new kind of narration, which is in turn capable of further refinement.

There are many problems of narration which have not even been opened in this chapter—problems which nobody has managed to resolve. To tell a story is to assemble a group of mutually relevant facts. But what is involved in the idea of relevance? "There are few problems in philosophy which merit closer analysis than the question of relevance," Arthur Danto has written.[63] And few have received so little attention. Now that relevance has become the rallying cry of a younger generation, perhaps it will be properly investigated.[64]

Narrative also involves the idea of connectedness among relevant events. But what is the nature of connections in a narrative series? "Tended, grew out of, developed, evolved, trend, development, tendency, evolution, growth," J. H. Hexter has written. "Such words are like sealed junction boxes on the complex circuits of history. One knows that inside the boxes there are connections which induce the currents of history to change direction; but the boxes conceal rather than reveal how these connections are made."[65]

63. Danto, *Analytical Philosophy of History*, p. 132.
64. For some observations on this subject, see above, Chapter 3, "Fallacies of Factual Significance."
65. Hexter, *Reappraisals in History*, p. 213.

Hexter's electric imagery might be extended to describe other dimensions of difficulty in this subject. There are not merely junction boxes in narrative circuits, but transformers, capacitators, generators, relays, breakers, and resistance coils—and there are radial circuits and ring circuits and many other kinds as well. In common practice, the problem of narrative connections is resolved by the use of an additional device which is our business for the next chapter—causality.

CHAPTER VI

FALLACIES OF CAUSATION

ও৯

What is called Wisdom is concerned with primary causes.
> —Aristotle

Der Glaube an den Kausalnexus ist der Aberglaube.
[Belief in the causal nexus is superstition.]
> —Ludwig Wittgenstein

The causal principle is, in short, neither a panacea nor
a myth; it is a general hypothesis . . . having an approximate validity in its appropriate domain.
> —Mario Bunge

Today's historians tend, characteristically, to combine generalization, narration, and causation in a single explanation model. But it is not self-evident that problems of cause are properly a part of a historian's work. Can any causal question be answered by an empirical method? Can any existing model of causal explanation survive a rigorous logical and linguistic analysis? These doubtful issues have occasioned a large literature, but little agreement.

There was a time when nearly everybody believed, as some still do, that *the* task of an historian was "to establish facts and to marshal them in a sequence of cause and effect."[1] But early in the twentieth century the idea of cause was widely condemned by scientists such as Mach and Helmholz, by historians such as Beard and Teggart, by novelists such as Kafka and Sartre, and by philosophers such as Wittgenstein and Russell. The latter wrote, for example, "The law of causality, I believe, like much that passes muster among philosophers,

1. Fritz Fischer, *Germany's Aims in the First World War* (New York, 1967), p. xxi.

is a relic of a bygone age, surviving, like the monarchy, only because it is erroneously supposed to do no harm."[2] Another philosopher has argued that "causality may have no more reality than a dragon or a mermaid."[3]

Recently, however, causation has regained respectability and more refinement than it ever possessed before, in discussions by philosophers, physicists, and social scientists. But historians are, as usual, a generation behind. A few continue to condemn the whole idea. Professor Howard Zinn has written,

> I will not tangle with *cause*, because once you acknowledge cause as the core of a problem, you have built something into it that not only baffles people, but, worse, immobilizes them. Causation is not merely complex—it is a problem impossible of solution according to some of the new [sic] philosophers. Perhaps it is one of those metaphysical conundrums created by our own disposition to set verbal obstacles between ourselves and reality.[4]

Other historians have responded in a different way. They have eliminated the word "cause" from their vocabulary, but they have continued to construct cryptocausal interpretations. They have camouflaged causation behind words such as "influences," "impulses," "elements," "master symptoms," "prodromes," "mainsprings," "roots," "bases," "foundations," "undercurrents," "fountainheads," "fertilizing factors," etc. All the synonyms in all the thesauri have been exhausted by historians, in their efforts to avoid an explanation form they distrust but have not been able to discard.

The most common semantical subterfuge is "factor." G. R. Elton has observed that

> The concept of cause being under a cloud (because it used to be employed too crudely) historians have for a time been hunting for a substitute. Wherever one turns in history today, one runs head-on into factors. There are no longer any causes of the Reformation; instead there are factors that made it possible. This is to go from the tolerably dubious to the quite abominable. A cause is something real: people do things in order to get results. A factor—outside mathematics, and trading stations and Scottish estates—is a meaningless piece of tired jargon. Events are not the product of simple causes but of complex situations in which a variety of people and circumstances participates, but this does not mean that they are produced by factors. A word to be forgotten.[5]

2. Bertrand Russell, "On the Notion of Cause," *Mysticism and Logic* (London, 1958), pp. 180–208. This work was first published in 1917.
3. William P. Montague, *The Ways of Knowing, or The Methods of Philosophy* (New York, 1958), p. 199.
4. Howard Zinn, *The Southern Mystique* (New York, 1964), p. 7: see also the statement by Charles Beard and Alfred Vagts in the Social Science Research Council's report, *Theory and Practice in Historical Study*, Bulletin 54 (1946), pp. 136–37.
5. G. R. Elton, *The Practice of History* (New York, 1967), p. 101.

The problem is more than merely semantical. Historians have recently responded to the problem of cause in the way that American statesmen have reacted to the problem of China. Formal nonrecognition masks a functional obsession. The results in both cases are some very odd goings-on, which would be wonderfully entertaining, if their effects were not so destructive.

There are, of course, many modes of historical explanation which are noncausal in nature. But I have never read an extended historical interpretation which does not include causal statements, or cryptocausal statements, in at least a peripheral way. Whether or not historians ought to do causal history, the plain fact is that almost all of them do it, and some do it better than others. Someday soon we shall probably see the refinement of a genuine and consistent noncausal history. But even then, causal interpretations will probably coexist with other forms, because causal relationships are something real in the world. Causation is an idea which is generally used because it is generally useful. In some of its renderings, it may be able to coexist with logic and empiricism. In others, it is clearly fallacious. The object of this chapter is to identify a few of the most common fallacies of causal analysis and then to conclude with a few affirmative remarks.

§• The *fallacy of post hoc, propter hoc* is the mistaken idea that if event *B* happened after event *A,* it happened because of event *A.* An example is provided by a female passenger on board the Italian liner *Andrea Doria.* On the fatal night of *Doria's* collision with the Swedish ship *Gripsholm,* off Nantucket in 1956, the lady retired to her cabin and flicked a light switch. Suddenly there was a great crash, and grinding metal, and passengers and crew ran screaming through the passageways. The lady burst from her cabin and explained to the first person in sight that she must have set the ship's emergency brake![6]

There are many *post hoc* fallacies in historical scholarship. Consider, for instance, one major interpretative problem—the defeat of the Spanish Armada in 1588. Some scholars have suggested that this event caused the decline of the Spanish empire and the rise of the British. But Garrett Mattingly replies that "it is hard to see why they think so. By 1603, Spain had not lost to the English a single overseas outpost, while the English colonization of Virginia had been postponed for the duration." Others have argued that the defeat of the Armada transferred control of the seas from the Spanish to the British. Professor Mattingly replies that before 1588 "English sea power in the Atlantic had usually

6. Alvin Moscow, *Collision Course* (New York, 1959), p. 85.

been superior to the combined strengths of Castile and Portugal, and so it continued to be, but after 1588 the margin of superiority diminished. The defeat of the Armada was not so much the end as the beginning of the Spanish navy."

Still others have attributed to the defeat of the Armada the dislocation of the Spanish economy by the disruption of communications with America. Mattingly: "In fact, more American treasure reached Spain in the years between 1588 and 1603 than in any other fifteen years in Spanish history." Others still have argued that the Armada "led to the great explosion of literary genius which marked the last fifteen years of Elizabeth's reign." Mattingly: "The assertion of a causal connection between the defeat of the Armada and the flowering of Elizabethan drama, is hard to refute; even harder, except by the method of *post hoc, propter hoc,* to prove. There is no link in England between the Armada campaign and any literary work as clear as one [*Don Quixote*] we can find in Spain."

Mattingly himself believed that there was something more to the thesis that the Armada "decided that religious unity was not to be reimposed by force on the heirs of medieval Christendom." But this assertion, moderate though it is in Mattingly's book, can be dealt with and dismissed by the method of *pro hoc*. The permanence of the fragmentation of Christendom was surely clear before the Armada sailed. If there were many Catholics or Protestants who remained blind to that fact, the scales would not fall from their eyes for many years after the Armada. A better argument can be made for the causal role of the Armada in the growth of English nationalism, but even this would have to be qualified both by stirrings of national spirit before 1588 and by the persistence of subnational and supernational attachments in England after that date.

In short, it appears that the defeat of the Armada, mighty and melodramatic as it was, may have been remarkably barren of result. Its defeat may have caused very little, except the disruption of the Spanish strategy that sent it on its way. That judgment is sure to violate the patriotic instincts of every Englishman and the aesthetic sensibilities of us all. A big event *must* have big results, we think. But this is the fallacy of identity, which we shall come to directly.[7]

&֍ The *fallacy of cum hoc, propter hoc* mistakes correlation for cause. Every textbook on statistics warns solemnly against this fallacy.[8]

7. Garrett Mattingly, *The Armada* (Boston, 1959), pp. 397–402.
8. Frederick E. Croxton, Dudley J. Cowden, and Sidney Klein, *Applied General*

And, indeed, some very silly errors have flowed from it. Robert Garland, the promoter of daylight-saving time, seriously suggested that boys who lived in daylight time zones had bigger feet than boys in other areas, and moreover that "bigger feet make better men." He concluded therefore that daylight time caused better men.[9]

Another example is supplied by a statistician who reports that there is a high positive correlation between the number of storks' nests and the number of human births in various parts of northern Europe. The apparent explanation is not that storks bring babies, but that population increase correlates with an increase in building construction, and that more buildings mean more places for storks to nest.[10]

After the assassination of President Kennedy, many commentators solemnly observed that since 1840, every President elected in a year ending in 0 has died in office—William Henry Harrison (1840), Abraham Lincoln (1860), James A. Garfield (1880), William McKinley (1900), Warren G. Harding (1920), Franklin D. Roosevelt (1940), and John F. Kennedy (1960). A few lunatic numerologists were quick to suggest a causal relationship.

There are many other examples in historiography. The Italian economic historian Amintore Fanfani seriously argued that capitalists tended to have longer heads than other people, and that therefore long-headed people had better heads for business than shortheaded people.[11] More recently, Lee Benson has attempted to answer questions such as "What was the cause of the Republican victory in 1860?" or "Was the candidacy of James G. Blaine the cause of the Republican defeat in 1884?" strictly by means of correlation.[12]

Correlation by itself can never establish a cause. It can disestablish one—for there can never be a *regularistic* causal relationship without correlation. But there can often be a regular correlation without a cause. If X and Y occur together with perfect regularity, X may be the cause of Y, or Y may be the cause of X, or Z may be the cause of X and Y, or there may merely be a coincidence. Near-perfect correlations exist between the death rate in Hyderabad, India, from 1911 to 1919, and

Statistics, 3d ed. (Englewood Cliffs, N.J., 1967), pp. 9, 406–7; W. Allen Wallis and Harry V. Roberts, *Statistics, A New Approach* (New York, 1956), pp. 527, 529, 544; A. L. O'Toole, *Elementary Practical Statistics* (New York, 1964), p. 243.

9. O'Toole, *Elementary Practical Statistics*, p. 243.
10. Wallis and Roberts, *Statistics*, p. 79.
11. Amintore Fanfani, *Catholicism, Protestantism, and Capitalism* (New York, 1938).
12. Lee Benson, "Research Problems in American Political Historiography," in Mirra Komarovsky, ed., *Common Frontiers of the Social Sciences* (Glencoe, Ill., 1957), pp. 113–81.

variations in the membership of the International Association of Machinists during the same period. Nobody seriously believes that there is anything more than a coincidence in that odd and insignificant fact.[13]

To establish the regularistic causal proposition that X caused Y, three things must be demonstrated. First, there must be a correlation between X and Y. Second, there must be a proper temporal relationship in their occurrence. X_1 must occur before Y_1. Third, there must be at least a presumptive agency which connects them. There is solid evidence that drunken driving causes accidents. A correlation has been observed beyond all doubt; the proper temporal relationship exists, and there is a chemical and physiological agency which is well understood. There is pretty good evidence that cigarette smoking causes lung cancer. The correlation is high, the temporal relationship is correct, and there is a reasonable presumption of an agency in inhalation of tobacco smoke and the deposit of carcinogens in the lung. The precise nature of that agency is not as clearly understood as in the case of alcohol and accidents, but the fact of its existence seems clear beyond a reasonable doubt.

Sometimes the question of causality can be by-passed by an investigator. In my opinion, whenever it can be avoided, it should be.

> In statistical work [one scholar has written] it is not necessary to prove that there are cause-and-effect relationships in every situation. Often, the establishment of the fact that there exists an association, and the measurement of its degree or intensity, are all that the investigator needs for the purposes of estimation and prediction. The statistician often is more interested in what he can accomplish by using observed associations or relationships than he is in assigning cause-and-effect or other explanations to them.[14]

This is surely true, and important. And yet, if an observer wishes to get beyond estimation and prediction to the problem of control, or to the problem of super- or extraregularistic explanation, then he must address himself to the problem of causality, however irritating it may be. And correlation, in conclusion, is only a necessary part of regularistic causal explanation. It is not sufficient, in itself, to resolve such issues.

&✿ The *fallacy of pro hoc, propter hoc* consists in putting the effect before the cause. It is an embarrassing error, which violates one of the few simple and self-evident rules of causality: if event E happened before event C, it cannot have happened because of it. In history, there

13. Harold A. Larrabee, *Reliable Knowledge* (Boston, 1954), p. 368.
14. O'Toole, *Elementary Practical Statistics*, p. 243.

are no prior effects and no instantaneous causes. The effect must always follow the cause, and it must be separated by a temporal interval, be it ever so slight.[15]

The fallacy of *pro hoc* is the sort of blunder which always leaves its perpetrator feeling a little queasy after it is pointed out to him. But its absurdity is more apparent in a general description than in particular instances. It has, indeed, been committed by two of the most able academic historians who are writing in America today: C. Vann Woodward and David M. Potter.

Woodward made this mistake in an essay called *The Age of Reinterpretation*, which first appeared as an article in *The American Historical Review* in October, 1960, and subsequently as a separate imprint by the American Historical Association. In an argument as comprehensive as Frederick Jackson Turner's interpretation of the significance of free land in American history, Woodward suggested that there was a comparable importance in the existence of an alleged "free security" for the development of American culture. Separated from its enemies by three oceans, and protected by the ships of the Royal Navy, the American Republic grew and prospered, Woodward believed, without having to pay for a military establishment, such as less fortunate nations required. It never had to pay a cost which was as heavy in political and psychological and social and cultural terms as it was in dollars.

From this supposed cause, Woodward reasoned to many broad effects: to the pace of American economic development, the prevalence of light taxes and limited government, the indiscipline of American youth, and other national characteristics which Woodward collectively called the "sunnier side of the national disposition—the sanguine temperament, the faith in the future, what H. G. Wells once called our 'optimistic fatalism.' "

It is a splendid argument. But unfortunately, the author is forced to make one concession which is both empirically necessary and logically fatal to his thesis. He concedes that before 1815 (or thereabouts), there was little "free security" for Anglo-America. Our oceanic moat was, in the first two centuries of our history, a great common, as Captain Mahan once called it, which did not protect the colonies but exposed them to their enemies. And there were enemies aplenty—formidable Indian tribes, the Dutch, the French, the Spanish, and after 1775 the British themselves. The southern colonies felt a continuous threat of

15. It is possible, of course, to have a cause C_1 and an effect E_1, and a C_2 and an E_2, which happened precisely in that temporal order. C_2 thus happened after E_1, and C_1 and C_2 may be indistinguishable in all respects—all except one. C_1 caused E_1, and C_2 did not, and could not.

domestic insurrection by its black labor force. And all the colonies were menaced by privateers and pirate fleets which were sufficiently powerful to lay siege to colonial capitals.

From the beginnings of settlement to 1815, there was a war in every American generation, and some of these wars were cruel and bloody. It is unlikely that a civilized society, anywhere in the world, has ever survived losses in proportion to those Virginia experienced in its first half century. And the deaths which New England suffered during King Philip's War were greater in proportion to its population than those which Russia or Germany sustained in World War II. The Anglo-American population, of course, was very much smaller than these great nations, but the social impact must have been comparable.[16]

Anglo-America fought its earliest and bloodiest wars without much help from the mother country, except in the French and Indian War. It was forced to conquer its own peace, at a heavy cost in blood and treasure. Something near to universal military service was forced upon it, and military expenditures which it could ill afford. And yet, in the midst of many tribulations, the phenomena which Woodward interprets as the fruit of free security developed swiftly: freedom and individuality, limited government, rapid economic growth, and all the rest. The "sunnier side" of the national disposition is perfectly personified by Benjamin Franklin, who lived much of his life in a world of war. It is precisely described by Crèvecoeur, who suffered severely in the Revolution.

In short, Woodward, who has worked mostly in the period since 1876, made a mistake which is all too common among students of the recent past. He forgot the first half of American history—the period from the Virginia massacre to the battle of New Orleans, which is longer than the interval between the battle of New Orleans and the siege of Khesanh. Woodward's oversight might be politely described as dysfunctional to his thesis, for it was the first half of American history which marked the emergence of his effect, and the second half which included the appearance of the alleged cause.[17]

16. The casualties of Germany and Russia in World War II are estimated at one in twenty-five and one in twenty-two of 1940 population. New England's losses in King Philip's War were at least one in twenty. See Douglas E. Leach, *Flintlock and Toma-hawk* (New York, 1966), pp. 10, 243.

17. Woodward could conceivably salvage something from the wreckage by making two major alterations in his argument. He could claim that there was a certain measure of "free security" in England before the colonization of North America and that the culture of the colonists was affected by it. And he could argue that "free security," in the period 1815–1949, had an intensifying or conservatizing effect with respect to the many qualities which he attributes to it. But neither of these refinements appears in his essay.

David Potter's fine book *People of Plenty* is also a splendid speci-men of a *pro hoc* for our collection of logical curiosities. Potter makes abundance the cause of much that is American. But America has not always been possessed of abundance, or affluence. In the first two centuries of our colonial and national existence, there were few great American fortunes, nor was there much of a surplus of anything, except rocks, trees, and trouble. The portraits of our ancestors have a lean and hungry look. It might be said that they became American, and *then* they became affluent. It is interesting to note that two centuries ago many students of American society believed that its free institutions were sustained by poverty rather than by wealth. From John Winthrop to John Adams, Americans thanked God that they were not a wealthy nation, for they believed that wealth spawned luxury and corruption and despotism and all the other ugly things that the Old World allegedly was and the New World wasn't—yet. The many national characteristics Potter identifies came early in our history (except for things like the advertising industry, which is my candidate for an un-American activ-ity). Americanism came early; abundance came late. And a good many Americanisms may be surviving in spite of our abundance—not because of it.

ﻉﺪ The *reductive fallacy* reduces complexity to simplicity, or diversity to uniformity, in causal explanations. It exists in several common forms, none of which can be entirely avoided in any historical interpretation. As long as historians tell selected truths, their causal models must be reductive in some degree. But some causal models are more reductive than others. When a causal model is reductive in such a degree, or in such a way, that the resultant distortion is dysfunctional to the resolution of the causal problem at hand, then the reductive fallacy is committed.

One common form of the reductive fallacy is the confusion of necessary with sufficient cause—the confusion of a causal component without which an effect will not occur, with all the other causal com-ponents which are required to make it occur. This sort of error appears in causal explanations which are constructed like a single chain and stretched taut across a vast chasm of complexity. The classic example is the legendary battle that was lost for the want of a horseshoe nail: for the want of a nail the shoe was lost, for the want of a shoe the horse was lost, for the want of a horse the rider was lost, for the want of a rider the message was lost, for the want of a message the regiment was lost, and for the want of a regiment the battle was lost.

This exemplary anecdote has probably been told to every quarter-master in the Western world—no doubt with a salutary effect upon the supply of military horseshoe nails. I am told that our army still possesses a considerable quantity of them. But it has not helped our sense of history.

In the late summer of 1862, for example, the Confederate army of Northern Virginia suddenly crossed the Potomac River and marched north into Union territory, threatening Baltimore, and Washington, and the rich farming country of south-central Pennsylvania. No Union commander could be certain of Robert E. Lee's intentions, which were in fact to concentrate his army near a small Maryland town and to march into Pennsylvania. Lee so informed his lieutenants in a document well known to Civil War buffs as Special Orders no. 191, copies of which were made for all Confederate division commanders. By chance two copies reached General D. H. Hill. One copy was carefully preserved; the other was used by a staff officer to preserve his cigars against the dews and damps of a September morning in Maryland. Somehow the packet—cigars, special order, and all—slipped out of his pocket, and into the hands of the Union general George B. McClellan. A few Union special orders were promptly issued, and there was a fight which the North called Antietam and the South called Sharpsburg and many a weary infantryman on both sides must have known by yet another name. It was the bloodiest day of the war, and a black one for Confederate arms. When it was over, General Lee was forced to retreat into Virginia. It is often said that Antietam was *the* decisive battle of the war. Many historians believe that it ended all chance of European intervention on the side of the Confederacy. Some are also of the opinion that this victory permitted Abraham Lincoln to gain a critical measure of control over his domestic opposition. Moreover, a few days after the engagement, Lincoln issued his preliminary Emancipation Proclamation.

Are we to conclude from this story that *the* cause of Northern victory in the Civil War was the loss of Special Orders no. 191? The answer depends upon the causal model which is at hand. There is, I think, no *prima facie* case against the validity of such a causal interpretation, if it is clearly understood that everything depends upon the acceptance of a contingent-series model of causality, and if the question at hand can be fairly and fully met by such an explanation. But there are many other kinds of causal models (at the end of this chapter an attempt will be made to identify them), and the questions which many historians choose to ask today are not of the sort which can be satisfied by a "want-of-a-nail" explanation. The reductive fallacy might therefore be redefined as the asking of one kind of causal question, and the answering of it with another and less comprehensive kind of causal explanation.

Other examples of reduction are undeniably fallacious in many of their applications. There is the classical case of Actium, Antony, and Cleopatra's nose. Why, one wonders, is Cleo's nose singled out for special attention? Surely other anatomical parts were more important to a red-blooded Roman.

Another famous example is supplied by Winston Churchill. In 1920, King Alexander of Greece died of blood poisoning, having been bitten by a pet monkey. This event was followed by a plebiscite, and a new king, and a bloody war with the Turks. Churchill wrote, "A quarter of a million persons died of that monkey's bite."[18]

There are endless other instances—Bajazet's gout, which allegedly interrupted his ambition to feed his horse upon the altar of St. Peter and prompted Gibbon to comment that "the disorders of the moral, are sometimes corrected by those of the physical world; and an acrimonious humor falling on a single fibre of one man may prevent or suspend the misery of nations."[19] One thinks also of the Duchess of Marlborough's gloves, and the Holy Roman Emperor's mushrooms, and Robert the Bruce and the spider, and an endless miscellany of other reductive curiosities.

Whole schools of historiography are grounded in the fallacy of reduction. One of them is Marxist Leninism, which in Leonard Krieger's phrase "is reminiscent of a Rube Goldberg mechanism in which a fat nobleman opens the door at one end of a corridor and sets off a chain reaction which explodes Nicolai Lenin out the door at the other end."[20] Similar errors appear in psychoanalytical history, which would in some of its forms reduce the cause of the reformation to Martin Luther's toilet training. Good Marxists and good psychoanalytic historians recognize this form of error and repudiate it, but as long as they hold to their various monisms, their explicit rejection of reduction is contradicted by the implicitly reductive nature of their interpretations.

The most stubborn and dangerous forms of reduction appear not in the works of historians of any persuasion but in the ravings of various ideological true believers, for whom history is "a thin thread of evidence taken from selected literary works."[21] Everybody, I suspect, has had some familiarity with such people, who carry their archives in

18. *The World Crisis: The Aftermath* (London, 1929), p. 386.
19. Gibbon, *The Decline and Fall of the Roman Empire,* ed. J. B. Bury, 3 vols. (New York, 1946), 3, chap. 64, p. 2236.
20. Leonard Krieger, "A View from the Farther Shore," *Comparative Studies in Society and History* 5 (1963): 269.
21. George Thayer, *The British Political Fringe* (London, 1965), p. 31.

their pockets—a few dog-eared clippings from periodicals and other people's books, snippets and shreds of evidence which they are likely to drag out on any argumentative occasion.

A curious backhanded twist upon the reductive fallacy occurs in a recent book by William and Paul Paddock, ominously titled *Famine— 1975!* (Boston, 1967). These authors attempt to demonstrate the inevitability of this disaster, by taking up one by one the various devices and tactics which have been proposed to forestall it. They consider the potential impact of various population limiting devices—IUD, the pill, sterilization, and others. And they separately examine the probable result of rising literacy rates and living standards, and various agricultural innovations—synthetic proteins, vitamins, incaparina, hydroponics, desalinization, the expansion of fisheries, the extension of agricultural research, the increased use of fertilizers, irrigation systems, land reform, government bounties and controls, private enterprise, and finally the "panacea of the unknown panacea." Each of these panaceas is separately rejected as insufficient to resolve the problem. The authors conclude that the problem is therefore insoluble. But they do not consider the effect of all of these measures, simultaneously applied—as they are likely to be. In other words, they study the possible effects of these measures reductively without considering their collective, interactive effect.[22]

ৡ The *fallacy of indiscriminate pluralism* is the converse of the reductive fallacy. It appears in causal explanations where the number of causal components is not defined, or their relative weight is not determined, or commonly both. The resultant explanation, for all its apparent sophistication and thoroughness, is literal nonsense. It is also self-contradictory, for an indiscriminate pluralism is not really a pluralism at all, but a perverse kind of monistic unity comparable to William James's idea of an infant's idea of the universe—"one big blooming buzzing Confusion."[23]

Indiscriminate pluralism is an occupational hazard of academic historians, who are taught to tell comprehensive truths. It is particularly powerful in the present generation, when all monisms are under the ban, and a "single-factor" thesis rarely appears without an extended prefatory apology. One hardly ever sees a contemporary reference to *the* cause of an event, but often to a multiplicity of "causes," "factors," "elements," "origins," "influences," "impulses," "stimuli," etc. As

22. Pp. 62–97.
23. William James, *Psychology* (Cleveland, 1948), p. 16.

pluralism becomes more popular, indiscriminate pluralism becomes more prevalent. It is understandably common among undergraduates and graduate students who are more than a little bewildered by the mass of competing interpretations which they are required to integrate into a coherent pattern. Every generation of history graduate students confronts twice as many books as the generation which preceded it. The number of titles has doubled every twenty years (roughly) since the invention of the printing press, and the number of monographs and learned journals has recently been rising even faster.

An apprentice historian also faces a great and growing eclecticism of method, technique, style, subject, and interpretation among the master craftsmen whom he must satisfy before he is admitted to the guild. Indiscriminate pluralism thus becomes functional to his professional purposes, at the same time that it is dysfunctional and deleterious to his interpretations. An example, possibly apocryphal, is a history graduate student in a great American University, who is said to have equipped himself for his General Examination with a set of cards, each of which carried a single word—"political," "economic," "constitutional," "religious," "military," "intellectual," "educational," "diplomatic," "demographic," "cultural," "social," and "miscellaneous." He is reputed to have responded to each question which was put to him by consulting his cards and enumerating "factors" in every category, giving equal time to each of them, and he passed with distinction!

But the fallacy of indiscriminate pluralism is not confined to students. Many skilled and mature historians have allowed it to creep into their work. One instance is an excellent book on the coming of the American Revolution by Bernhard Knollenberg. The author is not an academic historian but a lawyer by profession. He is, however, a fine scholar, and a worthy successor to the tradition of the great nineteenth-century gentleman-historians—an *amateur* in all the best senses of that battered word, and none of the worst.

Knollenberg's book, the first volume of a projected series, is an account of British imperial policy and American colonial politics from 1759 to 1766. He rejects several monist interpretations which have located *the* cause of the war in economics, or the alleged closing of the frontier, or politics. Instead, he offers a long list of irritants, which cover every category in our graduate student's cards, including "miscellaneous." But he does not carefully weigh one against the other in an integrated and refined interpretation. The result is more useful in its various parts than in the whole, which is shapeless and diffuse.[24]

24. Bernhard Knollenberg, *Origin of the American Revolution: 1759–1766*, rev. ed. (New York, 1961).

Indiscriminate pluralism is often implicit in works of narrative synthesis. One example, in a beautiful piece of narrative craftsmanship, is Johan Huizinga's *The Waning of the Middle Ages*, in which things have, in the author's words, "all sorts of causes of a general nature— political, economic, ethnographic," etc. etc.[25]

&~ The *fallacy of identity* is the assumption that a cause must somehow resemble its effect. It is related to the idea which explicitly underlay many folk remedies, the so-called doctrine of signatures, which was a belief that "every natural substance which possesses any medicinal virtue indicates by an obvious and well-marked external character the disease for which it is a remedy, or the object for which it should be employed."[26] Examples are the idea that turmeric is a cure for jaundice, or bloodstone for bleeding.

When the fallacy of identity appears in modern historical scholarship, it is apt to be implicit, rather than explicit, but its effects are no less troublesome for that fact. One example is the historiography of early inhabitants of Scotland. The Picts constructed brochs and souterrains which are small, dark, and mysterious. From this, some have concluded that the Picts themselves were small, dark, and mysterious— an inference which is described as "romance" by a good historian.[27]

A more common form of the fallacy of identity is the idea that big effects must have big causes, or that big events must have big consequences. We have already met this assumption in the historiography of the Spanish Armada. What was the cause of the collapse of the Manchu dynasty? One historian has written, "So swift a decline, so unexpected a reversal of fortune must have some deep-seated cause."[28] But *must* it?

An even more common form of the fallacy of identity appears often in what J. H. Hexter has called Tunnel History. There is a tendency in topical works to assume that economic effects have primarily economic causes, and that the origins of a religious phenomenon are necessarily religious, and that the great happenings in the history of education are to be explained primarily in terms of earlier great happenings in the history of education. The narrowness of such thinking is to be explained in a variety of ways, which we shall consider in a

25. Johan Huizinga, *The Waning of the Middle Ages* (Garden City, N.Y., 1954). p. 20.
26. John Stuart Mill, *A System of Logic*, 9th ed. (London, 1875), p. 502.
27. J. D. Mackie, *A History of Scotland* (Baltimore, 1966), p. 27.
28. C. P. Fitzgerald, *The Birth of Communist China* (Baltimore, 1964), p. 30.

later chapter. But part of the explanation, perhaps, is the hold which the doctrine of signatures still has upon our thought.

మ్ The *fallacy of absolute priority* assumes that there must be an absolute first term in any causal series, and that if event A_1 causes event B_1, the same cannot be true of B_1 and A_2.[29]

There are many problems of historical causality in which an interactive relationship between A_n and B_n makes better sense than any other. Did Protestantism cause capitalism to develop swiftly in America and Europe? Or did capitalism cause Protestantism to expand? Historians have been arguing about this problem, sometimes in these terms, for three generations. Surely, there was an interaction between these two great movements. It is impossible to say which came first, for there were proto-Protestantisms and proto-capitalisms which can be traced back to the Book of Genesis.

American historians seem equally determined to find a first cause in another problem, which is also three historiographical generations old. Did the inferiority of American Negroes cause anti-Negro prejudice or did prejudice cause inferiority? Arguments have been advanced for both of these positions. But Gunnar Myrdal has argued more persuasively that there was a vicious circle, in which prejudice caused inferiority and inferiority caused prejudice. There was intense anti-Negro feeling in Anglo-America from the very beginning, but also the nature of an African Negro's cultural heritage, the nature of Anglo-American culture, and the nature of the acculturative process were such that a Negro was in a position and in a condition of cultural (but *not* racial) inferiority from the very start.

మ్ The *fallacy of the mechanistic cause*, so-called by R. M. MacIver,

> treats the various components of a social situation, or of any organized system, as though they were detachable, isolable, homogeneous, independently operative, and therefore susceptible of being added to or subtracted from the causal complex, increasing or decreasing the result by that amount. But even a slight acquaintance with the mechanism itself should teach us to avoid this fallacy. We find writers who tell us that juvenile delinquency is due so much to this factor and so much to that and so much to this other. But no mechanic would make the mistake of saying that the carburetor contributed so

---

29. Morris R. Cohen and Ernest Nagel, *Introduction to Logic and Scientific Method* (New York, 1934), p. 385.

much and the ignition system so much and the gasoline so much to the speed of the car.[30]

MacIver's analogy is unfortunate, but his point is sound, in its relevance to historical explanations. There is, I think, an unhappy tendency for historians to break down the components of a causal complex and to analyze them separately, and even to assess separately their causal "influence," independent of other elements with which they interact. Almost any major causal problem can serve as an example—the cause of the American Civil War or the cause of World War I. Historians have formed the habit of speaking of the causes of these and other events—a usage which is technically incorrect, and also misleading in its implication that the various "causes" can be individually analyzed and assessed, and that somehow if one of the "causes" were removed, the effect would be diminished in the proportion of that causal component to other causal components. Imagine that an effect E was caused by A, B, C, and D. If all of these four causal components were necessary to that effect, then the removal of any one of them would not diminish E by one-fourth. Its absence would make E impossible. On the other hand, it is easy to imagine that A, B, C, and D, though not individually necessary to E, nevertheless interacted in a geometrical ratio. If there were only A, then E would be of a magnitude 1. If there were only A and B, then the effect would be not 2 but 2^2, or an E of magnitude 4. A, B, and C would produce an E of 9, and all four causal components, an E of 16. This is an involved way of saying that a causal complex is something other than the sum of its parts.

Three examples of the mechanistic fallacy are provided by Morton White. One is from the work of a great classicist, J. B. Bury, who eliminated depopulation, the Christian religion, and the fiscal system as causes of the dismemberment of the Roman empire. "If these or any of them were responsible for [the Empire's] dismemberment by the barbarians in the West, it may be asked how it was that in the East, where the same causes operated, the Empire survived much longer intact and united."[31] But this is a mistake. The three causal elements which Bury rejects may have interacted with each other, and with still other elements, in such a way as to produce very different results in the West and the East.

Another example is the criticism of Herbert Baxter Adams's explanation of the cause of America's early democratization in terms

30. R. M. MacIver, *Social Causation*, rev. ed. (New York, 1964), p. 94.
31. J. B. Bury, *History of the Later Roman Empire*, 2 vols. (New York, 1958) 1: 308–9; quoted in Morton White, *The Foundations of Historical Knowledge* (New York, 1965), p. 65.

of the "Germanic tradition." Many critics of this thesis have replied that
the "Germanic tradition" must be present in Germany, which is not
notorious for its democracy. But, White observes, "these supposed
refutations of singular explanatory statements are faulty if they proceed
on the assumption that Herbert Baxter Adams, when he said that the
presence of the Germanic tradition was responsible for American democratic institutions, necessarily implied that *wherever* the Germanic tradition is present, democracy arises."[32] It is possible that such a cause as
this could produce very different results in different contexts.

A third example is from the great French medievalist, Marc Bloch.
White writes:

> Even Marc Bloch, who was so much more concerned with the logic of his
> discipline than most historians, seems to have been involved in a logical in-
> consistency in his treatment of two distinct explanatory statements, just be-
> cause he seems to attack one by fallaciously arguing that it implies a false
> generalization but fails to use the same fallacious method of refutation on
> another. In his *Feudal Society* he considers as an explanation of the *cessation*
> of Scandinavian pillaging in the Middle Ages the fact that the Scandinavians
> were converted to Christianity, and apparently rejects this explanation on
> the ground that it implies the false generalization that no Christian people
> would engage in pillaging. He says: "As we shall often have occasion to ob-
> serve in the following pages, among the peoples of the West during the feudal
> era there was apparently no difficulty in reconciling ardent faith in the Chris-
> tian mysteries with a taste for violence and plunder, nay even with the most
> conscious glorification of war." On the other hand, when Bloch tries to ex-
> plain the *beginning* of the Scandinavian invasions, he is prepared to accept
> as its explanation the fact that the Scandinavian countries were overpopulated
> at the time, though he surely would deny that the people of *every* overpopu-
> lated country invade in the manner of the medieval Scandinavians. What we
> have here is a kind of double standard.[33]

&~ The *fallacy of reason as cause* mistakes a causal for a logical
order, or vice versa. It is a form of error for which the ambiguity of
the term "because" may be partly responsible. We use that word both
as a conjunction in a causal proposition and as a conjunction in a logical
proposition. It is easy, in practice, to confuse the two. Consider the
following statements:

1. Cromwell died because he caught intermittent fever.
2. Cromwell died because all men die, and Cromwell was a
man.

The first sentence supplies a causal explanation which is acceptable to

32. White, p. 64.
33. White, pp. 65–66; quoting Marc Bloch, *Feudal Society* (Chicago, 1961), pp. 35–38.

historians but syllogistically invalid.[34] The second sentence is syllogistically valid but historically insignificant and causally meaningless. To mistake it for a causal explanation is fallacious.

Sometimes the error runs in the opposite direction, and a causal explanation is mistaken for a reasoned argument. This was the case in the doctrines of historical relativism, which were fatally flawed by a classic example of the fallacy of reason as cause. Relativism confuses two very different problems—the problem of how knowledge is acquired and the problem of the validity of that knowledge. The fact that historical knowledge is itself historically caused by the situation of the historian does not in any degree imply that it is false. Blind patriotism may cause a Polish historian to assert that a German army invaded Poland in 1939. That statement possesses a truth value which is independent of its origins. A German historian might be similarly motivated to insist that a Polish army invaded Germany in 1939. That statement, whatever its cause, is false. The same logic equally applies to factual statements of every magnitude, though its application becomes more complex in a geometric ratio to the increase in size.

There are many other errors in relativism—errors which have been discussed at considerable length by competent philosophers.[35]

34. Some philosophers think that causal explanations of this sort are enthymenes—abbreviated syllogisms, in which a premise is not made explicit. But this, I think, is wrong. There could be an implied general premise here, but not one which will sustain a syllogism. The implied premise might be something like, "Some men who catch intermittent fever die." Or it might be "Most men (of great age, frail frame, etc.) who catch intermittent fever die." But these statements cannot satisfy a rule of syllogistic reasoning which requires that the middle term must be "distributed" at least once—i.e., that it must refer to everything in its range of reference, and not merely to some or to most things. Without a distributed middle term, a deductive syllogism collapses. No statement of statistical regularity can be properly distributed, and yet, no other kind of regularity statement is possible in historical writing.

But even a statement of statistical regularity is not, I think, what a historian commonly has in mind in causal propositions of this sort. He means rather to say that intermittent fever is a disease which *can* kill a man, and it *did* kill Cromwell. That it can be fatal is something which he might learn from merely a single instance, by an empirical understanding of the causal linkages, even though it may only have killed one man and no others. It is not always necessary, in history, or the natural sciences, or daily life, to have a causal explanation which includes either a general statement or deductive certainty. All that is required in many cases is a demonstration that the causal relationship is *possible*, and that it *probably* happened. I suspect that analytical philosophers who have attempted to impose the so-called covering law model upon this species of explanation are guilty of an inverse form of the fallacy of reason as cause, in their confusion of two different forms of thought.

35. A good critique of Charles Beard's relativism appears in Arthur C. Danto, *Analytical Philosophy of History* (Cambridge, 1965), chap. 6; and Mannheim's "relationism" is refuted in Charles Frankel, *The Case for Modern Man,* 2d ed. (Boston, 1959), chap. 7. See also, Christopher Blake, "Can History Be Objective?" *Mind* 72 (1955): 61–78; Ernest Nagel, "Some Issues in the Logic of Historical Analysis,"

And there is also something which is true and important. It is surely correct that no historian can know the totality of history as actuality. And it *is* a plain fact that history is something which happens even to historians. But the corrosive skepticism which relativism engendered was both logically deficient and practically deleterious to the progress of historical knowledge.

& profit; The *fallacy of responsibility as cause* confuses a problem of ethics with a problem of agency in a way which falsifies both. It often consists in merging two different questions and demanding a single answer: "How did it happen?" and "Who is to blame?" This pernicious practice is particularly common in attempts to explain disagreeable events, which are mostly contemporary events. An economist ran into it in a practical situation. Paul Samuelson writes,

> In some traditions a responsible and free human agent has come to be re-garded as the "cause" of anything. When Professor Jacob Viner and I served on the advisory board to the Commission on Money and Credit, I was in-terested in hearing him remark that there was good precedent in the fields of jurisprudence and torts to lay any possible blame for postwar inflation upon the Federal Reserve Board rather than on such factors as the backlog of demand or level of public debt, since "they" were responsible agents whose duty it was to prevent the evil.[36]

The most glaring example in American historiography is the at-tempt to explain the course of Reconstruction after the Civil War. The question of cause is no sooner raised than it is transformed from "What caused it?" to "Who is to blame?" The answers are numerous, but nearly all of them seek to impose responsibility upon some human agent, who has been specifically identified as Andrew Johnson, or Thaddeus Stevens, or the Radical Republicans collectively, or intransigent white Southern-ers, or Northern businessmen, or carpetbaggers, or scalawags, or drunken Negro legislators.

But it is quite impossible to locate any individuals who were re-sponsible in both a moral and a causal sense for what happened in this painful chapter of our past. The cause of the failure of Reconstruction race policy must surely be sought in general phenomena for which no

Scientific Monthly 74 (1952): 162–69; Jack W. Meiland, *Scepticism and Historical Knowledge* (New York, 1965); and Cushing Strout, *The Pragmatic Revolt in American History* (New Haven, 1958), p. 59. passim.
36. Paul A. Samuelson, "Some Notions on Causality and Teleology in Economics," in Daniel Lerner, ed., *Cause and Effect* (New York, 1965), p. 100 n.

free and responsible human agent can be held to blame. First, there was an intensity of Negrophobia in the nation, which resisted all correction. The real sovereigns of the United States, the white majority, were unable to accept the fundamental proposition that Negroes were people. Second, there was the prevalence of a tacit moral philosophy in the United States which was very close to that of Jefferson and Adam Smith—a philosophy which held that governmental power could not help people who were unable to help themselves, without destroying their moral fiber. Third, there was the ugly but undeniable fact of the brutalization of black slaves, who were incompetent as citizens of a free republic. None of these conditions was subject to modification by any act of any leading statesman. To argue the proposition "Was Andrew Johnson to blame, or Thaddeus Stevens?" is to manifest an empirical limitation and perhaps a moral blindness as well. It is also logically indefensible.

ɛↄ What is a causal explanation? It is an attempt to explain the occurrence of an event by reference to some of those antecedents which rendered its occurrence probable. This definition is ambiguous as to the number and nature of the antecedents. The ambiguity is deliberate, because historians do different things when they attempt to construct causal explanations. I can find no a priori superiority in any one of these different causalities. But it is important to recognize their differences, for error has often resulted from confusing one kind of causal explanation with another.

John Stuart Mill believed that "the real cause is the whole of these antecedents, and we have, philosophically speaking, no right to give the name of cause to any one, exclusively of others."[37] This assertion may be true, but it is not very useful. For some small events, a historian may hope to recover all of the antecedents which rendered the effect possible, or probable, or necessary. But in most causal problems which historians actually confront, selection is not merely desirable but inescapable.

Which antecedents should be selected? Philosophers and, implicitly, historians have developed many different criteria. R. G. Collingwood alone has suggested three of them. First,

> that which is "caused" is an event or state of things standing to it in a one-to-one relation of causal priority; i.e., a relation of such a kind that (a) if the cause happens or exists the effect also must happen or exist, even if no further conditions are fulfilled, (b) the effect cannot happen or exist unless the cause

37. Mill, *A System of Logic*, p. 214.

happens or exists, [and] (c) in some sense . . . the cause is prior to the effect, for without such priority there would be no telling which was which.[38]

Collingwood calls this a "theoretical natural science" type of causal explanation. But it is sometimes used in history, as when an economic historian explains the fact of inflation by the quantity theory of money.[39] The regularistic relationship in this model is always of a statistical sort, and a *ceteris paribus* clause must always be included. This requires an amendment in Collingwood's definition. A historian, and indeed a natural scientist, can never assert that an effect will always happen but only that it will probably happen. The connection between cause and effect is not necessary but probabilistic.

Collingwood identified a second kind of causal explanation, in which "that which is 'caused' is an event in nature, and its 'cause' is an event or state of things by producing or preventing which we can produce or prevent that whose cause it is said to be." He attributes this kind of causal explanation to "practical science," but it is also found in history. It is used, I think, by Eric McKitrick in his causal explanation of the course of Reconstruction after the American Civil War.[40] This model of causal explanation as controllable antecedents raises a problem of reference—namely, controllable by whom? Collingwood's answer is a relative one, in which every man becomes a historian, and the controllable antecedents are those he can control:

> A car skids while cornering at a certain point, strikes the kerb, and turns turtle. From the car-driver's point of view the cause of the accident was cornering too fast, and the lesson is that one must drive more carefully. From the county surveyor's point of view the cause was a defect in the surface or camber of the road, and the lesson is that greater care must be taken to make roads skid-proof. From the motor-manufacturer's point of view the cause was defective design in the car, and the lesson is that one must place the centre of gravity lower.[41]

In actual road accidents, however, a variant upon this causal criterion is regrettably more common. People involved in accidents tend to assume that the cause of their misfortune was an antecedent which somebody else could control. The driver would blame the surveyor for the condition of the road or the manufacturer for the quality of the

---

38. R. G. Collingwood, *An Essay on Metaphysics* (Oxford, 1940), pp. 285–86. All quotations from Collingwood in this section are from this source, unless otherwise attributed.
39. Earl J. Hamilton, *American Treasure and the Price Revolution in Spain, 1501–1560* (Cambridge, 1934), p. 301. Compare, however, J. H. Elliott, *Imperial Spain*, pp. 189–94.
40. Eric L. McKitrick, *Andrew Johnson and Reconstruction* (Chicago, 1960), passim.
41. Collingwood, *An Essay on Metaphysics*, p. 304.

car. The surveyor would condemn the driver, or the manufacturer. The manufacturer would point to the surveyor, or the driver.

A historian uses neither of these variants, for he is not a participant and there is rarely an antecedent which he personally can control. He conventionally chooses some or all of the principal participants and identifies controllable antecedents by reference to them, as McKitrick did. The same strategy is also used in daily practical decision making.

A third form of causal explanation is one which Collingwood believed to be *the* historical form, and one which he used himself. In "historical causation," he wrote, "that which is 'caused' is the free and deliberate act of a conscious and responsible agent, and causing him to do it means affording him a motive for doing it." This, of course, applies *only* to deliberate and free acts, which comprise but a small fraction of events which historians actually attempt to explain. But within this limit, it is a form of causal explanation which is widely used.

A fourth form of causal explanation has also been suggested—one which consists in the identification of abnormal antecedents.[42] An exponent of this view, R. M. MacIver, explains that an abnormal phenomenon is one which "intrudes on a relatively constant system or disturbs a relatively constant equilibrium. . . . Man has set up within or upon the order of nature a vast number of temporary operative systems, subject in their degree and after their kind to disturbances from within and from without." It might appear that this position entails a powerful metaphysical bias toward equilibrium as normal, and so it does in MacIver's version of it. But it need not do so. A historian could explain the phenomenon of political stability in terms of an abnormal equilibrium between economic and demographic growth.

In any case, causal explanation is often understood, in ordinary historiographical practice, to mean the identification of abnormal antecedents. Pirenne uses it, in precisely the terms of MacIver's model, to explain the cause of the disruption of the "Mediterranean commonwealth" by the invasion of Islam: "Now, all of a sudden, the very lands where civilization had been born were torn away; the Cult of the Prophet was substituted for the Christian Faith, Moslem law for Roman law, the Arab tongue for the Greek and Latin tongue."[43]

Still other historians have assumed that a causal explanation is one that identifies "underlying conditions" which were of such a nature that

---

42. MacIver, *Social Causation*, p. 186; H. L. A. Hart and A. M. Honoré, *Causation and the Law* (Oxford, 1959), pp. 31–38.

43. Henri Pirenne, *Medieval Cities* (Garden City, N.Y., 1956), p. 16. For this example, and much more on the problem of causation, I am obliged to White, *Foundations of Historical Knowledge*, p. 116.

they rendered the effect probable. This is perhaps the most common of all forms of causal explanation in historical scholarship. Indeed, causal explanations that depart from this model are commonly condemned in professional journals, for superficiality. An earlier generation of historians tended to use a different causal model, which was constructed of a series of contingent events, rather than underlying states.[44] Finally, some historians seek the precipitant cause. Kenneth Stampp did something like this in *And the War Came*.

These various attempts to resolve the problem of which causal antecedents should be included in a causal explanation yield eight answers:

1. All antecedents
2 Regularistic antecedents
3. Controllable antecedents
4. Rational and/or motivational antecedents
5. Abnormal antecedents
6. Structural antecedents
7. Contingent-series antecedents
8. Precipitant antecedents

There are undoubtedly other criteria, and subdivisions of these, and also ways of combining some of them with others. But this analysis may serve to make the major point, which is that there are many different kinds of causal explanation, and that they have different requirements and different uses. The specific kind of causal explanation a historian employs must be selected according to the nature of the effect to be explained and the nature of the object of the explanation. Every causal explanation should be an explanation to some purpose. There is no such thing as *the* cause, and no cause for all occasions.

Most of the trouble historians get themselves into in causal explanation consists in asking one kind of causal question and seeking another kind of causal answer. Or it consists in a stubborn determination to locate *the* cause. And both of these problems are aggravated by the unfortunate tendency of historians to hide their causal models from everybody—including themselves.

44. An excellent discussion, with examples, appears in White, *Foundations of Historical Knowledge*, pp. 133–47.

CHAPTER VII

FALLACIES OF MOTIVATION

ह्य

Men are not machines. . . . They are men—a tautology
which is sometimes worth remembering.
                              —Gilbert Ryle

Motivational explanation might be understood as a special kind of causal
explanation in which the effect is an intelligent act and the cause is the
thought behind it. Or it might be conceived in noncausal terms, as a
paradigm of patterned behavior. My own preference runs to the second
of these propositions, but there is no need to argue their relative merits
here. The following observations are consistent with both.

Historians have often used motivational explanations in their work.
Almost always, they have used them badly. Problems of motive in
academic historiography tend to be hopelessly mired in a sort of simple-
minded moralizing which is equally objectionable from an ethical and
an empirical point of view. Lord Rosebery once remarked that what
the English people really wished to know about Napoleon was whether
he was a good man.[1] The same purpose often prevails among professional scholars who are unable to distinguish motivational psychology
from moral philosophy, and even unwilling to admit that there can
be a distinction at all. Moreover, many scholars tend to find flat, monistic answers to complex motivational problems, which further falsifies
their interpretations.[2]

1. Quoted in E. H. Carr, *What Is History?* (New York, 1962), p. 97.
2. See, e.g., C. A. Macartney, *Hungary: A Short History* (Chicago, 1962), in which

Secondly, the quality of motivational explanation in history has been diminished by the rationalistic bias of historians. William L. Langer complained of his colleagues in 1957 that "Almost without exception . . . they have stuck to the approach and methods of historicism, restricting themselves to recorded fact and to strictly rational motivation."[3] Langer proposed that the historian's "next assignment" was a "deepening of our historical understanding through exploitation of the concepts and findings of modern psychology." But ten years after his address, few historians have acted upon his advice. Many scholars, of course, have made use of the classic mechanisms of psychoanalytic theory—compensation, repression, identification, projection, sublimation, displacement. It is rare to find a historical biography which does not introduce these ideas. But they are used superficially, crudely, and inconsequentially, as rhetorical supplements to motivational explanations which are still predominantly rationalist.

A minority of historians have attempted to deal with the problem of motivation in a more satisfactory way, by applying Freudian theory directly to their scholarship. As early as 1913, an American historian tried his hand at a psychoanalytic interpretation of Martin Luther.[4] There have been many other projects of a similar nature in the past half century, and a few have generated useful and constructive insights into historical problems.[5]

But these experiments have ended in failure more often than success. They have commonly consisted either of Freudian raids upon history, or of historians' raids upon Freud. The results have ranged from the highly dubious to the downright preposterous.

If we are wise, we might learn something from both the successes and

---

principal figures are categorized in a spirit suggestive of *1066 and All That*. We are solemnly informed that "Stephen II was almost entirely bad." Louis I, on the other hand, was "a true paladin," and Ladislas I was "a true paladin and a gentle knight" (pp. 20, 42).
3. William L. Langer, "The Next Assignment," *The American Historical Review* 63 (1958): 283–304.
4. Preserved Smith, "Luther's Early Development in the Light of Psychoanalysis," *American Journal of Psychology* 24 (1913): 360–77.
5. Alexander and Juliette George, *Woodrow Wilson and Colonel House: A Personality Study* (New York, 1956); William B. Willcox, *Portrait of a General: Sir Henry Clinton in the War of Independence* (New York, 1964); Fawn Brodie, *Thaddeus Stevens* (New York, 1959); Erik Erikson, *Young Man Luther, A Study in Psychoanalysis and History* (New York, 1962); E. R. Dodds, *The Greeks and the Irrational* (Berkeley, 1951); Lewis J. Edinger, *Kurt Schumacher: A Study of Political Behavior* (Stanford, 1965); Rudolph Binion, *Frau Lou: Nietzsche's Wayward Disciple* (Princeton, 1968); Lewis Namier, "King George III: A Study of Personality," *Personalities and Powers* (London, 1955), pp. 39–58; and despite criticism from the *cognoscenti*, Ernest Jones, *The Life and Work of Sigmund Freud*, 3 vols. (New York, 1953–1957).

the failures of Freudian historiography. Maybe the latter derive in some degree from limitations in psychoanalytic method, as well as from the poverty of historiographical procedure. Perhaps the utility and relevance and accuracy of Freudian theory is seriously diminished by five substantial failings. First, it is in its aboriginal condition narrowly culture-bound. I think it is significant that the success of psychoanalytic history has tended to vary inversely with the temporal and spatial and cultural distance between the subject and Freud. Second, psychoanalytic theory has, in effect, extrapolated normative patterns from a study of neurotic behavior. It is, again, no accident that psychoanalytic history has been successful in proportion to the degree of serious mental disturbance in the subject. For an investigation of motivation in stable, integrated personalities, its value has been nearly nil. Third, psychoanalytic theory places an excessive interest in childhood. This imbalance is untenable in itself, and also exceedingly inconvenient to historians who cannot hope to find the kind of evidence which psychoanalytic interpretations require. Fourth, a similar problem derives from the hypersexuality of Freudian theory, which is inherently indefensible and inapplicable to historians' problems. Finally, psychoanalytic theory has often been built into a closed deterministic system. Its enthusiasts have insisted that historians must take all or nothing. Many scholars have chosen the latter alternative, as the lesser evil.

These thoughts, of course, are not new. They have often been articulated in the past fifty years. Too often, they have been offered as excuses for a total rejection of psychological insights of all kinds into history. The argument here is something different. It is not for ante-Freudian history, or anti-Freudian history, or sub-Freudian history, but rather for post-Freudian or super-Freudian historical scholarship.

Historians might be able to make much more effective use of post-Freudian psychoanalytic literature than they can of the work of Freud himself. One historian of modern America[6] has already discovered a special relevance in the neo-Freudian thought of Karen Horney, who attempted to adjust psychoanalytic theory to the cultural conditions she discovered in the United States.

Moreover, historians might have more to learn from recent work in social psychology than in psychiatry. The problems of social psychology are closer to those of history, and the methods are more compatible. At the end of this chapter, I shall have some more specific things to say about the relevance of work by Abraham Maslow and David C. McClelland.

6. David M. Potter, *People of Plenty* (Chicago, 1954), pp. 34, 54–72, passim.

Finally, if historians have much to learn from psychology, they also may have something to teach. Psychology and psychoanalysis have both been diminished by a temporal provincialism of the sort which only historical scholarship can correct. But first, historians must put their own house in order. Let us proceed to some common fallacies in motivational explanation, and then to a few proposals for their correction.

&· The *pathetic fallacy* is the ascription of animate behavior to inanimate objects. In Arnold Toynbee's definition, it is "imaginatively endowing inanimate objects with life."[7] Most commonly, the pathetic fallacy takes the form of anthropomorphism and anthropopathism, in which human form and human feelings are given to gods, groups, objects, etc.[8] There are many examples of the pathetic fallacy in explicitly historical writing—by conservatives who fear the beast of Bolshevism, liberals who complain of the cunning of capitalism, intellectual historians who speak of the mind of the Enlightenment, and institutional historians who would have a bare-breasted Madame Liberty hitch up her skirts and hurdle the barricades, as in Delacroix's famous version of the Revolution of 1830.

It is often difficult to distinguish this fallacy from what may be merely an overblown figure of speech. And it is equally problematical to locate the point at which the behavior patterns of individuals can be transferred to groups. Is there such a thing as a national character? For better or for worse, many historians and social scientists believe that there is, and some of them speak of it as if it were a person. Sometimes the intention is merely metaphorical. But it is an exceedingly doubtful and dangerous image to introduce into one's thought, for it has a way of spreading swiftly out of control. Consider the case of Henry Steele Commager's book, *The American Mind*. In his preface, the author explicitly acknowledged the fictional quality of his title. But in his first chapter the fiction was reified, as Commager began to sketch with bold, quick strokes of his pen a portrait of "The American." Sixty million

7. Arnold J. Toynbee, *A Study of History*, 12 vols. (New York, 1935–61), 1:8; 12:45, 116.
8. Sometimes other forms of life become the model, as when Theodore Roosevelt wrote a speech in which he made the world into a menagerie, and compared all the nations to specific animals such as monkeys, hyenas, and hippopotami—an interpretative device which his wise friend Elihu Root discouraged, not for its logical deficiencies, but simply for the sake of its diplomatic shortcomings. Root solemnly suggested that Roosevelt should strike out all sentences which might bring war between the United States and other countries.

minds magically became one, and a long list of singular characteristics was recited:

> The American was incurably optimistic. . . . He had little sense of the past. . . . The American had spacious ideas, his imagination roamed a continent, and he was impatient with petty transactions. . . . He preached the gospel of hard work. . . . All this tended to give a quantitative cast to his thinking. . . . Theories and speculations disturbed the American, and he avoided abstruse philosophies of government or conduct. . . . His religion, too, notwithstanding its Calvinist antecedents, was practical. He was religious rather than devout. . . . The American's attitude toward culture was at once suspicious and indulgent. Where it interfered with more important activities, he distrusted it; where it was the recreation of his leisure hours or of his womenfolk, he tolerated it. . . . The sense of equality permeated the American's life and thought. . . . The American was good natured, generous, hospitable, and sociable. . . . Carelessness was perhaps the most pervasive and persistent quality in the American. . . . The American's attitude toward authority, rules, and regulations was the despair of bureaucrats and disciplinarians. . . . The American was at once intelligent and conservative, independent and reliable. . . . The American was romantic and sentimental. . . . The American had a strong sense of fair play. . . .[9]

All of these qualities were undoubtedly possessed by some Americans, and some perhaps were statistically descriptive of most Americans. But in Commager's book, they comprise a single autonomous superbeing called "The American," a creature who appears to possess not merely a set of normative mental characteristics, but a mind and will of its own. Commager's use of personification makes it impossible for a reader to distinguish a rhetorical device from a conceptual structure. Moreover, it made it difficult for Commager himself to do so.

A second and similar form of the pathetic fallacy was recognized more than sixty years ago by G. K. Chesterton, who called it "the fallacy of the young nation."

> It is a childish blunder, built upon a single false metaphor. I refer to the universal modern talk about young nations and new nations; about America being young, about New Zealand being new. The whole thing is a trick of words. . . . Of course we may use the metaphor of youth about America or the colonies, if we use it strictly as implying recent origin. But if we use it (as we do use it) as implying vigour or vivacity, or crudity, or inexperience, or hope, or a long life before them, or any of the romantic attributes of youth, then it is surely as clear as daylight that we are duped by a stale figure of speech.[10]

9. Henry Steele Commager, *The American Mind, An Interpretation of American Thought and Character Since the 1880's* (New Haven, 1950), pp. 3–40, passim.
10. G. K. Chesterton, *Heretics* (New York, 1905), pp. 256–7. Attacks upon anthropomorphism were not, of course, inaugurated by Chesterton. Other examples were identified as early as the sixth century B.C., by Xenophanes of Colophon, who was an outspoken critic of the anthropomorphism and anthropopathism in Greek religion.

Chesterton was mistaken in one respect—anthropomorphic ideas of nations and cultures are not merely semantical tricks but serious substantive errors. There have been many mistakes of this sort in historical writing—both in the work of traditional historians, such as Hippolyte Taine, and in the monographs of sophisticated social scientists, such as Karl Deutsch, who has written about the "wills" of nations. Deutsch defined those national "wills" as "the set of constraints acquired from the memories and past experiences of the system, and applied to the selection and treatment of items in its later intake, recall and decisions." But nations do not make decisions—only people do. Sometimes people may tend to make similar decisions within a national group, but that kind of normative decision making is very different from Deutsch's collective national will.[11]

A third subspecies of the pathetic fallacy appears in many absurd modern attempts to psychoanalyze historical events, institutions, cultures, or nations. An English social scientist, Geoffrey Gorer, has explained the historical relationship between Anglo-America and Europe in terms of a national Oedipus complex, in which "England, the England of George III and Lord North, takes the place of the despotic and tyrannical father, the American colonists that of conspiring sons."[12] In Mr. Gorer's interpretation, the Revolution was a great archetypical event, which has been perpetually re-enacted in the psyches of American patriots ever since.[13] The mother in this unhappy family is difficult to locate. Sometimes she seems to be the Statue of Liberty, and sometimes the Republic itself. If she is either of these things, then there would appear to be more than a little sexual and generational confusion in Gorer's rendering of American history, for by his logic the son becomes the father of his own mother. Social scientists have turned up some curious family relationships in their researches, but none as odd as this one.

Gorer is by no means alone in his errors. A learned student of Freud, Manfred Guttmacher, has done much the same thing, on the same subject. And Max Lerner has solemnly written of a national compensation for "the sacrificial slaying of the European father."[14]

---

11. Karl Deutsch, *Nationalism and Social Communication* (New York, 1953), p. 151. For an example of anthropomorphism in traditional historiography, see H. A. Taine, *The French Revolution*, 3. vols. (Gloucester, Mass., 1962), 2:358; and see also Gordon Shepherd, *The Austrian Odyssey* (London, 1957), pp. 3–22, passim, in which a rounded personality is attributed to Austria itself, or herself or himself.
12. G. Gorer, *The American People: A Study in National Character,* rev. ed. (New York, 1964), pp. 29–30.
13. This, by the way, is a fine example of the fallacy of archetypes, discussed above.
14. Max Lerner, *America as a Civilization,* 2 vols. (New York, 1961), 1:28.

Gorer also applied the same method to the problems of Russian history, explaining the success of Bolshevism in terms of the child-rearing practices which are inflicted upon Young Russia. One critic has commented that "there are more steps in any logic that leads from, say, swaddling to the Politburo than this sort of explanation dreams of."[15]

The author of that remark, Donald B. Meyer, has made very good sense in his attempt to distinguish legitimate from illegitimate uses of psychoanalytic analysis in history. "Efforts to transport vocabulary, to locate a social unconscious, a collective ego, a community superego, to equate social events with processes discovered by clinicians in individual dynamics, are no good; these are analogies as dubious as analogies drawn from Newton and Darwin," he has written. Psychoanalytic history must be biographical in its orientation. It must deal with individuals. Meyer hastens to add,

> It hardly follows from this, however, that psychoanalysis, even though it might be thoroughly adequate for the study of individuals, has no relevance to those social entities—institutions, states, classes, styles, cultures, groups, parties, churches, ideologies—which historians are anxious to illuminate. It follows rather that psychoanalytic biography constitutes a perspective, or a focus, from which history can organize all its narratives. . . . What do given institutions, states, styles, churches, etc., mean for the selves involved in them?[16]

The distinction is wire-drawn by Meyer, but it is indispensable to any attempt to use psychoanalytic analysis in history. If a historian wishes to work with a group, he must remember that his method applies to the individuals who compose the group, and *not* to the group itself. We might conclude with a wise comment by Richard Pares. With nice British understatement, he remarked that "the collective unconscious is somewhat overrated."[17]

ஃ The *apathetic fallacy* is defined by Arnold Toynbee as the error of "treating living creatures as though they were inanimate."[18] Leaving Toynbee's animus out of account, this form of error might be more satisfactorily specified as treating rational men as if they were not rational. One familiar form of this fallacy is the doctrine of historical

15. Donald B. Meyer, "A Review of Young Man Luther," in Bruce Mazlish, ed., *Psychoanalysis and History* (Englewood Cliffs, N.J., 1963), p. 178.
16. Ibid., pp. 177–78, 174–80.
17. Richard Pares, "Human Nature and Politics," in *The Historian's Business and Other Essays* (Oxford, 1961), p. 34.
18. Toynbee, *A Study of History*, 1:8.

materialism. Another is classical Freudian theory. The fallaciousness of these schools of thought is succinctly explained by W. H. Walsh:

> Marxists and Freudians, in their different ways, have taught us all to look for non-rational causes for ideas and beliefs which on the surface look perfectly rational, and have convinced some that rational thinking as such is an impossibility. But though we cannot (and should not) return to the naïve confidence of our grandfathers in these matters, it must none the less be pointed out that the anti-rationalist case here cannot be stated without contradiction. It undermines not only the theories of which its proponents disapprove, but itself as well. For it asks us to believe, as a matter of rational conviction, that rational conviction is impossible. And this we cannot do.[19]

Neither historical materialism nor psychic determinism can be proved or disproved by appeals to historical fact. They are metahistorical doctrines which transcend empiricism. But they cannot transcend their own logical assumptions, which are simply suicidal, as Mr. Walsh indicates. The complaint against these delusions consists not in the fact that they are empirically false but rather in the fact that they are logically absurd. I can see no room for compromise on this point.

The logical deficiencies of historical materialism have been discussed elsewhere at great length. They surely require no refutation here.[20] But there is no adequate discussion, to my knowledge, of the deficiencies of psychic determinism in historical thought. The fallacy appears in several works of otherwise distinguished scholarship. It is dysfunctional to the interpretation of E. R. Dodds, in an excellent but imbalanced book on the Greeks and the irrational. The author approvingly quotes William James's remark that "the recesses of feeling, the dark, blinder strata of character, are the only places in the world in which we catch real fact in the making."[21]

Some of the more picturesque examples of the same error appear not in monographs but in metahistorical interpretations. One extreme specimen is Gordon Rattray Taylor, *Sex in History* (New York, 1954). Taylor believes that "Eros and Thanatos permeate every compartment of human activity,"[22] a proposition which is defensible. But Taylor seeks to

19. W. H. Walsh, *Philosophy of History* (New York, 1960), pp. 102–3.
20. An excellent critique is H. B. Acton's *The Illusion of the Epoch* (London, 1955). See also M. M. Bober, *Karl Marx's Interpretation of History*, 2d ed. (Cambridge, 1950). The extent to which Marx was consistent in the commission of this fallacy is of course highly controversial. See Erich Fromm, *Marx's Concept of Man* (New York, 1961). But Fromm's introductory interpretation is seriously strained, as a rounded interpretation of Marx's writings in this respect.
21. E. R. Dodds, *The Greeks and the Irrational* (Berkeley, 1951), p. 1; the same assumption appears in Binion, *Frau Lou*.
22. P. 17.

demonstrate not merely "how closely attitudes to sexual matters interlock with other social attitudes," but also how they "dictate them." All histories which contradict this thesis are appropriately denounced as "emasculated." If all thought is determined in this way, then Taylor's thought must be determined too. And if it is, then it is difficult to imagine how his historical inquiry is possible. In short Taylor's work is not empirically deficient but logically self-destructive.[23]

The apathetic fallacy also occurs in fragmented forms, when historians are unable to empathize sufficiently with specific human subjects. Consider, for example, Richard Hofstadter's collection of essays, published as *The Paranoid Style in American Politics* (New York, 1965). William Buckley has protested that, in the work of Hofstadter, moderate liberalism is analyzed, but radical conservatism is diagnosed. The complaint, I think, is fairly made. The thought of Barry Goldwater is no more paranoid than the thought of Hofstadter. If Goldwater's conservatism is "fundamentalist," what shall we say of a scholar who regards other peoples' ideologies as symptoms of a personality disorder? Surely, there are paranoid conservatives in America, and paranoid liberals as well. But conservatism itself, however immoderate, is not merely a form of irrationality. To categorize conservatives in those terms is to resort to a kind of motivational special pleading. It is also to commit the apathetic fallacy, in a particularized form.

ટ— The *idealist fallacy* consists in interpretations of human conduct which rest upon a conception of man as *Homo sapiens* in a narrow and exclusive sense. It is a double error, for it converts *homines* into *Homo*, and *Homo* into *Homo sapiens*. The absurdity of this reduction should be readily apparent. If any individual *Homo* is *sapiens* in some degree, he is also *furens*, and *prudens, diligens*, and *odiens, ludens, faber, amator*, and more. To isolate merely the rational component of human existence is to falsify both humanity and rationality. Gerald W. Chapman observed that "when history is reduced to intellectual environments . . . expository critics risk inventing an 'intellectual man' quite as arbitrary as

---

23. The same mistake appears in Herbert Marcuse's *Eros and Civilization* (Boston, 1955), which, with other work by the same author, seems to be an attempt to combine the metaphysical determinism of Hegel, the economic determinism of Marx, and the psychic determinism of Freud with a plea for human freedom! See also Norman Brown, *Life Against Death: The Psychoanalytic Meaning of History* (Middletown, Conn., 1959), which also combines the apathetic fallacy with the fallacies of metahistory (cf. Arthur C. Danto, *Analytical Philosophy of History* [Cambridge, 1965], chap. 1).

'economic man' in classical economics or 'political man' in classical utilitarianism."[24]

The idealist fallacy occurs both in general and particular forms. The most prevalent general form is the so-called "neo-idealism" of R. G. Collingwood, which is commonly understood to consist in the following propositions:

> 1. All history is the history of thought . . . not only of thought but of reflective thought, that is, one which is performed in the consciousness that it is being performed, and is constituted what it is by that consciousness.
> 2. The history of thought, and therefore all history, is the re-enactment of past thought in the historian's mind.
> 3. There is nothing other than historical thought itself by appeal to which its conclusions may be verified.[25]

Collingwood's conception of history is one in which thoughts alone are events and in which an historian knows them by a process of rethinking. He asserts that "the historian is not interested in the fact that men eat and sleep and make love and thus satisfy their natural appetites."[26] But this is simply mistaken. Historians *are* interested in these aspects of human behavior, and increasingly so.

And as to "rethinking," Collingwood's method calls to mind the New England cod fisherman in Kipling's *Captains Courageous*:

> When Disko thought of cod he thought as a cod. . . . Disko Troop stared forward, the pipe between his teeth, with eyes that saw nothing. As his son said, he was studying fish—pitting his knowledge and experience on the Banks against the roving cod in his own sea. . . . So Disko Troop thought of recent weather, and gales, currents, food, supplies, and other domestic arrangements, from the point of view of a twenty pound cod; was in fact, for an hour, a cod himself, and looked remarkably like one.[27]

To require a historian to rethink Brutus's thought before he killed Caesar is to require him to become Brutus. And this he cannot do, any more than Disko Troop could convert himself into a twenty-pound cod.

---

24. Gerald W. Chapman, *Edmund Burke: The Practical Imagination* (Cambridge, 1967), p. ix.

25. R. G. Collingwood, *The Idea of History*, ed. T. M. Knox (New York, 1946), pp. 215, 308, 215, 243. Collingwood's argument, in the epilegomena to this classic work, is a sore trial to a serious reader. *The Idea of History* was published posthumously, from several separate and inconsistent drafts. Many attempts at explication and systematization have recently appeared: among them, William Dray, *Laws and Explanation in History* (Oxford, 1957); William Debbins, *Essays in the Philosophy of History*, 2d ed. (New York, 1965); Alan Donaghan, *The Later Philosophy of Collingwood* (Oxford, 1962); and Louis O. Mink, "Collingwood's Dialectic of History," *History and Theory* 7 (1968): 3–37.

26. Collingwood, *The Idea of History*, p. 216.

27. Rudyard Kipling, *Captains Courageous* (London, 1897), pp. 47, 103–4.

For Brutus did not merely think different things than Collingwood thought—he thought them differently. The whole idea is antihistorical, antiempirical, and absurd. It is true, of course, that some history is the history of thought and that some kinds of thoughts can be re-enacted in the historian's mind. But some thought which interests historians cannot be separated from feeling, or from thinking structures which exist within limits of time and space. Collingwood's method, strictly applied, would exclude not merely the nonintellectual problems in which historians are actually interested but also many intellectual problems, which are characteristically neither rational nor irrational, but transrational.

The epistemological issues raised by idealism are remote from the daily thought of historians, but not from their daily work. The idealist fallacy is a very real occupational hazard of intellectual history—a danger from which not even the best are immune. None was better than Perry Miller, whose studies of New England Puritanism are a landmark of historical literature. But great though they are, these works remain deeply flawed by the fallacy of idealism.

One problem for an idealist epistemology is the group phenomenon. Can one rethink the thought of a collectivity? Only, it seems, by conjuring up the fiction of a "corporate mind," as Collingwood called it. Perry Miller did this explicitly in the first volume of *The New England Mind*, in which he wrote, "I have taken the liberty of treating the whole literature as though it were a single intelligence, and I have appropriated illustrations from whichever authors happen to express a point most conveniently."[28]

Many magnificent insights accompanied this impressionist method. But a serious flaw was embedded in it. New England Puritanism was an entity, but it was not an intellect. It was a cluster of many thousands of intellects. There were important normative patterns of behavior, but also a wide range of significant variations. Miller's method entirely prevented a clear recognition of norms, or variations.

The second volume of *The New England Mind* displays another major deficiency of the idealist method. In a preface to the paperback edition of this work, Miller disparaged "such topics as ships, trade routes, currency, property, agriculture, town government and military tactics." In an argument which would have warmed the cockles of Collingwood's heart, Perry Miller insisted that "while indeed these kinds of activity require an exercise of a faculty which in ordinary parlance may be called intelligence, such matters are not, and cannot be made, the central theme

---

28. Perry Miller, *The New England Mind: The Seventeenth Century*, 2 vols. (Cambridge, 1939–53), 1:vii.

of a coherent narrative. They furnish forth at their worst mere tables of statistics, on the average meaningless inventories, and at their best only a series of monographs."[29] This argument is not only deficient in itself, but dysfunctional to Miller's work, for Volume Two, by the nature of its thesis, requires a good deal of discussion of these topics which the author despised.

Third, both volumes of the *New England Mind* tend, in the fashion of idealist history, to consider narrowly rational thought. Another student of Puritanism, Alan Simpson, has complained of Miller's work,

> He has told us too much about the Puritan mind and not enough about the Puritan's feelings. If the seventeenth century Puritan, with his formal training in scholasticism, usually tries to give a rational account of his faith, it is the stretched passion which makes him what he is. They are people who suffered and yearned and strived with an unbelievable intensity; and no superstructure of logic ought to be allowed to mask that turmoil of feeling.[30]

This turmoil of feeling cannot, ever, be re-enacted in the mind of a historian. It can only be *studied,* in its behavioral expressions. And Puritanical reasoning cannot be separated from it, without gross interpretative error. Miller made much—too much—of fine-drawn dichotomies, but not enough of the emotional cement which was the inner bond of Puritan belief.

A fourth common consequence of the idealist fallacy appears in Miller's monograph on Roger Williams. In this work, the author attempted, in effect, to re-enact Roger Williams's thought in his own mind. But if a historian is to operate merely by this method, how does he measure his success? By some sort of intuited congruence of one thought to another? Collingwood had no answer to this problem. He was true to the logic of his argument when he asserted that "I am now driven to confess that there are for historical thought no fixed points thus given: in other words, that in history, just as there are properly speaking no authorities, so there are properly speaking no data."[31] Nothing would bind a historian to his subject, but a gossamer web of intuited understanding. Miller trusted to this method sans method in his understanding of Roger Williams and paid a price for it. His thesis is wonderfully co-

29. Perry Miller, *The New England Mind, From Colony to Province* (Boston, 1961), Preface. Perry Miller began this book with an epigraph from Jeremiah: "And the Lord put forth His hand, and touched my mouth." *Vox Milleri, vox Dei est?*
30. Alan Simpson, *Puritanism in Old and New England* (Chicago, 1955), p. 21.
31. Collingwood, *The Idea of History*, p. 243. An example of the consequences which flow from this difficulty is Collingwood's explanation of King Arthur's behavior, which he reached by attempting to rethink Arthurian thoughts. The result has been described as "a new Arthurian legend, worthy to stand beside the inventions of Tennyson and Geoffrey of Monmouth," by Mortimer Wheeler in *Journal of Roman Studies* 29 (1939), 87–93, reviewing R. G. Collingwood and J. N. L. Myres, *Roman Britain and the English Settlements* (Oxford, [1936]).

herent; he successfully rethinks thoughts that Williams *might* have thought. Miller argued that Williams and the leaders of Massachusetts quarreled primarily over a method of biblical exegesis. Specifically, he believed that Williams favored a typological interpretation of the Bible, which threatened to destroy the very foundations of Puritan thought. But unfortunately for his thesis, there is a good deal of evidence that typology was favorably regarded by those Puritans who banished him from the Bay Colony. In short, by adopting a nonempirical idealist method, Miller permitted himself to become committed to an intuited interpretation which is empirically false.[32]

Finally, historical idealism is antihistorical in its very nature, for it would make a historian and his subject contemporaries. This actually happens in Perry Miller's biography of Jonathan Edwards. Miller was guilty here of the fallacy of the counterquestion, too, for in a revision of Parrington's interpretation of Edwards, he stood Parrington on his head. Parrington had made Edwards into a living anachronism—a contemporary of Cromwell. Miller overreacted and made Edwards into a contemporary of Paul Tillich, or Marcel Proust.[33] This error was sustained by his idealist method, which permitted him to move Jonathan Edwards through time, without being aware of the mistake he was making.

An idealist could conceivably claim, even assuming all these complaints against Miller's work are well founded, that its undoubted excellence is a vindication of idealism, fallacy or not. If Perry Miller's scholarship rests upon a fallacy, then one might wish that logical disorders were contagious. I am inclined to disagree. The power of Miller's thought is perfectly consistent with a better method—a method which would have corrected deficiencies without destroying strengths. Everything that Miller did right could have been done better in an inquiry which took a more rounded view of human beings and a less naïve view of their condition.

A slightly different form of the idealist fallacy consists in a presumption of rationality in human behavior. One historian of ideas, C. B. Macpherson, has elevated this assumption into an explicit method. In a study of political thought from Hobbes to Locke he wrote, "I have found it a fruitful hypothesis that each of the thinkers tended to be consistent, or (which comes to the same thing) was consistent within the limits of his vision."[34]

32. Sacvan Bercovitch, "Typology in Puritan New England: The Williams-Cotton Controversy Reassessed," *American Quarterly* 29 (1967): 166–91.
33. Perry Miller, *Jonathan Edwards* (New York, 1959), pp. 190, 289, 315, passim.
34. C. B. Macpherson, *The Political Theory of Possessive Individualism: Hobbes to Locke* (Oxford, 1962), p. 7.

Macpherson used this method with a view to establishing with some precision the limits of vision in his subjects. He hastened to add that it was "no more than a useful approach." But I take it to be a very dangerous one. Surely many thinkers have been *in*consistent within their own limits. A presumption of logical consistency is as unjustified as a presumption of the opposite.

A final example of the idealist fallacy suggests still another variation. It occurs in the following assertion by a biographer of Ivan the Great. J. L. I. Fennell writes,

> Ivan III, more clearly than any of his predecessors or followers on the grand princely throne of Moscow, knew precisely where he was going. He knew his goal, the means at his disposal, the obstacles to be encountered. He never over-estimated his own strength or under-estimated that of his enemies. His cold reasoning told him just how far he could abuse the freedom of his subjects and tamper with the sanctity of religious institutions. He never fought a war for the sake of fighting, sought a friendship from altruism, or disgraced a subject through spite. All the deeds of this dedicated, hard-headed ruler and shrewd diplomat were directed towards one goal only.[35]

I do not know for a fact that this characterization is false. Every account of Ivan III which I have seen speaks of his steely realism. Not much seems to be known of Ivan's personality. Fennell writes, "Seldom can a man have reigned for so long and achieved so much, and left so little impression on his contemporaries. Almost nothing is known of his personal qualities or of his private life."[36] Nevertheless, the cold realism which Fennell attributes to Ivan, and the Czar's alleged awareness of precisely where he was going, seems more than a little exaggerated. It is an established fact that Ivan spent many hours in his life so helplessly intoxicated that he did not know precisely where *anyone* was going. One suspects that there must have been other distractions, and maybe a few delusions as well.

ह्ल The *fallacy of the one-dimensional man* selects one aspect of the human condition and makes it into the measure of humanity itself. There are many variations, of which perhaps the most prevalent is still the fallacy of the political man. In one of its forms, this fallacy mistakes people for political animals who are moved mainly by a desire for power. It reduces the complex psychic condition of men merely to their political roles and shrinks all the components of the social calculus to a simple equation of power, ambition, and interest.

35. J. L. I. Fennell, *Ivan the Great of Moscow* (New York, 1962), p. 18.
36. Ibid., p. 354.

The classical example is provided by *Leviathan* and *Behemoth*, both by Thomas Hobbes. In *Leviathan*, that excellent philosopher made the error as explicit as it ever can be. "In the first place," he declared, "I put for a general implication of all mankind, a perpetual and restless desire of power after power, that ceaseth only in death." He allowed for other restless desires, but most were also cast in political terms, and subordinated to the primary one.[37]

Hobbes tried his hand at history in *Behemoth: The History of the Causes of the Civil Wars of England, and of the Counsels and Artifices by Which They Were Carried On from the Year 1640 to the Year 1660*. History, for Thomas Hobbes, was "a heap of evils." And historiography was "a short narration of the follies and other faults of men."[38] When he came to assess the cause of the English Civil Wars, all the soaring theological aspirations of the contending parties were reduced to the following proposition:

> The seducers were of divers sorts. One sort were ministers; ministers, as they called themselves, of Christ; and sometimes, in their sermons to the people, God's ambassadors; pretending to have a right from God to govern everyone his parish, and their assembly the whole nation. Secondly, there were a very great number, though not comparable to the other, which notwithstanding that the Pope's power in England, both temporal and ecclesiastical, had been by Act of Parliament abolished, did still retain a belief that we ought to be governed by the Pope, whom they pretended to be the vicar of Christ, and, in the right of Christ, to be the governor of all Christian people.[39]

The lofty return to political first principles by writers of that troubled generation came down merely to this, in Hobbes's understanding: "To these follies I might add the folly of those fine men, which out of their reading of Tully, Seneca, or other anti-monarchics, think themselves sufficient politicians, and show their discontents when they are not called to the management of the state, and turn from one side to another upon every neglect which they fancy from the king or his enemies." The Revolution itself, in Hobbes's pages, was but "a circular motion of the sovereign power through two usurpers, from the late king to this his son."[40]

Hobbes's interlocutor in *Behemoth* observed at one point, "If this be true, it is impossible any commonwealth in the world, whether monarchy, aristocracy, or democracy, should continue long without change, or sedition tending to change, either of the government or governors."

---

37. *Leviathan*, ed. Michael Oakeshott (Oxford, 1955), pt. I, chap. 11, p. 64.
38. *Behemoth*, in *English Works* (1840), 6:270, 309.
39. Ibid., 6:167.
40. Ibid., 6:358, 418.

Hobbes replied darkly, "It is true; nor have any of the greatest commonwealths in the world been long free from sedition."[41]

Thomas Hobbes, like an English mastiff, did grimly set his jaws upon a piece of the truth about humanity, but it was a piece from the hind end. He made men into beasts, braying and biting and trying their titles with their teeth. His political man was scarcely a man at all, but rather an untamed animal.

No historian of the twentieth century has, to my knowledge, built such an idea into such a system. But many historical interpretations are sometimes informed by a comparable assumption about a particular political man. It is often a variable thing, which appears and disappears in a single work. There are many examples in the historiography of the early republic. Scholars of a Federalist sympathy have committed the fallacy of the political man in their characterizations of Jeffersonians. And Jeffersonian historians, in turn, have introduced it to explain the behavior of Alexander Hamilton. An example of the latter is the writing of Adrienne Koch, who, in a recently published collection of essays called *Power, Morals and the Founding Fathers*, included a chapter called "Hamilton and the Pursuit of Power." The first Secretary of the Treasury becomes a power-worshiping fanatic, whose career is explained by this "all-consuming passion." His end is seen as a kind of poetic justice: "It was as if fate had come to punish him for his grave defect of character and consequent crimes with an early and violent death," she wrote piously.[42]

Adrienne Koch's monistic interpretation of a particular single individual in terms of "a perpetual and restless desire for power after power, that ceaseth only in death," is every bit as reductive as Hobbes's similar opinion of mankind in general. Many students of Hamilton's career— enemies as well as friends, and objective observers besides—would surely agree that he was consumed by many other passions besides a passion for power. Mrs. Reynolds could have named one. Moreover, Hamilton was also consumed by many altruisms and ideas and interests, some of which had nothing whatever to do with power in any meaningful sense of the word.

A second general species of the fallacy of the political man is that which reduces men merely to citizens, or subjects, or voters, or party functionaries, or officeholders. There was a good deal of this in many monographs published by constitutional and political historians fifty years ago, as well as in many general interpretations of American his-

41. Ibid., 6:252.
42. P. 77.

tory. It still appears more often than it should. Carl Prince's book *New Jersey's Jeffersonian Republicans* (Chapel Hill, 1967) is a case in point. The leading figures in this volume appear as political men on the make, mindless automatons programed for a maximization of political power. I regret that I did something of the same thing in a study of the Federalists. The complaint here is not about a special interest in political history but rather about the way in which that interest is developed, without sufficient attention to its cross-connections with other aspects of human conduct.

Other examples are discussed in an excellent analysis of motivation in writing on the Reconstruction era. What were the motives of Radical Republican politicians for enacting Negro suffrage? The answer, in many interpretations, is flat, simple, and monistic. Republican politicians wanted the political support of the Negro voters![43] This profundity can be taken not merely as a truth, but as a truism. And yet, it is all that a good many historians wish to know.

There are many other forms of the fallacy of the one-dimensional man. Everybody has some acquaintance with the fallacy of economic man—an idea steadfastly asserted by shabby scholars with holes in their socks. And besides *Homo economicus,* there is *Homo religiosus* and *Homo sociologicus,* and many more.[44] Some historians have even discovered *Homo historicus.* Bruce Mazlish appears to believe that *the* meaning of history consists in man's developing historical consciousness. What next![45]

ε&⯈ The *fallacy of the universal man* falsely assumes that people are intellectually and psychologically the same in all times, places, and circumstances. It is an error which has ruined the designs of innumerable utopians, revolutionaries, schematizers, prophets, preachers, psychiatrists, mystics, cranks, and social scientists of very shape and hue. Every unitary solution, without exception, which has ever been proposed as a panacea for the hopes and misfortunes of mankind, has been fatally flawed by this fundamental fallacy.

People, in various places and times, have not merely thought different things. They have thought them differently. It is probable that their

---

43. Lawanda and John H. Cox, "Negro Suffrage and Republican Politics: The Problem of Motivation in Reconstruction Historiography," *Journal of Southern History* 33 (1967): 303–30, discuss this error.
44. Ralf Dahrendorf, *Homo Sociologicus: Ein Versuch zur Geschichte Bedeutung und Kritik der Kategorie der sozialen Rolle* (Cologne, 1960).
45. Bruce Mazlish, *The Riddle of History* (New York, 1966).

most fundamental cerebral processes have changed through time. Their deepest emotional drives and desires may themselves have been transformed. Significant elements of continuity cannot be understood without a sense of the discontinuities, too.

The problem is immensely difficult, and highly doubtful. There is no primary evidence for the past thought of any man, at any time in history—though psychologists and biologists are beginning to discover paths into this inner wilderness. But there is accumulating evidence of expressions of thought and feeling which make no sense unless we allow a wide latitude for change in the nature of cerebral activity through space and time. The range of this change is as obscure as its nature. But its existence is, in my opinion, a historical fact which is established beyond a reasonable doubt.[46]

The fallacy of the universal man appeared in much eighteenth-century historiography. David Hume declared that "Mankind are so much the same, in all times and places, that history informs us of nothing new or strange in this particular. Its chief use is only to discover the constant and universal principles of human nature."[47] Voltaire was equally of the opinion that "Man in general has always been what he is now; this does not mean that he has always had fine cities . . . and convents full of nuns. But he has always had the same instinct which leads him to find satisfaction in himself, in the companion of his pleasures, in his children, in his grand children and in the work of his hands. Here is something that will never change from one end of the world to another."[48] But "man-in-general" changed from one wing of the Enlightenment to another. Much of what Voltaire described as universally present in human nature was, for example, conspicuously absent from the nature of Jean Jacques Rousseau, who derived mostly pain from the companions of his pleasure and gave his own children to an orphanage. Rousseau and Voltaire themselves are two clear examples of men who did not merely think different things but thought them differently.

In our own time, there are many other examples of the fallacy of the universal man. Its progress has been much encouraged by two hopeful tendencies in the modern world. The first is a powerful reaction against the fatal fallacy of racism. The repudiation of this bloody error by most historians, and many others, is surely cause for rejoicing. But some have overreacted and insufficiently allowed for the

46. For a preliminary attempt to deal with this problem in some detail see J. H. Van den Berg, *The Changing Nature of Man* (New York, 1961).
47. Hume, *Essays* (1767), II, 94.
48. Voltaire, *Selected Writings*, ed. J. H. Brumfitt (New York, 1963), pp. 260–62.

existence of cultural differences among men. Consider, for example, the historiography of Negro slavery in America. Historians have disputed many aspects of that mournful institution. Most bitter, and most fundamental, have been their quarrels over the nature of men who were slaves. In 1918, a very great historian of this problem operated upon an explicitly racist premise. "The slaves were negroes," wrote Ulrich B. Phillips, "who for the most part were by racial quality submissive rather than defiant, light-hearted instead of gloomy, amiable and ingratiating instead of sullen."[49]

More recently, the author of another standard history of the same subject began with a very different assumption, which was actively anti-racist. "I have assumed," wrote Kenneth Stampp, "that the slaves were merely ordinary human beings, that innately Negroes *are*, after all, only white men with black skins, nothing more, nothing less."[50]

Therein lies our fallacy. Stampp assumes, throughout his book, that an African Negro slave responded to his predicament much as Stampp himself might have done. It is as if that white liberal professor of history who worked in twentieth-century Berkeley, California, were somehow shackled, and put upon the block, and sold to a nineteenth-century plantation owner in Bibb County, Alabama (a thought which, by the way, might not seem so ridiculous to the incumbent governors of those two states). In the pages of Stampp's *Peculiar Institution*, the mark of Cain has disappeared from the brows of his protagonists. But every Negro is, as it were, Stampped into a white liberal stereotype which may be equally false.

It is more sensible, in my opinion, to operate upon a different assumption, which was more closely approximated in a brilliant essay by Stanley Elkins, published since Stampp's book appeared. Though there are surely many flaws in Elkins's approach, some of which are discussed in this book, he has opened most impressively one important line of inquiry in his suggestion that the nature of the acculturation process through which Negro slaves passed from one culture into another, and the role expectations which were ruthlessly enforced upon them, may have served to create a pattern of psychological and intellectual behavior which was very different from that of whites in this country, a pattern which was so deeply and powerfully ingrained in the nature of American Negroes that they did not begin to break out of it in significant numbers until a century after emancipation. Maybe that behavior pattern resembled in a superficial way the qualities which Ulrich Phillips and many

49. Ulrich B. Phillips, *American Negro Slavery* (Baton Rouge, La., 1966), pp. 341–42.
50. Kenneth Stampp, *The Peculiar Institution* (New York, 1965), p. vii. This work was first published in 1956.

others described in Negroes whom they knew—docility, dependence, irresponsibility, imitativeness. Beneath these mannerisms, there may have been a more fundamental set of psychic determinants and dynamics. Perhaps this behavior pattern, though not racially inherent in the nature of black men, nevertheless inhered to his cultural condition throughout his period of bondage, and for many years thereafter. Many Negroes today have clearly broken out of this psychic pattern; the black militant movement is a striking case in point. But maybe many others are still caught up in it and must still be emancipated from the worst shackles of all—shackles of the mind.

This view of Negro history is understandably unpopular among militant blacks. They insist that such personality stereotypes as Ulrich Phillips described and Stanley Elkins has begun to explain were merely social masks, if they existed at all—masks that blacks wore in the presence of whites. But maybe these manners ran deep in the minds of the enslaved.

Elkins seems to suggest in his book that the institution of slavery in the United States was such that it might have made Sambos of any slave, white or black or red, African or European or American. But maybe there were African cultural determinants which made blacks particularly vulnerable. There is good evidence that American Indians behaved very differently in slavery—so differently that they could not be successfully enslaved on a large scale, though many attempts were made.[51]

To represent Negroes merely as "white men with black skins," in Stampp's unfortunate phrase, is to deny their history. It is moreover to disguise the full dimensions of their modern dilemma, which cannot be dealt with merely by a neutral kind of equality of opportunity in an open and competitive society. If it is true that Negroes, by reason of their African inheritance, their acculturative experience, and their centuries of bondage, do not merely think different things but think them differently, then that fact has a most profound relationship to modern policies which have been designed to deal with the so-called race problem. The fact has two implications, which do not easily coexist. First, any simple attempt to assimilate Negroes into white society, on the ground that they are really white inside, is a threat to black identity more serious even than that which was posed by Ulrich Phillips's racism. There is no greater disservice to a black American than to call him a white man with a black skin. On the other hand, it may be true that Africans in America historically *became* people of such a nature that many of them are still un-

---

51. Cf. Stanley Elkins, *Slavery: A Problem in American Institutional and Intellectual Life*, 2d ed. (New York, 1963), pp. 81–139.

equipped to function in the modern world on a basis of equality. What would be required is some radical form of compensatory opportunity which would provide assistance without assimilation, a helping hand without homogenization. Stampp's well-intended liberal interpretation of the peculiar institution is, in short, doubly objectionable. It fails to perceive the greatest evil of slavery, which was not the use it made of men but the kind of men it made. And it obscures the nature of the problem with which America is presently faced, as well as offering a false solution. It is, I believe, America's glory that no other nation, anywhere on the face of the planet, has ever attempted to create a free, open, and equal society from such disparate materials. If the attempt is to succeed, we *must* have a sufficient sense of those disparities, as well as a respect for the integrity of the various individuals who are involved. In such a situation, the fallacy of the universal man is not merely a delusion but a danger. It is not, as its well-meaning proponents imagined, a tool of international peace and brotherhood, but the very opposite—a formidable threat to these lofty ideas.

ह≫ The *fallacy of the mass man*, in the words of E. H. Carr, confuses anonymity with impersonality.[52] It commonly happens when millions of individual living men are changed into "masses" and are thereby deprived of individuality and life itself. John Stuart Mill wisely observed in his *System of Logic* that "Men are not, when brought together, converted into another kind of substance." And yet they often are, when brought together for the purpose of historical analysis.

A few historians have been protesting against this practice for years. Carlyle, in his *French Revolution*, wrote,

> With the working people, again, it is not so well. Unlucky! For there are twenty to twenty-five millions of them. Whom, however, we lump together into a kind of dim compendious unity, monstrous but dim, far off, as the canaille; or, more humanely, as the "masses." Masses indeed, and yet, singular to say, if with an effort of imagination, thou follow them, over broad France, into their clay hovels, into their garrets and hutches, the masses consist all of units. Every unit of whom has his own heart and sorrows; stands covered there with his own skin, and if you prick him, he will bleed.[53]

So it was and is in history, but rarely in historiography. There is less humanity in billions of bloodless historiographical John Does and

52. Carr, *What Is History?*, p. 61.
53. Thomas Carlyle, *The French Revolution*, Modern Library ed. (New York, n.d.) p. 28.

Juan de la Cruzes than in a single prince or priest. Political historians of a conservative persuasion have received a good deal of deserved abuse for this detestable practice. But the error is not theirs alone. It commonly occurs in radical social history, too. Consider a recent work by Jesse Lemisch, on merchant seamen in colonial America.[54] Lemisch belongs to a small sect of scholarly dissenters who are commonly called New Left historians. He has actively repudiated the elitism of most academic historiography, but only to stand it on its head. In the essay at hand, he has homogenized a good many merchant seamen into a mass man who is explicitly called Jack Tar. This abstraction is not quite as dim or compendious as the mass men of conservative historians, but it is equally artificial. Lemisch's Jack Tar has about as much empirical validity as Jack and the Beanstalk—whom we might expect to meet when he gets to agricultural workers of the colonies. His Jack Tar is quite a jolly fellow, curiously comparable to the eighteenth-century country-gentleman abstractions celebrated by conservative scholars—a little on the rough side, but fair and firm and virtuous and manly and quick to resent restraints upon his liberties. In all of this, the range of individual acts and thoughts and feelings tends to disappear.

No denigration of Lemisch's work is intended, for he has carried our understanding of an important problem far beyond all earlier efforts. But in his writings the myth of the mass man remains—an affectionate abstraction which, whatever its connotation, remains an empty stereotype. A better strategy than the one Lemisch adopted—from an empirical point of view—would surely have been to conceptualize his problem in terms of ranges of normative behavior of individual merchant seamen.

&ᴗ The *fallacy of the man-mass* conversely converts a singular individual, with all his quirks and idiosyncrasies, into a collectivity of individuals. It appears in an unfortunate stylistic habit of Louis Hartz, who likes to couple a definite noun with an indefinite article. In his *Liberal Tradition in America*, "the joy of *a* Dewey meets the anguish of *a* Fenimore Cooper," and a good many metaphorical sparks fly, at least in the mind of this reader. He also writes of "*a* Jefferson" and "*a* Franklin," of "Harringtons and Machiavellis and Rousseaus," or "*a* Duke of Wellington" and "*an* Abbot Lawrence," of "*a* Flocun" and "*a* Ledru Rollin," "*an* Edmund Burke" and "*a* Thomas Paine," of "Benthams,

54. Jesse Lemisch, "Jack Tar in the Streets," *The William and Mary Quarterly*, 3d ser. 25 (1968): 371–407.

Mills and Carlyles," of "Disraelis and Bonalds," and even of "*a* Calvin" and "*a* Lenin."[55]

A contextual examination of these monstrosities suggests that Hartz's confusion is more than merely grammatical. It consists in the way in which he conducted both his conceptualization and his research. Hartz repeatedly took an available individual and enlarged him into a group. The result is that all the Federalists become "an Ames" or "a Hamilton," which is humbug. Having homogenized his subject in this way, Hartz proceeds to proclaim to all the world that his subject was homogeneous: America, it seems, was really just *a* Locke, to which *a* Beard had lost the key.

To complain of this practice is not to protest against all generalization but merely against a species of false generalization in which an individual is puffed up like a balloon and mistaken for a class of individuals. This error is common among both social scientists and historians. It appears in the writing of behaviorists like David Easton, who has referred to "a Walter Bagehot"; and also in the work of a traditional historian such as F. C. Lane, who speaks of "a John Adams."[56]

ʒ› The *historians' fallacy* is suggested by William James's "psychologists' fallacy," which he defines as the error of assuming that a man who has a given psychic experience knows it, when he has it, to be all that an observing psychologist would know it to be.[57] In precisely the same way, the historian's fallacy is the error of assuming that a man who has a given historical experience knows it, when he has it, to be all that a historian would know it to be, with the advantage of historical perspective.

One common form of this fallacy consists in the tendency of historians, with their retrospective advantages, to forget that their subjects did not know what was coming next. This sort of error is ludicrous, in an abstract way. Imagine a letter written in France, on May 24, 1337, which announced "the Hundred Years' War began here today." But the historians' fallacy is often an insidious form of error, which is exceedingly difficult to recognize or correct. A case in point is the continuing controversy over the surprise which we received from the Japanese

55. Louis Hartz, *The Liberal Tradition in America*, pp. 39, 46, 59, 107, 116, 120–21, 141, 148, and 157. Italics added.
56. David Easton, *A Framework for Political Analysis* (Englewood Cliffs, N. J., 1965), p. 81; and Frederic C. Lane, "At the Roots of Republicanism," *The American Historical Review* 71 (1966): 420.
57. James, *Principles of Psychology*, I, 196.

at Pearl Harbor, on December 7, 1941. Before the bombs began to
fall, there were many clear signals of an impending attack—so many,
and in retrospect so clear, that many people have suspected some sort
of foul play. Almost every historian of this event has recorded the accurate information which Ambassador Grew collected in Japan months
before Pearl Harbor Day. Everybody remembers the wealth of information collected from MAGIC, and the army radar operator who actually
tracked the incoming Japanese planes. But our memory does not extend
with equal clarity to many other signs and signals which pointed unequivocally in the opposite direction. An excellent recent monograph has
contributed considerably to our understanding of the problem by analyz-
ing it precisely in these terms. Its author, Roberta Wohlstetter, sensibly
observes that the

> signals announcing the Pearl Harbor attack were always accompanied by
> competing or contradictory signals, by all sorts of information useless for
> anticipating this particular disaster. . . . To understand the fact of surprise
> it is necessary to examine the characteristics of the noise as well as the
> signals that after the event are seen to herald the attack. . . . In short, we
> failed to anticipate Pearl Harbor not for the want of the relevant materials,
> but because of the plethora of irrelevant ones.[58]

Mrs. Wohlstetter's method might be studied with profit by many professional historians—and intelligence analysts. It is a very useful corrective
to a very common form of error.

The historians' fallacy appears full-blown in Louis Hartz's *The
Liberal Tradition in America,* which denounces Hamilton and Adams,
and Federalists and Whigs, for failing to understand their society. "They
deserve all of the criticism they have received," he writes, "but not for
the reason they have received it. Their crime was not villainy but stupidity. . . . What is remarkable is how long the American Whigs managed to
endure the strange abuse of a liberal community without waking up to
the logic behind it."[59] Now, Hamilton and Adams can be accused of a
good many things, but *not* stupidity. If Hartz's charge says anything
coherently, then I think it consists in an indictment of the founding
fathers for failing to read the future. In retrospect, we can find clear
signs in the early republic which point to the direction of change in
nineteenth-century America. But there were also many other signs, which
pointed in different directions. When Hartz denounces the Federalists as
a pack of dunces for failing to read the right signs, he reflects not so
much upon the limits of their perspicacity as upon the limits of his own.

58. Roberta Wohlstetter, *Pearl Harbor: Warning and Decision* (Stanford, 1962), pp.
3, 387, passim.
59. P. 101

On the other hand, there are many historians who have also committed the historians' fallacy by celebrating the cerebration of the Founders. Marvin Meyers, in a paper presented to the American Historical Association in December, 1967, came close to interpreting John Adams in such a way that Adams recognized himself to be a Founding Father with the clarity that we possess in retrospect. Mr. Meyers suggests that Adams had a clear and accurate sense of the way in which the Republic would develop after its founding, and that both of these insights were intertwined in his motivational patterns and ideological responses. It is as if the American revolutionary slogan were "Liberty, Equality, Paternity" and the Fathers of the Republic were driven by a sense of fatherhood and by an accurate premonition of the career of their republican child.

Still other historians' fallacies have been committed in the historiography of the early Republic, when scholars of many different political persuasions have analyzed the great party conflicts of the 1790s as if the participants knew what was going on with great clarity and precision. But the reality, I suspect, was a little like that which Herbert Feis describes in a meeting between Franklin Roosevelt and Herbert Hoover on January 20, 1933. Feis has written,

> Of the many confused scuffles it has been my professional pleasure to study, the one that ensued is the hardest to relate with confident accuracy. It was reminiscent of a naval engagement on a foggy night between two opposed fleets, each ship firing a gun whenever a flash was seen, being quite as likely to blow up a friend as an enemy. In this instance as well, the proponents were shooting at shadows and hitting the air.[60]

Feis's analysis is precisely applicable to the party battles of the early Republic, and to many other conflicts as well—political, intellectual, constitutional, military, economic, etc., etc. To apply this insight is, however, extraordinarily difficult. Nothing is more elusive than the information which somebody did not have, and yet nothing is more useful to a coherent and accurate historical interpretation.

Another specimen of the historians' fallacy is Philip C. Ritterbush's *Overtures to Biology: The Speculations of Eighteenth Century Naturalists* (New Haven, 1964), a useful and important book. But a reviewer has complained that "at least twice the author falls into one of the worst blunders that a historian of science can commit: hindsighted contempt for the ignorance of past investigators. Vaillant 'should not have expected' something to happen that we know (but he did not) could never happen. Linnaeus was guilty of an 'outrageous' assumption of something

---

60. Herbert Feis, *1933: Characters in Crisis* (Boston, 1966), p. 69.

that we know to be impossible."[61] The critic, Donald Fleming, needn't have been quite so self-righteous about it. But the critical point is soundly taken.

Still another example is Jack Lindsay, *Leisure and Pleasure in Roman Egypt* (New York, 1966), which a reviewer, Ramsay MacMullen, criticizes as follows:

> Though factual errors are few, and minor, yet a broader fault lies in the recurrent tendency to attribute to people of the time an informed awareness of their own culture now matched only by some curator of Egyptian antiquities. How many of us, however, know why we greet a sneeze with "Bless you!" or why we deck a pine tree at Christmas? The man in the street of Roman Egypt cannot have responded much more sensitively to the fascinating cultural lights, meanings and connections that the author detects.[62]

Curators of Egyptian antiquities, of course, are something less than omniscient within their chosen field. There is surely much that "the man in the street of Roman Egypt" knew about his own culture that no scholar will ever succeed in reconstructing. But there are other analytical advantages which operate on the opposite side, and they are a mighty snare and a delusion, in any retrospective inquiry.

A final example of the historians' fallacy is a borderline case. An excellent narrative historian, George Dangerfield, has written of Andrew Jackson that "the General seemed to regard himself as an extragovernmental force, a special spirit, unaccountable to anyone or anything but the nation and the frontier."[63] The meaning of this statement is a little obscure, but it comes close to suggesting that Andrew Jackson carried the collected works of Frederick Jackson Turner in his saddlebag.

Many historians have been conscious of the historians' fallacy. A few, indeed, have become so obsessively conscious of it that they have fallen into a counterfallacy. Douglas Southall Freeman made a determined effort to avoid it in his great biography of Robert E. Lee by the desperate expedient of telling his readers no more about a given situation than Lee himself knew. According to this method, which is called the "fog-of-war" technique by military historians, the object is to help the reader to find a rapport with Lee by providing a common bond of collective ignorance. It is, paradoxically, an effort to refine the clarity of our understanding of Lee by experiencing his own confusion. But this method, I think, is a mistake. There are certain items of information which every reader of *R. E. Lee* will bring to the book, such as who won

61. The *American Historical Review* 71 (1965): 113.
62. Ibid., 72 (1966): 139.
63. George Dangerfield, *The Awakening of American Nationalism* (New York, 1965), p. 47.

the Civil War and what happened at Gettysburg. To try to put the reader in Lee's place, and to seek a sort of historiographical high fidelity by many ingenious methodological tweeters and woofers, simply won't work; there is an irretrievable artificiality which cannot be overcome. Moreover, we possess many advantages in retrospection that ought not be relinquished.

–∗ If the reader is willing to accept the fallaciousness of these putative fallacies, then perhaps he will also accept a set of affirmative propositions which they suggest. These propositions are derived, in part, from a reading of some recent work in motivational psychology. That discipline has been exceedingly dynamic in past decades, as psychological thought has developed from the "instinct" orientation of James and Thorndike and MacDougall, through a stage in which "drives" were conceptually central, to a third stage in which the predominant idea appears to be "goal-directed" activity—which is to say, motivation in a more precise and literal sense.[64]

The work of Abraham Maslow and David McClelland might be particularly pertinent to historians' purposes and particularly valuable as a basis for rapport between psychology and history. Maslow and McClelland, if I understand them, have created a new synthesis of psychological thought, in which consciousness plays an ever larger role, though the importance of the unconscious is not repudiated. This general tendency is apparent in the general transformation of "instincts" to "drives" to "motives." As such, it brings psychological theory closer to the problems historians actually face in their work. A work such as David McClelland's *The Achieving Society* speaks directly to classic historiographical issues and suggests the possibility of a bridge between historical research and psychological theory. If these opportunities for a genuine interdisciplinary interaction can be exploited, then we may anticipate the refinement of motivational theory and motivational explanation by a union of psychology of history, which might begin with the following assumptions, all of which are the converse of the fallacies discussed in this chapter.

1. Motives are properly understood in terms of anticipatory goal states which are often physiologically associated in ways which we are only beginning to understand *but* which are never mere reflexes of biological or external stimuli.

64. See generally, Chalmers L. Stacey and Manfred F. Demartino, eds., *Human Motivation*, rev. ed. (Cleveland, 1963), esp. pp. 5–11; and David C. McClelland, ed., *Studies in Motivation* (New York, 1955), esp. pp. 226–34.

2. Only intelligent individual beings have motives—not sub-intelligent beings, not things, not groups. There are, however, normative motivational patterns which some individuals share with others in some degree.

3. Every motive is learned. David McClelland writes that "it must involve two points on an affective continuum: a present state (either positive, negative or neutral) which redintegrates through past learning a second state."

4. Motives have been learned differently in different times and places, so as to require conceptualization in developmental terms and in terms which respect the variability and mutability of particular cultural and physical environments. Psychological normality and abnormality are themselves temporally and culturally relative ideas which must be located in time and space.

5. Motives are usually pluralistic in both their number and their nature. Abraham Maslow writes, "Typically an act has more than one motive." To this, one might add that it has motives of more than one kind.

6. In any given motivational pattern, conscious and unconscious motives tend to coexist and interact. Neither consciousness nor the unconscious should be understood as prior states. Men are neither perfectly rational nor perfectly irrational but imperfectly both.

7. Conscious motives and unconscious motives are themselves pluralistic. In the realm of consciousness, a man who does something does it for every reason he can think of, and a few unthinkable reasons as well. Similarly to search for *the* motivational key in the unconscious is to commit the reductive fallacy.

8. Motivational pluralism must not, however, become an indiscriminate pluralism. There are what Maslow calls "hierarchies of prepotency" in motivation. There are many different levels of priority, intensity, and specificity. Moreover, in Maslow's words, "the appearance of one need usually rests on the prior satisfaction of another, more preponderant need."

9. Motive sets are never, ever, inalterably fixed in a living individual—not in the first six years, not in adolesence, and not in early adulthood. Karl Jaspers has written that "Man . . . is not what he is simply once and for all, but is a process."[65] His psychic process may, perhaps, be arrested for analytical purposes, but only in a fictional way. In fact, it is always in motion.

10. Similar sets of motives express themselves in similiar ways;

65. Karl Jaspers, *Man in the Modern Age* (Garden City, N.Y., 1957), p. 159.

different sets, in different ways. But single motives can be combined in different sets.

11. Motive sets affect, and are affected by, an entire man and not some segment of his self, or some fragment of his social existence. If any part is singled out for special study, it always remains a part—not the whole.

12. An empirical understanding of normal motivation must be derived from the study of normal men. The work of psychologists is diminished by its dependency upon the behavior of animals and undergraduates. The work of psychiatrists is narrowly based upon neurotic behavior, from which norms have been inaccurately extrapolated.

13. There can be no primary, direct evidence of any past motive. But there is a tacit logic of inference which can attain a high degree of probable accuracy. It is a logic which in its very nature appears to commit the fallacy of the consequent (in the form "if X, then probably Y; Y, therefore probably X"). But this form of reasoning is a useful tool of empirical inquiry.

Bland as these statements may seem, they contradict many—perhaps most—historical interpretations. They cannot coexist with Marxian historiography, or with classical Freudian theory, or with much conventional wisdom of academic history. Moreover, if they are correct, then interdisciplinary efforts in history and psychology would not take the form of mere consumption of psychological insights by historians, but rather a flow of fact and theory in each direction, with mutual benefits accruing to both disciplines.

CHAPTER VIII

FALLACIES OF COMPOSITION

ૐ

> It is one of the basic characteristics of history that the his-
> torian is concerned with human beings but that he does not
> deal with them primarily as individuals, as does the psy-
> chologist or the biographer or the novelist. Instead he deals
> with them in groups—in religious groups, in cultural groups,
> in ideological groups, in interest groups, in occupational
> groups, or in social groups.
> —David M. Potter

The subject matter of history is always men in the midst of other men—
men in collectivities and groups. A human group is something more than
merely a heap of people and something other than an organism or a
machine or a great person or an idea. A group is not exactly born, and
it does not precisely die. It has a beginning and an end, but no life cycle,
no organic pattern of growth and decay. It has no roots or branches; no
fruits or flowers; no mind or heart or soul; no cogs or gears or wheels
or levers. It does not possess a will or a personality.

Human groups exist in their own right and must be understood in
their own terms. We might define them in terms of five properties: a
finite membership of particular individuals, a regular structure of interaction, a normative pattern of behavior to which its members conform in
some degree, a set of functions which it performs for its constituents or
for other groups, and a sequence of development through time. An innumerable variety of group types have actually engaged the interest of
historians. The following are merely a few in common use.

1. Cultural groups, subcultures, communities, civilizations, *Gemein-
schaften.*

2. Social groups, societies, *Gesellschaften.*

3. Political groups, nationality groups, states, nations, polities,

political cultures, republics, kingdoms, parties, factions, parliaments, congresses, caucuses, conventions, cabals, camarillas.

4. Economic groups, exchange groups, investment groups, consumer groups, consortiums, combinations, communes, collectives, manors, plantations, farms.

5. Religious groups, religions, churches, denominations, sects, communions, congregations, cults.

6. Enculturative groups, educational groups, language groups, schools, colleges, faculties, student-groups.

7. Ideological groups, belief units, value units.

8. Reference groups, classes, castes, cliques, coteries.

9. Kinship groups, families, clans, tribes, gens, septs, connections.

10. Generational groups, age groups, peer groups, gangs.

11. Residential groups, hamlets, villages, towns, cities, suburbs.

12. Vocational groups, occupations, professions, guilds, crafts.

13. Military groups, armies, officer castes.

14. Voluntary associations, fraternities, fellowships, bands, clubs.

15. Temporary group aggregates, crowds, caravans, committees, etc.[1]

Each of these group terms has a broad range of meanings in common usage. Two anthropologists have located more than 160 different working definitions of "culture" alone in the literature of social science.[2] Sometimes these terms refer not to a group itself but to a set of group possessions. But always the existence of some sort of group, in the fivefold definition given above, is at least tacitly implied.

The purposes of group study have been as various as the groups themselves. Sometimes groups are important to historians merely as contexts in which individuals acted or in which particular events happened. Other historians are increasingly engaged in the history of groups themselves. In political history, for example, a predominant concern with individual acts and particular events is yielding to an interest in what are called political cultures. These entities are set in motion and themselves become the central object of historical inquiry. The same trend is apparent in social history, which too often in the past meant merely an interest in all the discrete happenings which political historians had

1. This list is provided for purposes of illustration, not formal classification. Though there is a large sociological literature on the subject, no definitive taxonomy of groups is possible, for new groups are always in the process of formation, and new group types, too. Cf. Robert K. Merton, *Social Theory and Social Structure*, rev. ed. (Glencoe, Ill., 1957), pp. 309–10n.

2. A. L. Kroeber and Clyde Kluckhohn, *Culture: A Critical Review of Concepts and Definitions* (Cambridge, Mass., 1952).

ignored. Today, however, social history is becoming a sophisticated study of the lineaments of society itself, as they have changed through time. The new economic historians, the new historians of education, the demographic historians, the new diplomatic historians, and the new historians of science are all moving on parallel lines.[3]

3. Cf. R. W. Fogel, "The New Economic History: Its Findings and Methods," *Economic History Review*, 2d ser. 29 (1966): 624–56; Allan G. Bogue, "United States: The 'New' Political History," *Journal of Contemporary History* 3 (1958): 5–27; Philip J. Greven, Jr., "Historical Demography and Colonial America," *William and Mary Quarterly*, 3d ser. 23 (1966): 627–34; Wilson Smith, "The New Historian of American Education," *Harvard Educational Review* 31 (1961): 136–43; Kuhn, *The Structure of Scientific Revolutions*, passim; Lawrence Stone, *The Crisis of the Aristocracy*, passim; T. Scott Miyakawa, *Protestants and Pioneers*, passim. This new work appears not merely in manifestoes but in monographs. It is sustained not by mere aspiration but by solid achievement. And it is happening in every historical field. One finds, for example, studies of social mobility in ancient China and modern America; and monographs on authority and alienation in ancient Rome and modern Australia. See, e.g., Cho-yun Hsu, *Ancient China in Transition* (Stanford, 1965); Stephan Thernstrom, *Poverty and Progress* (Cambridge, 1964); Ramsay MacMullen, *Enemies of the Roman Order* (Cambridge, 1966); and Michael Roe, *Quest for Authority in Eastern Australia* (Parkville, Australia, 1965).

This new history is an international phenomenon, which first became quantitatively significant in France and has since spread to other nations. One finds it in the great French journal, *Annales*, and in the major work of Marc Bloch and Fernand Braudel. Many new historical journals, mostly founded in the 1950s and 1960s, are similarly oriented. One thinks of *Past and Present* (1952, Oxford), *Saeculum* (1950, Munich), the *International Review of Social History* (1956, Amsterdam), *History and Theory* (1960, Middletown, Conn.), *Comparative Studies in Society and History* (1958, Ann Arbor, Mich.), and *The Journal of Contemporary History* (London, 1966). I am told that the same trends are apparent in Russian journals, too—*Novaia i Noveishaia Istoriia* (Modern and Contemporary History) (1958, Moscow); and *Vestnik Istorii Mirovoi* (Journal of the History of World Culture) (Moscow, 1957).

The new history seems to be moving very fast in France, the United States, and also the developing nations. In the latter, there is a curious kind of combined development, in which exceedingly primitive attitudes toward history exist side by side with the most sophisticated projects. In Indonesia, there are still interdisciplinary disputes between history and magic, at the same time that there are some remarkable projects in social and cultural history. See Soedjatmoko, ed., *An Introduction to Indonesian Historiography* (Ithaca, 1965). Some groups of historians are more laggard than others; German academic historiography may be the most backward in the world. But even in Germany there are stirrings by both history-minded sociologists and society-conscious historians. See for example, Ralf Dahrendorf, *Gesellschaft und Demokratie in Deutschland* (Munich, 1965), and Helmut Böhme, *Deutschlands Weg zur Grossmacht* (Cologne, 1966).

The old, agonized discussions of the relationship between history and the social sciences are increasingly irrelevant, as disciplinary lines are not merely being crossed but trampled under foot. The arbitrary institutional distinction between history and sociology simply disappears in monographs by Charles Tilly and Elinor Barber. Economic theory and economic history are closely integrated by scholars such as Douglass North, Albert Fishlow, Peter Temin, and many others. The academic difference between political science and history vanishes in work by William Nisbet Chambers, Samuel Beer, Stein Rokkan, Giovanni Sartori, and Hans Daalder. Demog-

Some historians study groups as particular events. Others are increasingly interested in the regularities of group types. Many scholars merely attempt empirical descripitions of human groups. A few construct group patterns as paradigmatic explanation models for the resolution of problems of individual behavior or of collective social needs.

But whatever purpose may prevail, and whatever group type may be chosen, there is a tacit logic which attaches to all group description or group explanation—a logic which is relevant to most historical inquiry. And there are also many forms of illogic, which are more easily identified than the logic which they imply. The following fallacies are common cases in point.

৪৯ The *fallacy of composition* consists in reasoning improperly from a property of a member of a group to a property of the group itself. This form of error is not restricted to groups of human beings but extends to all classes of things. And as such, it occurs in two varieties: First, it falsely extrapolates a quality of one group member to all group members. A hypothetical example would be committed by a man who observes that a particular American is rich and infers that all Americans, individually, are rich. Second, it is possible to transfer a quality of a member to the group itself. The man observes one rich American and concludes that America itself, as a group, is rich.

An actual example of the fallacy of composition appears in a book about the American South. The subject is a tough one, much complicated by the fact that, though there is a group of people (as well as a geographical region) which can be collectively identified as *the* South, there are also many subgroups: the tidewater-Chesapeake South, the Appalachian South, the Carolina low-country South, the Kentucky bluegrass South, the Mississippi levee-and-delta South, the Alabama-Georgia blackbelt South, the Texas cow-country South, the Ozark South, several distinct Floridian Souths, and sundry others. All of these various Souths have certain qualities in common, which mark them off from the various Norths, but they are also unlike each other in many different ways.

W. J. Cash's *Mind of the South* is a classic attempt to characterize the collective group which is the South. But its thesis is deeply flawed by the fallacy of composition. Cash was himself a product of the Appalachian

---

raphy and history are one in the scholarship of Louis Henry, Etienne Gautier, Pierre Goubert, D. E. C. Eversley, D. V. Glass, Angel Rosenblatt, and many others. All of these works have one quality in common—they are all addressed to one or more of the five aspects of group behavior listed in our definition above.

South. He was born in Gaffney, South Carolina, educated at Wofford College and Wake Forest, and was a resident of Charlotte, North Carolina. His perspective has been unkindly called the "Hillbilly view" of Southern history. For Cash, "the man at the center" of Southern culture was the man who scratched out his living on an Appalachian hillside. The inhabitants of the other Souths are seen at a distance, like people from a mountaintop. From that range they look small and insignificant—the "Virginians and their artificial influence," the Charlestonians, and the "Orleannais" who crawl around the edges of Cash's book. A critic of the book, C. Vann Woodward, has observed that "Cash knew nothing firsthand of the Tidewater, the Delta, the Gulf, the Blue-Grass or the Trans-Mississippi south. But the hill country had heard quite enough of the pretensions and poses of folk from those remote and high-living parts, and Cash figured it was time to let them have an unbiased history of the south from the hillbilly point of view."[4] More than that, when Cash studied a low country nabob, he saw a hillbilly in disguise. And when he studied a Negro he saw—he knew not what. Some strange creature whose innards were a mystery to him, and whose presence was largely ignored.

There are other complaints to be entered against Cash's idea of the South. There is a certain disturbing time'essness in his conceptualizations. The first half of Southern history is forgotten, and the second half seems to float in a great fluffy cloud of eternity. The mind of Cash's South is a singular thing, without spatial variations or temporal refinements. Moreover, there is something of the fallacy of the counterquestion in his book. Cash took the plantation legend and turned it upside down. He stood Scarlett O'Hara on her head. When the crinolines billowed out and down, there wasn't much to be seen of Scarlett's upper parts, but there was a considerable display of her lower ones, which some innocents in our own century naïvely persist in mistaking for reality. Scarlett's lower parts make a splendid spectacle. But it is a little disconcerting to find, in a book called *The Mind of the South*, so little brain and so much bottom.

Cash's book, for all its flaws, remains a very great book indeed. For anybody who is interested in the hillbilly South, it remains the indispensable guide—a veritable Baedecker to the boondocks. And anybody who is interested in Southerners has to know about hillbilly Southerners. We can say without condescension that Cash's *Mind of the South* is still supreme in this more restricted field. But as for the rest of the South . . . The author himself mentions Lula Vollmer's mountain woman, "who

---

4. C. Vann Woodward, "White Man, White Mind," *The New Republic*, December 9, 1967, pp. 28–30.

knew of France only that it was 'somers yan side of Asheville.' " Cash may have had the same impression of Charleston, and New Orleans, and Williamsburg, and the other distant places. He never even knew how far away they were from his Man at the Center.[5]

A second cluster of examples of the fallacy of composition appears in the historiography of the eighteenth-century Enlightenment—an international phenomenon if ever there was one. And yet in most accounts there is usually a Man at the Center, as in Cash's book, or a small group of Men at the Center, whose characteristics are generalized into the characteristics of the Enlightment itself. Ernst Cassirer organizes his understanding of the Enlightenment around a linear progression from Leibnitz to Kant. The development of Kantian thought predominates. For the English historian Alfred Cobban, the emphasis is different. "It seems to me, on the contrary, that such thinkers as Bacon, Newton, Locke, Hume and Bentham occupy key positions in the whole evolution of 'enlightened' Europe," he writes. Carl Becker's Enlightenment meant Montesquieu and Voltaire and Rousseau, Diderot, Helvetius, Holbach, Turgot, Quesnay, and Condorcet. France, he wrote, was "the mother country and Paris the capital." J. L. Talmon's Man at the Center is Robespierre. Lester Crocker's is, in one work, the Marquis de Sade. There are many similar absurdities in the literature on a subject which cries out for a careful, balanced, comparative study.[6]

ello The *fallacy of division* is the converse of the fallacy of composition. It occurs when somebody reasons falsely from a quality of the group to a quality of a member of the group. Once again, it applies to all kinds of classes of things, as well as to groups of people. A hypothetical example is an argument such as:

> A schooner is a common type of sailing craft.
> A bugeye is a schooner.
> Therefore, a bugeye is a common type of sailing craft.

5. W. J. Cash, *The Mind of the South* (New York, 1941), p. 47. A new study of Cash which agrees with none of these observations is Joseph L. Morrison, *W. J. Cash: Southern Prophet* (New York, 1967). I am much indebted to the insights of C. Vann Woodward, in the article cited above.
6. Ernst Cassirer, *The Philosophy of the Enlightenment*, trans. Fritz C. A. Koelln and James P. Pettegrove (Boston, 1951); Alfred Cobban, *In Search of Humanity: The Role of the Enlightenment in Modern History* (New York, 1960), pp. 7–8; Carl Becker, *The Heavenly City of the Eighteenth Century Philosophers* (New Haven, 1932), pp. 33–34; J. L. Talmon, *The Origins of Totalitarian Democracy* (New York, 1960); Lester G. Crocker, *Age of Crisis: Man and World in Eighteenth Century French Thought* (Baltimore, 1959).

Both of the premises are empirically true. But the conclusion, which is false, commits the fallacy of division.

One common form of the fallacy of division is an argument that a quality which is shared by some or many members of a group is shared by all of them, or that a quality which is shared by most members is possessed by any one of them. Vernon Parrington often committed this mistake in his great *Main Currents of American Thought*, where he formed the habit of conceptualizing a problem in group stereotypes and transferring the stereotype to individual members. Thus,

> Most Calvinists were theological determinists.
> Most New England Puritans were Calvinists.
> Therefore, most New England Puritans were theological
>   determinists.

But if a good deal of recent scholarship is right, New England Puritans were not determinists, or at least they were determinists with a difference.

A second type of the fallacy of division is an inference from a property of the group itself to a property of the member of the group. Thus, again from Parrington (2:179),

> The fortunes of the Federalists decayed after 1800.
> Joseph Dennie was a Federalist.
> Therefore, the fortunes of Joseph Dennie decayed after 1800.

There is only one remedy for this form of error—research.

&⤳ The *fallacy of difference* consists in a tendency to conceptualize a group in terms of its special characteristics to the exclusion of its generic characteristics.[7] This method is fallacious if the line of distinction between special and generic qualities cuts across the line of inquiry—as it almost invariably does. The group called Puritans serves as a useful example. Only a small part of Puritan theology was Puritan in a special sense. Much of it was Anglican, and more was Protestant, and most was Christian. And yet Puritanism is often identified and understood in terms of what was specially or uniquely Puritan.

The fallacy of difference is often an attempt at a definition by genus and difference, in which the genus is omitted or forgotten. "Such a reduction," writes Ralph Barton Perry, "is not only narrow, but false; because

7. It is identified and labeled by Ralph Barton Perry, in *Puritanism and Democracy* (New York, 1964), p. 82.

the differences lose their meaning when divorced from the genus."[8] A specimen is John F. H. New's *Anglican and Puritan: The Basis of Their Opposition, 1558–1640* (Stanford, 1964). If New merely meant to establish the points of conflict between Puritanism and Anglicanism, there would be nothing fallacious in his approach. Everything, as ever, depends upon purpose. But he moves beyond this purpose to another, for which his procedure is fallacious and seriously inconsistent—an attempt to generalize about the theology and psychology of Puritanism, which he undertakes to do in a rounded way but accomplishes only in terms of the points of conflict between Anglicans and Puritans. Many common commitments which appeared in both Anglicanism and Puritanism, however, are relevant to this larger purpose. In many respects, most Puritans *were* Anglicans. They were not Anglican in the same way as Archbishop Laud, but neither were they antithetical in all respects.

Another example of the fallacy of difference is identified by Barrington Moore, in the historiography—and sociology—of India, with respect to the significance of the caste system. "At least in its full ramifications," he writes, "the caste system is unique to Indian civilization. For this reason there is a strong temptation to use caste as an explanation for everything else that seems distinctive in Indian society. Obviously this will not do."[9] Moore notes that caste was used by historians to explain the apparent absence of religious warfare in India, but more recently religious warfare has become a problem of major proportions in India, and the caste system remains. I suspect that the caste system has been exaggerated not merely as an explanation of other distinctive aspects of Indian civilization but as an explanation of characteristics which were not distinctive as well.

ࠇࠇ The *converse fallacy of difference,* on the other hand, renders a special judgment upon a group for a quality which is not special to it. Commonly, this error appears in condemnatory judgments. Once again, the historiography of Puritanism provides an example. In America today, it is probable that Puritans are better known for the burning of witches than for anything else (except, perhaps, the baking of turkeys).

But by the standards of their own time, New England Puritans appear to have been extraordinary for the fact that they killed few witches and burned none. The incidence of executions for witchcraft seems to have been lower, per capita, in New England than in Old England, and

8. Ibid., p. 82.
9. Barrington Moore, *Social Origins of Dictatorship and Democracy* (Boston, 1966), p. 334.

much lower in America than in the countries of continental Europe. Estimates by able historians vary from a low of several hundred thousand executions for witchcraft in Western Europe in the early modern period to a high of several million. The few dozen murders in New England were modest by comparison. None of this, of course, is meant to condone witch-craft executions or to vindicate Puritans. But it *is* meant to suggest that there was nothing specially Puritan about witch hunts, and that there was possibly an inverse correlation between the two phenomena.[10]

A comparable error also appears in the history of the South. John Hope Franklin, in a monograph called *The Militant South* (Cambridge, Mass., 1956), argued that Southern culture was pervaded by violence. Few scholars would, I think, challenge that conclusion. But Franklin also suggests that violence was Southern in a special sense and that it was a particular consequence of the South's Peculiar Institution. The infer-ence is surely mistaken. Much of what Franklin found might be described as a Western as well as a Southern phenomenon. And in the cities of the Northeastern states, violence in the streets during the period 1800–1861 was a common and ordinary fact of life. Baltimore was not the only city that deserved the name of "Mob-town." There were many ugly and bloody disturbances in the streets of New York, Philadelphia, and even Boston.

There was also much violence in the Old Northwest. A history of one Illinois county is suitably titled *Bloody Williamson*. Franklin's study of violence is not quantitative—nor is anybody else's in this period. Until a controlled investigation is completed, it appears exceedingly unlikely that a high incidence of violence was uniquely Southern in the period 1800–1861. Maybe there was something specially Southern about the *quality* of violence below the Mason-Dixon line. And there is some evidence that violence may have been institutionalized in the South in ways which were not apparent in the Northeast or Northwest—in the establishment of military schools for example, and in the ritualized violence of the Southern elite. But in its impressionistic conclusions as to the incidence of violent acts, Franklin's *Militant South* seems to be in error.

⇛ The *fallacy of ethnomorphism* is a form of error which is worth distinguishing from ethnocentrism for analytical purposes, though the two are often compounded in a single name, and sometimes in a single act. Ethnomorphism is the conceptualization of the characteristics

10. George L. Kittredge, *Witchcraft in Old and New England* (Cambridge, Mass., 1929); H. R. Trevor-Roper, *Religion, the Reformation, and Social Change* (London, 1967), pp. 90–192.

of another group in terms of one's own. This pernicious error was recognized and repudiated two hundred years ago, but a perceptive English historical critic, Bolingbroke, complained that "There is scarcely any folly or vice more epidemical among the sons of man, than that ridiculous and hurtful vanity by which the people of each country are apt to prefer themselves to those of every other, and to make their own customs and manners and opinions the standards of right and wrong, of true and false."[11]

In historiography, the same error appears not merely in moral judgments but also in behavioral understandings. It is committed by primitive and civilized people alike. When the Puritans began to settle in Massachusetts, their Indian neighbors watched them move in and wondered why they had come. The Narraganset finally decided that the English must have burned up all the firewood in the old country and had moved to find more. "This was one of the Indians' chief reasons for removal," a historian explains, "and they naturally projected it to the white man."[12] The Puritans, in turn, pondered the presence of the red man in America, and some persuaded themselves that the Indians were descendants of the ten lost tribes of Israel—a historical interpretation which retained its popularity in Protestant America for the next two centuries. Cotton Mather had a slightly different thesis. "Though we know not when or how these indians first became inhabitants of this mighty continent," he wrote, "yet we may guess that probably the devil decoyed those miserable savages hither, in hopes that the Gospel of the Lord Jesus Christ would never come here to destroy or disturb his absolute empire over them."[13]

There are many modern examples. In ancient historiography, Gilbert Murray once asserted that Homeric religion was "not a religion at all." He meant that it did not meet the descriptive definitions of religion in modern Western culture.[14] Similarly, Lewis Mumford has complained of ethnomorphic conceptions in modern interpretations of the history of ancient technology, which sometimes reads like the chapter from *The Natural History of Iceland* that Dr. Johnson discovered—a chapter which which was called "Concerning Snakes," and read in its entirety: "There are no snakes to be met with throughout the whole island."[15] Mumford observed,

11. Henry Bolingbroke, *Letters on the Study and Use of History* (London, 1870), pp. 9–10.
12. Alden Vaughan, *The New England Frontier* (Boston, 1965), p. 62.
13. Ibid., p. 20.
14. Gilbert Murray, *Tradition and Design in the Iliad*, p. 222.
15. James Boswell, *Life of Dr. Johnson,* Modern Library ed. (New York, n.d.,), p. 799.

What has misled judgment in our own age is that the greatest technological achievements of the ancient world were in the realm of statics, not dynamics, in civil, not mechanical engineering: in buildings, not machines. If the historian finds a lack of invention in earlier cultures, it is because he persists in taking as the main criterion of mechanical progress the special kinds of power-driven machine or automation to which western man has now committed himself, while treating as negligible important inventions, like central heating and flush toilets—or even ignorantly attributing the latter to our own "industrial revolution."[16]

Other examples of ethnomorphism appear in broad conceptions of historical development. To George Bancroft it seemed that all groups would gradually develop into the form of the American Republic circa 1840. To Leopold Von Ranke, the model was the Prussian monarchy. Each scholar made the mistake of assuming that the development of his own particular group was a prototype for the development of all groups.

There is a vast ethnomorphism in Freud's thought, in the form of assumptions that behavioral patterns which appeared in the members of his own culture were transferrable without major change to members of many other groups, far removed in space and time. When Freud himself did this in his analyses of Leonardo and Moses, the result was an interpretative atrocity. Similarly, Marx generalized certain group characteristics which did exist (some of them) in nineteenth-century England, France, and Germany into universal phenomena for all groups everywhere.

Today the most powerful form of ethnomorphism is the idea that Anglo-American and North European cultural characteristics are *the* cultural norm. This mistaken belief is not merely prevalent among Anglo-Americans and North Europeans. The painful zeal with which Negro ladies have their hair straightened, Jewish ladies have their noses straightened, and Oriental ladies have their eyes straightened suggests that this pervasive ethnomorphism is internalized by members of other groups. Reference-group theory helps us to understand that many human beings have arranged their lives with reference to groups to which they do not belong.[17]

જ્જ The *fallacy of ethnocentrism* is committed by a historian who exaggerates the role of his own group in its interaction with other groups. A historian may commit it by mistaking not the shape of another group

16. Lewis Mumford, *The Myth of the Machine* (New York, 1967), p. 244.
17. Herbert H. Hyman and Eleanor Singer, eds., *Readings in Reference Group Theory and Research* (New York, 1968).

but merely its size—much as the endpaper map in Cleveland Amory's *Proper Bostonians* deliberately changes the size of American states in proportion to the ethnocentric perceptions of the inhabitants of Boston.

A historiographical example is provided by Chester Wilmot, a British journalist who published an excellent military history of World War II. He made a serious mistake, however, in his suggestion that the Russo-German War was an extension and a consequence of a prior Anglo-German rivalry:

> This was Hitler's solution of the dilemma in which he was placed by Britain's refusal to yield. The essence [that wôrd!] of his problem was that he could not gain the resources for a prolonged struggle with the Anglo-Saxon powers without involving himself in that "war on two fronts" which he had sworn to avoid. He could not inflict a crippling defeat on the British, let alone the Anglo-American combination, until he had greatly expanded his Navy and Air Force and was free to concentrate the main strength of his Army against the West. This he could not do so long as the threat of hostile Soviet action in the East compelled him to divide his forces and to allocate to the army two-thirds of his mobilised manpower and of his armament production. Furthermore, he could not keep Occupied Europe fed and quiet during the conquest of Britain, nor could he wage the intensive air and naval warfare which alone could bring victory, unless he could be certain of two things: full control over the economy of the Balkans, and continued deliveries of grain and oil from the U.S.S.R.[18]

An opposite interpretation might be nearer the mark. Hitler's career was more clearly marked by an obsession with Eastern Europe and Bolshevist Russia, rather than by a prior determination to conquer England. Along the way, he appears to have found himself in the unwelcome position of being compelled to fight England, and not the other way around. Moreover, Wilmot's map of the struggle magnifies the size of the island of Britain, much as Mercator's projection enlarges the island of Greenland. At the same time, it shrinks the great land masses of Russia and the United States.

On the other side, the Russian version of the Second World War errs in the opposite direction, and in greater degree. In the U.S.S.R. the Second World War is known as the Great Patriotic War. The official multivolumed history provides factually inaccurate estimates of the number of German troops engaged in the East and in the West. And the world to the west is shrunk to the size of a Leningrad suburb. American authors, also, have made comparable mistakes in standard histories of the French and Indian War, the War for Independence, the Wars Against African Piracy, the War of 1812, World War I, and World War II. In all of

18. Chester Wilmot, *The Struggle for Europe* (New York, 1952), p. 57.

these instances, the importance of American groups is grossly exaggerated, and the roles of other groups are much diminished.

There are many other examples in military history. Field Marshal Slim once defined a battle as something which happens at the intersection of two or more maps. We might paraphrase his statement: a battle is something which is fought at the intersection of two or more cultural groups. The temptations of ethnocentrism in this situation are almost irresistible.

But military history is not unique in this respect. The same fallacy appears in social, cultural, and political history. A striking example is the historiography of modern Burma, which calls to mind the Hindustani fable of the Six Men and the Elephant. Many different national groups interacted in the history of Burma; besides the Burmese, there were Chinese, Indians, British, Americans, Frenchmen, Japanese, and others. Fine Anglocentric books about Burma have been written by Maurice Collis, John S. Furnivall, D. G. E. Hall, and G. E. Harvey, to name but a few of many English and Anglo-Burman authors. Other scholars have produced works on the same subject from an American perspective, notably John L. Christian and John F. Cady—works which tend perhaps to overemphasize the admittedly important role of American missionaries in Burma. There are a few histories of Burma from the Japanese point of view—Willard Elsbree's *Japan's Role in Southeast Asia* (Cambridge, 1953). Still other accounts are Sinocentric, Indocentric, or Francocentric. Each of these approaches tends to exaggerate the role of a particular ethnic group in a very complex pattern of multiethnic interaction.

We have heard from each of the Six Men in Burmese historiography —in this case an Englishman, an American, an Indian, a Japanese, a Chinese, and a Frenchman—all of whom tended to exaggerate the size and significance of that part of the elephant upon which his hands happened to rest. But recently we have begun to hear from the elephant. Histories of Burma by Burmese scholars and statesmen are beginning to appear in quantity.[19] These works are, if anything, more stridently ethnocentric than those which preceded them. They are painful works of pious devotion to the Burmese people— works comparable in spirit to the heroic acts of Burmese ladies of good breeding before the British

19. Maung Htin Aung, *A History of Burma* (New York, 1967); Maung Maung, *Aung San of Burma* (The Hague, 1961); U Nu, *Burma Under Japanese Rule* (London, 1954); Ba Maw, *Breakthrough in Burma: Memoirs of a Revolution, 1939–1946* (New Haven, 1968); U Ba U, *My Burma* (New York, 1959). For a review of earlier historical writing in Burma see Thaung Blackmore, "Burmese Historical Scholarship," in *Historical, Archaeological and Linguistic Studies on Southern China, Southeast Asia and the Hong Kong Region* (Hong Kong, 1967), pp. 310–20.

"intrusion," as Maung Htin Aung calls it (p. 210)—ladies who, "as an act of piety to obtain merit, volunteered to suckle infant elephants," which were the sacred symbols of Burmese culture and religion.[20] There is a good deal of vicarious elephant suckling in Burmese national history. But it is surely no worse than the ethnocentric effusions of historians in other nations.

There are other studies of Burmese history and culture which are remarkable for their comparative absence of ethnocentrism. A very great example is E. R. Leach's *Political Systems of Highland Burma* (London, 1954), which is sufficient evidence that this bias *can* be controlled. Leach has written of group interactions which are conceptualized in such a way as to neutralize his own ethnocentric bias. The same effect can be achieved in many contexts, with ingenuity and common honesty.

The problem which appears in Burmese historiography commonly occurs in much more aggravated forms elsewhere. A student of Indonesian history has observed with respect to this field that

> the fundamental historiographical problem is, then, to find the meeting point between the many local histories of the Indonesian people and colonial history and so to determine how to unite the two. What criteria are to be used in order to write a single narrative out of so many histories? Is it possible to blend a history of Indonesia which is Indonesian in character (Indonesia-centric) out of local histories which are regio-centric or ethnocentric and out of colonial histories which are to us essentially [that word again!] xenocentric in character?[21]

These are, indeed, hard questions. When they are cast in these terms, they are perhaps insoluble. Though an "Indonesia-centric" history of Indonesia may seem at first sight to be perfectly sensible and defensible, and though it is surely functional to nationalizing purposes, it is dysfunctional to sound scholarship. Indonesian history has been made, in an extraordinary degree, by the interaction of many different groups, cultures, and nations. The only defensible approach, and the only effective solution to the historiographical problem, is a balanced and refined polycentrism, difficult though that may be to sustain.

Another example of ethnocentrism appears in European historiography. A French historian of England, Elie Halévy, placed heavy emphasis upon the French Revolution of 1830 in his interpretation of the progress of English reform during the 1830s.[22] An English historian, Norman Gash, has made a persuasive argument for the proposition that

20. John F. Cady, *A History of Modern Burma* (Ithaca, N.Y., 1958), p. 7 n.
21. Mohammed Ali, "Historiographical Problems," in Soedjatmoko, ed., *An Introduction to Indonesian Historiography* (Ithaca, 1965), pp. 11–12.
22. Halévy, *The Triumph of Reform (1830–1841)* (London, 1961), pp. 3, 34–37, passim.

Halévy exaggerated the importance of French affairs in English politics, and particularly in the English General Election of 1830.[23] All Gaul may be divided into as many parts as one likes, but one of them is not England. Halévy's error (if error it is) is an aberration in a work which is remarkably clean of ethnocentric fallacies—and an extraordinary model of intercultural understanding.

 ஐ The *fallacy of elitism* consists in conceptualizing human groups in terms of their upper strata, or of casting belief units in terms of their most refined thoughts and elegant expressions. Elitism substitutes Society for society, Culture for culture, Civilization for civilization, Manners for manners, and Morals for morals. This semantical ambiguity appears in many languages. The terms "Civilization," "Civilisation," and "Civilización" are involved in the same contradictions in English, French, and Spanish. Dante used "Civiltà" in the same ambiguous way. And the Germans have assimilated a splendid variety of pedantical terms—"Kultur," "Civilisation," "Gesittung," "Bildung," "Ausbildung," "Sitte," "Gewohnheiten," "Gebrauche"—most of which are equally treacherous.

 There is, of course, no impropriety in a study of Proper People, or of their Best Thoughts. A history of Society can be quite as useful as a history of society. But there is a fallacy in a confusion of the two, which has often happened in historical writing. The results sometimes include serious substantive error, as well as conceptual superficiality. In the Bosporus there is a surface current which flows powerfully to the southwest. But beneath it the water speeds swiftly in the opposite direction. The same phenomenon sometimes appears in human groups.

 The fallacy of elitism appears in a great pioneer work of cultural history, Voltaire's *Age of Louis XIV*. Voltaire's interest in manners and customs constituted an important and constructive departure from political and dynastic history. But the transition was incomplete. In place of a history of a political dynasty, Voltaire wrote the history of a Cultural dynasty. Worse, he seems to have assumed that where there was no Culture, there was no culture. In his preface he wrote:

> The thinking man, and what is still rarer, the man of taste, numbers only four ages in the history of the world; four happy ages when the arts were brought to perfection and which, marking an era of the greatness of the human mind, are an example to posterity.

23. Norman Gash, "English Reform and the French Revolution in the General Election of 1830," Pares and Taylor, eds., *Essays Presented to Sir Lewis Namier* (London, 1956), pp. 258–64.

The first of these ages, to which true glory belongs, is that of Philip and Alexander, or rather of Pericles, Demosthenes, Aristotle, Plato, Apelles, Phidias, Praxiteles; and this honour was confined within the limits of Greece, the rest of the known world being in a barbarous state.

The second age is that of Caesar and Augustus, distinguished moreover by the names of Lucretius, Cicero, Livy, Virgil, Horace, Ovid, Varro and Vitruvius.

The third is that which followed the taking of Constantinople by Mahomet II . . . the hour of Italy's glory. . . .

The fourth age is that which we call the age of Louis XIV, and it is perhaps of the four the one which most nearly approaches perfection. Enriched with the discoveries of the other three it accomplished in certain departments more than the three together. All the arts, it is true, did not progress further than they did under the Medici, under Augustus or under Alexander; but human reason in general was brought to perfection.[24]

This statement is a little imperfect in its chronology and a little credulous in its ascription of greatness. How can Apelles be an example to posterity? None of his works is known to survive. But there are more serious objections. Always, as Voltaire himself privately said of the book, "the principal figures are in the foreground; the crowd is in the background." Everywhere the object was to celebrate genius and cultivation. If Culture did not exist, in Voltaire's narrow conception, then there was nothing. Cultural history became a learned society—a club with a very exclusive admissions policy. If the subject matter of Voltaire's work was different from that of so-called drum-and-trumpet history, the ruffles and flourishes still sound the same.

Voltaire's confusion of Cultural history with cultural history still appears in modern historical works by such so-called cultural historians as Jacques Barzun, to name but one. Barzun writes about great musicians the way drum-and-trumpeters celebrated great generals. To brass and percussion he adds strings and winds. But everything else is still the same. He professes cultural history, but produces Cultural history. Many cultural histories are still Cultural in their content. Examples are two recent volumes in Harper & Row's New American Nation series—Louis B. Wright's *The Cultural Life of the American Colonies* (New York, 1957) and Russel B. Nye's *The Cultural Life of the New Nation* (New York, 1960). Both books begin with prefatory promises of cultural history. But they describe Culture instead—a weary round of stale anecdotes and impressions, mostly about the Best People.

Another example is the writing of a Latin American historian, José Toribio Medina. His work excluded the lower classes, "from whom

24. Voltaire, *The Age of Louis XIV*, trans. Martyn Pollack. Everyman edition (London, 1961), p. 1.

we can learn nothing," he wrote.[25] It is something of an irony that this scholar, who so cavalierly dismissed the vast majority of humanity from history, should be celebrated by a band of admirers as the "Humanist of the Americas."[26]

ဆာ The *fallacy of racism* is a popular delusion, and all the more powerful for its tendency, increasingly, to run underground. It might be defined in three different ways:

1. A false classification of people into fixed biological groups.

2. A false explanation of culturally learned behavior in terms of a biological, physiological, or hereditary cause.

3. A false prejudice, for or against any genetic class or ethnic group of human beings.

These three forms of error commonly coexist. But any one of them alone is sufficient to constitute the fallacy of racism.

Everything about this subject is controversial. But some things seem reasonably clear. Thanks to the revolutionary progress of genetics in the past generation, it can be demonstrated beyond a reasonable doubt that there *are* classes of men which can be called races—classes which are most accurately called "gene pools," or "breeding populations." A race is a collection of people who share a common genetic heritage and certain statistical regularities in their genetic make-up, which distinguish them, in some degree, from other collectivities.[27]

But, having asserted this, we must quickly add three important

25. Arthur P. Whitaker, "Medina's Concept of History," in Maury A. Bromsen, ed., *José Toribio Medina, Humanist of the Americas* (Washington, D.C., 1960), p. 70.
26. There are many other examples. Prominent among them is Werner Jaeger, *Paideia: The Ideals of Greek Culture,* 3 vols., trans. Gilbert Highet (New York, 1936)— a heavily elitist view of Greek culture. Cf. Moses Hadas, *Hellenistic Culture: Fusion and Difference.*
27. I am following two moderate interpretations of race, Stanley Garn, *Human Races* (Springfield, Ill., 1961), and Theodosius Dobzhansky, *Heredity and the Nature of Man* (New York, 1964). There is a wide range of expert opinion. Some anthropologists and geneticists have, I think, allowed too little latitude to race. Prominent among them is M. F. Ashley Montagu, who comes very close to denying that race exists, in *Man's Most Dangerous Myth: The Fallacy of Race,* 3d ed. (New York, 1952). Montagu has also edited a collection of essays in the same vein by ten scholars, all of whom minimize race, in *The Concept of Race* (New York, 1964). On the other hand, Carleton S. Coon, in *The Origin of Races* (New York, 1962) and *The Living Races of Man* (New York, 1965), argues beyond his evidence, in an interpretation which allows too much latitude to race differences. Between Ashley Montagu and Carleton Coon, there is a mediating position—the position of Garn and Dobzhansky, if I understand them correctly—which is in my judgment more tenable than either extreme, in light of present evidence.

qualifications. First, there is no simple definitive taxonomy of these "breeding populations"—no clear and crisp set of classes. There are many different variations in the genetic make-up of men, and there is no easy way of sorting them out. Some careful students of race divide men into a mere handful of racial groups; others, into several hundred.[28] For Carleton Coon, there are five races in the world—Caucasoid, Mongoloid, Congoloid, Australoid, and Capoid,[29] with numerous "clines" or inter-racial shadings between. Other scholars distinguish many small and special "races," even such as "Pitcairn Islanders" and "Neo-Hawaiians."[30] Wherever there has been a group which has tended to inter-marry, there is likely to be a gene pool, which can be defined with respect to some particular genetic peculiarity. Jews appear to be genetically distinct with respect to a particular statistical predisposition to certain rare hereditary diseases, such as the Tay-Sachs disease, and familial dysautonomia. Ashkenazic Jews are genetically distinguishable from Sephardic Jews with respect to familial Mediterranean fever and favism. The Irish appear to have a monopoly on the rare hereditary disease called leprechaunism. Scandinavians are apparently unique in the inci-dence of Silferskiold's disease. But none of these groups are now known to possess sufficient genetic differences to warrant special identity as a "race."[31]

Second, in the past five hundred years breeding populations have been highly unstable. Many new gene pools have been formed; others have faded away. Research in biochemistry and genetics has demon-strated that races have been in process of rapid and complex genetic change—more rapid and complex than most scholars believed possible a generation ago.[32]

Third, races are not "groups" in our sense of the word. They do, beyond a doubt, meet two of our group criteria, but not others. Races do possess a finite membership which can be statistically specified. And they do possess a common history. But they have no group structure, and no group function, and probably no normative patterns of conduct.

It is readily apparent that race is more than skin-deep. Garn ob-serves that "racial differences are known to exist in almost every area of anatomy where comparative data have been accumulated, and there

28. Garn, pp. 12–38, 116–32.
29. Coon, *The Living Races of Man*, pp. 6–10, passim.
30. Garn, pp. 7, 132. There has even been a classification of classifiers into "lumpers" and "splitters"—the former preferring a few big categories, and the latter, many little ones (ibid., p. 12). No genetic differences between lumpers and splitters have been demonstrated.
31. Ibid., pp. 81–91.
32. Ibid., p. v.

is growing evidence for racial differences in biochemical functioning and in the constituents of cells and tissues."[33] Racial differences have been located with some precision in pigmentation, hair form and color and quantity, bone size and form, tooth structure, growth rates, blood groups, susceptibility to disease, adaptations to heat and cold, sensitivity to drugs, and even in the composition of earwax.

These physiological variations are established beyond cavil. More doubtful is the problem of racial patterns of temperament and intelligence. No such patterns have been proved to exist. But this is not to say that such patterns have been proved not to exist. Garn writes,

> Racial differences in measured intelligence thus remain neither proven nor disproved. There are differences, but like stature, they do not necessarily indicate the maximum level of capacity in the absence of standard or controlled conditions. To the confirmed believer in racial differences in intelligence, we can simply say that the more nearly two groups are matched in educational level, family background, opportunity and security, the closer they agree on averaged I.Q. scores. To the dedicated equalitarian, the believer in no race differences, the disparate levels in the currently best-matched Negro-white comparisons remain to be refuted. . . . A very reasonable guess is that races are comparable in the sum and total of what we call "intelligence," but differ in many interesting details. As with the automatic response patterns that so neatly differentiate one individual from the other, race differences may exist in form-discrimination, color-sense, tonal-memory, mechanical-reasoning, abstract-reasoning and with other special (rather than general) aspects of intelligence. This supposition, moreover, is directly susceptible to testing.[34]

It is, indeed, susceptible to testing, but as yet it has not been tested in a conclusive way. The question must, at this moment, remain unanswered. An open-minded historian will, I think, carefully follow the progress of biochemical genetics, which has already produced some findings which are directly relevant to major historical problems. The genetic adaptation of Negroes to humid heat has been demonstrated by careful research, as well as the so-called sickle-cell trait, which provides a defense against malaria. Both of these facts cannot be ignored by a historian of the institution of Negro slavery. They assume great importance in any study of the history of the Black Caribs, for example. It is likely that other genetic discoveries—possibly even with respect to intelligence and temperament—will prove relevant to many other historical problems.

But at the same time, a historian must take the full measure of much research in the past fifty years, which has demonstrated the extraordinary cultural malleability of men—all men. The famous alpha tests

33. Ibid., p. 37.
34. Garn, *Human Races*, pp. 110–15.

of the United States Army in World War I found that Negroes from some Northern states scored higher in one kind of intelligence than whites from some Southern states.[35] Many recent projects have produced similar results.

It is also important to guard against common errors of inference. First, genetic patterns are statistical in nature. One cannot assume that any given member of a breeding population, even if his membership can be clearly established, will possess the genetic make-up which is normal in his group. Second, one cannot conclude that a breeding population which is distinctive in some ways is therefore distinctive in all ways, or in any particular way which is not clearly and conclusively established. Third, the arbitrary nature of all taxonomies of race should be clearly recognized. If genetic patterns are sometimes useful to historical research, they must be carefully defined *ad hoc* and not converted into sweeping generalities about tendencies of all people of a given genetic class in all respects. Genetic classifications must not be misconstrued as fixed groups. Fourth, a level of performance is not a measure of capability. Fifth, genetic classes must not be confused with social and cultural groups. Historians have mistaken language groups such as Aryans and Semites for racial classes. Often, in the nineteenth century, they mistook national groups for races. Henry Cabot Lodge wrote frequently of the "English" race. There are laws in some American states which still speak of the "Chinese" race. An Italian novelist, Ignazio Silone, described in *Bread and Wine* the tendency of some people to confuse occupational groups with race:

> Don Paolo was suprised to observe the role that mustaches, beards, and hair still played in differentiating the professional class from the peasants and the landlords. He realized also why the various classes were indicated in dialect by the word "race"—the "race" of husbandmen, the "race" of "artists" (Artisans), the "race" of landowners. The son of a petty landowner who studies, and therefore inevitably becomes a state or municipal employee, promptly tries to obliterate the fact that he comes of the "race" of husbandmen by brushing his hair in the style of his new station.[36]

There are many comparable errors in historical scholarship.

Finally, a historian should beware of the counterfallacy of anti-racism, which has been committed by many well-meaning social scientists. "Racist" is today a pejorative term, as negative in its connotation as "nigger" used to be—if not more so. "Nigger" connoted incapacity;

35. Ashley Montagu, "Intelligence of Northern Negroes and Southern Whites in the First World War," *American Journal of Psychology* 68 (1945): 161–88.
36. Ignazio Silone, *Bread and Wine* (New York, 1946), p. 151; quoted in Montagu, *Man's Most Dangerous Myth*, pp. 83–84.

"racist" suggests depravity. For this remarkable change in meaning, within the span of a generation, Nazism may be primarily responsible. The discrediting of racism may, paradoxically, prove to be Hitler's most enduring accomplishment. But some people have reacted in a mistaken way to the terrible crimes and atrocities which were committed in the name of race. They have tended to repudiate the idea of all hereditary characteristics, and to dismiss race as a dangerous superstition. Some racist thought is dangerous, but genetics remains a science. Race itself, properly understood, is a reality—a historical reality—at the same time that racism is a profound and bloody error, which cannot be tolerated in the contemporary world. Men can live with other fallacies in this book. But racism kills and maims and mutilates. Against this form of error, there ought to be a law.

⅋⅋ The *fallacy of cross grouping* consists in the conceptualization of one group type in terms of another. Hypothetically, this form of error can occur in numerous ways—in n^2 ways, if n = the number of group types in the world, plus innumerable multiple combinations. Practically, however, historiographical cross-grouping tends to appear in one particular variety: the conceptualization of all group types in terms of the nation-state. There are, of course many useful particular problems which can and should be conceptualized in terms of the nation-state—mostly political and legal problems, for by definition a nation-state is a legal and political group. But there are many other problems which should be approached differently—problems about religious, economic, social, or cultural groups, which rarely coincide with the nation-state. It would make no sense to write a history of the German religion, the Swiss language, the Congolese society, or the Nigerian culture. There are no such things. There are religions in Germany, languages in Switzerland, societies in the Congo, and cultures in Nigeria. But these problems are not defined accurately by national frontier posts. They have boundaries of their own.

The preponderant majority of the 134 sovereign nation-states which exist at the time of this writing do *not* possess a clearly defined national culture, a single language, a national society, or a national economy. Most nation-states in the world today are extensions of the colonial administrations which preceded them, and they still retain much of the colonial regime's shape and substance. A few were physically formed by some forgotten European bureaucrat, thousands of miles away, who scratched lines upon the map of a continent which he had never seen, nor ever wished to.

Though national history is increasingly unfashionable nowadays, it still retains its hold upon historians. Historical records have been sorted into national piles; there is a bias in our source material which is not easily overcome. Many classic historiographic problems are problems of national history, not readily translated into other terms. In American universities, historians are still hired as specialists in national history, and they tend to be trained in that way as well. This is not commonly the case in ancient or medieval historiography, and not consistently the case in African, Asian, and Latin American historiography. But most historians in America are specialists in modern European and United States history, and as such they tend to be national historians.

Today, "cultural history" is replacing national history in much of the best historical scholarship. And a "culture" is often understood to mean an integrated group having a common political organization, a social structure, an economic system, a religion, and a common way of life that embraces every aspect of human existence. In this sense, "culture" is an abstraction, and an exceedingly dangerous one. Except, perhaps, on a few remote and primitive islands, it does not exist.

But historians are tending to graft this abstraction called culture upon the root of national history, with deleterious consequences for empirical research and with many classic examples of the fallacy of cross-grouping. There are some wise words in David Potter's essay, "The Historian's Use of Nationalism and Vice Versa,"[37] which identifies the common tendency of historians "to assume too simple an equation between nationality and culture. . . . Many 'nationalist' movements have a minimum of common cultural content . . . the impulse moving them is primarily a negative political reaction against an existing regime (especially a colonial regime)."[38]

This modern tendency has lent new life to an old error. The nation-

37. *American Historical Review* 67 (1962): 924–50.
38. Ibid., pp. 933–35. The problem of nationality in historical writing is complicated by the incorrigible habit which many historians have formed, of confusing different, and sometimes antithetical meanings and purposes in the use of that term:

1. A confusion of "nation" as an idea, with "nation" as a group, with "nation" as an institution. These meanings can coexist in some contexts, as Mr. Potter demonstrates, but they are sometimes contradictory.

2. A confusion of what is with what ought to be: Mr. Potter notes the tendency of "the historian to deny nationality to groups of whom he morally disapproves."

3. A confusion of what exists historically with what is thought to exist by historians. Potter himself makes this mistake when he writes, "National groups usually coincide with a political state, but it would be too restrictive to say that a national group is simply a political group, for very often the historian is not concerned with the political aspects of the history of the group" (p. 924). This is a lovely example of a *non sequitur*. Things that are, are not the same as things that are of concern to historians. Historiographical interest is not an index of historical reality.

state, in the new form of national culture, retains its power as the predominant unit of historiographical inquiry. Just how powerful national history still is appears in two recent attempts to escape from it. One is by Cyril Black, who in an important new book called *The Dynamics of Modernization* (New York, 1966) attempted to break the lockstep of national history by studying in a comparative way the phenomenon of modernization everywhere in the world. But the unit of his analysis is still the nation-state. In the words of a reviewer of the book, "he accepts the concept of the national state, which he identifies with politically organized societies as almost the only really significant classification of mankind, and this leads him to some rather odd taxonomies both of processes of development and of national states themselves."[39]

Black, in the usual way, grafts onto the main stem of the nation-state an economy, a society, and a culture. But always the nation-state retains its pre-eminence. The reviewer notes, "To select the national state as the unit of study in the process of modernization introduces a serious bias into the account at the very start. It makes the whole process look much more political and much more planned than it was." His reviewer, an economist, would have preferred, if I understand him, to make ecological groups into the primary units of analysis, which is equally mistaken. A phenomenon such as modernization, as it is usually conceived, involves political development, economic development, social development, and cultural development on many different axes. What is required, surely, is a more complex pattern of conceptualization to deal with this complex subject—a conceptualization in terms of a variety of group types, which conforms more closely to the reality of multigroup membership in the modern world. Maybe the political, economic, social, and intellectual categories are not the most suitable ones—they are merely a reflection of the organization of academic society. The point is not that these particular groups should become the units of analysis, but rather that the analytical strategy must be adjusted to the subject, and in the study of a polycentric phenomenon, a conceptual polycentrism is required. The complex cannot be reduced, for convenience, to the national state, or the ecological system, or any other monistic scheme.

A second attempt to break out of the narrow boundaries of national history is R. R. Palmer's *The Age of Democratic Revolution* (2 vols. [Princeton, 1959–1964]), an excellent and useful book, which attempts to conceptualize revolutionary change in the Western world in the period 1760–1800 in terms of a world revolution in which many nations participated. But the transition from national to supernational history is

39. Kenneth Boulding in *History and Theory* 7 (1968): 83–90.

incomplete. The nation-state is still, in most chapters of Palmer's book, the unit of analysis. He has advanced from national history to national histories, but not to the next step, genuine supernational history.

Palmer's positive achievement, and Black's, should not be minimized. They have both accomplished more in the way of diminishing national stereotypes and national limits in historical scholarship than any other historians who come to mind. The limits of their accomplishment are noted merely as a way of measuring the difficulty of the task.

Both Palmer and Black are Americans who specialize in aspects of the history of Europe. Palmer is a historian of France; Black, of Russia. In the disparity between their own national origins and their national specialties both men gained a certain cosmopolitan advantage. The worst cases of narrow nationalism in scholarship appear in the works of scholars who, like myself, are American historians of America, or English historians of England, or German historians of Germany. It is easy, in these circumstances, to submerge all group types into the nation-state without a second thought. There is no difficulty in finding an example— indeed, it is difficult to find a survey history of the United States which is *not* an example of cross-grouping in the form of submerging all groups into the nation. Morison and Commager, Hofstadter, Miller and Aaron, Williams, Current and Friedel—are all inveterate cross-grouping books. And these are probably the best available surveys of American history.

If cross-grouping is most common in the form of confusing many groups with nation-groups, it also appears in other forms. One of them is the confusion of social and cultural groups of many kinds with geographical groups. Consider a hypothetical example: the inhabitants of Manhattan, who are a geographical and a political group. But they are not a society or a culture. Nevertheless it would be possible for an anthropologist to attempt a study of the Manhattan Islanders, like the Trobriand Islanders, and the result might have a certain superficial plausibility. He could apply the rhetoric and the conceptualization of cultural anthropology to the Manhattan Islanders, and illustrate it graphically and persuasively with many bits and scraps of "evidence." He could begin by demonstrating that the Manhattan Islanders have an ecological base and a political structure, complete with sachems and chieftains and other picturesque functionaries. He could show that they have formed traditional rivalries with other people—with the Staten Islanders, and the Long Islanders, and the terrible Bronx People. He could "prove" that they share certain physical characteristics in common—blackened lungs, bloodshot eyes, bronchial congestion. He could locate a religious common denominator in the fact that nearly all of them worship one God at most (maximal monotheism, it might technically be called).

Our anthropologist concludes that children of the Manhattan Islanders play curious ritualized games which are not widely known in other "cultures"—stick ball, snatch-the-purse, buzz-the-fuzz, and other jolly diversions. Adult Manhattan Islanders faithfully observe certain strange taboos—custom forbids them to speak politely to a stranger, or to smile in public, or to say please and thank you under any circumstances. They also keep curious dietary laws, somehow involving lox and bagels. Their ethical practices are complex—stealing is forbidden to private citizens, but encouraged in chiefs and sachems. Special burial practices are customarily used for deviant Islanders, who are dropped into the river after midnight, with their feet encased in concrete—a probable symbol of disapproval.

All of this, of course, commits the fallacy of false culture. Manhattan is, I repeat, the name of an island, a borough, a geographical group, a residential group, a political group, and maybe an ecological group, but it is not the name of a cultural group. It would be a very great mistake to confuse one with the other. And yet, as "culture" gradually acquires the same mystique and the same elasticity among historians that "nation" is slowly losing, the danger of the fallacy of false culture is likely to grow.

Finally, we might note the existence of other, and special, forms of cross-grouping, with reference to a single illustrative example. In the introduction to this chapter we noted two different group types, among others: voluntary associations and residence groups. There is a recent and important book by Kenneth T. Jackson called *Ku Klux Klan in the City 1915–1930* (New York, 1967), which demonstrated what many American historians had forgotten or never known—that the Klan was an urban phenomenon as well as a rural one. But though Jackson's book was a useful corrective to old errors, there was always a tension in his conceptualization between the voluntary association called the Klan and the residential group called the city. The Klan was predominant in Jackson's inquiry, but most problems presented by the history of the Klan are not susceptible to resolution within the city limits. Maybe there is a cross-grouping fallacy here.

ᢒᜆ How are groups properly studied? In response to this question, an immense methodological literature has been spawned by sociologists. From the best of their work, historians have much to learn. No matter what kind of group is studied, certain questions are likely to be relevant. An able sociologist, Robert Merton, provides a useful checklist which historians might employ. Merton suggests that the study of the structure of groups involves the following problems:

1. Actual and expected duration of the group.
2. Actual and expected duration of membership within it.
3. Clarity or vagueness of definitions of membership.
4. Degree of engagement of members of the group.
5. Absolute size of the group and/or component parts.
6. Relative size of the group and/or component parts in reference to other groups.
7. Open or closed character of the group.
8. Completeness of the group; i.e., the ratio of actual to potential members.
9. Degree of differentiation; i.e., status and role as operationally distinguished within the group.
10. Shape and height of stratification.
11. Types and degrees of cohesion.
12. Potential for fission and unity within the group.
13. Extent and nature of interaction within the group.
14. Character of social relations obtaining in the group (see Parsons, *The Social System,* pp. 58–88).
15. Degree of conformity to group norms, toleration of deviant behavior, and institutionalized departures from group norms.
16. System of normative controls.
17. Degree of visibility and observability within the group.
18. Ecological structure of the group.
19. Autonomy and dependence of the group.
20. Degree of group stability.
21. Modes of maintaining stability.
22. Relative social standing of groups.
23. Relative power of groups.[40]

Merton is mostly interested here in group structure. Other questions would have to be framed for group function and dysfunction, with respect to members, nonmembers, and other groups. Moreover, a modification is required to accommodate historical questions. All of Merton's questions can be set in motion and studied on a temporal axis. A major flaw in sociology is its tendency to cast these problems in static forms. Historians, in this respect, can make a special contribution. But before they can do so, they must make their answers to Merton's questions clear, explicit, precise, and accurate.

Any student of groups must beware of many common kinds of

---

40. Merton, "Reference Groups and Social Structure," in *Social Theory and Social Structure,* pp. 308–25.

error which lie along the way. He should be careful not to homogenize individuals into groups, or one group into *the* group. Most people in complex environments have belonged to many different groups—to concentric series of groups, and eccentric clusters of groups, and ephemeral groups which appear and disappear within the span of a few moments. R. M. MacIver has remarked that "All community is a matter of degree. Our life falls within not one but many communities, and these stretch around us grade by grade, building associations of every kind." The homogenizing tendency has been encouraged by a good deal of romantic humbug in radical and conservative thought, which persists in regarding men as potential members of a single community. This ancient absurdity is increasingly anachronistic. It is deleterious to empirical scholarship and dangerous to peace and simple survival in the complex modern world, where multiple group membership is a great irreversible fact of life.

CHAPTER IX

FALLACIES OF
FALSE ANALOGY

ह्य

The chief practical use of history is to deliver us from plausible historical analogies.
—James Bryce

For epistemological puritans, analogies are not precisely explanations at all. They are devices for discovering explanations. But given our loose pragmatic everyday definition of explanation—i.e., "making clear, plain, or understandable"—analogies are very useful explanatory tools. The word "analogy," in modern usage, signifies an inference that if two or more things agree in one respect, then they might also agree in another. In its most elementary form, an analogy consists in a set of propositions such as the following:

> *A* resembles *B* in respect to the possession of the
>   property *X*.
> *A* also possesses the property *Y*.
> Therefore, it is inferred that *B* also possesses the
>   property *Y*.

The same thing can be said more succinctly in symbols:

$$AX : BX : : AY : BY$$

An unknown fourth term, *BY*, is thereby inferred from three known terms, on the assumption that a symmetrical due ratio, or proportion, exists.

Analogical inference plays an important, and even an indispensable, part in the mysterious process of intellectual creativity. Many great innovating minds have, in the words of Jean Perrin, a French philosopher

of science, "possessed to an extraordinary degree, a sense of analogy."[1]
The isochronous motion of a pendulum presented itself to Galileo in the
analogous behavior of a lamp swinging on its chain in the Pisa cathedral.
Recent scholarship has reinforced the legend of Sir Isaac Newton and the
great analogous apple. Benjamin Franklin operated by an analogy between electricity and a liquid; Huygens, by an analogy between ocean
waves, sound, and light; Van't Hoff, by an analogy between gases and
and solids in solution; Lord Kelvin, by an analogy between electricity
and heat; and Maxwell, by an analogy between light and electromagnet-
ism.

Analogies are equally useful and ornamental in the articulation of
ideas. They can do so in an internal way, by promoting an unconscious
or inchoate inference into the realm of rationality within a single mind.[2]
And they also operate externally, as a vehicle for the transference of
thought from one mind to another. Analogies can brilliantly reinforce a
reasoned argument. They suggest and persuade, inform and illustrate,
communicate and clarify. They are versatile and effective pedagogical
tools. The great popularizers of science, from Voltaire to George Gamow,
could scarcely have operated without them.

Historians use analogies widely both as heuristic instruments for
empirical inquiry, as explanatory devices in their teaching, and as embellishments in their writing. Often, analogies are used unconsciously—a
metaphor is an abridged form of analogy. Without analogies, creative
thought and communication as we know it would not be merely impracticable but inconceivable. The many uses of analogy, however, are
balanced by the mischief which arises from its abuse. Let us begin by
examining a few of them.

ട൛ The *fallacy of the insidious analogy* is an unintended analogical inference which is embedded in an author's language, and im-
planted in a reader's mind, by a subliminal process which is more powerfully experienced than perceived. The mistake is a simple one, but serious
in its effects; for analogies are widespread in historical thought and important in the shaping of its content. Whenever a historian uses a
metaphor, he draws an analogy. And he uses metaphors all the time.
George Santayana perversely believed that all human discourse is metaphorical, which is surely an overstatement. But much more of our discourse is metaphorical than we are apt to realize. And the metaphors we

1. Quoted in Maurice Dorolle, *Le Raisonnement par Analogie* (Paris, 1949), p. 61.
2. John Williamson, "Realization and Unconscious Inference," *Philosophy and Phenomenological Research* 27 (1966): 11–26.

use to describe an object also determine the quality of our understanding of it. Whenever an analogy is unconsciously used, so as to be dysfunctional to that understanding, the fallacy of the insidious analogy results.

Historians instinctively employ many insidious analogies without a second thought—or maybe even a first one. All of the following examples have caused trouble: Addled Parliament, Augustan age, avantgarde, Axis, Babylonian captivity, Barnburners, blank check, Boxer, Bloody Assizes, brinkmanship, Bubble Act, cameralism, capitalism, Carbonari, Cold War, cordon sanitaire, Croix de Feu, Dark Ages, Depression, Digger, doughface, Enlightenment, Fabian, Fauve, Federalist, feudalism, filibuster, Founding Father, Fronde, gag rule, gentlemen's agreement, Good Neighbor Policy, Grand Peur, Guelph, Hats and Caps, Heavenly Kingdom, imperialism, Industrial Revolution, Ironsides, Jacquerie, jazz, jeremiad, Judas, Know-Nothing, Kulturkampf, Lebensraum, Leveller, Loco-foco, logroller, Methodism, mother country, the Mountain, muckraker, mugwump, New Light, Old Believer, Open Door, papacy, Pact of Steel, puppet ruler, purge, Puritan, Quaker, quisling, Reconstruction, Renaissance, revolution, Rump Parliament, Roi de Soleil, Sea-Beggar, Spartacist, squatter, Take-Off, trust, Tory, the Sick Man of Europe, underground, university, utopia, vernacular, vigilante, Village Hamden, wobbly, Whig, Xanthippe, yahoo, yellow-dog contract, zambo, Zouave, Zionist.

Each of these terms contains within it an insidious analogy which has served to distort our understanding of the object it is supposed to describe. It would be absurd to suggest that any of these terms should be stricken from the lexicon of history. They have been beaten into our heads by many generations of well-meaning schoolmarms and driven so deep they could not be removed even if we wished to do so. One might, abstractly, wish to have a Jeffersonian revolution every nineteen years in our historical vocabulary, to avoid becoming captives of our language. But a more practicable solution would be for historians themselves to search out the metaphors in their language and raise them to the level of consciousness, where they can be controlled.

Other proper names are used in laymen's language as the *first* terms in an analogical inference, with equally serious effects, of an opposite nature. The common and customary meanings of Aristotelian, Benthamite, Ciceronian, Freudian, Jeffersonian, Machiavellian, Marxian, and Platonic have diminished our understanding of the thought of these men. Many a monograph on the Puritans has been motivated by a determination to demonstrate that the common metaphorical meaning of "puritanical" is seriously inaccurate as a description of the Puritans proper. We are beginning to see a similar scholarly phenomenon with

respect to the term "Victorian." And yet, so powerful are these metaphors that even the monographs which seek to correct them become
captives, too, and commit the fallacy of the counterquestion by merely
reversing the objectionable implication.

There are still other insidious analogies in the verbs, adjectives,
adverbs, and even prepositions that historians conventionally use. Revolutions tend to "break out," as if they were dangerous maniacs, locked
in a prison cell. Governments are overturned, like applecarts. Economies
boom and bust, like a cowboy on a Saturday spree. Cultures flower and
fade like a garden of forget-me-nots. Jefferson and Hamilton, or Pitt
and Fox, tend to "thrust and parry" through the history books, like
pairs of gentlemanly duelists. But Kennedy and Khrushchev, or Churchill and Hitler, bash and bludgeon like Friar Tuck and Little John.

Analogies of this sort are catching. And they serve to control
conceptualization. In histories of relations between Asia and the West,
door analogies are fashionable, as in Commodore Perry and the closed
door of Nippon, and the American Open Door Policy in China. In a
recent work on the history of China by an excellent Australian scholar,
one learns that "The Westerners banged heavily on the barred door of
the Chinese world; to the amazement of all, within and without, the
great structure, riddled by white ants, thereupon suddenly collapsed,
leaving the surprised Europeans still holding the door handle."[3] Such
analogies as this suggest that Asia is all structure and the West is all
function. They communicate a sense of clear and active purpose in the
latter and of mindless passivity in the former. Moreover, it is sometimes
assumed that China should swing freely before Western pressure, or
else it is slightly unhinged.

In the historiography of Poland, a different set of analogies is
customary. One is the traditional idea, deeply rooted in Polish literature,
that Poland is the "Christ among nations," a noble, transcendent being
which has suffered for the sins of all humanity, betrayed by the Jews
and crucified by the Romans. The result of this humbug is that history
becomes, in Namier's phrase, a visit of condolence. The Polish people
have been encouraged by their historians to develop a self-righteous
sense of persecution with few equals in the modern world. Every national
misfortune becomes a measure of the depravity of mankind—all mankind, that is, except the martyr nation, whose citizens are Poles apart.
This myth is profoundly dysfunctional to any constructive and statesmanlike attempt to deal with complex and critical diplomatic problems of
Eastern Europe.

3. C. P. Fitzgerald, *The Birth of Communist China* (Baltimore, 1964), p. 30.

Other studies of Polish history tend to adopt a very different kind of analogical imagery. It is historiographically conventional to compare Poland to a bird—all feathers and fragile bones, big-beaked and small-brained, beautiful but slightly weird, and sometimes a little sinister. Stanley L. Sharp, a collector of many picturesque examples, declares that "Ornithological comparisons seem traditional with reference to Poland." He notes that

> The ardent Polish nationalist Stanislaw Mackiewicz wrote in his critical study of Beck's foreign policy, "Poles, like certain beautiful birds, are apt to lose sight of their own surroundings, enraptured by their own song." . . . The romantic poet Juliusz Slowacki once called Poland "the peacock and the parrot of nations." The British writer John W. Wheeler-Bennett described Poland's policy as that of "a canary who has persistently but unsuccessfully endeavored to swallow two cats."

Sharp titled his own book, by the way, *Poland, White Eagle on a Red Field.*[4]

The complaint, in all of this, is not that analogies are used, but that they are used insidiously, and that many absurd biases are bootlegged into historical interpretations. An able scholar can, however, convert an offense into an opportunity. He can study the analogies and metaphors which he instinctively invokes and thereby learn much about the biases buried in his own mind, below the level of his consciousness.

We will never have historical writing without analogies. The next generation of historians may perhaps learn to communicate with more accuracy and precision by the use of mathematical symbols (unless they are reduced by a nuclear catastrophe to a primitive exchange of grunts and grimaces). But in either instance, there will still be analogies and metaphors in historical discourse. Let us hope that they will be developed with clarity, caution, and conscious reflection.

&ev The *fallacy of the perfect analogy* consists in reasoning from a partial resemblance between two entities to an entire and exact correspondence. It is an erroneous inference from the fact that *A* and *B* are similar in some respects to the false conclusion that they are the same in all respects. One must always remember that an analogy, by its very nature, is a similarity between two or more things which are in other respects unlike. A "perfect analogy" is a contradiction in terms, if perfection is understood, as it commonly is in this context, to imply identity.

4. (Cambridge, 1953), p. 150.

This sort of error often appears in attempts at evaluation by analogy, in arguments such as the following.

> *A* and *B* are analogous in some respects.
> *A* is generally a good thing.
> Therefore, *B* is generally a good thing.

This set of propositions is structurally fallacious, for it shifts the analogy from a partial resemblance to an identity, which is implied by the holistic value judgment. If *B* were existentially analogous to *A* in respect to *X* and *Y*, then it might be fairly though not conclusively inferred that it is evaluatively analogous in the same limited sense. But it can never be inferred that *B* is equivalent to *A* in either an existential or an evaluative way.

Two examples of invalid historical analogies of this sort have appeared in debates over American intervention in Vietnam. Spokesmen for the United States government have tended to find an analogue in Munich. A critic of the administration and its Vietnam policy, Arno J. Mayer, has accurately criticized this unfortunate comparison, which is, I think, not merely a rhetorical device, invoked by Washington policy makers to justify their acts, but rather an operating assumption, upon which their acts are based. Mayer protests that

> By its proponents, the Munich analogy is designed to stress the identity, not the similarity, of Hitler and Mao; of the Nazi German and the Communist Chinese political systems and foreign policy objectives as well as methods; and of externally incited subversion as well as the strategic significance of Czechoslovakia and South Vietnam. The ensuing lesson is presented as self-evident: no self-respecting American should want in the White House a Chamberlain or Daladier, who by surrendering South Vietnam to the Chinese-controlled North Vietnamese and Vietcong would encourage Peking to activate its timetable for aggressive expansion into Southeast Asia and beyond.[5]

Mayer proceeds to summarize the differences between Munich and Vietnam: the disparity between the Vietcong and the Sudeten Germans; the difference between the Czech government and the Saigon regime; the difference between the strategic significance of Czechoslovakia and Vietnam; the difference between the intentions of Nazi Germany and Communist China; the difference between the military capability of Anglo-French forces in 1938 and American power in the late 1960s. Mayer also challenges the assumption that Hitler would have changed his aggressive plans in any significant degree had the

5. Arno J. Mayer, "Vietnam Analogy: Greece, Not Munich," *The Nation*, March 25, 1968, pp. 407–10.

allies stood their ground at Munich, and suggests that the only effective deterrent would have been an effective alliance between Soviet Russia and the Western nations, with rights of transit for Soviet troops through Rumania and Poland. Such an alliance, he believes, was inconceivable, given the intense and obsessive anti-Bolshevism of the Western powers. Finally, Mayer denounces all "allegedly scholarly" historians and political scientists who have "accepted, legitimized and propagated the cold war eschatology according to which Nazism and Bolshevism were essentially identical totalitarian systems bent on unlimited expansion by a crude blend of outright force and externally engineered subversion."

Many details of Mayer's thesis are doubtful, as to his understanding of both the Czechoslovakia crisis and the war in Vietnam. But his protest is surely sound. There probably cannot be any sustained analogy which will stretch from Munich to Saigon without breaking down. But more important, there can never be an identical analogy, such as Cold Warriors customarily draw between the 1930s and their own predicament.

But Mayer is not done. He believes with E. H. Carr that the "current era is exceptionally history-conscious" and that "today's citizen has that pronounced need for and is peculiarly susceptible to analogies." On this assumption, he concludes that a historian's duty consists not merely in knocking over bad analogies but in setting up good ones, in order to provide "the citizen with alternate historical sign posts." His alternative to the Munich-Vietnam analogy is a Greece-Vietnam analogy, in which parallels are drawn between the "reticent role" of Stalin and Mao; between indigenous Greek guerrillas and the Vietcong; between Tito and Ho Chi Minh; between English retrenchment in Greece and the French retreat from Vietnam; between the temporary military and political weakness of Russia vis-à-vis the United States in the late 1940s and the temporary weakness of China twenty years later; between the domino theory of the Truman Doctrine and similar assumptions in what might be called the Johnson Doctrine for Southeast Asia. Mayer suggests that American policy—which includes containment of Communism, ordered modernization, and gradualist reform—is similar in Greece and Vietnam. He implies that it has failed in Greece and that it will fail in Southeast Asia as well. Moreover, "Not only Greece—as the recent coup demonstrates—but also many of the developing countries lack the political integration, the social cohesion, and the economic sinews to sustain gradual and ordered modernization and reform, even with considerable foreign aid."

But Mayer has refuted one bad argument only to replace it with a worse one. In his Greek analogue to Vietnam he commits the same fallacy that others have done by analogizing from Munich to Southeast Asia. Mayer concedes that there are "specific dissimilarities" between Greece and Vietnam, but nowhere in his article does he specify them. Instead, he tends to leap from analogy to identity, in the manner of his opponents.

There are, of course, many major differences which he does not take into account. Ho Chi Minh's concern with South Vietnam is of a very different order from Tito's interest in Greece. The political culture of Vietnam is far removed from that of Greece. The British presence in Greece was of a different nature from the French regime in Indo-China. American assistance to Greece was unlike our intervention in Vietnam, both in quantity and in quality. Most important, international political, military, and economic conditions have changed radically from the late 1940s to the late 1960s. Vietnam is a painful and difficult dilemma for the United States precisely because there is nothing in our recent or distant past (or anybody else's) which is more than incidentally and superficially similar.

Many analogues to Vietnam have been suggested—not merely Munich and Greece, but the Mexican War, the Philippine Insurrection, the Korean War, the insurgency in British Malaya, guerrilla warfare in German-occupied Europe, the American Revolution, the Spanish rising against Napoleon. In each of these instances, the analogy is very limited, if indeed it exists at all. And there is surely no identity between any of these happenings and the situation which American policy makers face in Vietnam. That problem must be studied and solved in its own terms, if it is to be solved at all. There are many particular historical lessons which might be applied, in many limited and special ways, with due allowance for intervening changes. There are restricted and controlled analogies which might suggest hypothetical policy commitments for possible use. But there are no comprehensive analogies which serve as a short cut to a solution. A satisfactory historical approach to the problem will not be oriented toward a search for an analogue but rather toward a sense of environing continuities and changes within which the present problem in Vietnam exists; combined with a keen and lively sense of treacherous anachronisms and false analogies such as have deluded so many well-meaning architects of American policy—and their critics, too.

There are many other examples of the identical analogy, a few of which might be briefly noted. Ranke supported his government in the Franco-Prussian war with the flat assertion that "We are fighting against Louis XIV." This is a classic case of the abuse of historical knowledge. A sophisticated sense of history consists not in the location of analogues such as this but rather in an ability to discriminate between sound analogies and unsound ones.

Another quaint example, by an able historian who ought to have known better, is the following assertion by Richard Pares: "It does help us if we can realize that Charlemagne was just like an enlightened American millionaire, for this recognition brings him into a class about which we may know something."[6] This curious comparison may tell us more about the extraordinary ideas which one British historian entertained on the subject of enlightened American millionaires. And as it stands, it is a false inference from resemblance to identity. Charlemagne may or may not have been like an enlightened American millionaire in some respect—though I cannot think of one, and Pares mentioned none in particular. But he was surely not "just like" an American millionaire. Therein lies a fallacy.

&> The *fallacy of the false analogy* is a structural form of error which occurs when the analogical terms are shifted from one analogue to another. Consider the following cases:

1. $AX : BZ : : AY : BY$
2. $AX : BX : : AY : BY$
3. $AZ : BZ : : AY : BY$

The second and third analogies are structurally sound. But the first example is a false analogy in that there is an inconsistency between X and Z.

This form of error is often exceedingly difficult to recognize, because it is often hidden in semantical ambiguity, or buried in some of the things which the author doesn't tell us. Let us consider an actual example of this fallacy, perpetrated by Richard Morris. In an essay called "Class Struggle and the American Revolution,"[7] Morris addresses himself to the sticky question of whether or not the War for Independence was, by the design of its agents, a social revolution. He argues that it was not directly, integrally, and aboriginally so, but rather engendered—indirectly, incidentally, and gradually—a set of revolutionary social and economic changes which were not among its "avowed objectives." This argument is sustained by an analogy between the War of Independence and the First World War.

6. Richard Pares, *The Historian's Business and Other Essays* (Oxford, 1961), p. 8.
7. *William and Mary Quarterly*, 3d. ser. 19 (1962): 3–29.

An analogy might be fairly drawn to World War I [Morris writes]. Perhaps the greatest change which came in the wake of that conflict, so far as America was concerned, was the emancipation of American women, an extraordinary phenomenon which liberated women from the home and thrust them into the factory. The revolutionary impact of this social upheaval on postwar life, politics, marriage, morals and the family is incalculable. And it never would have happened so fast had it not been for the manpower shortage during the war. But we have usually been taught that we went to war with Germany over her renewal of unrestricted submarine warfare or because the House of Morgan had floated loans to the Allies. I never realized that when Woodrow Wilson called upon the Congress to declare war he really intended to free American womanhood from the shackles of housework. Now within certain limitations [unspecified by M.], I think the analogy to the American Revolution is eminently fair. We did not declare our independence of George III in order to reform the land laws, change the criminal codes, spread popular education, or separate church and state. We broke with England to achieve political independence, freedom from external controls, emancipation, if you will, of the bourgeoisie from mercantile restraints.[8]

Morris's analogy seems to reduce itself to the following four propositions. The first three are factual. The fourth is an analogical inference.

1. World War I was a war which engendered revolutionary social change in the United States.

2. The American War for Independence was a war which engendered revolutionary social change in the United States.

3. Americans did not fight World War I to engender revolutionary social change in the United States.

4. Therefore, it is inferred that Americans did not enter the War for Independence to engender revolutionary social change in the United States.

This looks structurally sound, on first inspection. But a closer look suggests trouble. World War I was not the same kind of war as the War of Independence—it was a total war, in which the nation was enlisted with a degree of commitment which did probably not appear in any eighteenth-century war, and certainly not in the American War for Independence. And the engendering of revolutionary social change in World War I is functionally connected to its total aspect. Moreover, different processes of social change developed in the two cases. Morris's first two propositions are disparate, in that they describe two different things. They are to each other as AX is to BZ, rather than as AX is to BX. Therein lies a fallacy.

8. P. 26.

⅋ The *fallacy of the absurd analogy* is another structural form of analogical error, in which an inference is extended between two nonrelated characteristics. Consider two hypothetical examples:

> This rubber ball and that apple are both
> red, round, smooth, and shiny.
> That apple is very good to eat.
> Therefore, this rubber ball will be very good to eat.

Secondly:

> This rubber ball and that apple are both red, round,
> smooth, and shiny.
> That apple looks pretty in a Christmas stocking.
> Therefore, this rubber ball will look pretty in a Christmas
> stocking.

The first of these analogies is patently absurd. But the second, given certain aesthetic assumptions, is correct. The difference between them is that the qualities of the ball and the apple described in the first terms of the analogy are functionally relevant to aesthetics but not to edibility. There is, in short, a rule of relevance in analogizing, which must always be respected. In our elementary form:

$$AX : BX : : AY : BY$$

There must be a relationship between X and Y if there can be an analogy between A and B.[9]

The English historian G. M. Trevelyan recalls in his autobiography a character named Edward Bowen, an "eccentric genius" of "somewhat ascetic habits" who was Trevelyan's housemaster at school. But Bowen's genius did not consist in a talent for analogical inference. Trevelyan remembered that "He once said to me, some years after I had left school, 'O boy, you oughtn't to have a hot bath twice a week; you'll get like the later Romans, boy.' "[10]

⅋ The *fallacy of the multiple analogy* is a structural deficiency which occurs when a second analogy is bootlegged into the main analogy so as to undercut the basis of comparison. Consider the following hypothetical example, which comes from the work of an English phi-

9. For a suggestive discussion, see C. Mason Myers, "The Circular Use of Metaphor," *Philosophy and Phenomenological Research* 26 (1965–66): 391–402.
10. G. M. Trevelyan, *An Autobiography and Other Essays* (London, 1949), p. 11.

losopher, Alfred Sidgwick: "The growing size of London bodes evil to England because London is the heart of England and a swollen heart is a sign of disease."[11]

This statement might be broken down into three parts:

1. London is analogous to a heart (presumably in the sense that both perform a vital circulatory function).
2. A swollen heart is a sign of disease.
3. The growth of London bodes evil to England.

But between the second and the third statements, two other analogies are tacitly added:

2.1 Swelling is analogous to growing.
2.2 A sign of disease is analogous to that which bodes evil for England.

Assuming that an analogy is merely a partial resemblance and not an identity, neither of these two tacit pairs of analogues is interchangeable. There is, therefore, no continuity from proposition two to proposition three. The trouble is papered over by semantical ambiguity in the original statement, an ambiguity which serves to camouflage the additional analogies.

A historical example appears in George Rudé's *The Crowd in History*, in which the author solemnly asserts that "Thus, beheaded, the sans culotte movement died a sudden death; and having, like the cactus, burst into full bloom at the very point of its extinction, it never rose again."[12] This statement combines three disparate analogies. It is objectionable on both stylistic *and* substantive grounds. As a mixed metaphor, it is a literary monstrosity. As a multiple analogy, it is a logical absurdity. Many amusing examples appear from time to time in *The New Yorker*. The major complaint to be entered against these excrescences is not aesthetic but analytical. Vulgarity can coexist with empiricism; illogic cannot.

ᘐ❧ The *fallacy of the holistic analogy* is, I think, the fatal fallacy of metahistory, as it has been practiced by Spengler and Toynbee and a host of others. It is an attempt to construct an analogical inference from some part of history—to the whole of history. All metahistorians have built their interpretations upon a metaphor, for there is nothing else at hand. Empiricism is impossible if the object is to tell the whole

11. Alfred Sidgwick, *Fallacies* (London, 1883), p. 179.
12. P 106.

truth. Only some nonempirical method of inference, such as analogy, can be used.

A close student of analogy, Harald Hoffding, has observed that

> if analogy is employed metaphysically or cosmologically, it is not a *single* realm of Being serving to illuminate another *single realm;* it is a single realm that is used to express Being as a totality. This symbolism is of a different kind and has a different validity from that brought to bear on particular fields. It cannot be carried out to its full consequences and it cannot be verified. . . . In these respects, cosmological and metaphysical symbols are different from scientific ones. . . . Religious symbols share the fate of the metaphysical. In both cases the attempt is made to create absolutely valid final concepts; the only difference lies in the motive.[13]

The behavior of analogy in cosmology, metaphysics, and religion is the same as its behavior in metahistory. But in the latter, claims to empirical accuracy are entered. Empiricism fails, however, in the face of holistic problems, and the analogy alone is left to carry the weight. Arnold Toynbee has been fairly and fully criticized by many reviewers for this mythological use of analogy in *A Study of History.* He has entered a plea of guilty, but only to certain "excesses." The criticism, however, cuts deeper than that: it alleges that Toynbee's method is fundamentally analogical, and his analogies are fundamentally unsound, because they cannot be put to the test. To this, of course, Toynbee does not plead guilty, for he cannot, without repudiating the work of a lifetime.[14]

&❧ The *fallacy of proof by analogy* is a functional form of error, which violates a cardinal rule of analogical inference—analogy is a useful tool of historical understanding only as an auxiliary to proof. It is never a substitute for it, however great the temptation may be or however difficult the empirical task at hand may seem.

Humanity appears to have made a little progress in this respect. A student of Renaissance culture has written, "While modern thought is fully aware of the tentative nature of analogical reasoning, earlier thought tended to consider an analogy as an end in itself and to rest content in an aesthetic and essentially poetic awareness of the feeling of understanding the analogy brought."[15]

13. Harald Hoffding, *The Problems of Philosophy* (New York, 1913), p. 121; and *Der Begriff der Analogie* (Leipzig, 1914), passim.
14. Arnold J. Toynbee, *A Study of History*, vol. 12, *Reconsiderations* (New York, 1961), pp. 30–41.
15. Joseph A. Mazzeo, "Analogy and Renaissance Culture," *Journal of the History of Ideas* 15 (1954): 299–304. See also, Thomas De Vio, Cardinal Cajetan, *The Analogy*

But the progress is incomplete. So successful are analogies in creating the illusion of sense and certainty that they are widely used as a method of proof in their own right. I have heard a sociologist argue that, though an analogy never affords a "rigorous demonstration," it may nevertheless provide an "appreciable coefficient of affirmation," which can be cast in terms of probability. This is solemn nonsense. Analogical probability is altogether as elusive as analogical certainty, in the absence of an empirical test. The accuracy of that empirical test may be cast in probabilistic terms with precision, but not the analogy itself, which has finished its work after the empirical level is reached.

An example of this fallacy, in which an analogy is not transcended, is a controversial essay on slavery and Negro personality by Stanley Elkins—a work of which we have taken note several times.[16] Elkins establishes an analogy between two different institutions—plantation slavery in Anglo-America and concentration camps in Nazi Germany. The latter have been studied by many psychologists who were interested in the personality patterns the camps caused in their inhabitants. Elkins argues that the camps and slavery were analogous in several respects and that slavery created a "Sambo" personality which is comparable to the "old prisoner" mentality which some psychologists have found in the concentration camps.

Elkins's argument is plausible and highly persuasive. His analogy operates effectively as a heuristic device in his own inquiry and as a rhetorical instrument in his presentation. It suggests much but—it proves nothing. One might argue that his analogy is structurally imperfect in a variety of ways, and that the institutional parallels between slavery and concentration camps tend to dissolve on close inspection. But there is a more serious complaint to be made against Elkins's work. He does not move beyond his analogical insight to establish empirically the existence of the Sambo personality pattern. There are only a few casual snippets of impressionistic evidence, much of which is secondary or tertiary. Elkins has insisted that he did not mean to prove his argument by analogy, but he nevertheless does so implicitly in his book.

In my opinion, there is an important truth in Elkins's thesis. Many other historians seem to think so, too. The argument, analogy and all, is beginning to work its way into the textbooks, and even into historical novels, such as William Styron's *The Confessions of Nat Turner,* which appears to owe a special debt to Stanley Elkins and which may serve

---

of Names (1498), trans. E. A. Bushinski (Pittsburgh, 1953), a systematization of the so-called Thomistic theory of analogy.

16. Stanley Elkins, *Slavery: A Problem in American Institutional and Intellectual Life,* rev. ed. (New York, 1963).

to popularize his thesis. One of Elkins's students has even ground out a monograph, which echoes the master's expectations in the spirit of Sambo himself. But everything still hangs precariously upon an analogy, which, even if it were the best analogy in the world, would be insufficient to sustain it.

ᑫᐧᕽ The *fallacy of prediction by analogy* occurs when analogy is used to anticipate future events—as it often is, in the absence of anything better. H. W. Fowler observed that analogy "is perhaps the basis of most human conclusions, its liability to error being compensated for by the frequency with which it is the only form of reasoning available."[17]

The trouble with futurist analogies is not that they might be wrong, but rather that they must be utterly untestable and inconclusive. The problem is not that there is a probability of error within them, but that there is an indeterminancy of probability. It is not possible to distinguish a true historical analogy from a false one without an empirical test of its inference. As long as one of those parts remains in the future, the analogy is untestable.

A historiographical case in point is a collection of quasi-historical essays edited by Bruce Mazlish and published as *The Railroad and the Space Program: An Exploration in Historical Analogy* (Cambridge, Mass., 1965). Mazlish and his colleagues seriously attempted to estimate the future effect of the space program upon American society by means of an analogy with the past effects of the railroad in nineteenth-century America. The contributors were able scholars all, and their essays uniformly reached a high level of sustained and sophisticated cerebration. But with respect to the future consequences of the space program, they might as well have hired a gypsy to study the palm of Werner von Braun or invited an astrologer to contribute a paper to their project. Their conclusions about the space program are either tenuous in the extreme, or truistic, or else Delphic utterances of the sort which confidently predict with considerable semantical confusion that maybe X will happen, or maybe it won't.

The work of Mazlish and his colleagues, in short, is not very useful for serious students of the space program. But, significantly, the book is highly suggestive for students of the railroads. Most contributors devote much of their interest to the latter. The hypothetical heuristic construct provided by the space program has a stimulative effect in historical

17. H. W. Fowler, *Modern English Usage* (Oxford, 1926), p. 20.

inquiry, which is altogether independent of its truth value with respect to the space program itself. It provides many suggestive hints and hypotheses which might be put to an empirical test by an economic historian, with the possibility of new and important insights into economic development in the nineteenth century. In short, the Mazlish volume demonstrates explicitly a truth long implicit in the operations of historians—namely, that an analogy is a useful device for a sort of retrodiction of past events and for the generation of hypothetical interpretations which can be put to the test. One can reason from an idea of the future (however mistaken it may prove to be) to an insight into the past, and put the latter to the test. But the process is not reversible.

Mazlish might reply that there are no empirical ways of knowing the future. But this, I think, is a mistake. Two other methods are employed with increasing accuracy in a wide range of fields—in meteorology, economics, and demography. These methods are both historical in nature. One of them consists in the discovery of past trends and their extrapolation into the future, in some cases with determinable degrees of probability. The other is a kind of theoretical knowledge, or conditional knowledge, which takes the form of "If, then" propositions—empirical propositions which are tested by reference to past events. Forecasting of this sort can work—indeed, it does work—even with respect to events which are partly determined by willful acts of reasoning agents.

But a prediction by analogy is useless in itself. Sometimes the analogizer covers himself in the fashion of Mark Twain's weather forecaster: "Probable nor'east to sou'west winds, varying to the southard and westard and eastard and points between; high and low barometer, sweeping round from place to place, probable areas of rain, snow, hail, and drought, succeeded or preceded by earthquakes with thunder and lightning."[18]

Nothing else can improve his accuracy.

ළ The misuses of analogy are many and complex, but all fallacies in this chapter can be divided into two groups. First, there are structural fallacies of analogical inference—analogies which are imperfect in their form. Second, there are functional fallacies, in which sound analogies are applied to inappropriate purposes.

Any intelligent use of analogy must begin with a sense of its limits. An analogical inference between *A* and *B* presumes that those two

18. Quoted in D. S. Halacy, *The Weather Changers* (New York, 1968), p. 30.

objects are similar in some respects but dissimilar in others. If there were no dissimilarities, we would have an identity rather than an analogy. Analogical inference alone is powerless to resolve the critical problem of whether any particular point is a point of similarity or dissimilarity. It can never *prove* that because A and B are alike in respect to X, they are therefore alike in respect to Y. Proof requires either inductive evidence that Y exists in both cases, or else a sound deductive argument for the coexistence of X and Y. If either of these attempts at proof is successful, then the argument becomes more than merely analogical. If neither is successful, there is no argument at all.

In common practice, some deductive inference as to the connection between X and Y is commonly drawn. In empirical inquiry, an attempt must also be made to establish the existence of X and Y. Galileo, in the example of the analogy between the chain lamp and the motion of a pendulum, mentioned at the beginning of this chapter, immediately advanced beyond analogy to empiricism, by means of an experiment which he cleverly contrived on the spur of the moment. He timed the swings of the cathedral lamp by his own pulse beat. In the same fashion, Newton and Franklin and the others quickly proceeded to put their analogies to the test.

The psychological power of analogical explanation is dangerous both to logic and to empiricism. Many bad ideas have had a long life because of a good (effective) analogy. If analogy is used to persuade without proof, or to indoctrinate without understanding, or to settle an empirical question without empirical evidence, then it is misused. Sometimes the results are not merely disagreeable but downright dangerous. In the formation of postnuclear public policy, nothing is quite as lethal as a faulty prenuclear analogy. Fallacies of this sort are apt to be failures not of will but of understanding. In public questions of nuclear policy, they may be the last thing a well-meaning statesman ever intends to commit—the very last thing.

PART III
ARGUMENT

CHAPTER X

FALLACIES OF SEMANTICAL DISTORTION

ﻬ

Rightly to be great is not to stir without great argument.
—Shakespeare

The fallacies in this chapter are not particular to professional historians. But every historian runs the risk of committing them. All historical interpretations are arguments, and they must conform to a logic of argumentation if they are to cohere as truth. Many so-called historical facts are arguments, too. When a scholar makes a "factual mistake," he may actually have committed what is commonly called a fallacy of argument.

By argument, of course, I do not mean a controversy or a disagreement, but rather an attempt to proceed from premises to a conclusion by orderly and rational inference. Anyone who hopes to accomplish this object can get himself into three different kinds of trouble—structural distortion, semantical deception, and substantive distraction.

The first of these categories refers to *formal* fallacies of argument. There are many different systems of formal logic in the world—the canonical logic of ancient China, the grammatical logic of ancient India, the syllogistic logic of Aristotle, the dichotomous logic of Ramus, and the mathematical logic of Russell and Whitehead are among the most familiar. Surely there are more logical systems in heaven and earth than are dreamt of by any logician. If a visitor from another planet were to descend upon our world, he might bring with him a formal logic unlike anything an earthling knows. It is probable—indeed, almost certain—that our posterity will produce formal logical systems far different from those we now possess.

This book contains no discussion of formal logic for two reasons. First, every existing logical system has been fully discussed by logicians with more expertise than a historian can hope to attain. Second, and more significant, no presently articulated system of formal logic is really very relevant to the work historians do. The probable explanation is not that historical thought is nonlogical or illogical or sublogical or anti-logical, but rather, I think, that it conforms in a tacit way to a *formal* logic which good historians sense but cannot see. Some day somebody will discover it, and when that happens, history and formal logic will be reconciled by a process of mutual refinement. But at present, we must confine ourselves to a more humble task.

This chapter is about informal fallacies of a semantical nature. Many a ponderous volume has been produced on the subject of semantics. Our business, however, is with a small part of this large problem—the attainment of clarity and precision in historical prose. Imprecision in a sonnet may be the soul of art. But in a closely argued scholarly statement, its consequences are always inconvenient, and sometimes fatal. The first question to be asked of any expression, in every historical context, is not "Is it true?" but "Is it meaningful?" A meaningful expression, for present purposes, is merely one which successfully serves two purposes. First, it clearly and consistently communicates an author's intention to a reader's understanding. Second, it communicates, in the same fashion, an author's intention to his own understanding. The latter object is often more elusive than the former. The semantical deceptions in this chapter are mostly self-deceptions rather than deliberate attempts to mislead.

Meaning, in this limited sense, is mainly a definitional problem, which presents no difficulty in most ordinary words and word combinations. It is rarely necessary for a historian to analyze a statement such as "What is meaning?" in the manner of G. E. Moore, and ask, "What is the meaning of *meaning*? What is the meaning of *what*? What, indeed, is the meaning of *is*?" Most words in a historiographical argument are sufficiently clarified in a tacit way by the argument itself. In a famous phrase by P. W. Bridgman, "The true meaning of a term is to be found by observing what a man does with it, not what he says about it."[1]

Usually, what a man does with a term is a sufficient guide. Nothing more needs to be said. But some people do extraordinary things with their terms, and a good deal of confusion can result if definitions are not

1. Percy W. Bridgman, *The Logic of Modern Physics* (New York, 1946), p.7.

explicitly made and consistently used. We shall begin, in this chapter, with a review of the common fallacies of semantical deception, and then proceed to consider the process of definition itself in a more constructive way.

    م• The *fallacy of ambiguity* consists in the use of a word or an expression which has two or more possible meanings, without sufficient specification of which meaning is intended. In politics and poker, ambiguity has its uses, and even its justifications. Adlai Stevenson, in the presidential campaign of 1952, told a tale about his namesake, who was a candidate for Vice President in 1892:

> I have read a lot of stories about the time when my grandfather campaigned in the state of Washington for the Vice Presidency, exactly sixty years ago this month. The big issue, I am told, at that time was whether your majestic mountain was to be named Mount Tacoma or Mount Rainier. Apparently that was the only subject of interest in Washington at that time. Anyway, the views of Seattle and Tacoma were in violent disagreement and it seems that my adroit grandfather solved this difficulty by giving each audience from the back platform of his train an eloquent speech about the beauties of the mountain, and then went on to say, "And I want everyone to know, all of you good people, that I emphatically agree that this magnificent mountain should be named—" and just then they pulled the whistle on the train and it started with a puff, and the old man bowed to the audience graciously and they cheered ecstatically.[2]

But when the proverbial whistle is pulled in a train of scholarly argument, the results are not amusing. Simple semantical ambiguity develops in several different ways. It sometimes arises from the use of historical terms which have meant so many different things that they are meaningless until a specific meaning is clarified in context. A sophisticated stylist is able to accomplish this end tacitly, without a laborious and pedantic definition of terms. But an explicit formal definition, however clumsy it may be, is always preferable in historical writing to the most graceful ambiguity.[3] Words such as democracy, capitalism, nationalism, class, culture, education, party, feudalism, and romanticism—to name but a few—should never be employed without an *ad hoc* definition. An elaborate exercise in philology is rarely required—merely a simple working definition, or perhaps a set of definitions, which will provide a rapport between an author and his readers.

    Ambiguity also creates confusion in the relationship between a

---

2. Adlai Stevenson, *Major Campaign Speeches* (New York, 1953), p. 83.
3. Ambiguity can be a thing of beauty, in belletristic prose. See William Empson, *Seven Types of Ambiguity*, 3d ed. (Norfolk, Conn., 1953), for an extended discussion.

researcher and his sources. Giles Constable got into trouble in a monograph on monastic tithes in the early Middle Ages. A reviewer of his work complained that "More emphasis might also have been placed upon the basic ambiguity that persistently hovers around the word 'tithe,' particularly in private acts. The term could also mean a secular quitrent, and in scores if not hundreds of private documents, the historian simply cannot tell what type of rent the term is signifying."[4]

It is easy to shrug off such objections as this, as mere nitpicking pedantry. But the results can be destructive to otherwise excellent scholarship.

Another kind of ambiguity consists in the use of an old term in a new way without warning. Sir Lewis Namier provides an amusing example of a Victorian lady who complained that she did not like a house because it was "very romantic." Her correspondent responded, "I *don't* understand why you should wish it not to be *very romantic.*" The Victorian lady replied, "When I said romantic I meant damp."[5]

There is much of this sort of ambiguity in the writings of the so-called New Left in America. Every red-blooded radical knows that American libertarianism is really totalitarianism, and that American democracy is really tyranny, and that American freedom is really a species of slavery, and that American tolerance is really intolerance, and that an open society in the United States is really a gigantic concentration camp with invisible barbed wire. To the uninitiated, the meanings of these words appear to be bent beyond the breaking point. Perhaps the confusion is owing to the stubborn determination of American radicals to conceptualize their own society in terms taken from a very different one. The irrelevance of these terms is hidden by means of ambiguity from the people who invoke them.

A special form of ambiguity might be called the fallacy of etceteration. It occurs when a historian, enumerating evidence, or categories, or types, or reasons, seeks to disguise a problem, or perhaps the poverty of his materials, by employing the abbreviation "etc." An example is supplied by Maitland, who discovered that Elizabeth I was the first English monarch to add the words *et cetera* to her title. Maitland pondered the problem, and finally came to the following conclusion:

> No doubt she is Defender of the Faith, though we cannot be sure what faith she will defend. But is that all? Is she or is she not Supreme Head upon

---

4. David Herlihy in *The American Historical Review* 71 (1965): 134, reviewing Giles Constable, *Monastic Tithes: From Their Origins to the Twelfth Century* (New York, 1964).
5. Sir Lewis Namier, "History and Political Culture," in Fritz Stern, ed., *Varieties of History* (New York, 1956), p. 386.

earth of the Church of England and Ireland? . . . It was a difficult problem. On both sides there were men with extreme opinions, who, however, agreed in holding that the solution was not to be found in any earthly statute book. . . . Then a happy thought occurs. Let her highness etceterate herself. This will leave her hands free, and then afterwards she can explain the etceteration as occasion may require. And so, Queen Elizabeth I became the first English ruler to be "solemnly etceterated."

The *"et cetera"* probably meant, "and (if future events shall so decide, but not further or otherwise) of the Church of England and also of Ireland upon earth the Supreme Head."[6]

Other Englishmen solemnly etceterated George Washington during the American Revolution. In July, 1776, the Howe brothers addressed a peace feeler to "George Washington, Esq., etc., etc." The intended recipient refused to accept it, on the ground that he was General Washington. The senders blandly replied that "etc., etc." included all titles which Squire George chose to adopt. The fighting continued, in a decidedly unambiguous way.[7]

ह▸ The *fallacy of amphiboly* arises in an argument where meaning is muddled by slovenly syntax—bad grammar, or poor punctuation, or both. Trouble of this sort commonly develops in three specific ways. First, it may derive from a relative pronoun with more than one possible reference. The classic example is "He said, 'Saddle me the ass.' And they saddled him." Second, amphiboly may arise from a misplaced modifier, as in the proverbial definition of anthropology as "the science of man embracing woman." Third, amphiboly may be the result of an elliptical construction, as in a wartime poster which urged everyone to "Save Soap and Waste Paper." The following historiographical examples are hypothetical:

1. "Richly carved Chippendale furniture was produced by colonial craftsmen with curved legs and claw feet."

2. "Many Americans were outraged when President Theodore Roosevelt had a Negro for dinner."

3. "The measures of the New Deal were understandably popular, for many men received jobs, and women also."

4. "The ship was christened by Mrs. Coolidge. The lines of her bottom were admired by an enthusiastic crowd."

Sometimes an amphibolous operation is performed on a primary document by a careless editor. He makes a small change in grammar

6. Frederic W. Maitland, "Elizabethan Gleanings," *Collected Papers*, 3:157–65.
7. John R. Alden, *A History of the American Revolution* (New York, 1969), p. 265.

or punctuation, with a major alteration in meaning. Two nineteenth-century historians, Henry Cabot Lodge and Henry Adams, both inaccurately quoted a letter from a New England Federalist, Stephen Higginson, to Timothy Pickering, on the subject of disunion, as follows: "I have seen your letters to Mr. Cabot and Mr. Lyman on the question of separation, which is a very delicate and important one, considered in the abstract. We all agree there can be no doubt of its being desirable." But the manuscript actually read, "I have seen your letters to Mr. Cabot and Mr. Lyman on the question of separation, which is a very delicate and important one. Considered in the abstract we all agree there can be no doubt of its being desirable." Two petty changes in punctuation were made, together with other errors in other parts of the letter, with the result of making Higginson appear more favorable to disunion than in fact he was.[8]

ह~ The *fallacy of figures* is a form of ambiguity which consists in the abuse of figurative language, so that a reader cannot tell whether or not a literal meaning is intended; or if so, what that meaning might be. There are many figures of speech which are commonly used in conventional discourse without a second thought. Henry Peacham, in *The Garden of Eloquence* (London, 1577), named and defined more than two hundred of them, most of which are still often used, but not always recognized by the user. In another edition of the same work, Peacham provided "cautions" against the abuse of each figure—abuse which has become more common than correct and effective employment of these rhetorical devices.

Today, Henry Peacham's subject seems altogether as quaint as many of his examples. It has, indeed, been increasingly unfashionable since the late sixteenth century. Nevertheless, it is one which a historian might study carefully, for two purposes. First he can improve his style by controlled and conscious use of these embellishments. There is nothing necessarily fussy or false or weak about them. The greatest classics of Elizabethan and Jacobean literature, such as the King James Bible and the plays of Shakespeare, gained refinement, power, and honesty from frequent use of figures.

Second, a study of figures should help a historian to keep them out of his prose when he wishes to do so. Sometimes we must make

8. The letter, dated March 17, 1804, appears in Lodge, *The Life and Letters of George Cabot* (Boston, 1877), p. 453; and Henry B. Adams, ed., *Documents Relating to New England Federalism, 1800–1850* (New York, 1965), pp. 361–62. The original is in the Pickering Papers, Massachusetts Historical Society.

our writing as literal as possible. Clarity often requires the ruthless removal of every stylistic ornament from our prose. And yet these embellishments are so deeply rooted in our language—owing partly to the genius of Elizabethan literature, and partly to the nature of language itself—that it is as difficult to pull them out as it is to put them in. The following list (much shorter than Peacham's) includes a few figures which can cause great confusion in historical writing. Definitions and examples are taken from Fowler's *Modern English Usage*, from Thrall and Hibbard's *Handbook to Literature*, and from Henry Peacham.

Antiphrasis, the use of a word to convey its opposite meaning, as Antony's "such *honourable* men."

Apophasis, the making of an assertion while seeming to deny it. In the *American Historical Review*, 71 (1965): 147, one historian wrote of another, "It is no real criticism to say that the author does not equal Eileen Power in her ability to make the past come alive."

Aposiopesis, a sudden breaking off, in which the reader is required to supply the missing words, as "If he should fail—"

Catachresis, the misapplication of a word, perhaps for effect or possibly from ignorance, as "chronic" for "serious," or "decimate" for "slaughter," or "dilemma" for "difficulty," or "dock" for "pier," or "ratification" for the Senate's consent to a treaty.

Ellipsis, the omission of words necessary to the grammatical structure of a sentence, as Pope's "Where wigs [strive] with wigs, [where] with sword-knots sword-knots strive,/ [Where] Beaus banish Beaus, and [where] coaches coaches drive."

Euphemism, a word in which accuracy is sacrificed to taste, as "remains" for "corpse," or "passed on" for "died."

Hypallage, an inverted relationship between several words, as Virgil's "the trumpet's Tuscan blare," for "the Tuscan trumpet's blare."

Hyperbole, an exaggeration for effect, as "older than time."

Hysteron Proteron, the reversal of the logical order of ideas, as Dogberry's, "Masters, it is proved already that you are little better than false knaves, and it will go near to be thought so shortly."

Litotes, a double negative, or multiple negative, as in a sentence by Harold Laski: "I am not, indeed, sure whether it is not true to say that the Milton who once seemed not unlike a seventeenth-century Shelley had not become, out of an experience ever more bitter each year, more alien to the founder of that Jesuit sect which nothing could induce him to tolerate." This statement is discussed in a splendid essay by George Orwell, "Politics and the English Language," in *A Collection of Essays* (New York, 1954), pp. 162–76.

Meiosis, an understatement, as "altercation" for "fight."

Metonymy, thᴜ use of a substitute term for another which is suggested by it, as "The Pentagon announced today . . ."

Oxymoron, the joining of contradictory terms, as "cruelly kind," or "simply gorgeous," or "frightfully nice," or "make haste slowly," or "ordered confusion," or "deafening silence," or Michael Walzer's characterization of John Calvin's thought as "a theology antitheological," in *The Revolution of the Saints* (Cambridge, 1965), p. 24.

Persiflage, defined by H. W. Fowler as "irresponsible talk, of which the hearer is to make what he can without the right to suppose that the speaker means what he seems to say." An example is the argument of Carl Becker in *The Heavenly City of the Eighteenth Century Philosophers* (New Haven, 1932), pp. 30–31. The book is disguised as a historical interpretation, and yet on the flyleaf of a presentation copy, he wrote, "This certainly isn't history. I hope it's philosophy, because if it's not it's probably moonshine:—or would you say the distinction is oversubtle?"

Prolepsis, describing an event as happening before it could have done so. Fowler provides a poetic example: "So the two brothers and their murder'd man/ Rode past fair Florence."

Prosopopoeia, by which a person is made to represent a type, or an idea, or an institution, or a quality, as in "Hamiltonian" for Federalist, or "a Jefferson" for any democratic thinker.

Suggestio Falsi, a statement which is literally true, but which encourages a false inference, as to the question, "Is X a competent scholar?" the answer, "X is my friend; I'd rather not say."

Solecism, a violation of grammar or idiom, as "Winston tastes good, like a cigarette should." Richard Sherry, in *A Treatise of Schemes and Tropes* (1550, Gainesville, Fla., 1961), p. 36, defined it as "an unmete and unconvenient joynynge together of the partes of speech . . . which because it is used by famous authors, instead of faults, be called figures."

Soroesmus, in Peacham's phrase, "a mingling together of divers languages, as when there is in one sentence English, Latinne & French."

Synecdoche, a figure in which a part is used for the whole, as "bread" for "food" or "man" for "people."

Zeugma, the use of a single modifier for two terms, with one of which it seems logically connected: "See Pan with flocks, with fruits Pomona crowned."

If all this seems a little remote from the daily business of a historian, consider the following common uses of hyperbole, in which the author is often fooled as well as his readers. Historians have been known to write "always" for "sometimes," and "sometimes" for "occasionally," and "occasionally" for "rarely," and "rarely" for "once." In historical writing "certainly" sometimes means "probably," and "probably" means "possibly," and "possibly" means "conceivably."

Similarly the phrase "It needs no comment" should sometimes be translated as "I do not know what comment it needs." When a historian writes, "It is unknown," he might mean "It is unknown to me," or "I don't know," or even "I won't tell." The expression "in fact" sometimes means merely "in my opinion." And the phrases "doubtless" or "undoubtedly," or "beyond the shadow of a doubt" sometimes really should be read, "An element of doubt exists which I, the author, shall disregard."

Another familiar variation on this melancholy theme is the tendency to convert the verdict of a historian into "the verdict of history." Arthur Schlesinger, Jr., seems to be habitually attached to this ugly usage.[9] And when he writes, in the same volume, "And so Landon passed into history" (p. 232) he means, "I'm finished with Alf for a while."

Another figure of the similar sort is the hyperbole "every schoolboy knows." If any schoolboy knew all the things which Macaulay believed that every schoolboy knows, then that omniscient child might be awarded a university degree, *honoris causa*. "Every schoolboy knows . . . who strangled Atahualpa," Macaulay wrote. I doubt that any modern schoolboy outside of Peru even knows who Atahualpa was, much less how he died. Maybe things were different when Prescott was popular, and there were not so many strangulations to remember. But generally speaking, the phrase "every schoolboy knows" means "some very learned scholars have forgotten, or failed to emphasize sufficiently, the fact that."

All these figurative expressions are difficult to interpret in practice, because they are sometimes used figuratively and sometimes literally, and often there is no signal to tell the reader which sort of meaning is intended. It would, of course, be absurd to remove all figures of speech from historical usage merely because some figurative language is apt to confuse more than it clarifies. Figures are so deeply embedded in our language that they cannot be removed, even if one wished to do so. And they are not merely ornamental but also useful in enlarging the range of communication. But wherever they may be taken literally by an intelligent reader, and a literal reading of them falsifies or distorts the meaning, then the fallacy of figures results.

&ᴗ The *fallacy of accent* occurs in an argument when meaning is distorted by emphasis. Imagine a tabloid headline reading:

9. See, e.g., *The Coming of the New Deal* (Boston, 1959), p. 175, passim.

CATASTROPHIC CRIME WAVE IN CITY
predicted by prelate

Another example is provided by a historian of Salem, Massachusetts, who writes that

> Captain L—— had a first mate who was at times addicted to the use of strong drink, and occasionally, as the slang has it, "got full." The ship was lying in a port in China, and the mate had been on shore and had there indulged rather freely in some of the vile compounds common in Chinese ports. He came on board, "drunk as a lord," and thought he had a mortgage on the whole world. The captain, who rarely ever touched liquors himself, was greatly disturbed by the disgraceful conduct of his officer, particularly as the crew had all observed his condition. One of the duties of the first officer [i.e., the mate] is to write up the "log" each day, but as that worthy was not able to do it, the captain made the proper entry, but added: "The mate was drunk all day." The ship left port the next day and the mate got "sobered off." He attended to his writing at the proper time, but was appalled when he saw what the captain had done. He went on deck, and soon after the following colloquy took place:
>
> "Cap'n, why did you write in the log yesterday that I was drunk all day?"
>
> "It was true, wasn't it?"
>
> "Yes, but what will the owners say if they see it? 'T will hurt me with them."
>
> But the mate could get nothing more from the captain than "It was true, wasn't it?
>
> The next day, when the captain was examining the book, he found at the bottom of the mate's entry of observation, course, winds, and tides: "The captain was sober all day."[10]

Adlai Stevenson liked to tell a tale upon himself, which involves the fallacy of accent. During the 1956 presidential campaign he arrived at a Chicago airport to find a shouting mob waiting for him. In the front rank was an immensely pregnant lady, carrying a large sign reading "STEVENSON IS THE MAN."[11]

A historiographical example is suggested in an article by M. Rostovtzeff, "The Decay of the Ancient World and Its Economic Explanations." The author examined the accuracy of interpretations of "the decline of ancient civilization," and sensibly concluded that much depends upon the way in which that phrase is accented. To speak of the decline of *ancient* civilization is one thing. But to talk of the decline of ancient *civilization* is quite another. "Thus," Rostovtzeff wrote, "to apply to events in the ancient world in the centuries after Diocletian and Constantine the term

10. Charles E. Trow, *The Old Shipmasters of Salem* (New York, 1905), pp. 14–15.
11. Kenneth S. Davis, *The Politics of Honor: A Biography of Adlai Stevenson* (New York, 1967), p. 363.

'decay' or 'decline' is unfair and misleading. If, however, in the formula 'decay of ancient civilization' we lay stress on 'ancient' and not on 'civilization,' the formula hits the mark."[12]

Another example, this time from American history, has developed from a famous phrase in the Declaration of Independence, "All men are created equal." One wonders if Jefferson meant "All men are *created* equal" or "All men are created *equal*." If the former, then he might have agreed with Nathaniel Ames, who observed that

> All men are created equal,
> But differ greatly in the sequel.

If he intended the latter, however, a more extended idea of equality appears.

On the afternoon of July 4, 1826, the fiftieth anniversary of the Declaration of Independence, Jefferson and John Adams dramatically died within a few hours of each other. Adams's last words were spoken at noon, when he awakened briefly and said, "Thomas Jefferson survives," and slipped back into unconsciousness. Some historians have made this utterance into a noble tribute to the third President. But one wonders what precisely Adams intended by his delphic phrase. Maybe he said it with a groan, and meant, "Is that sandy-haired son of a bitch still alive?"

Innuendo is a form of the fallacy of accent. There are many refined examples of insinuated reflections oñ character and reputation in the writings of Tacitus. One student of his work has commented on "his readiness to tax to the uttermost every resource of Latin in the cause of antithesis or innuendo."[13] A less subtle specimen, which derives a certain illustrative clarity from its coarseness, was committed by a nineteenth-century New England clergyman and was described in a recent biography of the Grimké sisters:

> Traveling on a boat to New Haven, [James G.] Birney met the Reverend Leonard Bacon, pastor of the First Congregational Church of New Haven, and took occasion to question him about a remark attributed to him regarding Sarah Grimké.
>
> "And what was that?" asked Rev. Bacon.
>
> "I have been told," said Birney, "that in speaking of fanaticism, at one time in New England, you said a Quaker woman had been known publicly to walk through the streets of Salem, *naked as she was born*—But that Miss Grimké had not been known to make such an exhibition of herself *yet*. DiꞁJ you say this?"

12. M. Rostovtzeff, "The Decay of the Ancient World and Its Economic Explanations," *Economic History Review* 2 (1930): 197–99.
13. John Jackson, Introduction to Tacitus, *The Annals* (London, 1931), p. 238.

"I did," Bacon readily admitted and added after a pause: "And should I have said that she did?"[14]

If innuendo is understood in a more general way to mean any insinuation or connotation, then it cannot be eliminated from language. Some have tried to do so, by desperate expedients. It is said that Jeremy Bentham was so fearful of the fallacy of accent that he deliberately employed a reader with a perfectly monotonous voice. But even a monotone can commit a fallacy of accent in the rendering of a style which requires tonal variations, as all English style must. The only rational expedient is to strive for controlled connotation—even, one might say, controlled innuendo—so that veiled meanings are properly aligned with the author's purpose, and with reason and empirical accuracy. The fallacy of accent consists not in the use of emphasis, but in its unfair and inaccurate use.

֍ The *fallacy of equivocation* occurs whenever a term is used in two or more senses within a single argument, so that a conclusion appears to follow when in fact it does not. Sometimes, equivocation is deliberately employed for stylistic effect, without a significant substantive distortion. As such, it is the basis of much humor of a low kind. Witness the following "bon mot" by a "certain witty Lord" in eighteenth-century London: "His Lordship being informed, that a Lady, lately divorced, would probably be married to the Earl of Upper O——y, said that it is about time she was upper O——y for she has been under O——y long enough."[15]

Other equivocations are not intended. In a recent study in Sudanese history, Byron Farwell attempted to explain the alleged corruption of the Mahdi by the following extraordinary enthymeme: "Power, of course, corrupts, and luxury when available is a powerful temptation."[16] Therefore, by Farwell's logic, when luxury became available to the Mahdi, he became powerfully corrupt.

A more serious modern instance appears in Herbert Aptheker's *American Negro Slave Revolts* (2d ed. [New York, 1963]). Aptheker meant to prove that there were many revolts in the history of American Negro slavery—a revolt being defined at the outset as something involving "a minimum of ten slaves" with "freedom as its object." He concluded that there were some two hundred fifty of these happenings in less than

14. Gerda Lerner, *The Grimké Sisters from South Carolina* (Boston, 1967), p. 196.
15. D. Judson Milburn, *The Age of Wit* (New York, 1966), p. 45.
16. Byron Farwell, *Prisoners of the Mahdi* (New York, 1967), p. 24.

two hundred years. But if his original definition of revolts is respected, the number shrinks to fifteen or twenty—for as Aptheker proceeds, he loosens his definition of slave revolts to include events involving fewer than ten people, risings not directed toward freedom, revolts in French and Spanish colonies, conspiracies, and alleged conspiracies. Had Aptheker's definition been rigorously applied, his thesis would have been visibly untenable. Instead, it is obscurely so.

&» The *fallacy of quibbling* is a form of equivocation which involves two or more people in a single argumentative exchange. It occurs whenever the meaning of a term is changed as it changes hands, with a resultant argumentative distortion.

An intricate example appears in an answer to Max Weber's thesis in *The Protestant Ethic and the Spirit of Capitalism*, by a Swedish economic historian named Kurt Samuelsson. Weber's argument for a functional relationship between capitalism and the Protestant ethic rested upon a careful definition of these terms. Samuelsson subtly shifted those definitions in his attempt at refutation. In the end, he succeeded in refuting a thesis, but not the Weber thesis.

Weber defined capitalism in a special and limited sense, to mean the rational organization of formally free labor.[17] He specifically repudiated the more general and more common definition of capitalism as "the impulse to acquisition, pursuit of gain, of money, of the greatest possible amount of money." But Samuelsson substituted this latter definition for Weber's in his version of the Weber thesis, defining capitalism as "large scale accumulation," or "the growth of capital mobilisation and credit provision on a large scale."[18]

Samuelsson had no difficulty in demonstrating that there were many capitalists, in his sense, who had nothing to do with Protestantism. But this fact did not contradict Max Weber's argument—indeed, Weber specifically affirmed it. Samuelsson's work is useful in one respect, at least. Many others have also misread Weber; specifically, they have misunderstood it as an argument for a connection between Protestantism and the heaping up of riches, or Protestantism and the growth of the acquisitive impulse, or Protestantism and the growth of capital mobilization. To misread Weber in this way is to miss his point by a country

17. Max Weber, *The Protestant Ethic and the Spirit of Capitalism* (New York, 1948), p. 21.
18. Kurt Samuelsson, *Religion and Economic Action*, trans E. Geoffrey French (New York, 1961), pp. 84, 92.

mile. Samuelsson's iconoclastic essay might usefully serve as a reminder of this fact, and as a remedy for a vulgar version of the Weber thesis which has circulated widely in the universities.

&~ The *black-or-white fallacy* is a form of error which occurs in the misconstruction of vague terms—i.e., terms such as hot and cold, light and dark, good and bad, free and unfree, and right-wing and left-wing. There is no firm and fixed criterion for distinguishing between hot and cold, no sharp line which separates these two words, but an area of doubt between them. A precise distinction can be made for a particular purpose, but only by drawing an arbitrary line. And that practice is dangerous in two different ways.

First, it is sometimes argued that because such a distinction is arbitrary, and merely a matter of degree, that no "real" distinction exists. In other words, it might be asserted that there is no "real" difference between two different shades of gray, because they are both called gray, and only an arbitrary line can separate light gray from dark gray, the only "real" difference being between white and black. It is sometimes said, for example, that there is no "real" difference between the treatment of Negroes in Mississippi and Massachusetts, because Mississippi's record in this respect is not pitch-black, and Massachusetts' is far from being snow-white. But nevertheless, there *is* a difference between two shades of gray, a difference which this line of argument disguises by a semantical trick.

Conversely, it is possible to err in the opposite way and be deluded by language into a reification of the arbitrary line, in which case dark gray becomes black, and light gray becomes white. An example was recently perpetrated by two able American historians, Lee Benson and James P. Shenton. Both these scholars were enthusiastic supporters of Senator Eugene McCarthy and opponents of Senator Robert F. Kennedy. On March 20, 1968, the two historians published in *The New York Times* an advertisement which read as follows:

> The Responsibility of American Intellectuals is to tell the truth. Always. The truth is: The movement that has made Senator McCarthy its symbol exemplifies rationality, courage, morality. The movement Senator Kennedy commands exemplifies irrationality, opportunism, amorality. The truth is: To be moral and remain moral, movements must always choose moral men and moral means. The truth is: The end never justifies the means. Never. If American intellectuals do not know that, they have learned nothing from history. The truth is: In March 1968, history has caught up with American intellectuals. They must choose between morality and amorality, between McCarthy or Kennedy. And to act on their choice. Publicly. Unequivocally. Immediately.

The confusion in this extraordinary statement consists not merely in the fact that politicians do not behave according to these Manichaean expectations, but that language doesn't behave this way either. "McCarthy" and "Kennedy" are words of one sort; "moral" and "amoral" are of quite another. The latter are vague words, like hot and cold, which are qualities which exist in various degrees, and in various respects. If an arbitrary distinction is drawn between "moral" and "amoral," then it must be drawn clearly and explicitly, and its arbitrariness must be borne in mind. If it is not, two shades of gray are converted by semantical mumbo jumbo into black and white. When words are used as they are by Benson and Shenton, they become meaningless. Their statement is not merely false—it is solemn and literal nonsense.

Another example of this form of the black-or-white fallacy occurs in the preface to Sir Lewis Namier's *The Structure of Politics at the Accession of George III* (2d ed. [London, 1957]), in which the author declared, "I refrain from adding a bibliography. There can be none for the life of a community; I hardly remember having come across contemporary materials, or any book reproducing such materials, which did not contribute something to my information."[19] In other words, "I cannot list all of my sources; therefore, I need not list any of my sources." Everyone who has done the sort of research which Namier did will credit his statement that every piece of English evidence which was contemporary to his English subject became a source for his study. But some sources were more productive than others. A select bibliography of the most useful material would have been a good, gray middle ground between the black of no bibliography, and the white of a complete one.[20]

᳕ The remedy for all these informal fallacies is formal definition faithfully applied. There are many different kinds of formal definition. A historian ought to choose consciously and carefully from the range of possibilities available to him. Imprecision results not merely from an incomplete or inaccurate or inconsistent definition, but also from the use of an inappropriate definitional type. Suppose, for example, a definition of "Quaker" is required. It could be one or more of the following types, some of which overlap:

1. A *definition by genus and difference* locates a term within a larger class, and then supplies specific differences. Alan Simpson employs

19. P. xiv.
20. For a similar error, see William Appleman Williams's justification of the omission of footnotes from *The Contours of American History* (Cleveland, 1961), p. 491.

this method when he defines a Quaker as a member of the left wing of Puritanism. (*Puritanism in Old and New England*, p. 1.)

2. A *theoretical definition* might include a statement of principles involved in an idea. Frederick Tolles defines a Quaker as a man whose religious faith "represented an equilibrium of four elements—mysticism, prophetism, perfectionism, and universalism." (*Meeting House and Counting House*, p. 6.)

3. A *lexical definition* defines a word by explaining its common, ordinary, or accepted usage. In Webster, Quaker is defined as, "in common usage, a member of the Society of Friends." In seventeenth-century Massachusetts, however, Quaker was also used as a synonym for fanatic.

4. A *stipulative definition* introduces a wholly new expression into the language, or gives a new and special meaning to an old expression, as in the use of Quaker to mean "a dummy gun," or "a guessing game played with coins." (Mitford Matthews, *Dictionary of Americanisms*, p. 1337.)

5. A *precising definition* defines a word in a specific way for a special purpose. Imagine a handyman who is instructed to remove all the brush from a back lot, but to leave all the trees. In his instructions, a tree might be defined as anything more than three inches thick at the base. Similarly, a historian of the Pennsylvania Assembly in the mid-eighteenth century could conceivably define a Quaker as "an assemblyman who belonged to a political faction, of which the acknowledged head was Isaac Norris II."

6. An *enumerative definition* provides a complete list of every item to which a word applies. It is impracticable, of course, in the case of "Quaker," where it would have to be "George Fox, William Penn," etc., until all Quakers are named. For other purposes, however, such as defining the Big Three, an enumerative definition is natural and normal.

7. An *ostensive definition* is more generally useful, for it is a representative rather than a complete listing. Thus, a Quaker is "such a person as George Fox, or William Penn, or John Woolman."

8. A *genetic definition* describes the origin of the thing designated by a word: a Quaker is "a member of a sect founded (1647) by the English religious leader George Fox. . . ." (Thomas H. Johnson, *The Oxford Companion to American History*, p. 315.)

9. A *constructive definition* tells how a thing can be made—which is not very appropriate to the Quaker example, though it is often used in other contexts. But it might be applied even to "Quaker," as "a person who is admitted to a Society of Friends, either by means of birth to a member, or by signifying his willingness to join."

10. An *operational definition* specifies the tests which determine

whether or not a term applies to the thing in question. For example, "a person may be called a Quaker if he manifests the following behavioral characteristics: a tendency to gather in silent meetings, to dress plainly, to address others as thee, to refuse to doff his hat except in prayer, to refuse to bear arms, and to refuse to swear oaths."

11. A *synonymous definition* explains the meaning of a term by identifying other terms with the same meaning; as, "Quaker: Friend, Foxite, etc."

12. An *analytical definition* defines a thing by detailing its parts. "A Quaker believes in the doctrine of the Inward Light, the separation of church and state, the irrelevance of priests and creeds, the right and duty of conscientious objection, the responsibility of philanthropy and charity," etc.

13. A *synthetic definition* defines a thing by reference to other things. Robert Doherty used this method in a recent monograph, *The Hicksite Separation* (New Brunswick, 1967), in which he compiled such charts as the following, for Quakers and Non-Quakers in Philadelphia, circa 1828:

WEALTH: REAL ESTATE

Assessed value of real estate	Quaker		Non-Quaker	
	Number	Percent	Number	Percent
0	42	30	214	46
$ 1–999	18	13	92	20
1000–1999	16	11	46	10
2000–2999	11	8	41	9
3000–3999	10	7	29	6
4000–	43	30	43	9
Total	140	99	465	100

14. A *persuasive definition* defines a term in such a way as to induce a person to accept or reject some principle or value. An example would be John Morley's definition of Quakerism as "the most devout of all endeavours to turn Christianity into the religion of Christ." (*Oliver Cromwell*, p. 429.) Another example, on the other side, is the traditional definition of a Quaker as "a man who prays for his neighbors one day a week, and preys on them the other six."

15. A *figurative definition* defines a term in metaphorical terms, as, William Penn's definition of Quakers as "dissenters in our own land," or "the children of light," etc.

The term Quaker is one which presents comparatively few definitional difficulties. The reader is invited to try to define "Puritan," on the one hand, or "Hicksite," on the other. Historical definitions can be troublesome not merely because of the complexity of the historical process, but also because of the complexity of the definitional process. There is as much confusion between structural types of definition as between substantive definitions themselves.

A historian, however, will simplify his definitional responsibilities by observing a few simple but often neglected rules. First, he does not have to define a term for all eternity but merely for the limited context and purpose he has in mind. Failure to respect this common-sense principle has occasioned a good deal of semantical imprecision, and even some imprecision in the first degree—which is to say, willful and premeditated imprecision. A Dutch historian, Jan Romein, has written,

> The historian always works with vague notions. Race, people, nation, state. Nobility, bourgeoisie, small-middle class, proletariat. Republic, monarchy, dictatorship, democracy. Feudalism, capitalism, socialism, fascism. Renaissance, baroque, romanticism, liberalism. Where is the historian whose hand will not hesitate when venturing to define any of these conceptions? But where, also, is the historian who will refrain from using them as being too vague? The historian must work with vague notions because his object does not admit of exact ones.[21]

Romein used this argument to justify his favorite imprecision, the idea of a *Zeitgeist,* or spirit of an age. But his argument is absurd. The defining hand of the historian might well hesitate if indeed he had to define Romein's illustrative terms for all seasons, independently of historical context and historiographical purpose. But he is merely required to establish workable *ad hoc* definitions, which can be done with maximal precision and minimal effort.

Second, a historian should, where possible, define historical processes rather than nonhistorical states—things that happen rather than things that are. Many historians have labored long and hard to establish a definition of a static thing called political democracy, an atemporal entity which involves them not merely in vast metaphysical confusion but in a good deal of historical bewilderment as well—for political democracy has meant different things at different times. Their task is considerably eased if they think in terms of process, and conceptualize in terms of "democratization" rather than "democracy." I have found that historians will agree quickly on a workable definition of political democratization, with reference to a particular project—as, for example, the expansion of voter participation in an increasingly free electoral process; but they will argue for years over the meaning of "political democracy."

21. Quoted in Pieter Geyl, *Encounters in History* (New York, 1961), p. 326.

Third, contrary to the opinions of many logicians, a historian needs rarely to concern himself with finding a definition which is entirely commensurate or equivalent to the thing defined. And he should never try to define the "essential" qualities of a thing. The first is supremely difficult; the second is a superstition. Let us recur to the example of the handyman in the back lot, who was instructed to cut down all the brush but not to destroy any trees. For that purpose, a definition of a tree as anything more than three inches thick at the base is sufficiently precise, and perfectly satisfactory—though in many another context, to define a tree as anything more than three inches thick at the base is not merely false but meaningless.

Fourth, historians should supply an enumerative or ostensive definition for every doubtful proper noun of prominent importance in their writing. Often other kinds of definition are necessary, too. But these, I think, are always required, for a historian must establish clear links between language and reality, between the conceptual and the concrete. Consider, for example, the case of Herbert Butterfield's *The Whig Interpretation of History*. Butterfield's analytical terms are very clear, and for a historian, extraordinarily exact. But E. H. Carr has complained of the book that "though it denounced the Whig interpretation over some 130 pages, it did not, so far as I can discover without the help of an index, name a single Whig except Fox, who was no historian, or a single historian save Acton, who was no Whig."[22] Carr is not quite correct. Hallam is mentioned on page 4, and Hallam was a historian and a Whig, though he was both just barely. Two other names appear on page 96 of Butterfield's book. But these exceptions neither vitiate Carr's criticism, nor mitigate Butterfield's offense.

Fifth, though a historian is not required, as has been suggested, to find a fixed definition of a term for all time, he must find a definition which will remain constant and consistent through a single argumentative series. If he shifts to another argument in a single work, then the term might be changed in that transition. But it cannot be changed within an argument, if the term is functional to the reasoning process.

Sixth, a historian must openly and directly confront the problem of connotation and innuendo. Neither can be altogether eliminated. Words will always communicate meanings on many different levels. A historian should turn connotation and innuendo to constructive purposes. He should seek to control and direct them, rather than to remove them—to align the many-leveled meanings of his words with each other, and with his evidence, and with his logic.

22. Carr, *What Is History?*, p. 50.

CHAPTER XI

FALLACIES OF SUBSTANTIVE DISTRACTION

ह১

Nay, Sir, argument is argument. You cannot help paying regard to their arguments if they are good. If it were testimony, you might disregard it. . . . Testimony is like an arrow shot from a long bow; the force of it depends on the strength of the hand that draws it. Argument is like an arrow shot from a cross bow, which has equal force though shot by a child.

—Samuel Johnson

A second set of informal fallacies are substantive rather than semantical. They all operate by shifting attention from a reasoned argument to other things which are irrelevant and often irrational. A definitive catalogue of distractions is, of course, impossible and absurd. The following sixteen fallacies are merely a few common forms of error. Nearly all of them have been discussed before. The standard Latin nomenclature is adopted, for the sake of convenience.

The two most full and ample discussions in print are a collection of posthumous essays by William G. "Single-Speech" Hamilton called *Parliamentary Logic* (1808) and Jeremy Bentham's *Book of Fallacies* (1824).[1] Bentham's work is perhaps the more important of the two,

1. Both works have been reprinted, and Bentham's has appeared in different versions under different titles. The best is Bentham's *Handbook of Political Fallacies*, ed. Harold A. Larrabee (Baltimore, 1952). There are many other works of the same sort. Etienne Dumont's *Traité des Sophismes politiques* (Geneva, 1816) was a redaction prepared from Bentham's own unpublished notes. More recently Arthur Schopenhauer composed a similar work called *The Art of Controversy* which is available in an English translation. Of many modern works, Robert H. Thouless, *Straight and Crooked Thinking* (New York, 1932) and L. Susan Stebbing, *Thinking to Some Purpose* (Baltimore, 1938), might be specially recommended.

though Hamilton's is more readable, and in some technical respects more sound.

There are two serious errors in Bentham's work. First, he tended to assume that these forms of error are usually evidence of some sort of sinister interest in their authors. "Is it credible . . . that their inanity and absurdity should not be fully manifest to the persons who employ them?" he asked. "No," he answered in his solemn way, "it is not credible."[2] But this is a very great mistake. Many of the following examples, if not quite all of them, are clearly not the result of a deliberate attempt to deceive but rather of obscured understanding by authors who were themselves deceived—a condition which is far more common than Bentham was prepared to admit.

Bentham's second mistake was equally serious. He tended to assume that these fallacies were such that "their application affords a presumption either of weakness or of total lack of relevant arguments on the side on which they are employed."[3] But many a bad argument has been used in a good cause. It would be a very profound and pedantical mistake to presume that any of the fallacies in this book, if they appear in a historical interpretation, are prima-facie evidence that the interpretation is false in all respects, and utterly useless.[4]

&ᴗ The *fallacy of argument ad verecundiam* is an appeal to authority. The conventional Latin label means literally an argument to modesty, or shyness, or shame. This form of error is an egregious but effective rhetorical technique which puts an opponent in the awkward position of appearing to commit the sin of pride if he persists in his opposition.

The most crude and ugly form of an argument *ad verecundiam* in historical writing is an appeal to professional status. David Donald, for example, published an essay in which he attempted to analyze the leadership of the abolitionist movement in social terms, and concluded that most abolitionists were "descended from old and socially dominant Northeastern families, reared in the faith of aggressive piety and moral endeavor . . . an elite without function, a displaced class in American society . . . basically abolitionism should be considered the anguished

2. Bentham, *Handbook of Political Fallacies*, ed. Larrabee, p. 242.
3. Ibid., p. 227.
4. Bentham's book is mistaken in many other ways, which are less relevant to our inquiry. He believed that Parliamentary government was so constituted as to encourage the commission of fallacies, and that the congressional system of the American Republic was much superior in this respect. To this infatuation, a student of American politics can only add a sigh.

protest of an aggrieved class against a world they never made."[5]

Shortly after this thesis appeared in print, a young graduate student, Robert Skotheim, published a reply[6] in which he criticized Donald's sample of abolitionist leaders, the imprecision of his data, the absence of a control, and a false extrapolation from abolitionist leadership to all abolitionists.

Donald, unfortunately, lost his temper. His rebuttal consisted of a series of *ignoratii*, punctuated by an *ad verecundiam*. And he finished with the following salvo, aimed at Skotheim in particular, and uppity graduate students in general.

> Mr. Skotheim's criticisms raise the general problem, which Professor David M. Potter so cogently discussed not long ago in a review in the *Journal of Southern History*, of "how far it is possible to proceed in judging historians' interpretations without grounding these judgments in an understanding of the history which is being interpreted." Perhaps the teaching profession is at fault in encouraging young scholars like Mr. Skotheim to undertake studies in methodology and historiography before he has demonstrated his competence in research.[7]

Donald's unfortunate argument from professional status calls to mind an exchange in Lewis Carroll's *Sylvie and Bruno*:

> "Do you mean to say," said Lady Muriel, "that these manikins of an inch high are to *argue* with me?"
>
> "Surely. Surely!" said the Earl. "An argument doesn't depend for its logical force on the *size* of the creature that utters it!"
>
> She tossed her head indignantly. "I would *not* argue with any man less than six inches high!" she cried. "I'd make him *work!*"
>
> "What at?" said Arthur, listening to all this nonsense with an amused smile.
>
> "*Embroidery!*" she readily replied. "What *lovely* embroidery they would do!"[8]

In historiography, such crude forms of argument *ad verecundiam* are rarely to be met with—in print, at least. The explanation is not that scholars are gentlemen, but rather, as Bolingbroke noted many years ago, that "those who are not such, however, have taken care to appear such in their writings."[9]

---

5. David Donald, *Lincoln Reconsidered* (New York, 1956), pp. 19–36: "Toward a Reconsideration of Abolitionists."
6. *Journal of Southern History* 25 (1959): 356–65.
7. Ibid., 26 (1960): 156–57.
8. *The Complete Works of Lewis Carroll*, Modern Library ed. (New York, n.d.), p. 450.
9. Henry Bolingbroke, *Letters on the Study and the Use of History* (London, 1870), pp. 10 f.

&ᴖ» More common and more subtle forms of argument *ad vere-cundiam* appear in appeals to all the paraphernalia of pedantry. Among them are:

1. Appeals to pedantic words and phrases
2. Appeals to references
3. Appeals to quotations
4. Appeals to length
5. Appeals to detail and specificity
6. Appeals to mathematical symbols

The first of these forms of error is committed by scholars who never use a little word when a big one will do. Historians take a certain pride in their alleged immunity from this fallacy—in their freedom from jargon and academic affectation. But their conceit is not correct; indeed, it is growing increasingly inaccurate as an understanding of contemporary historiographical language. Ordinary everyday words like "simple" are replaced by monstrosities such as "simplistic" without any refinement of meaning. Special fields of historical inquiry are building pedantic vo-cabularies at an appalling rate. Urban historians, for instance, speak endlessly of "urbitecture," "areal differentiation," "ecosystems," "nodal points," "metropolitan matrices," "ruralization," "subareal mosaics," "conurbation," and other such neologisms, which are in some cases useful for their precision and defensible for their utility. But these terms are also used for purposes of legitimization, as ritual incantations which serve to camouflage doubt, confusion, illogic, imprecision, and igno-rance. One recent book about urban history blithely defines several of these terms in several different ways, and adds an unblushing explanation that "there is little consistency in the use of metropolitan nomenclature, and we have not attempted to be unduly precise here."[10] If professional jargon is imprecise, then I think it is utterly indefensible. There can be no complaint, of course, against the use of technical terms, but merely against their illegitimate use for effect.

Sometimes I suspect that Americans are particularly susceptible to this unfortunate fallacy. Bertrand Russell, in his memoirs, has recalled:

> In Chicago I had a large seminar, where I continued to lecture on the same subject as at Oxford, namely, "Words and Facts." But I was told that Ameri-cans would not respect my lectures if I used monosyllables, so I altered the title to something like "The Correlation between Oral and Somatic Motor Habits." Under this title, or something of the sort, the seminar was ap-proved.[11]

10. Charles N. Glaab and A. Theodore Brown, *A History of Urban America* (New York, 1967), p. 272n.
11. Bertrand Russell, *Autobiography, 1914–1944* (Boston, 1968), p. 331.

Be that as it may, there are many examples of labored pedantry which are equally objectionable for reasons of logic, rhetoric, and empiricism. One reads such a sentence as the following: "The philosophical anthropology pointed to here can perhaps best be described as a phenomenological anthropology: that is to say, a logos of the phenomenon of anthropos, which has its source and its 'subject matter' in the concernful questing for the being of man-in-quest himself,"[12] and one wonders why.

This humbug is common enough in history today. It will probably become more so. Already, we find a simple mutiny, on Drake's first circumnavigation voyage, ponderously and perhaps falsely discussed as a manifestation of status jealousy.[13] The pioneer of many fashionable historiographical techniques today might be heard in this connection. "The ABC of my trade," Marc Bloch wrote, "consists in avoiding big-sounding abstract terms. Those who teach history should be continually concerned with the task of seeking the solid and concrete behind the empty and the abstract."[14]

A second variety of an argument of the authority of learning symbols is named the "fallacy of references" by an irate philosopher[15] who was properly infuriated by the regrettable tendency of pedants of all persuasions to lard a lean thesis with fat footnotes which are irrelevant, or superfluous, or even something unmentionably worse. The hatefulness of this practice is compounded by the fact that there is often no effective defense. What can the most learned reader do when he is referred to a source which he cannot reach without organizing a scholarly safari? There is no clear and consistent way to distinguish useless references from useful ones which, however remote their sources may be, are often invaluable to specialists. But there are a few pernicious practices in citation which are obviously illegitimate, and easily avoided. Does an author cite the same sources over and over again with minor variations for the sake of appearance? Does he use multiple citations, inextricably entangled in a single note? Does he cite a primary source but quote a transcription from a secondary one? Does he supply a partial citation, which is enough to demonstrate his erudition but not enough to locate the source? These are merely a few of many forms of scholarly malpractice in the construction of references.

A third form of a pedantical *ad verecundiam* consists in the use of quotations, which are often employed for forensic rather than empirical

12. Richard M. Zaner, "An Approach to Philosophical Anthropology," *Philosophy and Phenomenological Research* 27 (1966): 55–68.
13. Kenneth R. Andrews, *Drake's Voyages* (New York, 1967), p. 67.
14. Marc Bloch, *Strange Defeat* (London, 1949), p. 27.
15. Richard Whately, *Logic*, p. 208.

purposes. In historical scholarship, this practice is widespread among young scholars, who have a way of articulating a thesis in series of quotations from older scholars and original sources—quotations which are strung together like beads on a necklace, with a few connections of their own invention. Their own best statements are sometimes buried in the notes, where nobody can find them. As historians gain maturity, they tend to become more assertive in their own right. But the habit is not easily broken.[16]

A variant upon this pedantic impropriety is the tendency of some historians to cast their own doubtful interpretations in the form of attribution. Manning Clark, in his *Short History of Australia* (New York, 1963), argues that "the life of the lower classes was all riot, revelry and drunkenness."[17] This dubious factual statement is accompanied by a more dubious causal explanation, which is in turn supported by a most dubious method of attribution. "Some observers attributed such behaviour to the discrepancy between the sexes, especially amongst the convicts," Clark wrote.[18] This, I think, is an argument *ad verecundiam*. It is certainly true that there was a skewed sex ratio in Australia during the period under discussion. But a causal connection cannot be sustained by attribution to "some observers." Such interpretations are not properly theirs, but the historian's and he must make an empirical case for them.

A fourth form of argument *ad verecundiam* consists in a thesis which is sustained by the length of its exposition. Richard Whately complained two centuries ago that "a very long discussion is one of the most effective veils of fallacy. . . . A fallacy which when stated barely . . . would not deceive a child, may deceive half the world if *diluted* in a quarto volume."[19] Many readers of Arnold Toynbee's *A Study of History* may have been persuaded principally by the monumental proportions of the work. Toynbee surely did not design this effect, but the results are the same as if he had deliberately done so. The sheer pedantic bulk of his many volumes is equally unnecessary to the articulation of his thesis, and unpleasant in its irrational effect upon an awed and ignorant public. At one point, Toynbee mentions "the Tarsian Jewish apostle of Christianity in *partibus infidelium.*" He means Paul. In this "ornate alias," as it has been called, nine pedantic words do the work of one. D. C. Somervell managed

16. For an example, see Donald Southgate, *"The Most English Minister . . ."* The *Policies and Politics of Palmerston* (New York, 1960), pp. 390, 392, 394, xxi, xxii, xxiii, xxviii, 6, 8, 9, 10, 12, 13, passim; and see also a review of E. P. Thompson, *The Making of the English Working Class* in the *Economic History Review*, 2d ser. 18, (1965): 632–43, for a discussion of the use and abuse of quotations by Thompson.
17. P. 73.
18. P. 73.
19. Whately, *Logic*, p. 151.

to shrink Toynbee's twelve volumes to two, largely by striking out the adjectives. Overwriting of this sort is objectionable not merely for stylistic reasons but also because of its rhetorical effect upon uncritical readers.

Isaac Disraeli, in his collection of literary curiosities, describes an eccentric gentleman who invited a number of authors to dinner and seated them in the order of the thickness of their publications. Precisely the same bias operates when thick, square, quarto books attract a quantum of enthusiasm out of all proportion to everything but their size. An example is a fourteen-volume study of *The British Empire Before the American Revolution,* by Lawrence Henry Gipson. The author is treated with extreme deference by his colleagues in colonial history, partly because he has written an extraordinarily long book and partly because he has lived an extraordinarily long time.[20] A more critical approach would surely be more appropriate and also more complimentary to Gipson, who is a good scholar and a tough old man. There are many methodological virtues in his work, and much that is useful as well. But there are also serious deficiencies which ought to be sorted out by critical reviewers. Instead, his well-meaning colleagues tend to avoid any criticism at all and yield to an unintended double *ad verecundiam* in their deference to the length of the work itself and the length of the author's life. If considerations of "taste" are to be consulted, then surely there is nothing as tasteless as unqualified encomia to old men and big books.

A fifth form of a pedantical *ad verecundiam* is an appeal to detail or specificity. The British philosopher, A. C. Bradley, has commented at some length upon the fact that "we generally, it is true, take forcible detail and strong particularity as a sign of fact."[21] Historians, especially, by the nature of their discipline, are prone to this prejudice. There can, of course, be no empirical proof without particularity, but there is often particularity without proof. The reader might examine Macaulay's memorable interpretations of Jeffreys, and Marlborough, and Penn, all of whom he deeply disliked. His descriptions gain their argumentative power and literary effect from a richness of controlled detail. But recent students of these three men, as well as of other personages who became the antagonists in Macaulay's work, have demonstrated that much of the detail is false, misleading, or merely irrelevant to the point at issue. Parrington was another, of many great historians, who had the same extraordinary gift, and who often misused it.

Sixth, there are arguments *ad verecundiam* in the form of an appeal to the authority of mathematics. There is an anecdote, undoubtedly

20. A specimen of this devotional literature is Richard B. Morris, "The Spacious Empire of Lawrence Henry Gipson," *William and Mary Quarterly* 24 (1967): 169–89.
21. A. C. Bradley, *The Principles of Logic,* 2d rev. ed., 2 vols. (London, 1922), 1:75.

apocryphal, which may nevertheless serve as a hypothetical illustration. It has often been said that Diderot once was asked in the court of Catherine II of Russia to debate the existence of God with a mathematician named Euler. The latter allegedly began by saying:

$$\frac{a + b^n}{n} = X$$

To this, he added, "Donc Dieu existe. Répondez!" According to the story, Diderot was so unnerved that he blushed and stammered and fled for France.

It is unlikely that this tale is true. Diderot was not merely a great controversialist but a good mathematician too. He would not have been flustered by so trivial a forensic tactic. But true or false, this anecdote is accurately descriptive of a common attitude among mathematical illiterates. These unfortunate people are not merely untaught, but unteachable—until the fear of numbers is somehow gotten out of them.

The converse of this fallacy consists in the categorical rejection of mathematical symbols. G. B. Shaw appears to have entertained a great contempt for numbers. He wrote,

> I somehow distrust mathematical symbols. I remember at school a plausible boy who used to prove to me by algebra that one equals two. He always began by saying, "Let x equal a." I saw no great harm in admitting that; and the proof followed with rigorous exactness. The effect was not to make me proceed habitually on the assumption that one equals two, but to impress upon me that there was a screw loose somewhere in the algebraic art, and a chance for me to set it right some day when I had time to look into the subject. And I feel bound to make the perhaps puerile confession that when I read Jevons's *Theory of Political Economy,* I no sooner glanced at the words "let x signify the quantity of commodity,' than I thought of the plausible boy, and prepared myself for a theory of value based on algebraic proof that two and two make five.[22]

There is something of this attitude in the response of historians to the use of mathematics in their discipline by econometricians and demographers. They might consider the reply to Shaw which was made by a friend of Jevons', Philip H. Wicksteed, who wrote,

> Mr. Shaw's youthful experience about x and a are so highly instructive that I cannot refrain from dwelling upon them for a moment. His friend induced him to "let $x = a$," and Mr. Shaw—not expecting that x would take any mean advantage of the permission—granted the request. But he did not understand that in letting $x = a$ he was also letting $xt - a = 0$, and the proof (of the proposition, $2 = 1$) that "followed with rigorous exactness,"

22. Philip H. Wicksteed, *The Common Sense of Political Economy*, rev. and enl. ed., 2 vols. (London, 1948), 2:726.

assumed that $x - a$ did *not* equal zero. Mr. Shaw arrived at the sapient conclusion that there was "a screw loose somewhere" not in his own reasoning
powers, but—"in the algebraic art"; and thenceforth renounced mathematical reasoning in favour of the literary method which allows a clever man
to follow equally fallacious arguments to equally absurd conclusions *without
seeing that they are absurd*. This is the exact difference between the mathematical and literary treatment of the pure theory of political economy.[23]

Finally, there is a common form of the fallacy of argument *ad
verecundiam*, which consists in the authority of the printed page over
ignorant minds. In most of us, there is a little of the legendary Caspar
Milquetoast, who believed anything he saw in writing—the blurb on
a book jacket, ballyhoo on a patent-medicine bottle, signboards, and
skywriting. Every teacher who has ever used a textbook has surely met
this form of error in some of his students.

There is also a counter fallacy which, according to Marc Bloch,
was popular among the *Poilus* of the 1914–1918 war.

> The prevailing opinion in the trenches [he wrote] was that anything might
> be true, except what was printed. . . . The role of propaganda and censorship
> was considerable, but in a way exactly the reverse of what the creators of
> these institutions expected of them. . . . The men put no faith in newspapers,
> and scarcely more in letters, for these, besides arriving irregularly, were
> thought to be heavily censored. From this there arose a prodigious renewal
> of oral tradition, the ancient mother of myths and legends. Wiping out by-
> gone centuries by a daring stroke, beyond the wildest dream of the boldest
> experimenters, governments reduced the front-line soldier to the means of
> information and the mental state of olden-times, before journals, before news
> sheets, before books.[24]

There is perhaps a similar tendency today, among a certain
portion of the younger generation, to disbelieve anything which they
find in print, particularly on the subject of drugs, education, and Vietnam, unless it is the purple prose which oozes from their own hectograph
machines. But these same students are apt to be extraordinarily credulous
of any fact communicated to them by electronic means. This form of
error is not the antithesis of the Caspar Milquetoast syndrome, but its
complement. Both habits of thought are equally inimical to rational
intelligence and disciplined creativity.

ह‍ॐ The *fallacy of argument ad hominem* occurs in many different forms, all of which serve to shift attention from the argument
to the arguer. Among its more common varieties are, first, the abusive

23. Ibid., 2:733.
24. Marc Bloch, *The Historian's Craft* (New York, 1953), pp. 107–8.

ad hominem, which directly denounces an opponent. The classic example, perhaps apocryphal, is a note passed from one desperate lawyer to another: "No case; abuse plaintiff's attorney."

Abraham Lincoln did this once, with the adversarial roles reversed. Unhappily, he got away with it. Lincoln's law partner, William H. Herndon, remembered:

> In a case where Judge [Stephen T.] Logan—always earnest and grave—opposed him, Lincoln created no little merriment by his reference to Logan's style of dress. He carried the surprise in store for the latter, till he reached his turn before the jury. Addressing them, he said: "Gentlemen, you must be careful and not permit yourselves to be overcome by the eloquence of counsel for the defence. Judge Logan, I know, is an effective lawyer. I have met him too often to doubt that; but shrewd and careful though he be, still he is sometimes wrong. Since this trial has begun I have discovered that, with all his caution and fastidiousness, he hasn't knowledge enough to put his shirt on right." Logan turned red as crimson, but sure enough, Lincoln was correct, for the former had donned a new shirt, and by mistake had drawn it over his head with the pleated bosom behind. The general laugh which followed destroyed the effect of Logan's eloquence over the jury—the very point at which Lincoln aimed.[25]

A second variety of argument *ad hominem* is circumstantial. It consists in a suggestion that an opponent's argument is merely a reflection of his interest. Adlai Stevenson attacked the arguments of the Republican party in 1952 with the assertion that it was "out of patience, out of sorts, and out of office."[26]

Third, there are associative *ad hominem* arguments, which attempt to undercut an opponent by reference to the company he keeps. There is an example, in doggerel, from English politics:

> If the Devil has a son,
> It is surely Palmerston.

A pictorial specimen from American politics was the attempt by Senator Joseph McCarthy and his staff in 1950 to end the political career of a consistent and courageous critic—Senator Millard Tydings of Maryland—by distributing a doctored photograph showing Tydings tête-à-tête with a prominent American Communist, Earl Browder. The attempt was successful.[27]

Fourth, there are arguments *ad hominem* in the form of *tu quoque* ("you too"), in which it is suggested that an opponent has sometimes held the view which he now opposes, or that he has adopted the practice

25. Paul M. Angle, ed., *Herndon's Life of Lincoln* (New York, 1965), p. 291.
26. Adlai Stevenson, *Major Campaign Speeches* (New York, 1953), p. 4.
27. Richard Rovere, *Senator Joe McCarthy* (New York, 1959), pp. 160–61.

which he new condemns, or that his argument applies to himself as well as to his opponent. A *graffito*, scrawled upon the wall of a New York subway station, read:

God is Dead: Nietzsche

To this, some subterranean pilgrim made the reply:

Nietzsche is Dead: God

One of the great *ad hominists* of all time was Dr. Johnson. Oliver Goldsmith was driven to complain that "there is no arguing with Johnson: for if his pistol misses fire, he knocks you down with the butt end of it."[28] Johnson employed this brutish tactic not merely in the form of argument *ad hominem*, but *ad feminam* as well. It is reported that "Once, upon hearing a lady from the provinces complain of how she disliked London because there her fingernails were always dirty, he remarked, 'Perhaps, Madam, you scratch yourself.' "[29] In a more famous encounter, he was conversing with Mrs. Catherine Macaulay, a female historian of radical Whiggish principles, and an enthusiast for the American Revolution—which is to say that by her very existence she infuriated her bearish antagonist in seven different ways. When Mrs. Macaulay argued boldly for the equality of mankind—in the presence of her servants—Dr. Johnson replied by asking her to allow a footman to sit down beside her.[30]

Once Dr. Johnson got as good as he gave, from another female of his acquaintance. In conversation with Miss Seward, a lady poet from his native Lichfield, he asserted, "I am willing to love all mankind, *except an American*." Then, according to Boswell,

> his inflammable corruption bursting into horrid fire, he "breathed out threatenings and slaughter;" calling them, "Rascals—Robbers—Pirates;" and exclaiming, he'd "burn and destroy them." Miss Seward, looking to him with mild but steady astonishment, said, "Sir, this is an instance that we are always most violent against those whom we have injured."—He was irritated still more by this delicate and keen reproach; and roared out another tremendous volley which one might fancy could be heard across the Atlantick. During this tempest I sat in great uneasiness, lamenting his heat of temper; till, by degrees, I diverted his attention to other topicks.[31]

Arguments *ad hominem* sometimes run in reverse, in which case they are, I suppose, arguments *de homine*. The French historian Alphonse Aulard made a career of attacking Hippolyte Taine. Aulard

---

28. James Boswell, *The Life of Dr. Johnson*, p. 361, Oct. 26, 1769.
29. D. Judson Milburn, *The Age of Wit* (New York, 1966), p. 24.
30. Boswell, *The Life of Dr. Johnson*, p. 660, 1776.
31. Ibid., p. 806, April 15, 1778.

even went so far as to assert that "a candidate for a history degree at the Sorbonne would not make a good impression if he quoted Taine as an authority."[32]

There are many arguments *ad hominem* in historiographical exchanges. The nature of this fallacy is, I hope, sufficiently clear not to require additional examples. If anybody is interested, he might consult the "Communications" section of the *American Historical Review*, in which *ad hominem* arguments are exchanged as regularly as a ball in a tennis match. But an *ad hominem* debate is unlike tennis in one respect—it is a match which everybody loses: players, referees, spectators, and all.[33]

 ℞ The *fallacy of argument ad crumenam* makes money into a measure of truth and right. A vulgar example is the proverbial retort which finds a regrettable popularity in this republic—"If y'r so smart, why ain't ya rich?" I had not expected to find an instance of this error in the work of academic historians, whose economic status is a sufficient discouragement. Indeed, among threadbare academic gentlemen, the counterfallacy of an argument to poverty is perhaps more popular, except when it is used by college presidents, as it actually was by Harvard's Charles W. Eliot, as an excuse to keep down faculty salaries.

But an unexpected example of argument *ad crumenam* turned up in the work of President Eliot's kinsman—Samuel Eliot Morison. In a plea for the excellence of old-fashioned narrative writing, Morison argued that narratives were better than monographs, partly because they were worth more money to their authors.

> The tremendous plowing up of the past by well trained scholars is all to the good, so far as it goes [he wrote]. Scholars know more about America's past than ever; they are opening new furrows and finding new artifacts, from aboriginal arrowheads to early 20th century corset stays. But they are heaping up the pay dirt for others. Journalists, novelists and free-lance writers are the ones that extract the gold, and they deserve every ounce they get because they are the ones who know how to write histories that people care to read. What I want to see is a few more Ph.D.'s in history winning book-of-the-month adoptions and reaping the harvest of dividends. They can do it, too, if they will only use the same industry at presenting history as they do in compiling it.[34]

32. Pieter Geyl, *Encounters in History* (New York, 1961), p. 132. Aulard's attack appeared at greatest length in *Taine: Historien de la Révolution Française* (Paris, 1907).
33. See, e.g., *The American Historical Review* 73 (1968): 996, 1710, passim.
34. Samuel Eliot Morison, "History as a Literary Art," *Old South Leaflets*, series 2, number 1 (n.d.): 5.

The reader will note that an argument *ad crumenam* is grafted on to an argument *ad populum*. Morison has other arguments for history as literary art, most of which are equally mistaken. He meant well, and the stylistic deficiencies of much professiorial prose are a common scandal. But this argument for the merits of literary history might be translated precisely into the vulgar terms of our first example: "If y'r so smart, why ain't ya rich?"

ह The *fallacy of argument ad baculum* (literally, to a big stick) is an appeal to physical force, actual or implied, in order to sustain an argument—a crude tactic not commonly employed in American academic disputes today, unless students are the disputants. Tempers have flared to a fever heat in many a fierce interpretative exchange. But never, to my knowledge, have historians of slavery attempted to settle the profitability question at twelve paces; nor have embattled Turnerians and anti-Turnerians ever conducted a gouging contest on a prairie campus. No critic of the New Political History has been defenestrated from Pittsburgh's tower of learning; nor has a graduate student ever actually been pressed to death beneath a folio set of the *Monumenta* for standing mute on a doctoral examination.

But it was not always so. The most powerful piece of historical writing in Western culture ends, characteristically, with an omnibus threat of bodily injury and spiritual harm to all would-be revisionists. The reader of the Book of Revelation, 22:18–19, is solemnly warned: "I testify unto every man that heareth the words of the prophecy of this book, If any man shall add unto these things, God shall add unto him the plagues that are written in this book: And if any man shall take away from the words of the book of this prophecy, God shall take away his part out of the book of life, and out of the holy city, and *from* the things which are written in this book."

Today a soft sell is thought to be more effective. But there have been many disagreeable instances of an argument *ad baculum* in the great disturbances which have disrupted the peace of the world in the past few generations. In Japan, during the reign of the present emperor, a scholar who doubted the accuracy of the standard genealogical history of the imperial family was threatened with assassination. In Soviet Russia, and other Communist nations, more than a few chapters of historiographical revisionism have ended in the rattle of machine-gun fire. German historiography has perhaps suffered more severely in this respect than that of any other nation. Sixty years ago, its historians set standards for the world. Thirty years ago, its great centers of learning were purged of every vestige of open anti-Fascism. Today in historical scholarship, Germany is a stagnant backwater. This great reversal cannot be attributed solely to the nihilistic violence of Nazism; other agents have contributed to the effect. Nevertheless, the decline of the German universities since 1932 testifies to the dangerous power of an argument *ad baculum*, not merely over the specific victim, but over everybody in the vicinity.

These examples are not likely to be very disturbing to liberal Americans—Fascist beasts and fanatic Bolsheviks are *supposed* to misbehave. But there have also been many regrettable examples in modern America. James W. Silver, a historian in Mississippi, had the temerity, a few years ago, to speak openly and honestly of the culture in which he lived. He was threatened forthwith with bodily violence by the people who set the tone of public discussion in that state. There are such primitives living in the nooks and crannies of every civilized society. But society in Mississippi is so organized as to magnify their power and their opportunities to act. More recently, in many universities throughout the western world, radical students have disrupted classes, damaged buildings, destroyed books, and injured people, and committed many outrages when instructors made statements with which they disagreed. In Massachusetts recently, students answered an unpopular speaker by thrusting a banana in his mouth. In California, other people have been killed in these violent disturbances. Three years ago, when I began work on this book, I had planned to omit argument *ad baculum*, on the ground that it occurred too infrequently in American universities to warrant mention. How wrong I was! Today, it constitutes a more immediate threat to rational processes than any other error which I have included.

What is a rational man to do, in the face of an appeal *ad baculum*? Knock-down arguments, alas, must be overcome not with a syllogism but a stick. Liberty *and* order are the prerequisites of reason. Let us hope that the senseless and suicidal misbehavior of a small number of immature students, and of a still smaller number of irresponsible adults who have urged them on, will awaken the great moderate mass of free men in this republic to protect and defend our rare and happy heritage of freedom and stability. Let us have the courage, patience, and wisdom to *enforce* restraint (without repression) upon our erring children. Then, only then, can the dialogue of reason continue.

There is, by the way, a counterfallacy which consists in an appeal not to a big stick but to a little one. Americans who pride themselves upon a proverbial sympathy for the underdog are perhaps particularly vulnerable. There is surely no a priori reason for taking up the cause of the underdog, who may be a dirtier dog than the top dog. Critics of the war in Vietnam have raised the cry of "Bully" against American intervention. But right does not vary with might—even inversely.

౾ఌ The *fallacy of argument ad temperantiam* is an appeal to moderation, on the apparent assumption that truth, in Burke's phrase, is always a "sort of middle." In academic scholarship it commonly occurs in two forms. The first is stylistic; the second, substantive.

The prevalance of a prejudice toward stylistic moderation in academic historiography explains the monumental dullness of its monographic literature. The problem is not that historians do not know how to write, but rather that they are actively discouraged from indulging in any stylistic practice which might be interpreted as literary intemperance. Historians write dull books not because they are dull fellows, but because they have formed the stupid habit of confusing dullness with detachment. A clear example of an excess of stylistic moderation is the good, gray, *Cambridge History of British Foreign Policy*, or the *Cambridge Modern History*. An editor of these excruciating works, the English diplomatic historian A. W. Ward, is alleged to have revised one chapter on the ground that "It's a bit lively."[35]

An exceedingly lively American scholar, Charles A. Beard, may have operated upon the same assumption in his most important work, *An Economic Interpretation of the Constitution*. Several scholars have pondered an odd fact about that work. Eric Goldman observes,

> For a man like Charles Beard, who could write with either a shillelagh or a stiletto, the *Economic Interpretation* was a triumph in dullness. Not a single departure from catalogue organization, not a single bright sentence, enlivened the book, which carefully described itself as an "arid survey." Max Lerner, who believes that the *Economic Interpretation* influenced his own thinking enormously, has described the volume's strategy of flatness. "Beard must have had a premonition of the desperate resistance he would run into," Lerner commented. ". . . It is almost as if the author had set out with a deliberate severity to strip the book of every adornment, on the theory that a plain woman would be less suspected of being a wanton than an attractive one."[36]

If liveliness is thought to be unbecoming in a monograph, enthusiasm appears to be unforgivable. One of Beard's most outspoken critics, Robert Brown, failed to bend before his colleagues' bias toward moderation and published several volumes in a spirit of furious revisionism, which are sometimes condemned not for their substance but for their

35. S. C. Roberts, *Adventures with Authors* (Cambridge, 1966), pp. 112–13, quoted in G. R. Elton, *The Practice of History* (New York, 1967), p. 108.
36. Eric Goldman, *Rendezvous with Destiny* (New York, 1952), p. 153.

style. A conservative scholar has written, "What mars Professor Brown's important contributions to our understanding of the late colonial period is a certain belligerence toward fellow workers in this field."[37] I hold no brief for Brown, who does indeed make himself more than a little disagreeable by a strident, self-righteous style. But that aspect of his work has nothing whatever to do with its interpretative merit.

A second form of the fallacy of argument *ad temperantiam* consists in substantive moderation. "*N'ayez pas de zéle*," said Talleyrand. Many historians have made this *mot* into a motto. Ranke was one of them. Beard sneered that "he could write of popes in a manner pleasing to both Catholics and Protestants of the upper classes." That fact was owing not merely to an elitist common denominator but to an excess of substantive moderation. Ranke, I think, sometimes imagined that he had unlocked the inner secret of objectivity, when he had merely found a middling subjectivism.

Another example was Macaulay, who condemned historians who believed that to be impartial was "to intersperse in due proportion epithets of praise or abhorrence." Macaulay himself operated on a different assumption. To be impartial was, for him, to intersperse, in due proportion, epithets of abhorrence for all extremes. A recent work has analyzed the importance of "middlingness" in his thought.[38]

&❧ The *fallacy of argument ad antiquitam* is an illegitimate appeal to ages past in order to justify acts present or future. Jeremy Bentham called it the "Chinese argument" in his *Handbook of Political Fallacies*, which is both inaccurate and unfair in its implication that this fallacy is a logical disorder to which orientals are especially susceptible. Bentham's own hilarious examples suggest that an argument *ad antiquitam* has perhaps been brought to its highest level of refinement by lily-white Anglo-Saxon gentlemen on both sides of the Atlantic Ocean. Constitutional law in both England and America might be conceived as one prolonged and preposterous argument to antiquity by inscrutable occidentals in flowing judicial robes. "Men love old truths," said Billy Herndon, as he traveled the circuit in frontier Illinois, and they love old errors, too. There is scarcely a corner of the world in which men do not, in some degree, bow down before absurdities inherited from their ancestors.

37. Lawrence Henry Gipson, *The British Empire Before the American Revolution*, vol. 13 (New York, 1967), p. 453.
38. Vincent E. Staizinger, *Middlingness: Juste Milieu Political Theory in France and England, 1815–1848* (Charlottesville, Va., 1965).

An argument to age is not merely irrelevant to many of the issues which it has been used to defend. It is also, in its usual form, inconsistent with itself. Let us assume for the moment that age *is* wiser than youth, presumably because of its experience. If our ancestors were alive today, they would be venerable indeed, and their opinions should carry considerable weight. But they are not alive, an obvious fact which is often forgotten by ancestor-worshiping fanatics. Now let us add a second premise which is also necessary in an argument to age—namely, that men can and do learn from the experience of others, and that there is a kind of collective experience which customarily attaches to all mankind, and which is commonly called its history.

Now, when our ancestors lived, they were as young as we are (younger on the average), and the world was younger still. The collective experience of mankind was less extended in their time than ours. Their opinions, therefore, partook more nearly of the youth of mankind than ours do. As the date of their opinions is distant from the present, so in the same proportion are their opinions less mature than our own. An eighteenth-century idea, in this sense, is not two centuries older than a twentieth-century idea, but two centuries younger. If the premises of an argument to age are granted, then the distance of an ancestor's opinions from the present should be in the same degree a presumption against their validity rather than for it.[39]

It is possible, of course, to make a different kind of argument to ancestors, which is logically more tenable, if empirically more preposterous. Such an argument might begin with Henry Adams's assumption that there is an equivalent to the second law of thermodynamics in history, so that the energy and wisdom of all mankind are always running downhill. But this is an argument to youth, and not to age.

However absurd these thoughts may be, many intelligent historians have followed them. In another work, I have argued at some length that Henry Cabot Lodge, a Harvard Ph.D. in history and a competent historian in his own way, did this, with profoundly deleterious results for his own career. He attempted to apply the precepts of his great-grandfather in a political world where practices were very different.[40]

In our own time, it is a rare political proposal which is not, in some fashion, legitimized by an out-of-context quotation from the Founding Fathers. Consider, for instance, the rhetorical raids which have been made upon the writings of Thomas Jefferson. His works

39. William P. Montague, *The Ways of Knowing, or the Methods of Philosophy* (New York, 1958), p. 44.
40. David Hackett Fischer, "Founding Fathers and Great Grandsons" (in *Life and Letters of George Cabot,* by Henry Cabot Lodge forthcoming).

have been ransacked by Democrats and Republicans, liberals and conservatives, radicals and reactionaries, New Englanders and Southerners, to sustain elitism and equality, capitalism and socialism, states' rights and interventionism, isolationism and internationalism, rationalism and romanticism, atheism and Christianity, agrarianism and urban development. He has been quoted at length by Earl Browder in defense of Communism, and by Ezra Pound in the cause of Fascism; by Sukarno in the interest of "guided democracy," and even by Ho Chi Minh in the name of Vietnamese nationalism. All of this, of course, has often been abetted by historians, who have too often allowed themselves to be seduced into an essay called "Thomas Jefferson survives," or some such thing. Among the perpetrators of these wretched little essays are some of the most able historians in the Republic—Ralph Henry Gabriel, Henry Steele Commager, Julian Boyd, Dumas Malone, Charles A. Beard, C. M. Wiltse, A. M. Simons, and many others.[41]

ತಾ The *counterfallacy of argument ad novitam* is an appeal to modernity, or novelty, or youth. Its popularity among historians is perhaps partially explained by Marc Bloch's anecdote about another great scholar.

> I had gone with Henri Pirenne to Stockholm. We had scarcely arrived, when he said to me: "What shall we go to see first? It seems that there is a new city hall here. Let's start there." Then, as if to ward off my surprise, he added: "If I were an antiquarian, I would have eyes only for the old stuff, but I am an historian. Therefore I love life."[42]

Whatever the explanation may be, arguments *ad novitam* appear in several forms in historical writing. One of them is the unfortunate habit, which historians have formed and which the public has encouraged, of assuming that special significance attaches to a subject if it can be proved to be chronologically first in some respect. David Marshall Lang, author of a fine biography of Alexander Radischev, argues in his title for the significance of his protagonist by calling him *The First Russian Radical* (London, 1959). But if "radical" means "a person who favors rapid and sweeping changes in laws and methods of government," as Webster defines it, then there were surely Russian radicals before Radischev, and others after him. It could be argued that each of them was "first" in some respects but not in others. However that may be, Radischev retains a historical significance for the kind of radical that he

41. See, generally, Merrill Peterson, *The Jeffersonian Image in the American Mind* (New York, 1960).
42. Bloch, *The Historian's Craft*, p. 43.

was and for the radical things that he did. The question of firstness is a minor matter, of much less importance.

Another common historiographical form of an *ad novitam* is the excessive weight which often attaches to the most recent interpretation of any given subject. In one sense, this is the very opposite of firstness, for the blue ribbon is awarded to the book in last place. But, looking backward, it is the first book—the newest and most novel. "The judgment that earlier accounts are untrue, or at best inaccurate, is common to historians in all periods," Frederick Teggart complained in 1925. "The remarks of Thucydides on Herodotus, of Polybius on Timaeus, of Lucian on Ctesias, are typical of ancient historiography. In modern times, the same attitude has been maintained. Macaulay and Froude are the butt of every novice. Round calls Freeman "a superseded fossil."[43]

It is true that the best studies of certain historical problems are often the most modern studies. But there is no necessary causal or logical connection between modernity and excellence. There are many cases in point, within my own field. The best survey of the political history of the American Republic in the 1790s is still Richard Hildreth's account, published more than a century ago. The best general history of the Jeffersonian era is still Henry Adams's, despite many flaws. The best single book on the so-called Age of Jackson is still Tocqueville's, by a long shot. There are many other examples. The best history of medieval Florence is still the great work of Davidsohn; the best history of the Spanish Inquisition, in my opinion, is still Llorente's; the best history of the origins of the Seven Years' War is still Ranke's; the best military history of the Crimean War is surely Kinglake's. A competent scholar has written that there are "aspects of the history of pre-Columbian America in which the last, best work is still the first serious work—Alexander von Humboldt's extraordinary *Vues de Cordillères et Monuments des Peuples Indigènes de l'Amerique* (1814)."[44]

There is also a good deal of the fallacy of argument *ad novitam* in the absurd child worship of the late 1960s—in its juvenile fashions and fads, and in the infantile conceit that nobody over thirty can ever be trusted. Surely an inverse age requirement for integrity is as absurd as Noah Webster's idea that franchise should be restricted to people over forty-five.

  ಕ್ಞ The *fallacy of argument ad consequentiam* is an attempt to prove or disprove a reasoned argument by reference to the consequences

43. Frederick J. Teggart, *Theory and Processes of History* (Berkeley, 1962), p. 13.
44. Leo Deuel, *Conquistadors Without Swords: Archaeologists in the Americas* (New York, 1967).

which flow from its acceptance or rejection. One example is the verdict which an English historian, G. R. Elton, passed upon Erik Erikson's psychoanalytic interpretation of Martin Luther. "I cannot feel that the much-praised Freudian effort of E. H. Erikson, *Young Man Luther: A Study in Psychoanalysis in History* (London, 1959), contributes anything of value to an understanding of Luther or his age," Elton wrote, "In so far as it has been responsible for John Osborne's play, it may even need condemnation."[45]

Elton is, of course, entitled to his opinion, which must be regarded with respect, particularly when it refers to European history in the sixteenth century. But his second sentence is surely illegitimate. Maybe Mr. Erikson's essay *was* responsible, in some degree, for John Osborne's play, in the sense that the playwright may have derived many of his ideas and most of his facts from the psychiatrist. (I don't know that this is the case.) And maybe Osborne's play itself calls for condemnation as a historical work. Its interpretation of Luther is at least as strained as it alleges the Lutheran bowels to have been. But one cannot reason from these premises to the conclusion that Erikson's monograph should be condemned for the deficiencies of an unfortunate melodrama which may have been based upon it.

Other historiographical examples of an argument to consequences appear in attempts by conservative or chauvinist historians to justify the United States' war with Mexico. A nineteenth-century German scholar, Hermann von Holst, believed that Polk's policy was a Good Thing, because it caused the civilization of California, which was a Very Good Thing.

> In the hands of Mexico [he wrote] California was not only as good as lost to civilization, but it also lay exposed, a tempting prey, to all the naval and colonial powers of the world. . . . In whatever way the ethics of ordinary life must judge such cases, history must try them in the light of their results, and in so doing must allow a certain validity to the tabooed principle that the end sanctifies the means. Its highest law is the general interest of civilization, and in the efforts and struggle of nations for the preservation and advancement of general civilization, force not only in the defensive form, but also in the offensive, is a legitimate factor.[46]

Von Holst's interpretation is doubly objectionable, on ethical and logical grounds. The end may or may not justify the means, but it cannot sanctify them. Even assuming the validity of Von Holst's absurd premise that Mexico's loss was civilization's gain—an assumption which

---

45. Elton, *The Practice of History*, p. 25.
46. Hermann von Holst, *The Constitutional and Political History of the United States*, 8 vols. (Chicago, 1881) 3:268–73.

is not likely to survive a cultural comparison of Los Angeles and Mexico City—it does not follow, that a quality which attaches to an effect is transferable to the cause, or that a line of reasoning is valid or invalid because we happen to approve or disapprove of its practical consequences.

A superpatriotic American historian has taken a similar position on the same issue. Samuel Flagg Bemis commemorated the expansionism of President Polk with a combination of an argument *ad consequentiam* and an argument *ad populum*. To critics of the aggressive acts which led to the Mexican cession, Bemis asked if they would wish to give it back. "Notwithstanding all this," he wrote at the end of his account of the aggression of the United States against its neighbor, "Notwithstanding all this it would be well-nigh impossible today to find a citizen of the United States who would desire to undo President Polk's diplomacy, President Polk's war, and the treaty of Guadeloupe Hidalgo."[47]

ßÞ The *fallacy of argument ad nauseam* might serve, tongue in cheek, as a tag-name for a serious form of error, in which a thesis is sustained by repetition rather than by reasoned proof. This strategy was a favorite of Lewis Carroll's immortal Bellman, in *The Hunting of the Snark*.

> "Just the place for a Snark!" the Bellman cried
>   As he landed his crew with care;
> Supporting each man on the top of the tide
>   By a finger entwined in his hair.

> "Just the place for a Snark! I have said it twice:
>   That alone should encourage the crew.
> Just the place for a Snark! I have said it thrice:
>   What I tell you three times is true."[48]

The absurdity of this ludicrous device appears merely in its description. But it should not be lightly dismissed. Its popularity among advertising executives, public relations specialists, and professional propagandists is sustained by the solid fact that it works. Recent research in psychology has suggested something of the subliminal mechanisms by which repetition erodes critical resistance to the most absurd assertions.

Everybody, I suspect, has met this fallacy in various forms. An example is provided by an American historian, Oscar Handlin. There is a

47. Samuel Flagg Bemis, *A Diplomatic History of the United States*, 4th ed. (New York, 1955), p. 244.
48. *The Complete Works of Lewis Carroll*, p. 757.

salutary unwritten rule in the historian's code of professional ethics that forbids him to review the same book more than once. But there is no comparable taboo against his writing the same book as many times as he likes. Handlin's bibliography is enormous. But his many titles are mostly variations on a few themes.

The most prominent theme is the immigration of non-English people to America, mostly since 1820, which Handlin has implicitly elevated into the central "factor" in American history in his works. This argument has not been received with enthusiasm by critics, one of whom fairly complained that Handlin tended to ignore the contribution of the Anglo-Saxon element to American culture. But Handlin does not reply—he republishes. The result is a bibliography which reads a little like the *Bobbsey Twins* series. *The Uprooted* is followed by *Sons of the Uprooted; Boston's Immigrants* by *Positive Contributions by Immigrants* and *Immigration as a Factor in American History*. The same arguments also appear in *The Americans: A New History of the People of the United States*, which is about "the influence of migration upon the people of the United States"; and in *The American People in the Twentieth Century*, which might be called "Immigration as a Factor in Twentieth-Century America," and *Al Smith and His America*, which is about "Immigration as a Factor in Al Smith's America."

Similarly, Handlin has argued that the predicament of Negroes in twentieth-century America is closely comparable to that of immigrant groups. He has been sharply criticized for underestimating the duration and intensity of race prejudice and the significance of race slavery in America; and also for tending to mistake Negroes for Jews, and maybe for German Jews—a good example of the culture-bound fallacy. Again, Handlin responds by reiteration: *Race and Nationality in American Life* (1957); *The Newcomers: Negroes and Puerto Ricans in a Changing Metropolis* (1959); *Fire Bell in the Night* (1964); and many short essays besides. The words of Tristram Shandy come to mind:

> Tell me, ye learned, shall we for ever be adding so much to the bulk—so little to the stock?
>
> Shall we for ever make new books, as apothecaries make new mixtures, by pouring only out of one vessel into another?
>
> Are we for ever to be twisting, and untwisting the same rope? for ever in the same track—for ever at the same pace?
>
> Shall we be destined to the days of eternity, on holy-days as well as working-days, to be shewing the relics of learning, as monks do the relics of their saints—without working one—one single miracle with them?[49]

49. Laurence Sterne, *The Life & Opinions of Tristram Shandy, Gentleman*, Modern Library ed. (New York, 1950), pp. 355–56.

ह৶   There are many similar distractive fallacies of argument: *ad misericordiam* (an appeal to pity); *ad odium* (to hatred); *ad superstitionem* (to credulity); *ad modum* (to gradualism, due measure, or proportion); *ad metum* (to fear); *ad superbiam* (to snobbery, or pride); *ad invidiam* (to envy), and others, without limit. Many of them are discussed at length by Jeremy Bentham in his *Handbook of Political Fallacies*.

All of these forms of error are committed in historiographical as well as forensic disputation. Consider, for instance, the historiography of one great historical event—the French Revolution. A major component of Michelet's interpretation is an argument *ad misericordiam* in the name and interest of "the people," most of whom appear to have been hungry widows and orphans.

Carlyle's *The French Revolution* is equally an argument *ad odium*. His hatred is visited upon the alleged chaos of the Revolution itself, that great madness, "World Bedlam," and also upon its greatest personality, Robespierre, "seagreen Pontiff," "most consistent, incorruptible of thin, acrid men." Even his virtues are converted into objects of loathing.

Foes and friends of the Revolution have both resorted to an argument *ad superstitionem*. In the vanguard of the former marched the pious Abbé Barruel, who thought that the Revolution was the dark spawn of an unnatural union between the Incubus of Freemasonry and the Bitch-Goddess Liberty. On the other side, the Christian socialist Buchez interpreted the French Revolution as the institutionalization of Christianity. Some parts of his forty volumes read like an extended commentary on the New Testament.

The biases which inform Tocqueville's *Old Regime and the French Revolution* are a clear example of argument *ad modum*. Taine's history, on the other hand, is an extended *ad metum*. That great historian—a moderate without moderation, and a liberal without liberality—will long be remembered for his hair-raising descriptions of insane rationalism of the social contract, for his horror tales of the flashing bright blade of the guillotine, and for his interpretation of the people as a great beast, *"l'animal primitif, le signe grimaçant, sanguinaire, et lubrique."* All of these images are symbols not merely of hatred, but fear. Taine had witnessed some similar sights in his own time—and he was afraid.

Arguments *ad superbiam*, in the form of class pride, fill the books of conservative critics—Maistre and many since. As culture pride, the same form of error appears in the works of Renan and Flaubert. As race pride it is deeply rooted in Maurras, Gaxotte, and Bainville. On the other side, arguments *ad invidiam* appear on occasion in a sequence of socialist historians from Louis Blanc to Mathiez and Georges Lefebvre.

&~ By way of a conclusion, there is nothing to add on the dismal subject of substantive distractions except a few tedious platitudes which have undoubtedly suggested themselves already to every serious reader. Instead, I shall end this chapter and the main body of the book by cataloguing one final fallacy of distraction to which a fallacist himself is especially susceptible. It is offered as a byword and a warning to every reader who has responded in the wrong spirit to this work. The *fallacist's fallacy* consists in any of the following false propositions:

1. An argument which is structurally fallacious in some respect is therefore structurally false in all respects.

2. An argument which is structurally false in some respect, or even in every respect, is therefore substantively false in its conclusion.

3. The appearance of a fallacy in an argument is an external sign of its author's depravity.

4. Sound thinking is merely thinking which is not fallacious.

5. Fallacies exist independent of particular purposes and assumptions.

All of these propositions are profoundly wrong. Let us examine them briefly. First, an argument which is fallacious in one of its parts is not necessarily fallacious in others. All great historical and philosophical arguments have probably been fallacious in some respect. But it is unlikely that any extended argument has ever actually been fallacious in all respects. Complex theses are great chains of reasoning. The fact that one link in the chain is imperfect does not mean that other links are necessarily faulty, too. If the argument is a single chain, and one link fails, then the chain itself fails with it. But most historians' arguments are not single chains. They are rather like a kind of chain mail which can fail in some part and still retain its shape and function. If the chain mail fails at a vital point, woe unto the man who is inside it. But not all points are vital points.

Second, even if an argument is structurally fallacious in such a way that it collapses as an argument, the conclusion may still be substantively correct. Many false arguments have yielded true conclusions. An eighteenth-century New England physician studied the origin of the American Indians and arrived at the accurate conclusion that they were of Mongol extraction. His reasoning was roughly as follows: Noah had three sons: Japhet, Shem, and Ham. Everywhere, the children of Ham must serve the children of Japhet. The Indians have no Negro slaves, and therefore they must be the children of Shem. Thus, they are of Mongol extraction.[50] There is nothing good to be said for this argument

50. Sir Lewis Namier, in *Personalities and Powers* (London, 1955), "Human Nature in Politics," p. 6.

from either a logical or an empirical point of view. But its conclusion is substantively valid, even though every one of its premises is false, and the method of inference as well.

Third, a fallacy is not an emblem of depravity, or evidence of deliberate deceit. We have already noticed this error in Jeremy Bentham's *Book of Fallacies*. It is a common mistake. One of my colleagues examined an example of a fallacy which appears in an earlier chapter of this book—a fallacy from the work of *X*, a distinguished American historian. The colleague commented, "What you really mean to say, is that *X* is a *Bad* historian!" And his expression implied, "A Bad Man, to boot." I meant no such thing. All examples of fallacies in this book are drawn from the work of competent historians. Some are from the work of great historians. None, to my knowledge, were deliberately concocted to deceive a reader.

Fourth, the incidence of empirical and logical error in a work is not an inverse measure of its excellence. There are no rules of reason for distinguishing a shallow argument from a profound truth. There are no axioms of logic which can measure the gift of creativity or wisdom.

Finally, forms of illogic are always relative to specific logical assumptions and objects. They do not possess an independent existence. Aristotle's "fallacy of accident" is dependent upon the assumption that there are distinct differences between "essential" and "accidental" qualities. But if one disbelieves in the existence of essences, then the fallacy of accident has no meaning. Some of the fallacies in this book may be as empty to some readers as the fallacy of accident is to me.

The thesis of this book is something distinct from all these errors. It is a simple proposition that historians, and all men who seek to think historically, tend to make certain assumptions in their work, and that these assumptions have logical consequences which must be respected. Every historical work has a logical dimension. Of course, it has many other dimensions, too. If there is a logic of historical thinking, there is equally a grammar and a rhetoric of historical expression. And if there is a historiographical trivium, there is much more besides which belongs to the realm of psychology, epistemology, ethics, and metaphysics. But of all these many components of historical thinking, none is more susceptible to control and refinement than the logical component. Logic is not everything. But it *is* something—something which can be taught, something which can be learned, something which can help us in some degree to think more sensibly about the dangerous world in which we live.

CONCLUSION

ॐ

History is not only a particular branch of knowledge, but a particular mode and method of knowledge in other branches.

—Lord Acton

Any serious attempt to answer the question "What is good history?" leads quickly to another—namely, "What is it good for?" To raise this problem in the presence of a working historian is to risk a violent reaction. For it requires him to justify his own existence, which is particularly difficult for a historian to do—not because his existence is particularly unjustifiable, but because a historian is not trained to justify existences. Indeed, he is trained not to justify them. It is usually enough for him that he exists, and history, too. He is apt to be impatient with people who doggedly insist upon confronting the question.

Nevertheless, the question must be confronted, because the answer is in doubt. In our own time, there is a powerful current of popular thought which is not merely unhistorical but actively antihistorical as well. Novelists and playwrights, natural scientists and social scientists, poets, prophets, pundits, and philosophers of many persuasions have manifested an intense hostility to historical thought. Many of our contemporaries are extraordinarily reluctant to acknowledge the reality of past time and prior events, and stubbornly resistant to all arguments for the possibility or utility of historical knowledge.

The doctrine of historical relativism was no sooner developed by historians than it was seized by their critics and proclaimed to the world as proof that history-as-actuality is a contradiction in terms, and that history-as-record is a dangerous delusion which is, at best, an irrelevance to the predicament of modern man, and at worst a serious menace to his freedom and even to his humanity. A few of these people even believe, with Paul Valéry, that

> History is the most dangerous product which the chemistry of the mind has concocted. Its properties are well known. It produces dreams and drunkenness. It fills people with false memories, exaggerates their reactions, ex-

acerbates old grievances, torments them in their repose, and encourages either a delirium of grandeur or a delusion of persecution. It makes whole nations bitter, arrogant, insufferable, and vainglorious.[1]

These prejudices have become a major theme of modern literature. Many a fictional protagonist has struggled frantically through six hundred pages to free himself from the past, searching for a sanctuary in what Sartre called "a moment of eternity," and often finding it in a sexual embrace.[2]

In Aldous Huxley's *After Many a Summer Dies the Swan*, Mr. Propter is made to say, "After all, history isn't the real thing. Past time is only evil at a distance; and of course, the study of past time is itself a process in time. Cataloguing bits of fossil evil can never be more than an ersatz for eternity."[3] In the same author's *The Genius and the Goddess*, John Rivers compares history to a "dangerous drug" and dismisses it as a productive discipline of knowledge:

> God isn't the son of memory: He's the son of Immediate Experience. You can't worship a spirit in spirit, unless you do it now. Wallowing in the past may be good literature. As wisdom, it's hopeless. Time Regained is Paradise Lost, and Time Lost is Paradise Regained. Let the dead bury their dead. If you want to live at every moment as it presents itself, you've got to die at every other moment. That's the most important thing I learned.[4]

Some entertaining errors of the same sort appear in John Barth's splendid picaresque novel, *The Sot-Weed Factor*, where, in sixty-five chapters, Clio is ravished as regularly as most of the major characters. In an epilogue, the author writes,

> Lest it be objected by a certain stodgy variety of squint-minded antiquarians that he has in this lengthy history played more fast and loose with Clio, the chronicler's muse, than ever Captain John Smith dared, the Author here posits in advance, by way of surety, three blue-chip replies arranged in order of decreasing relevancy. In the first place be it remembered, as Burlingame himself observed, that we all invent our pasts, more or less, as we go along, at the dictates of Whim and Interest. . . . Moreover, this Clio was already a scarred and crafty trollop when the Author found her; it wants a nice-honed casuist, with her sort, to separate seducer from the seduced. But if, despite all, he is convicted at the Public Bar of having forced what slender virtue the strumpet may make claim to, then the Author joins with pleasure the most engaging company imaginable, his fellow fornicators, whose ranks include

1. Paul Valéry, *Regards sur le Monde Actuel* (Paris, 1949), p. 43.
2. Jean Paul Sartre, *The Reprieve* (New York, 1947), p. 352.
3. Aldous Huxley, *After Many a Summer Dies the Swan*, Harper & Row ed. (New York, 1965), p. 81.
4. Aldous Huxley, *The Genius and the Goddess*, Bantam Books ed. (New York, 1956), p. 4.

the noblest in poetry, prose and politics; condemnation at such a bar, in short, on such a charge, does honor to artist and artifact alike.[5]

Other literati have set their sights on historians, rather than history. Virginia Woolf asserted, "It is always a misfortune to have to call in the services of any historian. A writer should give us direct certainty; explanations are so much water poured with the wine. As it is, we can only feel that these counsels are addressed to ladies in hoops and gentlemen in wigs—a vanished audience which has learnt its lesson and gone its way and the preacher with it. We can only smile and admire the clothes."[6] Similar sentiments are cast as characterizations of historians in Sartre's *Nausea*, Kingsley Amis's *Lucky Jim*, George Orwell's *1984*, Aldous Huxley's *Antic Hay*, Wyndham Lewis's *Self-Condemned*, Anatole France's *Le Crime de Silvestre Bonnard*, Edward Albee's *Who's Afraid of Virginia Woolf?*, Stanley Elkin's *Boswell*, and Angus Wilson's *Anglo-Saxon Attitudes*. "It's so seldom that Clio can aid the other muses," says one character in the latter work. "Bloody fools, these historians," growls another.[7]

The antihistorical arguments of our own time have infected historians themselves, with serious results. Historical scholarship today is dominated by a generation (born, let us say, between 1900 and 1940) which has lost confidence in its own calling, lost touch with the world in which it lives, and lost the sense of its own discipline. Historians have failed to justify their work to others, partly because they have not even been able to justify it to themselves. Instead, when academic historians explain why they do history, there is a narrow parochialism and petty selfishness of purpose which surpasses rational belief. I have heard five different apologies for history from academic colleagues—five justifications which are functional in the sense that they permit a historian to preserve some rudimentary sense of historicity, but only at the cost of all ideas of utility.

First, there are those who claim that history is worth writing and teaching because, in the words of one scholar, "It is such fun!"[8] But this contemptible argument, which passes for wisdom in some professional quarters, is scarcely sufficient to satisfy a student who is struggling to master strange masses of facts and interpretations which are suddenly dumped on him in History I. It is unlikely to gratify a graduate student,

5. John Barth, *The Sot-Weed Factor*, Grosset and Dunlap ed. (New York, 1964) p. 793.
6. Virginia Woolf, "Addison," *Essays*, 4 vols. (London, 1966), 1:87.
7. Angus Wilson, *Anglo-Saxon Attitudes* (London, 1956), pp. 11, 364.
8. Fritz Stern, ed., *Varieties of History: From Voltaire to the Present* (New York, 1956), p. 30.

who discovers in the toil and loneliness of his apprenticeship the indispensable importance of a quality which the Germans graphically call *Sitzfleisch*. It will not be persuasive to a social scientist who is pondering the pros and cons of a distant journey to dusty archives. It cannot carry weight with a general reader, who is plodding manfully through a pedantic monograph which his conscience tells him he really ought to finish. Nor will it reach a public servant who is faced with the problem of distributing the pathetically limited pecuniary resources which are presently available for social research. And I doubt that it has even persuaded those historiographical hedonists who invoke it in defense of their profession.

For most rational individuals, the joys of history are tempered by the heavy labor which research and writing necessarily entail, and by the pain and suffering which suffuses so much of our past. Psychologists have demonstrated that pleasure comes to different people in different ways, including some which are utterly loathesome to the majority of mankind. If the doing of history is to be defended by the fact that some historians are happy in their work, then its mass appeal is likely to be as broad as flagellation. In all seriousness, there is something obscene in an argument which justifies the pedagogic torture inflicted upon millions of helpless children, year after year, on the ground that it is jolly good fun for the torturer.

Another common way in which historians justify historical scholarship is comparable to the way in which a mountain-climbing fanatic explained his obsession with Everest—"because it is there." By this line of thinking, history-as-actuality becomes a Himalayan mass of masterless crags and peaks, and the historian is a dauntless discoverer, who has no transcendent purpose beyond the triumphant act itself. If the object is remote from the dismal routine of daily affairs, if the air is thin and the slopes are slippery, if the mountain is inhabited merely by an abominable snowman or two, then all the better! If the explorer deliberately chooses the most difficult route to his destination, if he decides to advance by walking on his hands, or by crawling on his belly, then better still! By this convenient theory, remoteness is a kind of relevance, and the degree of difficulty is itself a defense.

This way of thinking is a tribute to the tenacity of man's will but not to the power of his intellect. If a task is worth doing merely because it is difficult, then one might wish with Dr. Johnson that it were impossible. And if historical inquiry is merely to be a moral equivalent to mountaineering for the diversion of chairborne adventurers, then historiography itself becomes merely a hobbyhorse for the amusement of overeducated unemployables.

A third common justification for history is the argument that there are certain discrete facts which every educated person needs to know. This view has been explicitly invoked to defend the teaching of required history courses to college freshmen, and to defend much research as well. But it is taxonomic in its idea of facts and tautological in its conception of education. What it calls facts are merely the conventional categories of historians' thought which are reified into history itself. And what it calls education is merely the mindless mastery of facts—a notion not far removed from the rote learning which has always flourished in the educational underworld but which no serious educational thinker has ever countenanced.

There are *no* facts which *everyone* needs to know—not even facts of the first historiographical magnitude. What real difference can knowledge of the fact of the fall of Babylon or Byzantium make in the daily life of anyone except a professional historian? Facts, discrete facts, will not in themselves make a man happy or wealthy or wise. They will not help him to deal intelligently with any modern problem which he faces, as man or citizen. Facts of this sort, taught in this way, are merely empty emblems of erudition which certify that certain formal pedagogical requirements have been duly met. If this method is mistaken for the marrow of education, serious damage can result.

Fourth, it is sometimes suggested that history is worth doing because it is "an outlet for the creative urge."[9] Undoubtedly, it is such a thing. But there are many outlets for creativity. Few are thought sufficient to justify the employment of thousands of highly specialized individuals at a considerable expense to society.

Tombstone rubbing is a creative act. So is the telling of tall stories. If history is to be justified on grounds of its creative aspect, then it must be shown to be a constructive, good, useful, or beautiful creative act. Most people who use this argument seem to be thinking in aesthetic terms. But if aesthetic principles become a justification for history, then surely 99 percent of the monographs which have appeared in the past generation are utterly unjustified. Most historians publish a single book in their lifetime—usually their doctoral dissertation. I cannot remember even one of these works which can be seriously regarded as a beautiful creative act. There have been a good many manifestoes for creative history in the past several decades, and more than a few essays which fulsomely describe the potential of history as art. But the number of modern histories which are worth reading on any imaginable aesthetic standard can be reckoned

9. Norman Cantor and Richard I. Schneider, *How to Study History* (New York, 1967), p. 3. For a more extended argument, see Emery Neff, *The Poetry of History* (New York, 1947).

on the fingers of one hand. Painful as the fact may be, historians must face up to it—literary history as a living art form is about played out. In an earlier generation, it was otherwise. But today this tradition is either altogether dead or sleeping soundly. An awakening has been confidently predicted from time to time, but with every passing decade the anticipated date has been postponed. Historians, for the past several generations, have been moving squarely in the opposite direction. There is nothing to suggest a change, and there are a good many hints of continuity in years to come. Until there is a reversal, or some sort of revival, or even a single serious and successful creative act, history as it actually is today, and as it is becoming, must be justified by another argument.

A fifth justification for history is cast in terms of the promise of future utility. I have heard historians suggest that their random investigations are a kind of pure research, which somebody, someday, will convert to constructive use, though they have no idea who, when, how, or why. The important thing, they insist, is not to be distracted by the dangerous principle of utility but to get on with the job. It is thought sufficient for an authority on Anglo-Saxon England to publish "important conclusions that all Anglo-Saxonists will have to consider."[10] If enough historians write enough histories, then something—the great thing itself —is sure to turn up. In the meantime we are asked to cultivate patience, humility, and pure research.

This argument calls to mind the monkeys who were set to typing the works of Shakespeare in the British Museum. So vast is the field of past events, and so various are the possible methods and interpretations, that the probability is exceedingly small that any single project will prove useful to some great social engineer in the future. And the probability that a series of random researches will become a coherent science of history is still smaller.

A comparable problem was studied by John Venn, some years ago. He calculated the probability of drawing the text of *Paradise Lost* letter by letter from a bag containing all twenty-six signs of the alphabet— each letter to be replaced after it is drawn, and the bag thoroughly shaken. Assuming that there were 350,000 letters in the poem, Venn figured the odds at 1 in $26^{350,000}$, which if it were written out, would be half again as long as the poem itself.

This operation is in some ways analogous to the method of historians who hope to construct a science of history by reaching into the grab bag of past events and hauling out one random project after another. The analogy is not exact—the probability of success in history is even more

10. *The American Historical Review* 71 (1966): 529.

remote than Venn's. If *A* is the number of possible methods (a large number), *B* is the number of possible topics (even larger), *C* is the number of possible interpretations (larger still), and *D* is the length of a sufficient series, then the odds are 1 in $(ABC)^D$. Now *D* may be as small as 1, but *A, B,* or *C* may equal infinity. If any one of them does, then the odds are infinitely improbable, in the sense of an infinite regression toward zero. In this context, infinite improbability will serve as a working definition of practical impossibility.

A series of researches can be expected to yield a coherent result only if they are *not* random. If a historian hopes that his work will promote some future purpose, then he must have some idea of what that purpose might be. The question cannot be postponed to another day. It must be faced now. And yet historians who justify their work as "pure research" deliberately avoid it. Their lives are wasted in aimless wanderings, like those which Bertrand Russell remembers from his childhood. "In solitude," he writes, "I used to wander about the garden, alternately collecting birds' eggs and meditating on the flight of time."[11] When grown men carry on in this way, the results are not amusing but pathetic.

All five of these justifications for history are functional to historical scholarship, but only in the sense that they serve to sustain a rough and rudimentary historicity in the work of scholars who have lost their conceptual bearings. But these attitudes are seriously dysfunctional in two other ways. First, they operate at the expense of all sound ideas of social utility. Secondly, they stand in the way of a refinement of historicity, beyond the crude level of contemporary practice.

Academic historians have been coming in for a good deal of abuse lately, and with a great deal of justification. There is a rising chorus of criticism which is directed principally against the sterility and social irrelevance of their scholarship. Only a few professional pollyannas would assert that these complaints are without cause.

But the reform proposals that accompany these protests are worse than the deficiencies they are designed to correct. Historians of many ideological persuasions are increasingly outspoken in their determination to reform historical scholarship, and often exceedingly bitter about the willful blindness of an alleged academic establishment which supposedly stands in their way. But these reformers are running to an opposite error.

Historians are increasingly urged to produce scholarship of a kind which amounts to propaganda. There is, of course, nothing new in this

11. Bertrand Russell, *Autobiography, 1872–1914* (Boston, 1967), p. 14.

idea. It appeared full-blown in the work of James Harvey Robinson and other so-called New Historians more than fifty years ago.[12] There was much of it after the Second World War, in the manifestoes of conservative anti-Communist scholars such as Conyers Read,[13] and in the monographs of liberal activists during the 1950s. There is still a great deal of it today in Eastern Europe, where more than a few historians imagine that they are "scholar-fighters," in the service of world socialism. Today, in America and Western Europe, this idea is being adopted with increasing fervor by young radical historians, who regard all aspirations to objectivity as a sham and a humbug, and stubbornly insist that the real question is not whether historians can be objective, but which cause they will be subjective to.

These scholars[14] are in quest of something which they call a "usable past." But the result is neither usable nor past. It ends merely in polemical pedantry, which is equally unreadable and inaccurate.

There have always been many historians who were more concerned that truth should be on their side than that they should be on the side of truth. This attitude is no monopoly of any sect or generation. But wherever it appears in historical scholarship, it is hateful in its substance and horrible in its results. To make historiography into a vehicle for propaganda is simply to destroy it. The problem of the utility of history is not solved but subverted, for what is produced by this method is not history at all. The fact that earlier generations and other ideological groups have committed the same wrong does not convert it into a right.

Moreover, the "usable" history which is presently being produced by historians of the "New Left" is not objectionable because it is substantively radical but rather because it is methodologically reactionary. Radical historians today, with few exceptions, write a very old-fashioned kind of history. They are not really radical *historians*. A good many new procedural devices are presently in process of development—devices which may permit a closer approximation to the ideal of objectivity. But one rarely sees them in radical historiography, which is impressionistic, technically unsophisticated, and conceptually unoriginal—old conceptions are merely adjusted in minor respects.

If history is worth doing today, then it must *not* be understood either in terms of historicity without utility, or of utility without historicity.

12. James Harvey Robinson, *The New History* (New York, 1912).
13. See above, p. 86.
14. For a discussion of their work, see Irwin Unger, "The 'New Left' and American History," *The American Historical Review* 72 (1967): 1237–63. For a sample, see Barton J. Bernstein, *Towards a New Past: Dissenting Essays in American History* (New York, 1968).

Instead, both qualities must be combined. The trouble with professional historians is that they are not professional enough—and not historians enough. If they are to be useful as historians, then they must do so by the refinement of their professional discipline and not by its dilution.

History can be useful, as history, in several substantive ways. It can serve to clarify contexts in which contemporary problems exist—not by a presentist method of projecting our own ideas into the past but rather as a genuinely empirical discipline, which is conducted with as much objectivity and historicity as is humanly possible. Consider one quick and obvious example—the problem of Negro-white relations in America. It is surely self-evident that this subject cannot be intelligently comprehended without an extended sense of how it has developed through time. Negro Americans carry their history on their backs, and they are bent and twisted and even crippled by its weight. The same is true, but less apparent, of white Americans, too. And precisely the same thing applies to every major problem which the world faces today. Historians can help to solve them, but only if they go about their business in a better way—only if they become more historical, more empirical, and more centrally committed to the logic of a problem-solving discipline.

Historical inquiry can also be useful not merely for what it contributes to present understanding but also for what it suggests about the future. A quasi-historical method is increasingly used, in many disciplines, for the purpose of forecasting—for establishing trends and directions and prospects. Historians themselves have had nothing to do with such efforts, which many of them would probably put in a class with phrenology. Maybe they should bear a hand, for they have acquired by long experience a kind of tacit temporal sophistication which other disciplines conspicuously lack—a sophistication which is specially theirs to contribute.

Third, history can be useful in the refinement of theoretical knowledge, of an "if, then" sort. Econometric historians have already seized upon this possibility, and political historians are not far behind. What, for example, are the historical conditions in which social stability, social freedom, and social equality have tended to be *maximally* coexistent? No question is more urgent today, when tyranny, inequality, and instability are not merely disagreeable but dangerous to humanity itself. This is work which a few historians are beginning to do. Maybe it is time that more of them addressed such problems, more directly.

Fourth, historical scholarship can usefully serve to help us find out who we are. It helps people to learn something of themselves, perhaps in the way that a psychoanalyst seeks to help a patient. Nothing could be more productive of sanity and reason in this irrational world. Historians, in the same way, can also help people to learn about other selves. And nothing is more necessary to the peace of the world. Let us have no romantic humbug about brotherhood and humanity. What is at stake is not goodness but survival. Men must learn to live in peace with other men if they are to live at all. The difficulties which humanity has experienced in this respect flow *partly* from failures of intellect and understanding. Historical knowledge may help as a remedy—not a panacea, but a partial remedy. And if this is to happen, professional historians must hold something more than a private conversation with themselves. They must reach millions of men, and they will never do so through monographs, lectures, and learned journals. I doubt that they can hope to accomplish this object by literary history or by the present forms of popular history. Instead, they must begin to exploit the most effective media of mass communication—television, radio, motion pictures, newspapers, etc. They cannot assign this task to middlemen. If the message is left to communications specialists, it is sure to be garbled in transmission. All of these uses of history, as history, require the development of new strategies, new skills, and new scholarly projects.

In addition to these four substantive services which historians can hope to provide, there is another one which I regard as even more important. Historians have a heavy responsibility not merely to teach people substantive historical truths but also to teach them how to think historically. There is no limit to the number of ways in which normative human thinking is historical. Nobody thinks historically all the time. But everybody thinks historically much of the time. Each day, every rational being on this planet asks questions about things that actually happened—questions which directly involve the logic of inquiry, explanation, and argument which is discussed in this book.

These operations rarely involve the specific substantive issues that now engage the professional thoughts of most historians. They do not touch upon the cause of the First World War, or the anatomy of revolutions, or the motives of Louis XIV, or the events of the industrial revolution. Instead, this common everyday form of historical thought consists of specific inquiries into small events, for particular present and future purposes to which all the academic monographs in the world are utterly irrelevant.

Historical thought ordinarily happens in a thousand humble forms—when a newspaper writer reports an event and a newspaper reader peruses it; when a jury weighs a fact in dispute, and a judge looks for a likely precedent; when a diplomat compiles an *aide-memoire* and a doctor constructs a case history; when a soldier analyzes the last campaign, and a statesman examines the record; when a householder tries to remember if he paid the rent, and when a house builder studies the trend of the market. Historical thinking happens even to sociologists, economists, and political scientists in nearly all of their major projects. Each of these operations is in some respects (not all respects) historical. If historians have something to learn from other disciplines, they have something to teach as well.

The vital purpose of refining and extending a logic of historical thought is not merely some pristine goal of scholarly perfection. It involves the issue of survival. Let us make no mistake about priorities. If men continue to make the *historical* error of conceptualizing the problems of a nuclear world in prenuclear terms, there will not be a postnuclear world. If people persist in the *historical* error of applying yesterday's programs to today's problems, we may suddenly run short of tomorrow's possibilities. If we continue to pursue the ideological objectives of the nineteenth century in the middle of the twentieth, the prospects for a twenty-first are increasingly dim.

These failures—failures of historical understanding—exist everywhere today. Frenchmen, in pursuit of their venerable vision of Gallic grandeur, combine a *force de frappe* with the fallacy of anachronism—a lethal combination. Arabs cry up a *jihad* against the infidels, as if nothing had changed in nine hundred years but the name of the enemy. On the other side of the Jordan River, Jews nurse their bitter heritage of blood and tears, without any apparent sense of how the world has changed. In Moscow and in Washington, in London and in Bonn, in Peking and New Delhi, statesmen and citizens alike are unable to adjust their thoughts to the accelerating rate of changing realities.

That people will learn to see things as they are—that they will understand the world as it is, and is becoming—that they will become more rational and empirical in their private thoughts and public policies —that these things will come to pass, is not what Damon Runyon would have called a betting proposition. He might have figured the most favorable odds at six to five, against. But if people continue to commit their fatal fallacies at something like the present rate, the odds for their survival will become a long shot.

Responsible and informed observers have estimated that by the 1990s as many as forty-eight nations may possess nuclear weapons.[15] As the number of these arsenals increases arithmetically, the probability of their use grows in geometric ratio. Biological and chemical weapons of equal destructive power and even greater horror are already within the reach of most sovereign powers, and many private groups as well.

15. Sir John Cockcroft, "The Perils of Nuclear Proliferation," in Nigel Calder, ed., *Unless Peace Comes* (New York, 1968), p. 37.

Natural scientists have helped to create this deadly peril; now it is the business of social scientists to keep it in bounds. Here is work for historians to do—work that is largely educational in nature—work that consists in teaching men somehow to think reasonably about their condition. Reason is indeed a pathetically frail weapon in the face of such a threat. But it is the *only* weapon we have. To the task of its refinement, this book has been addressed.

INDEX

ॐ

INDEX OF FALLACIES

ﻬ

(in order of appearance)